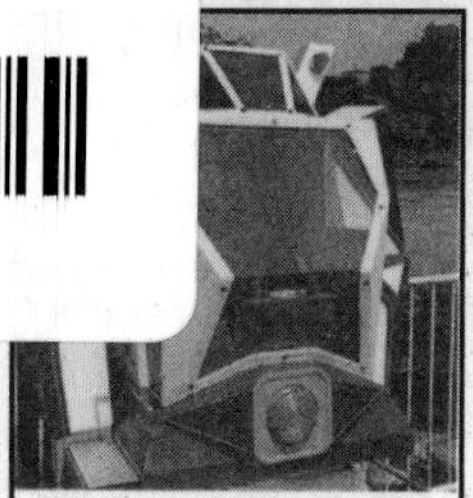

武井宏之

There are some vintage rides in tiny amusement parks on the roofs of old department stores. A lot of them have nice designs, and many people collect the American '50s-style ones, but I like these other guys. Like this one, emulating certain robots from '80s anime TV shows, except built with '70s-style craftsmanship. I would very much like it for the *Takei Collection.*

—*Hiroyuki Takei*

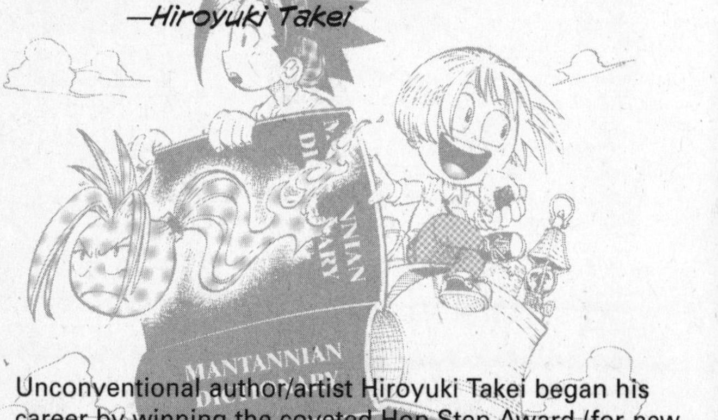
MANTANNIAN

Unconventional author/artist Hiroyuki Takei began his career by winning the coveted Hop Step Award (for new manga artists) and the Osamu Tezuka Award (named after the famous artist of the same name). After working as an assistant to famed artist Nobuhiro Watsuki, Takei debuted in **Weekly Shonen Jump** in 1997 with **Butsu Zone**, an action series based on Buddhist mythology. His multicultural adventure manga **Shaman King**, which debuted in 1998, became a hit and was adapted into an anime TV series. Takei lists Osamu Tezuka, American comics and robot anime among his many influences.

SHAMAN KING VOL.11
The SHONEN JUMP Manga Edition

This graphic novel contains material that was originally published in English in **SHONEN JUMP** #45-48.

STORY AND ART BY
HIROYUKI TAKEI

English Adaptation/Lance Caselman
Translation/Lillian Olsen
Touch-up Art & Lettering/Kathryn Renta
Additional Lettering/Josh Simpson
Design/Sean Lee
Editors/Pancha Diaz & Joel Enos

Managing Editor/Frances E. Wall
Editorial Director/Elizabeth Kawasaki
VP & Editor in Chief/Yumi Hoashi
Sr. Director of Acquisitions/Rika Inouye
Sr. VP of Marketing/Liza Coppola
Exec. VP of Sales & Marketing/John Easum
Publisher/Hyoe Narita

Printed in the U.S.A.

Published by VIZ Media, LLC
P.O. Box 77010
San Francisco, CA 94107

SHONEN JUMP Manga Edition
10 9 8 7 6 5 4 3 2 1
First printing, January 2007

www.viz.com

PARENTAL ADVISORY
SHAMAN KING is rated T for Teen and is recommended for ages 13 and up. This volume contains violence.

THE WORLD'S MOST POPULAR MANGA

SHONEN JUMP

www.shonenjump.com

SHONEN JUMP MANGA

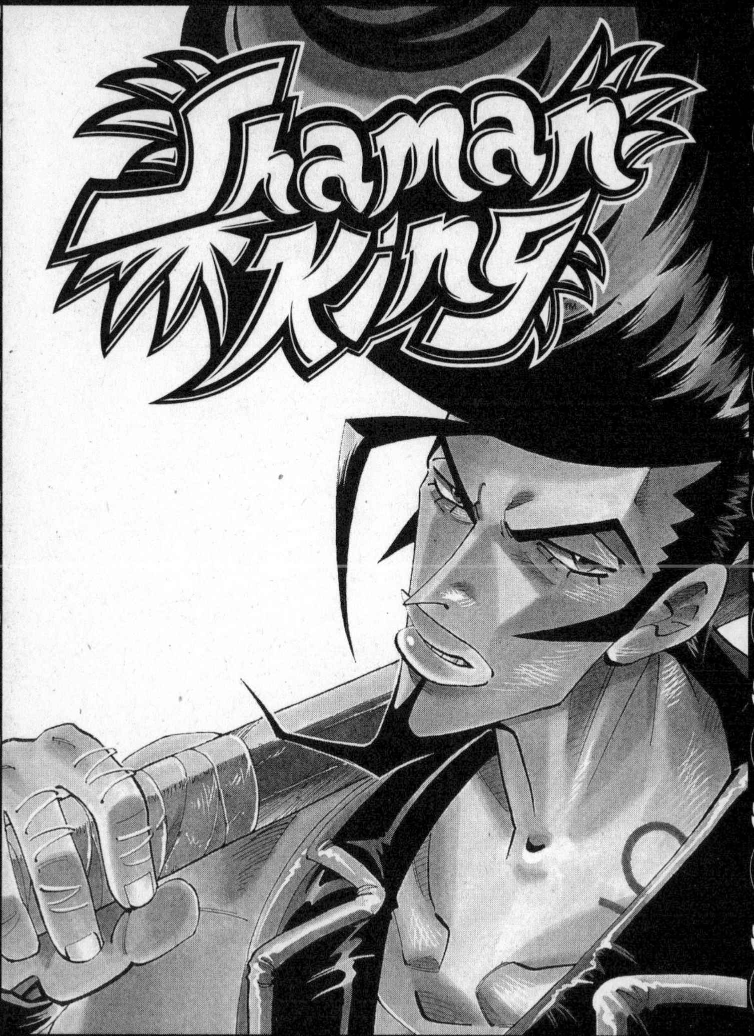
Shaman King

VOL. 11
BLOOD AND POMPADOURS

STORY AND ART BY
HIROYUKI TAKEI

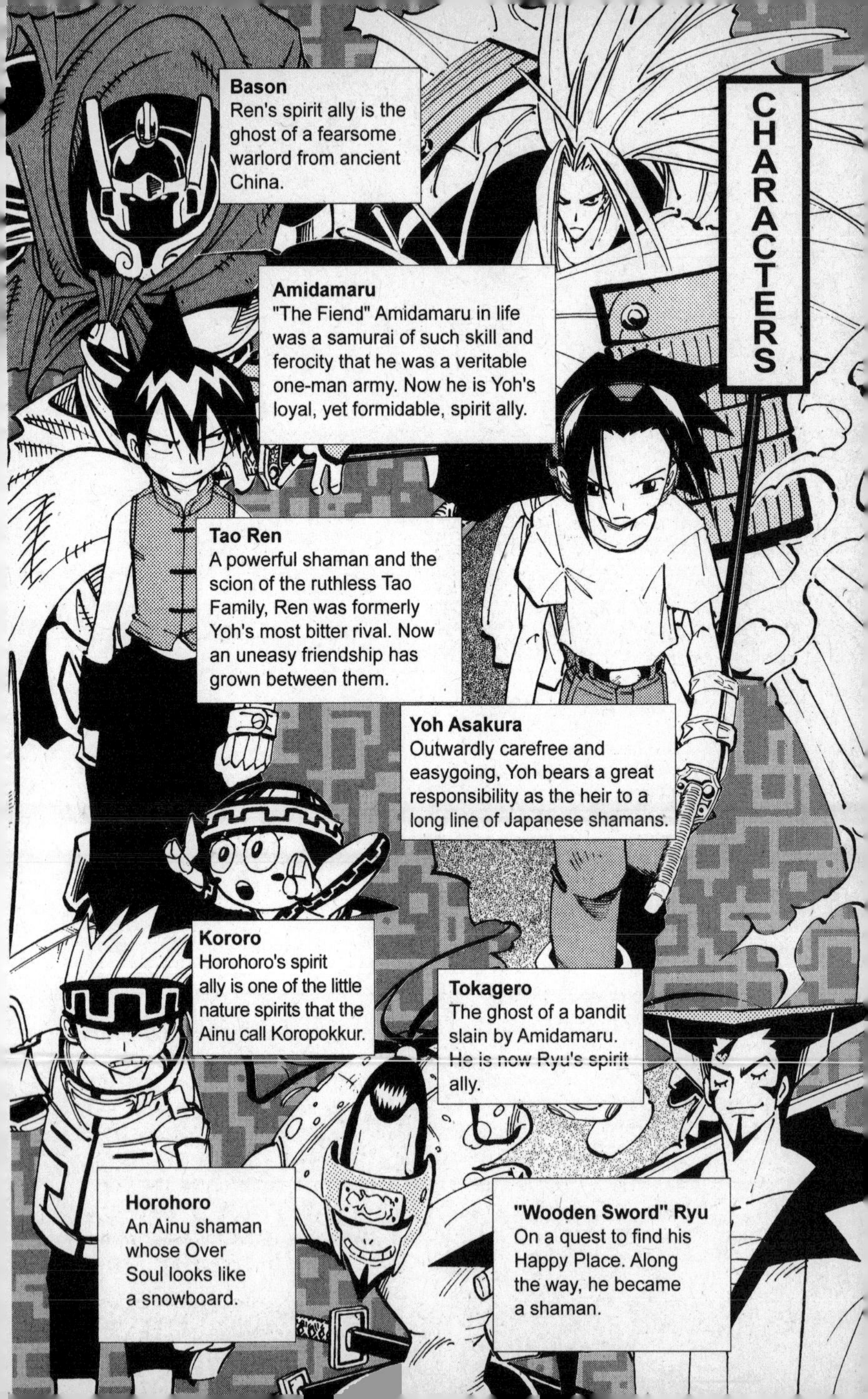
CHARACTERS
Bason
Ren's spirit ally is the ghost of a fearsome warlord from ancient China.
Amidamaru
"The Fiend" Amidamaru in life was a samurai of such skill and ferocity that he was a veritable one-man army. Now he is Yoh's loyal, yet formidable, spirit ally.
Tao Ren
A powerful shaman and the scion of the ruthless Tao Family, Ren was formerly Yoh's most bitter rival. Now an uneasy friendship has grown between them.
Yoh Asakura
Outwardly carefree and easygoing, Yoh bears a great responsibility as the heir to a long line of Japanese shamans.
Kororo
Horohoro's spirit ally is one of the little nature spirits that the Ainu call Koropokkur.
Tokagero
The ghost of a bandit slain by Amidamaru. He is now Ryu's spirit ally.
Horohoro
An Ainu shaman whose Over Soul looks like a snowboard.
"Wooden Sword" Ryu
On a quest to find his Happy Place. Along the way, he became a shaman.

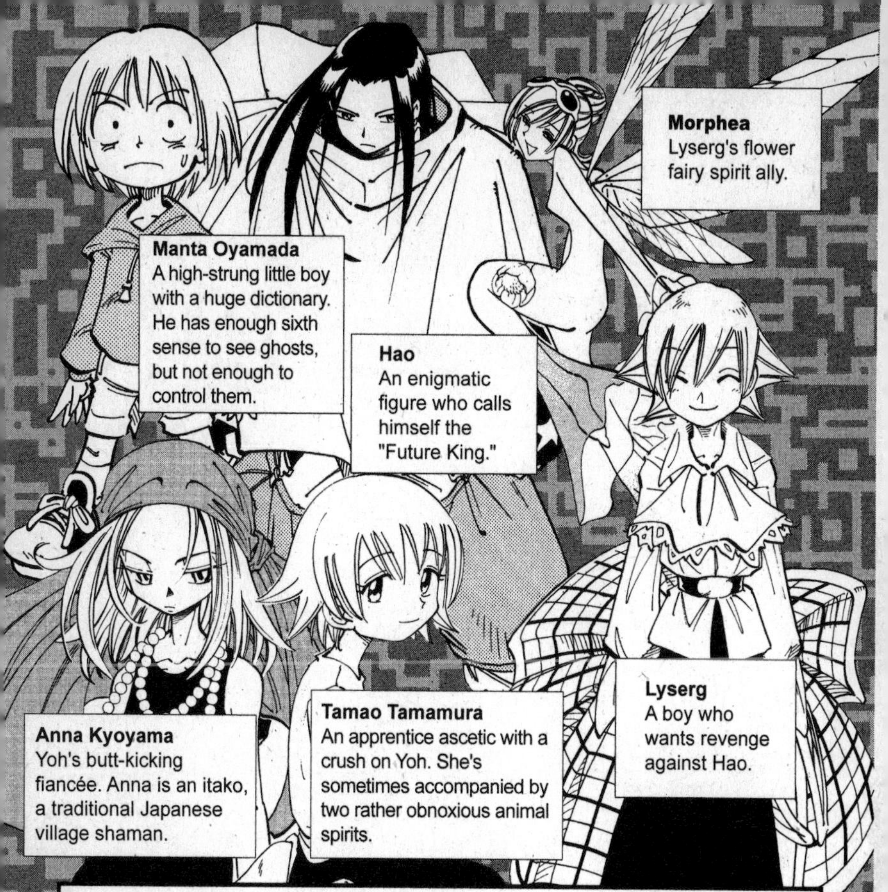
Morphea
Lyserg's flower fairy spirit ally.
Manta Oyamada
A high-strung little boy with a huge dictionary. He has enough sixth sense to see ghosts, but not enough to control them.
Hao
An enigmatic figure who calls himself the "Future King."
Lyserg
A boy who wants revenge against Hao.
Tamao Tamamura
An apprentice ascetic with a crush on Yoh. She's sometimes accompanied by two rather obnoxious animal spirits.
Anna Kyoyama
Yoh's butt-kicking fiancée. Anna is an itako, a traditional Japanese village shaman.

THE STORY THUS FAR

Yoh Asakura not only sees dead people, he talks and fights with them, too. That's because Yoh is a shaman, a traditional holy man able to interact with the spirit world. Yoh is now a competitor in the "Shaman Fight," a tournament held every 500 years to decide who will become the Shaman King and shape humanity's future.

Having passed the fierce preliminaries, the contestants set out for the main competition at the Patch Village. But en route, they suddenly find themselves dropped into the wilds of North America with instructions that they must find their way on their own. Yoh and the others meet Lyserg, a boy with a vendetta against Hao. After a brief battle, he joins the group. Meanwhile, Yoh's grandfather reveals an ancient family secret to Anna...

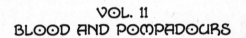

VOL. 11
BLOOD AND POMPADOURS

CONTENTS

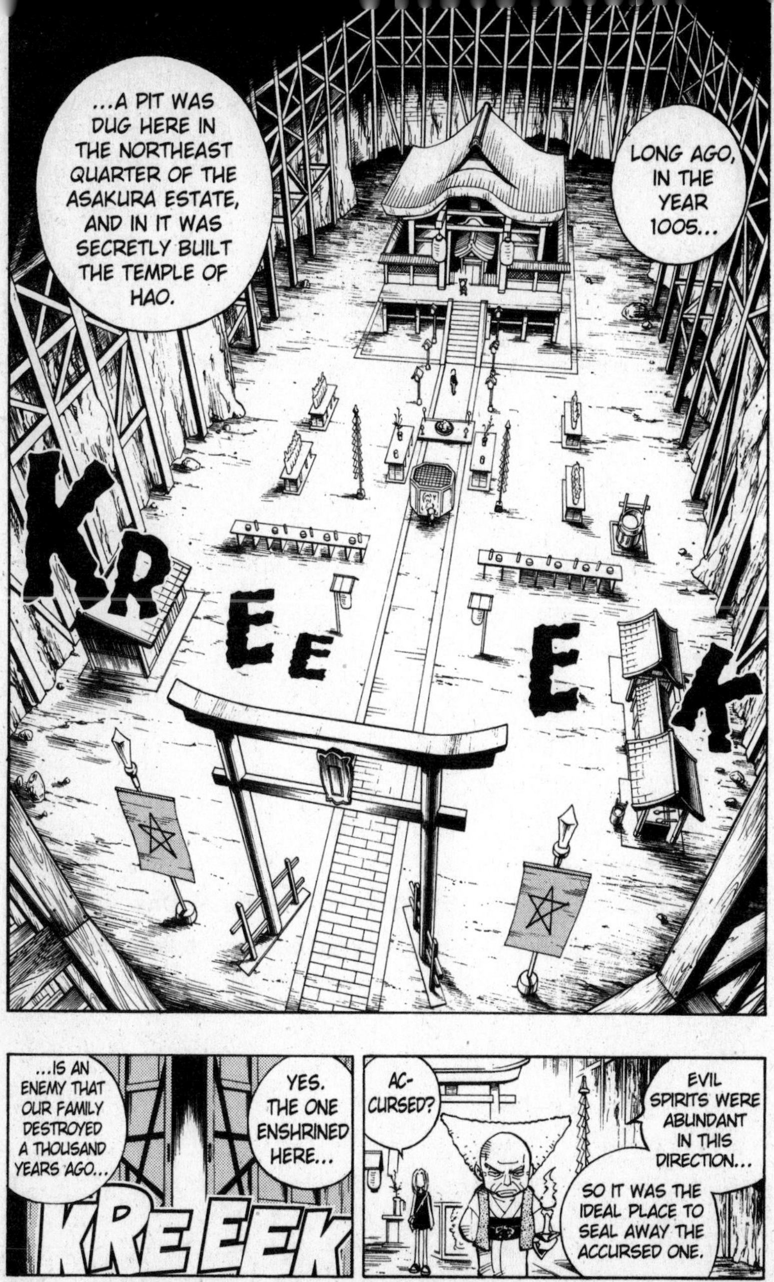
LONG AGO, IN THE YEAR 1005...
...A PIT WAS DUG HERE IN THE NORTHEAST QUARTER OF THE ASAKURA ESTATE, AND IN IT WAS SECRETLY BUILT THE TEMPLE OF HAO.
KREEEK
EVIL SPIRITS WERE ABUNDANT IN THIS DIRECTION...
SO IT WAS THE IDEAL PLACE TO SEAL AWAY THE ACCURSED ONE.
AC-CURSED?
YES. THE ONE ENSHRINED HERE...
...IS AN ENEMY THAT OUR FAMILY DESTROYED A THOUSAND YEARS AGO...
KREEEK

Reincarnation 90: Ominous Stars

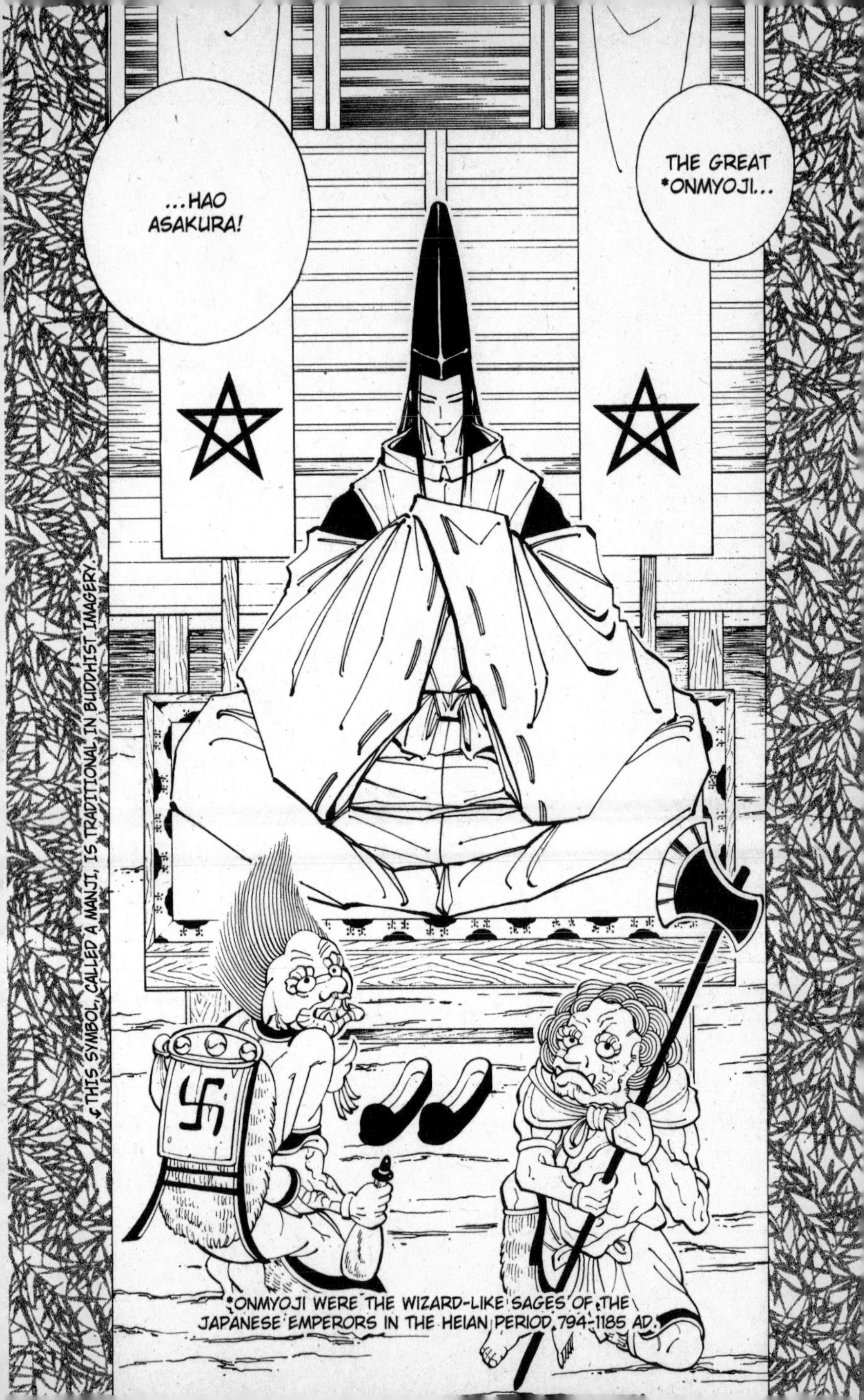
THE GREAT *ONMYOJI...
...HAO ASAKURA!
*ONMYOJI WERE THE WIZARD-LIKE SAGES OF THE JAPANESE EMPERORS IN THE HEIAN PERIOD 794-1185 AD.
↲THIS SYMBOL, CALLED A MANJI, IS TRADITIONAL IN BUDDHIST IMAGERY.

Reincarnation 90: Ominous Stars

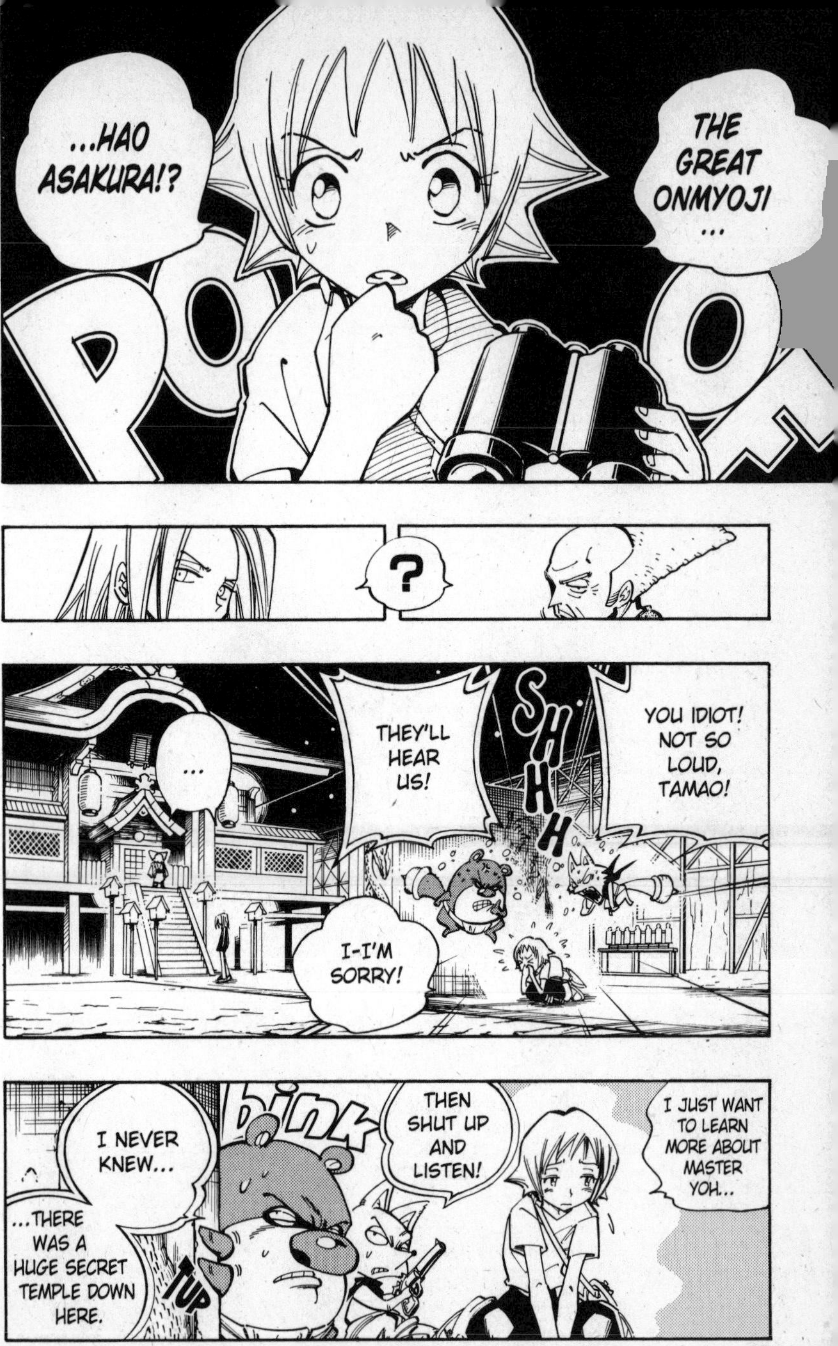
THE GREAT ONMYOJI...
...HAO ASAKURA!?
POOF
?
YOU IDIOT! NOT SO LOUD, TAMAO!
SHHH
THEY'LL HEAR US!
...
I-I'M SORRY!
I JUST WANT TO LEARN MORE ABOUT MASTER YOH...
THEN SHUT UP AND LISTEN!
bink
I NEVER KNEW...
...THERE WAS A HUGE SECRET TEMPLE DOWN HERE.
TUP

READ THIS WAY

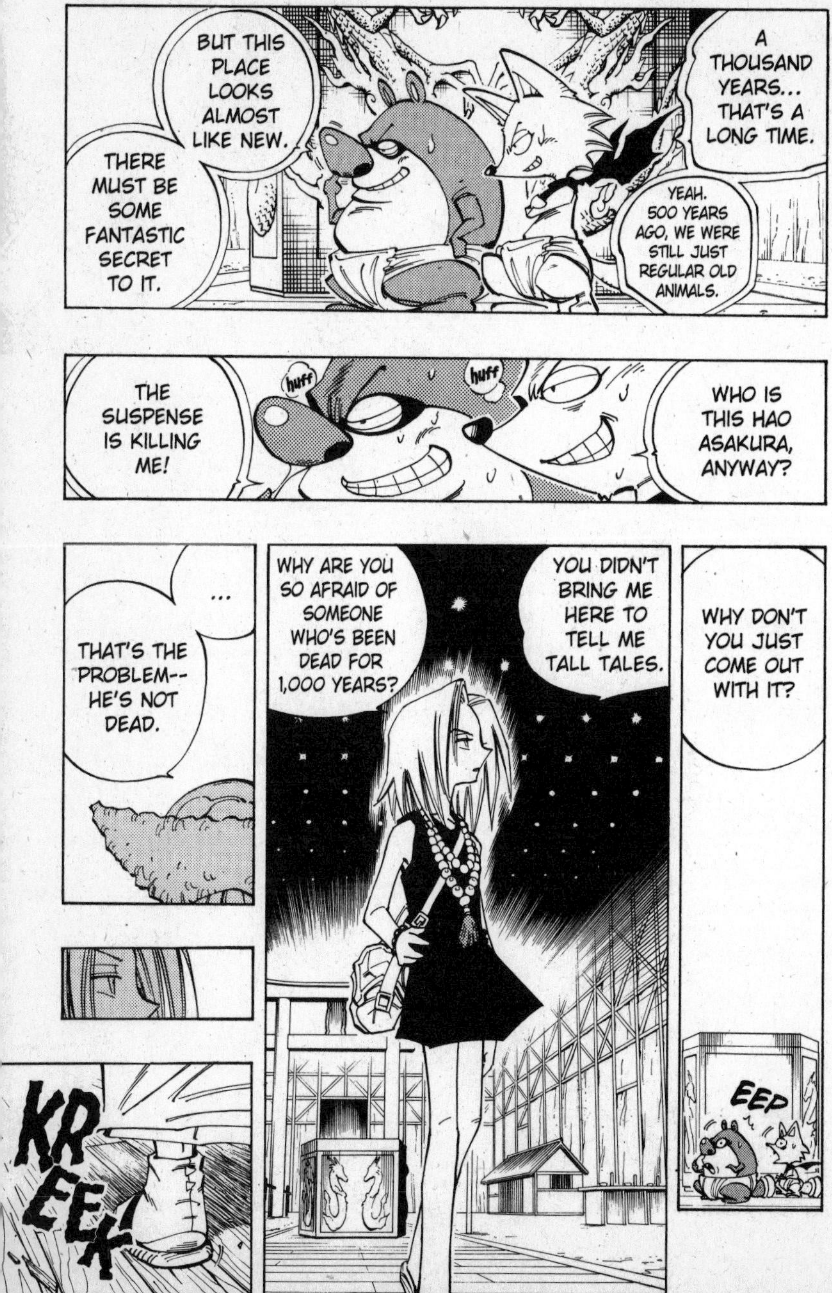

A THOUSAND YEARS... THAT'S A LONG TIME.
YEAH. 500 YEARS AGO, WE WERE STILL JUST REGULAR OLD ANIMALS.
BUT THIS PLACE LOOKS ALMOST LIKE NEW.
THERE MUST BE SOME FANTASTIC SECRET TO IT.
WHO IS THIS HAO ASAKURA, ANYWAY?
huff
huff
THE SUSPENSE IS KILLING ME!
WHY DON'T YOU JUST COME OUT WITH IT?
EEP
YOU DIDN'T BRING ME HERE TO TELL ME TALL TALES.
WHY ARE YOU SO AFRAID OF SOMEONE WHO'S BEEN DEAD FOR 1,000 YEARS?
...
THAT'S THE PROBLEM-- HE'S NOT DEAD.
KREEK

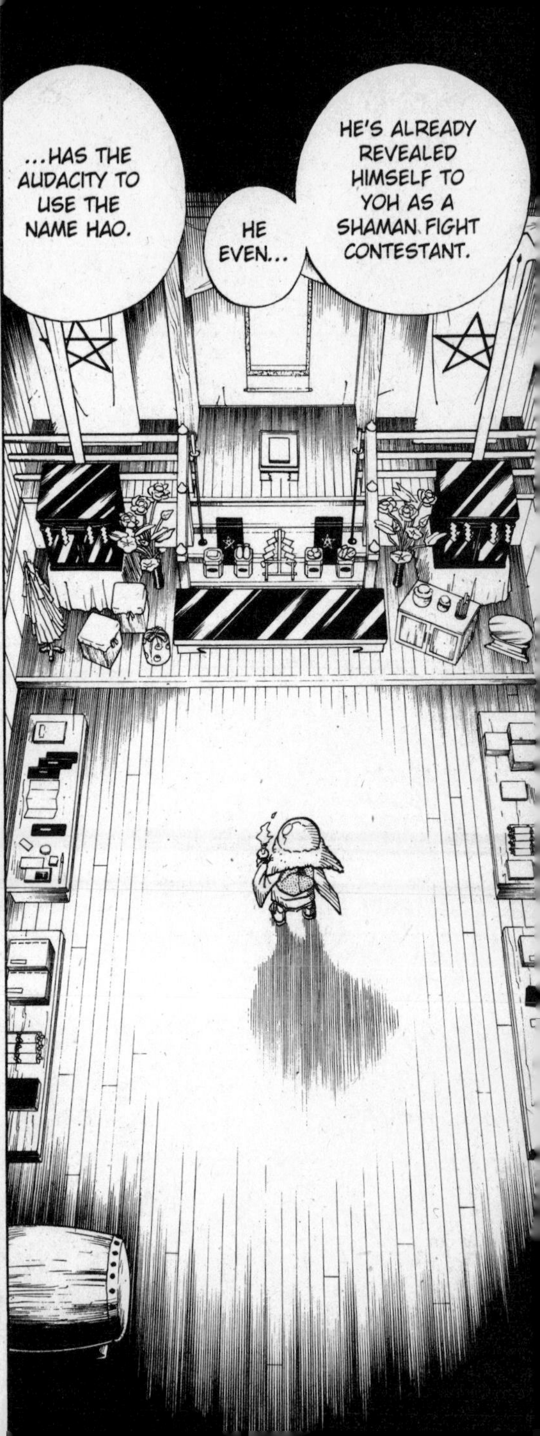
HE'S ALREADY REVEALED HIMSELF TO YOH AS A SHAMAN FIGHT CONTESTANT.
HE EVEN...
...HAS THE AUDACITY TO USE THE NAME HAO.

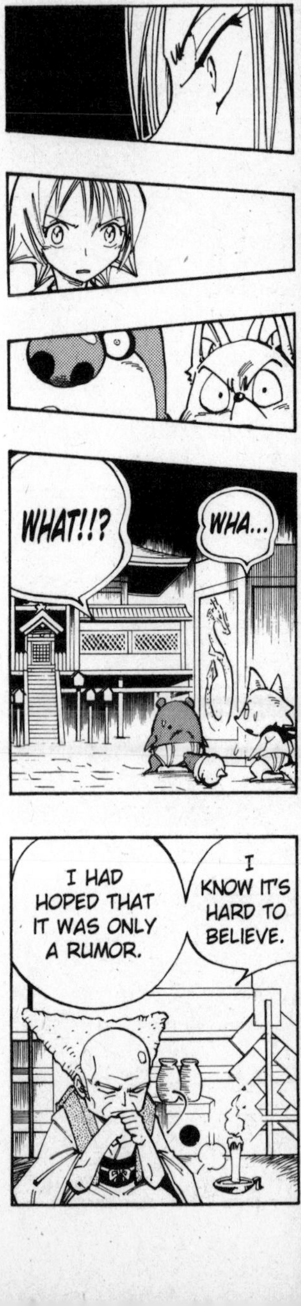
WHA...
WHAT!!?
I KNOW IT'S HARD TO BELIEVE.
I HAD HOPED THAT IT WAS ONLY A RUMOR.

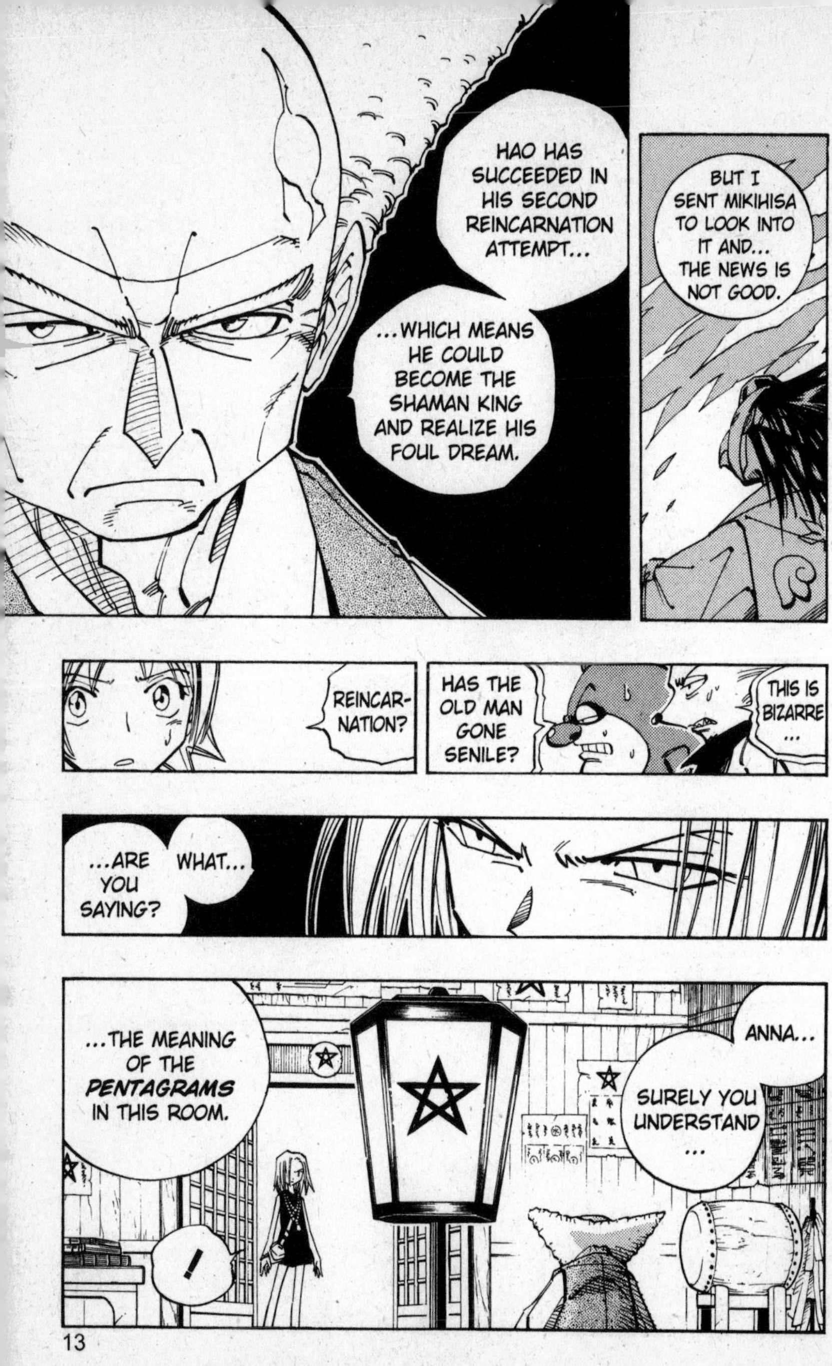
BUT I SENT MIKIHISA TO LOOK INTO IT AND... THE NEWS IS NOT GOOD.
HAO HAS SUCCEEDED IN HIS SECOND REINCARNATION ATTEMPT...
...WHICH MEANS HE COULD BECOME THE SHAMAN KING AND REALIZE HIS FOUL DREAM.
THIS IS BIZARRE ...
HAS THE OLD MAN GONE SENILE?
REINCAR-NATION?
WHAT...
...ARE YOU SAYING?
ANNA...
SURELY YOU UNDERSTAND ...
...THE MEANING OF THE *PENTAGRAMS* IN THIS ROOM.
!

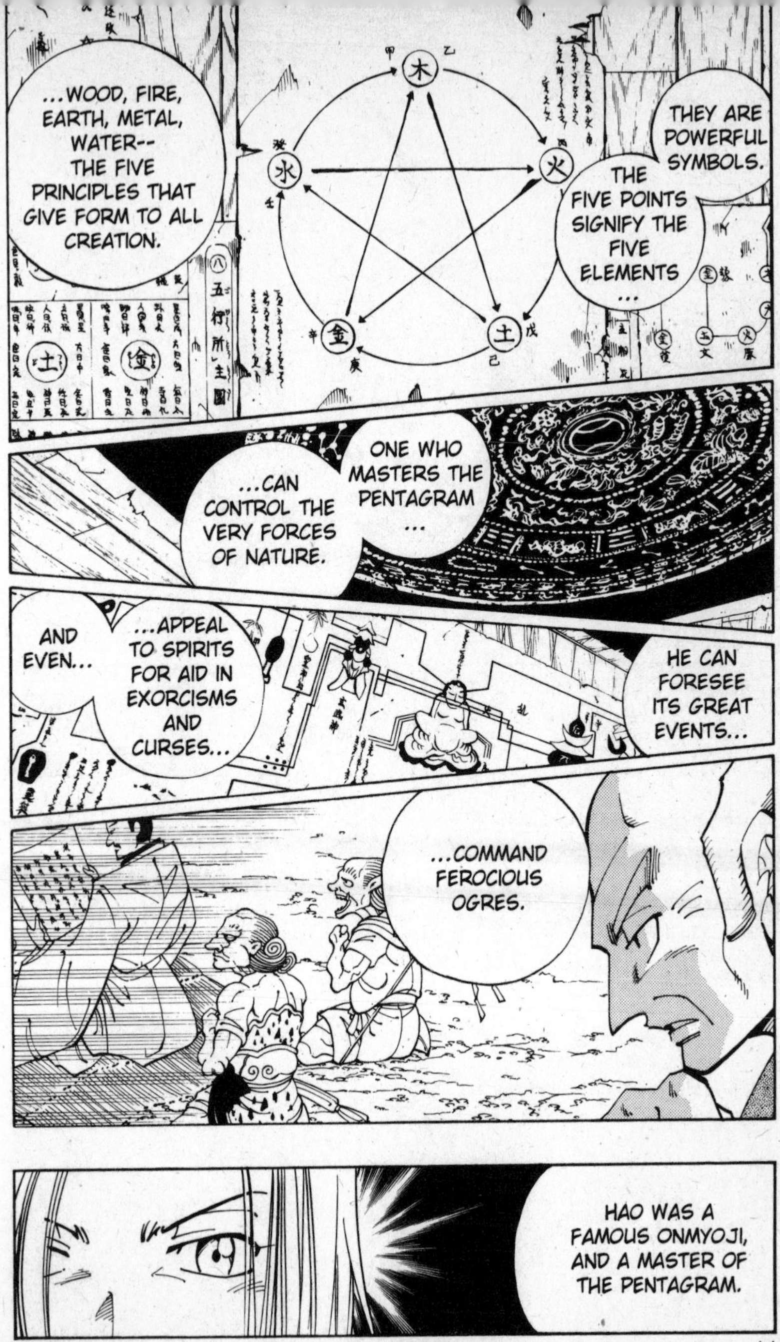
THEY ARE POWERFUL SYMBOLS.
THE FIVE POINTS SIGNIFY THE FIVE ELEMENTS...
...WOOD, FIRE, EARTH, METAL, WATER-- THE FIVE PRINCIPLES THAT GIVE FORM TO ALL CREATION.
ONE WHO MASTERS THE PENTAGRAM...
...CAN CONTROL THE VERY FORCES OF NATURE.
HE CAN FORESEE ITS GREAT EVENTS...
...APPEAL TO SPIRITS FOR AID IN EXORCISMS AND CURSES...
AND EVEN...
...COMMAND FEROCIOUS OGRES.
HAO WAS A FAMOUS ONMYOJI, AND A MASTER OF THE PENTAGRAM.

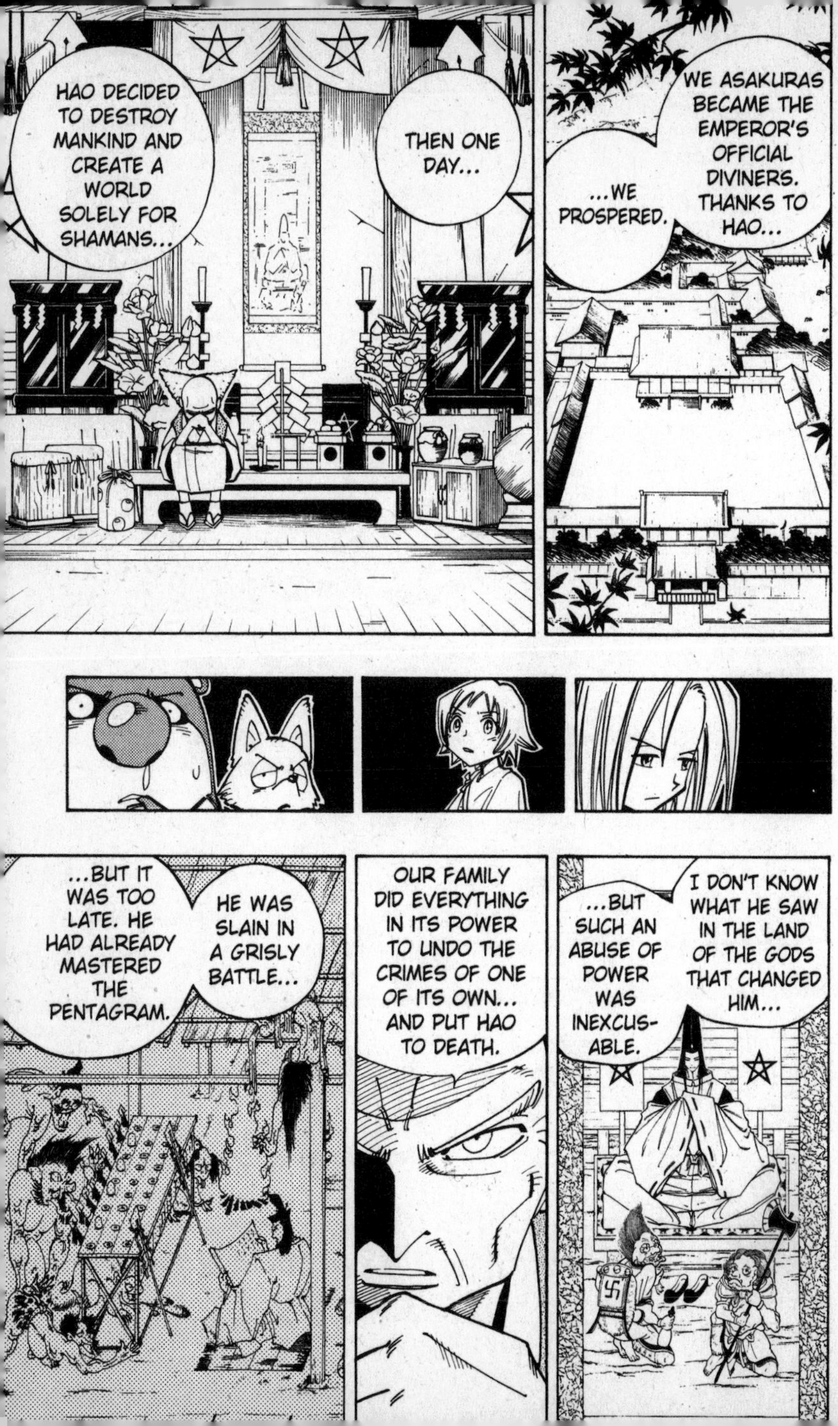
WE ASAKURAS BECAME THE EMPEROR'S OFFICIAL DIVINERS. THANKS TO HAO...
...WE PROSPERED.
THEN ONE DAY...
HAO DECIDED TO DESTROY MANKIND AND CREATE A WORLD SOLELY FOR SHAMANS...
I DON'T KNOW WHAT HE SAW IN THE LAND OF THE GODS THAT CHANGED HIM...
...BUT SUCH AN ABUSE OF POWER WAS INEXCUS-ABLE.
OUR FAMILY DID EVERYTHING IN ITS POWER TO UNDO THE CRIMES OF ONE OF ITS OWN... AND PUT HAO TO DEATH.
HE WAS SLAIN IN A GRISLY BATTLE...
...BUT IT WAS TOO LATE. HE HAD ALREADY MASTERED THE PENTAGRAM.

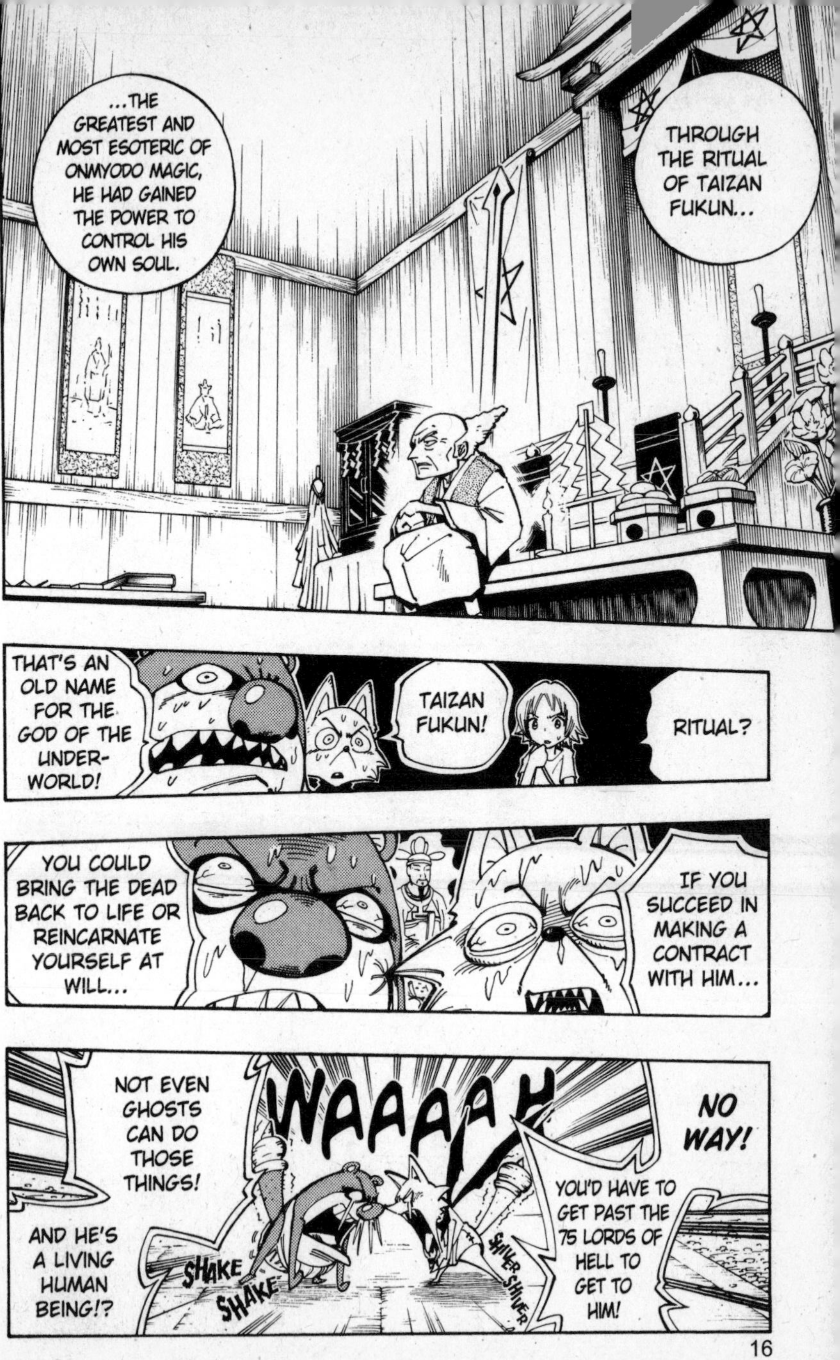
THROUGH THE RITUAL OF TAIZAN FUKUN...
...THE GREATEST AND MOST ESOTERIC OF ONMYODO MAGIC, HE HAD GAINED THE POWER TO CONTROL HIS OWN SOUL.
RITUAL?
TAIZAN FUKUN!
THAT'S AN OLD NAME FOR THE GOD OF THE UNDER-WORLD!
IF YOU SUCCEED IN MAKING A CONTRACT WITH HIM...
YOU COULD BRING THE DEAD BACK TO LIFE OR REINCARNATE YOURSELF AT WILL...
NO WAY!
YOU'D HAVE TO GET PAST THE 75 LORDS OF HELL TO GET TO HIM!
WAAAAH
SHIVER SHIVER
SHAKE SHAKE
NOT EVEN GHOSTS CAN DO THOSE THINGS!
AND HE'S A LIVING HUMAN BEING!?

READ THIS WAY

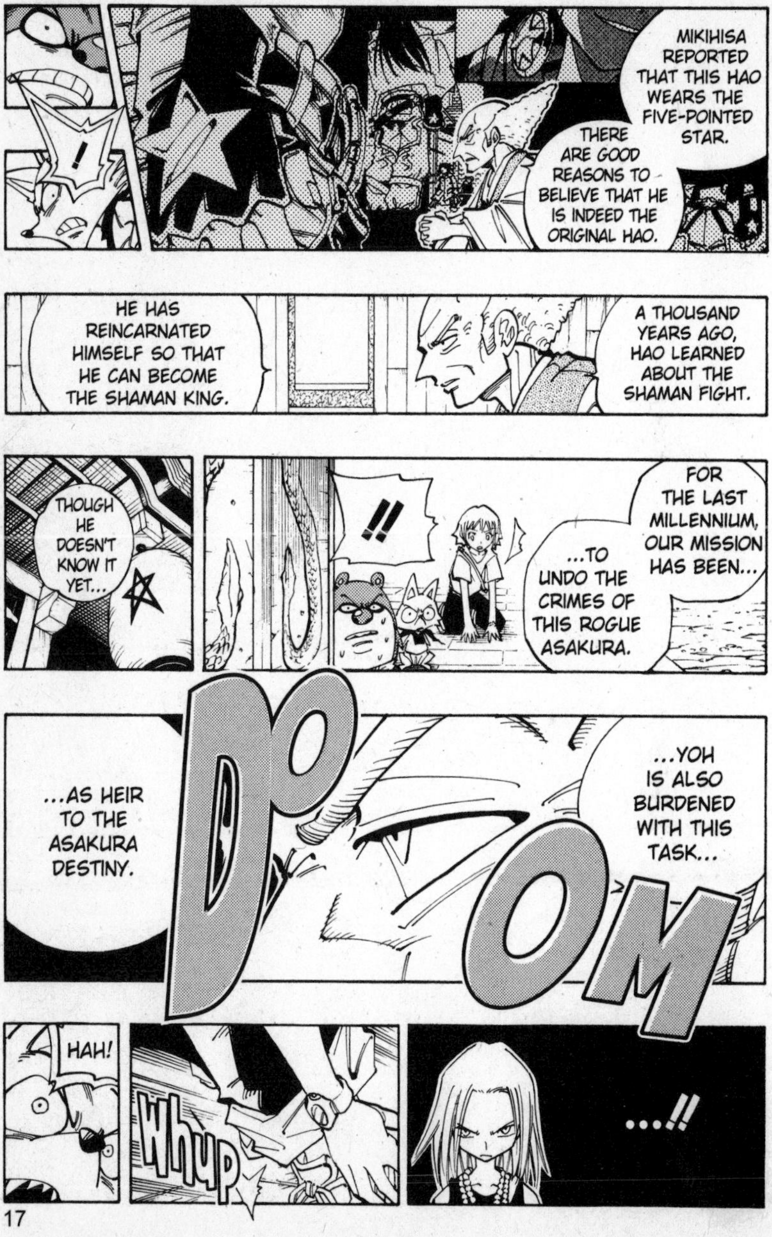

MIKIHISA REPORTED THAT THIS HAO WEARS THE FIVE-POINTED STAR.
THERE ARE GOOD REASONS TO BELIEVE THAT HE IS INDEED THE ORIGINAL HAO.
!
A THOUSAND YEARS AGO, HAO LEARNED ABOUT THE SHAMAN FIGHT.
HE HAS REINCARNATED HIMSELF SO THAT HE CAN BECOME THE SHAMAN KING.
FOR THE LAST MILLENNIUM, OUR MISSION HAS BEEN...
...TO UNDO THE CRIMES OF THIS ROGUE ASAKURA.
!!
THOUGH HE DOESN'T KNOW IT YET...
...YOH IS ALSO BURDENED WITH THIS TASK...
...AS HEIR TO THE ASAKURA DESTINY.
DOOM
...!!
Whup
HAH!

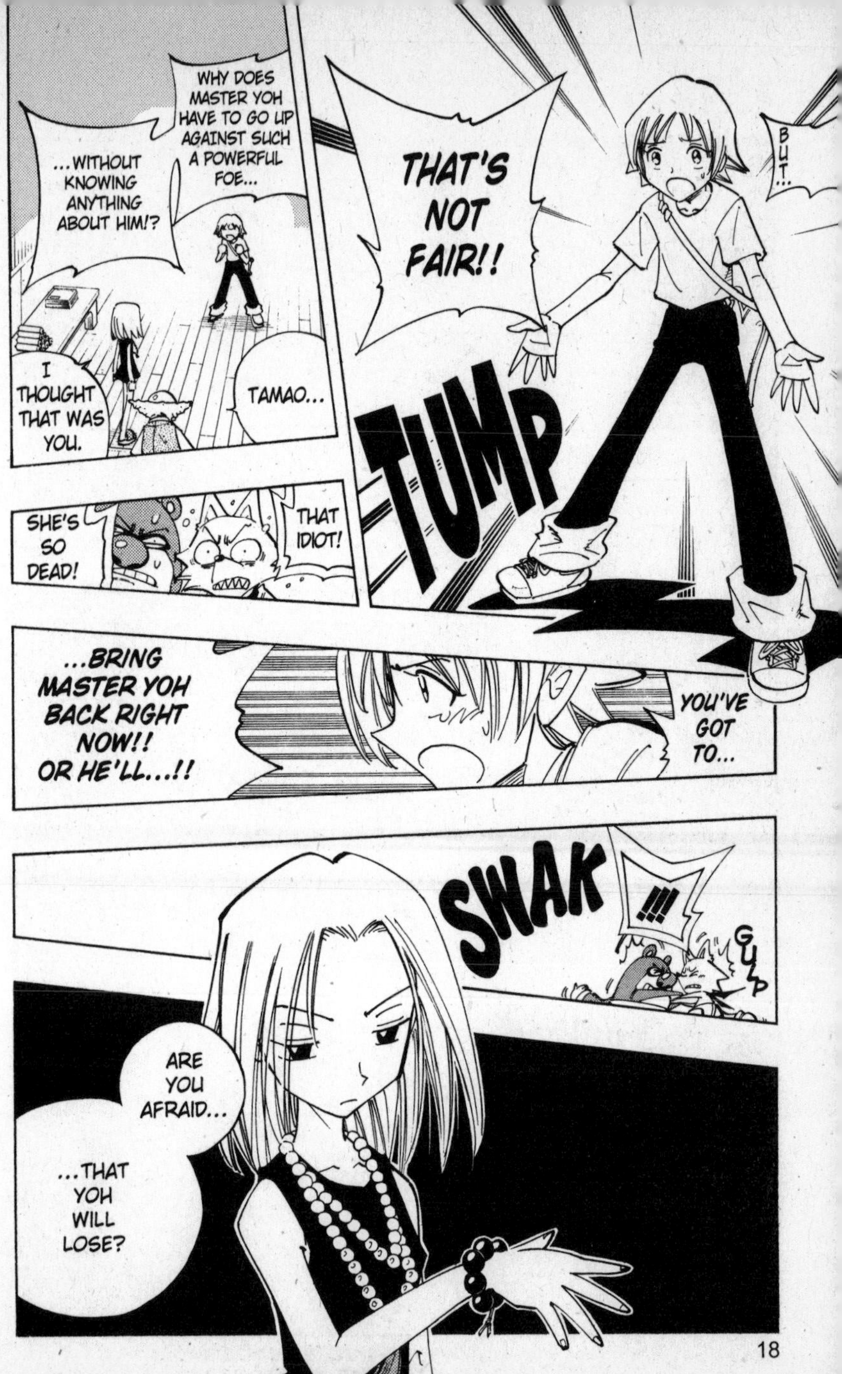
BUT...
THAT'S NOT FAIR!!
TUMP
WHY DOES MASTER YOH HAVE TO GO UP AGAINST SUCH A POWERFUL FOE...
...WITHOUT KNOWING ANYTHING ABOUT HIM!?
TAMAO...
I THOUGHT THAT WAS YOU.
THAT IDIOT!
SHE'S SO DEAD!
YOU'VE GOT TO...
...BRING MASTER YOH BACK RIGHT NOW!! OR HE'LL...!!
SWAK !!!
GULP
ARE YOU AFRAID...
...THAT YOH WILL LOSE?

READ THIS WAY

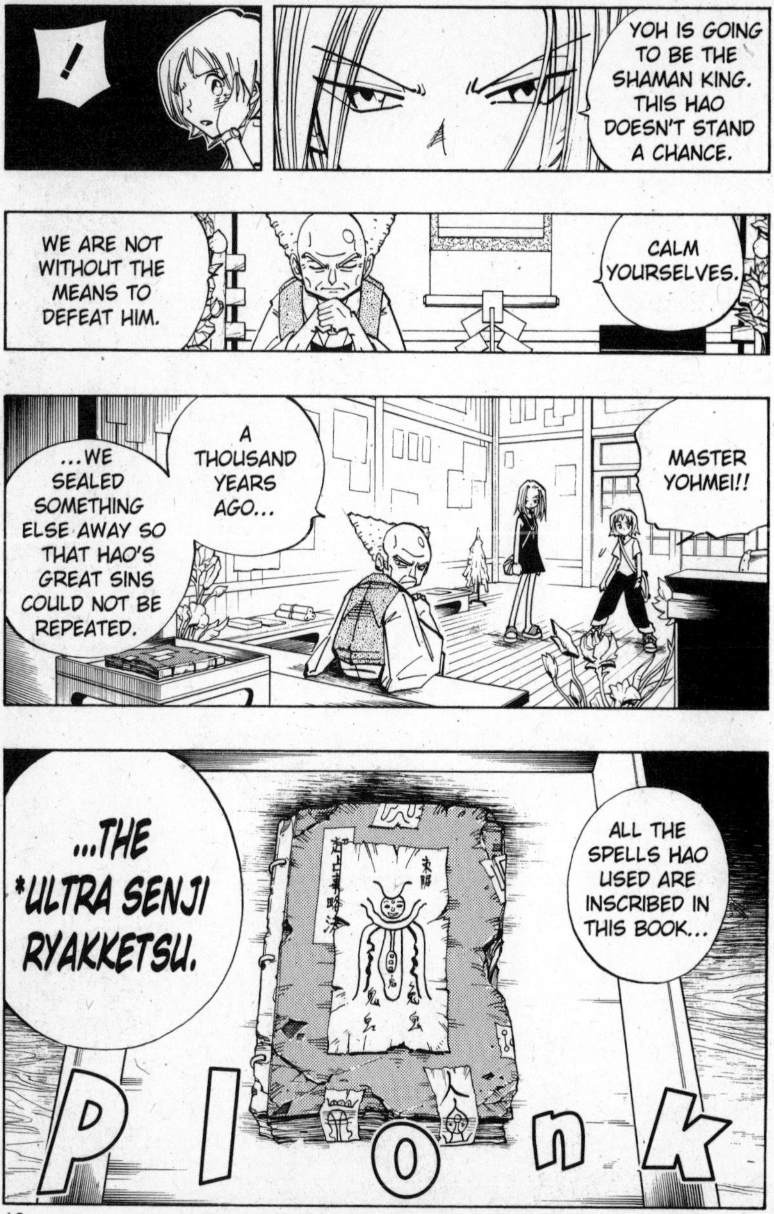

YOH IS GOING TO BE THE SHAMAN KING. THIS HAO DOESN'T STAND A CHANCE.
!
CALM YOURSELVES.
WE ARE NOT WITHOUT THE MEANS TO DEFEAT HIM.
MASTER YOHMEI!!
A THOUSAND YEARS AGO...
...WE SEALED SOMETHING ELSE AWAY SO THAT HAO'S GREAT SINS COULD NOT BE REPEATED.
ALL THE SPELLS HAO USED ARE INSCRIBED IN THIS BOOK...
...THE *ULTRA SENJI RYAKKETSU.
Plonk

*THE REGULAR SENJI RYAKKETSU WAS AN ONMYODO PRIMER WRITTEN BY THE FAMOUS ONMYOJI, ABE NO SEIMEI.

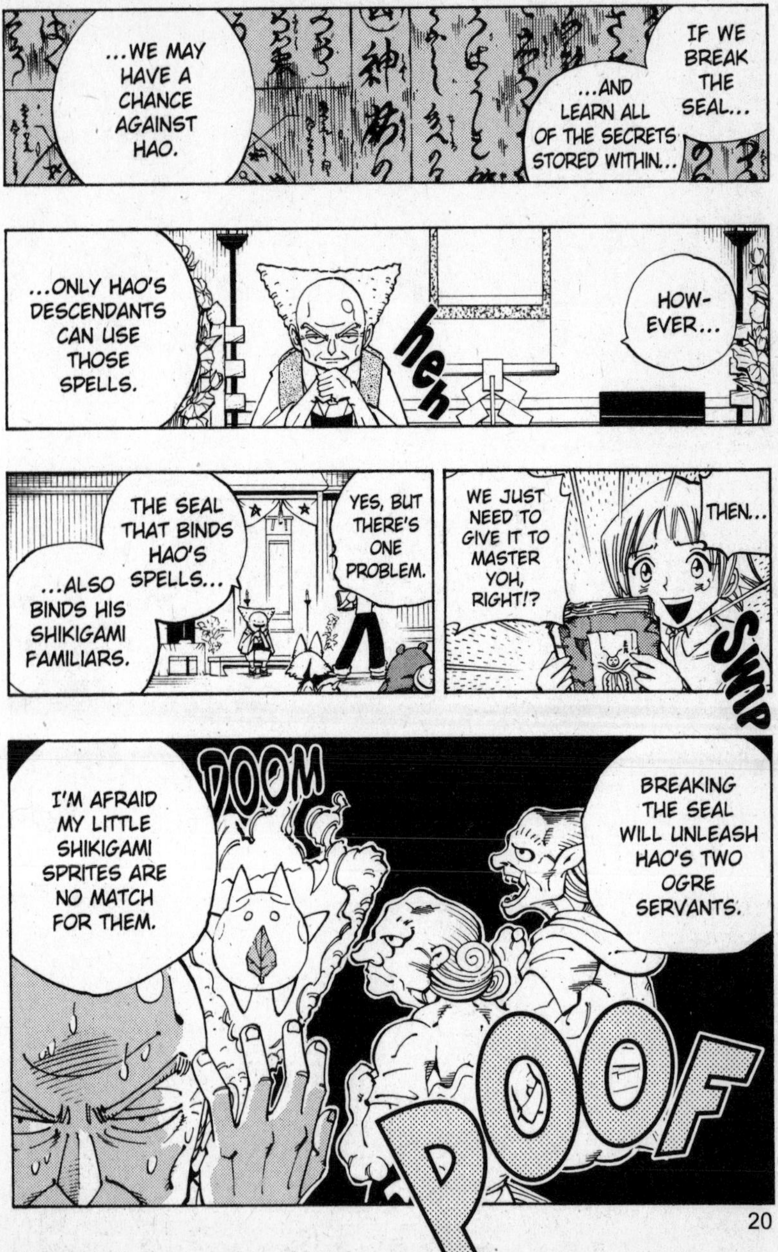
IF WE BREAK THE SEAL...
...AND LEARN ALL OF THE SECRETS STORED WITHIN...
...WE MAY HAVE A CHANCE AGAINST HAO.
HOW-EVER...
heh
...ONLY HAO'S DESCENDANTS CAN USE THOSE SPELLS.
THEN...
WE JUST NEED TO GIVE IT TO MASTER YOH, RIGHT!?
SWIP
YES, BUT THERE'S ONE PROBLEM.
THE SEAL THAT BINDS HAO'S SPELLS...
...ALSO BINDS HIS SHIKIGAMI FAMILIARS.
BREAKING THE SEAL WILL UNLEASH HAO'S TWO OGRE SERVANTS.
DOOM
I'M AFRAID MY LITTLE SHIKIGAMI SPRITES ARE NO MATCH FOR THEM.
POOF

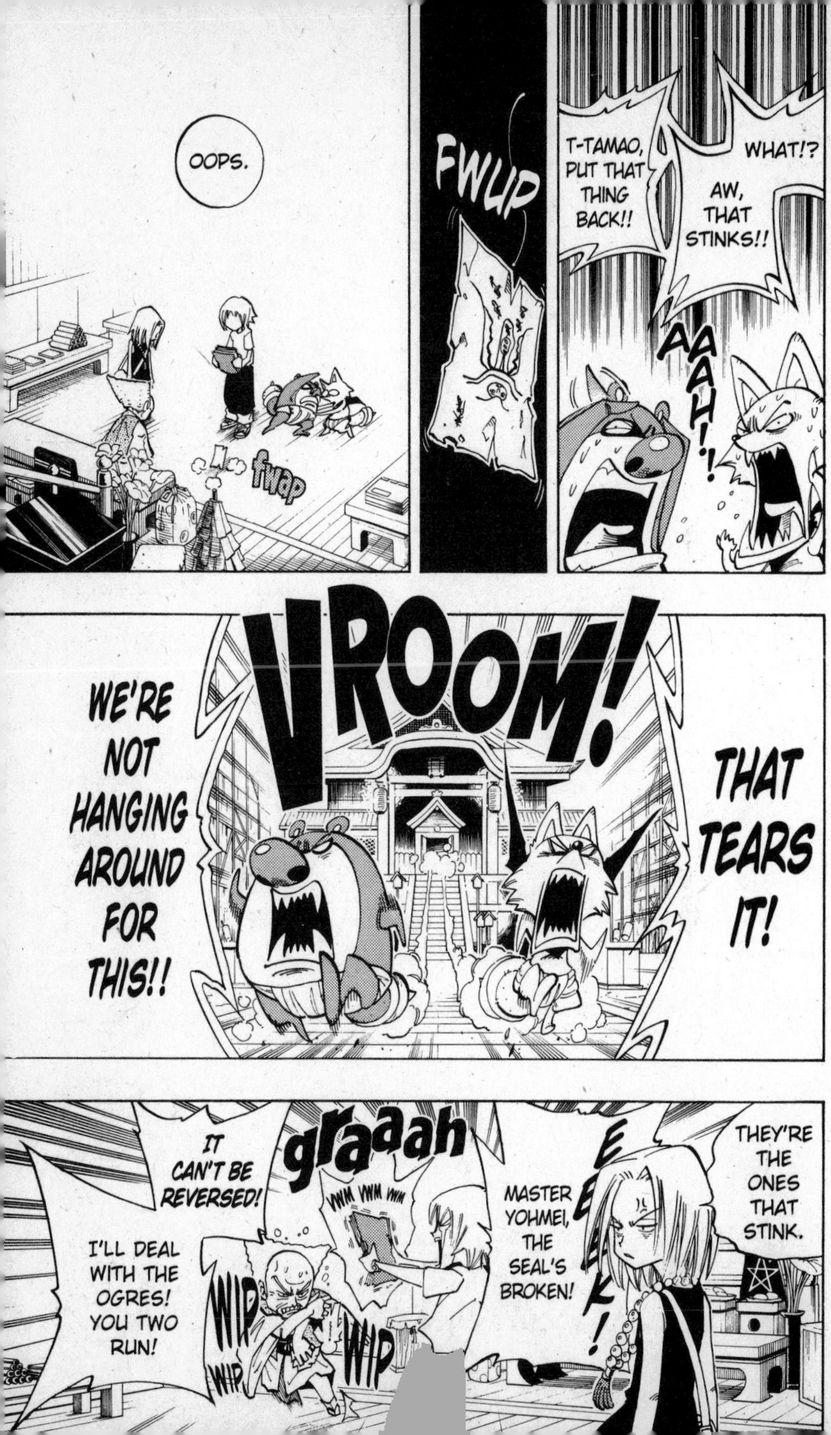
WHAT!?
AW, THAT STINKS!!
T-TAMAO, PUT THAT THING BACK!!
AAAH!!
FWUP
OOPS.
fwap
THAT TEARS IT!
VROOM!
WE'RE NOT HANGING AROUND FOR THIS!!
THEY'RE THE ONES THAT STINK.
EEEK!
MASTER YOHMEI, THE SEAL'S BROKEN!
graaah
VWM VWM VWM
IT CAN'T BE REVERSED!
I'LL DEAL WITH THE OGRES! YOU TWO RUN!
WIP
WIP
WIP

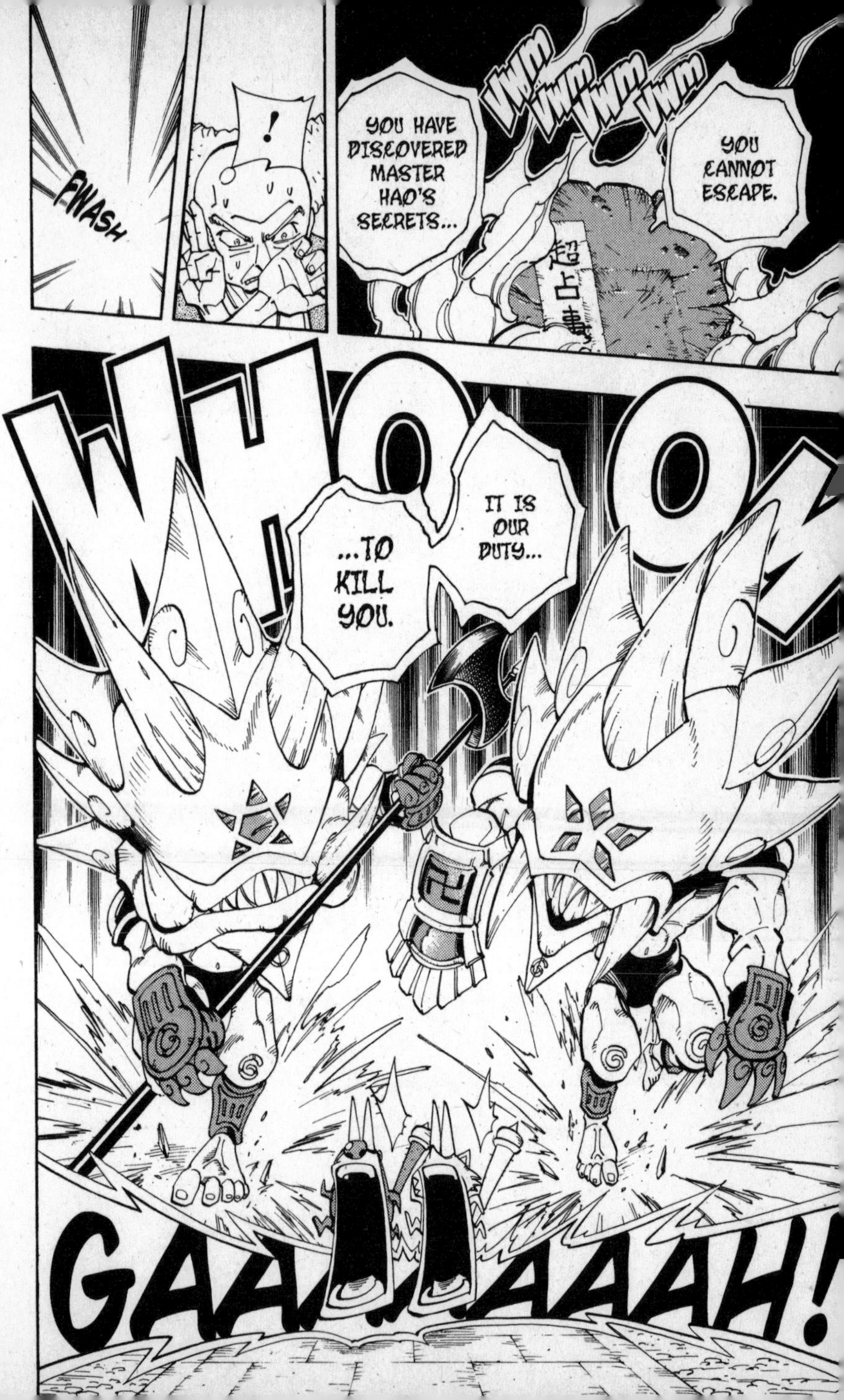
VWM VWM VWM VWM
YOU HAVE DISCOVERED MASTER HAO'S SECRETS...
YOU CANNOT ESCAPE.
!
FWASH
WHOOM
IT IS OUR DUTY...
...TO KILL YOU.
GAAAAAAH!

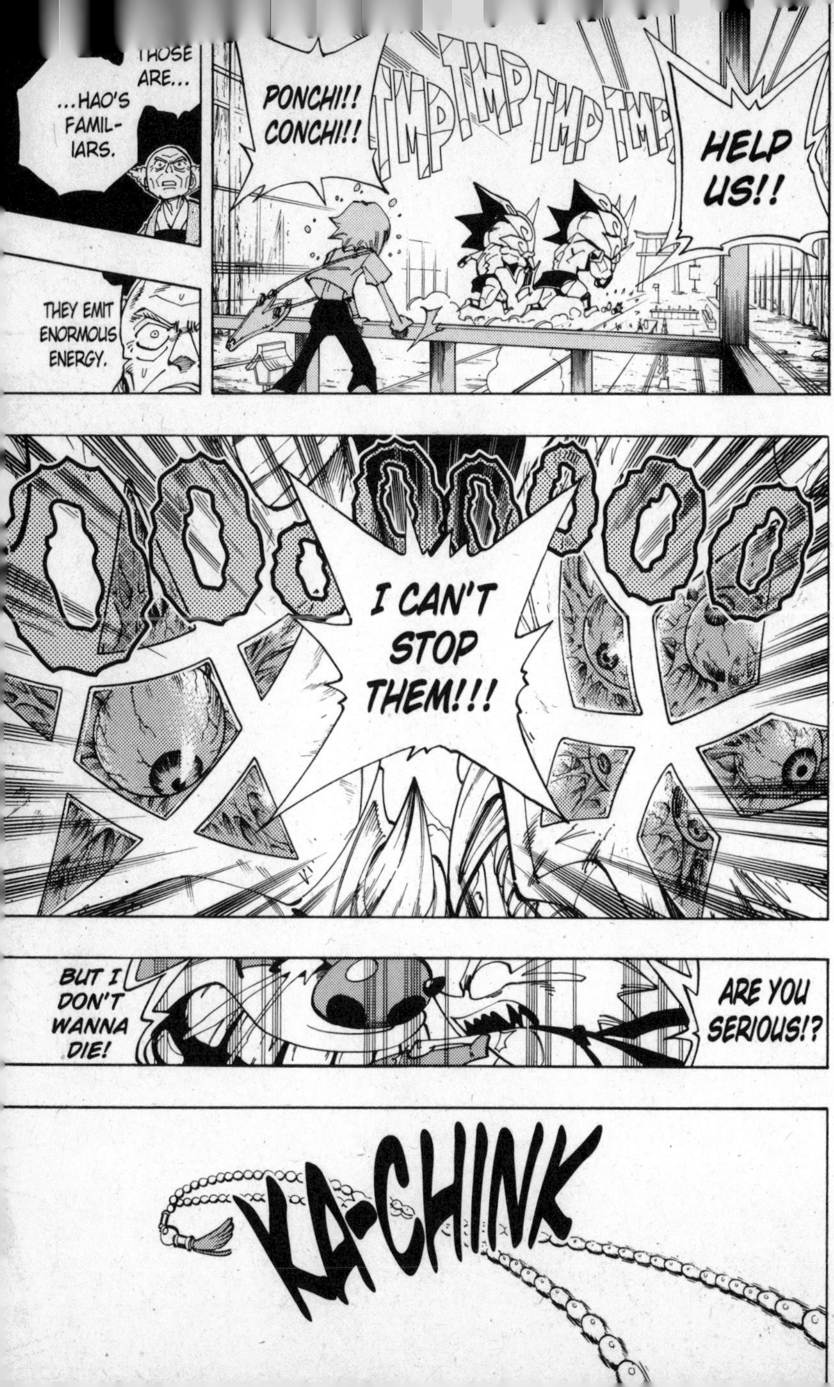
HELP US!!
TMP TMP TMP TMP
PONCHI!! CONCHI!!
THOSE ARE...
...HAO'S FAMIL-IARS.
THEY EMIT ENORMOUS ENERGY.
I CAN'T STOP THEM!!!
ARE YOU SERIOUS!?
BUT I DON'T WANNA DIE!
KA-CHINK

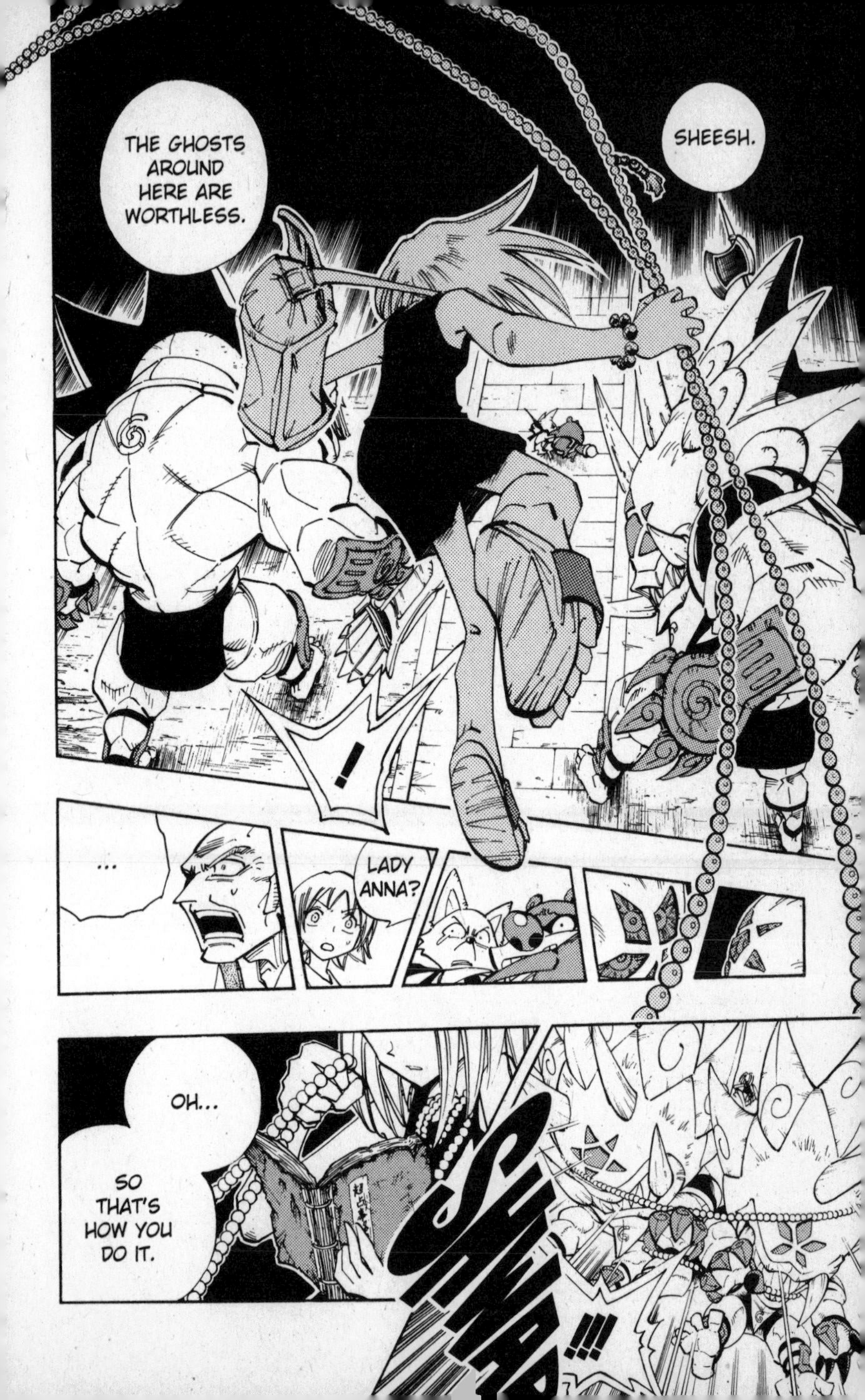
SHEESH.
THE GHOSTS AROUND HERE ARE WORTHLESS.
!
LADY ANNA?
...
SNAP!!!
OH...
SO THAT'S HOW YOU DO IT.

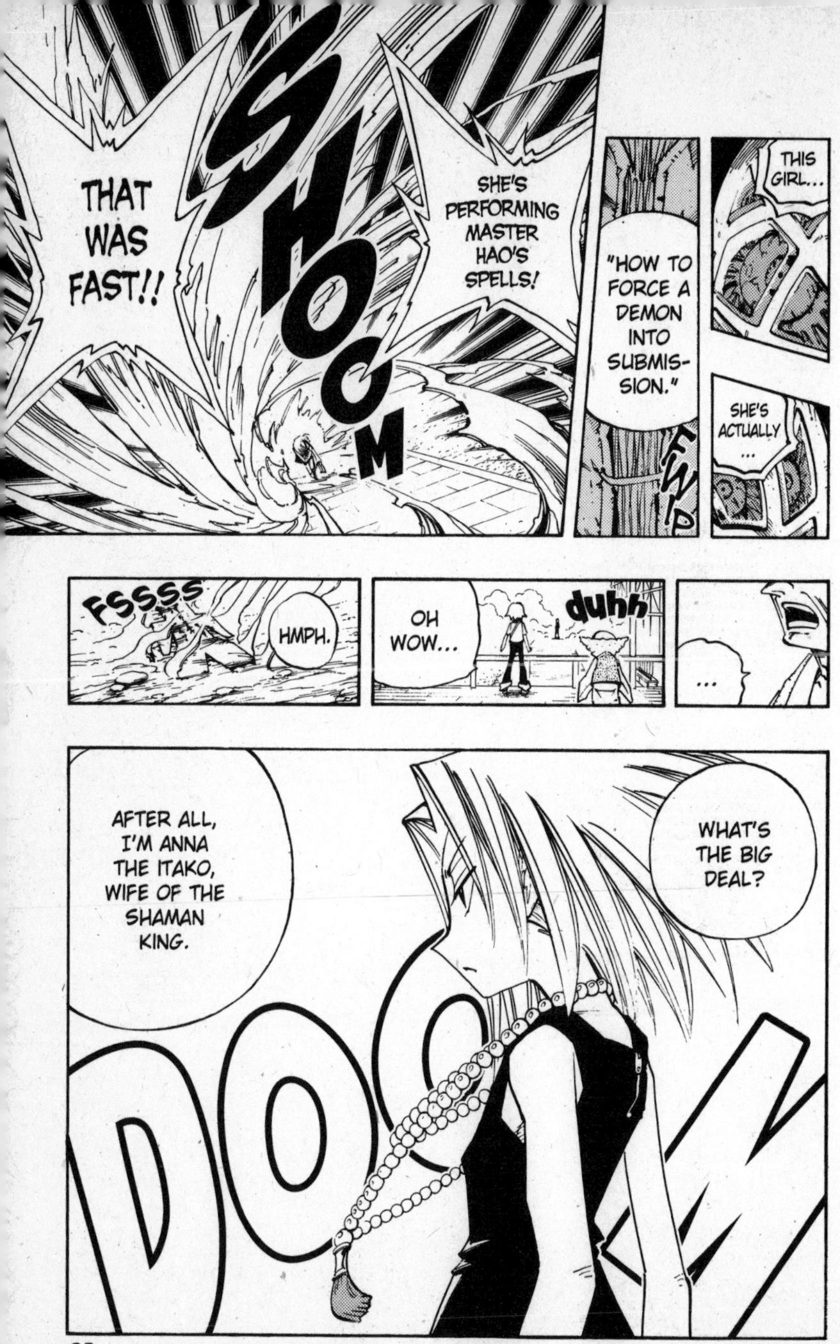
THIS GIRL...
SHE'S ACTUALLY ...
"HOW TO FORCE A DEMON INTO SUBMISSION."
FWIP
SHE'S PERFORMING MASTER HAO'S SPELLS!
SHOOM
THAT WAS FAST!!
...
OH WOW...
duhh
FSSSS
HMPH.
WHAT'S THE BIG DEAL?
AFTER ALL, I'M ANNA THE ITAKO, WIFE OF THE SHAMAN KING.
DOOM

SHAMAN KING CHARACTER FILE No.47

麻倉木乃
KINO ASAKURA

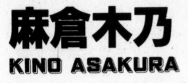

2000
(Nov)

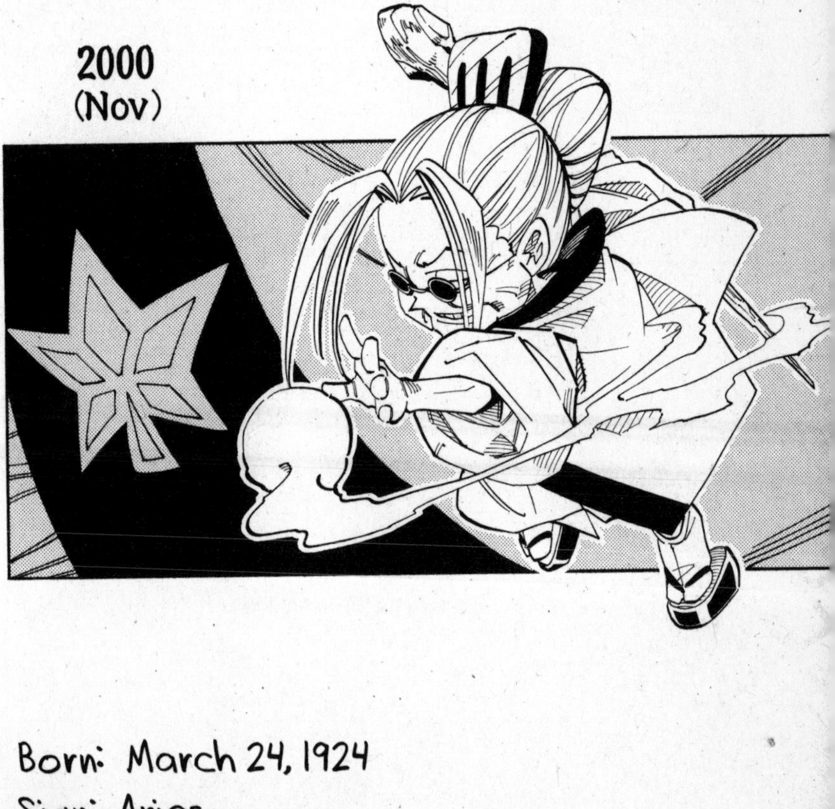

Born: March 24, 1924
Sign: Aries
Blood type: A
Age: 76

Reincarnation 91: When the Pieces Come Together

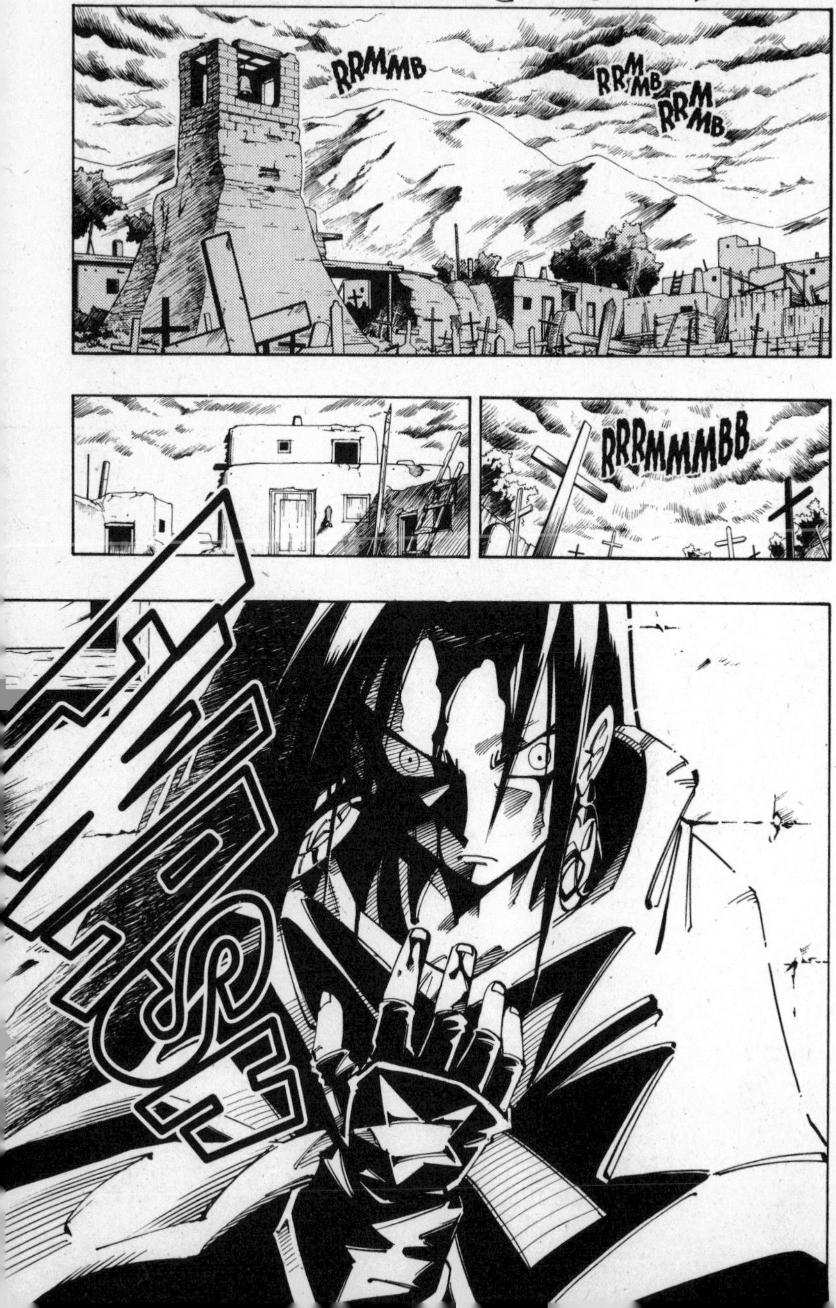
RRMMB
RRMMB
RRMMB
RRRMMMBB

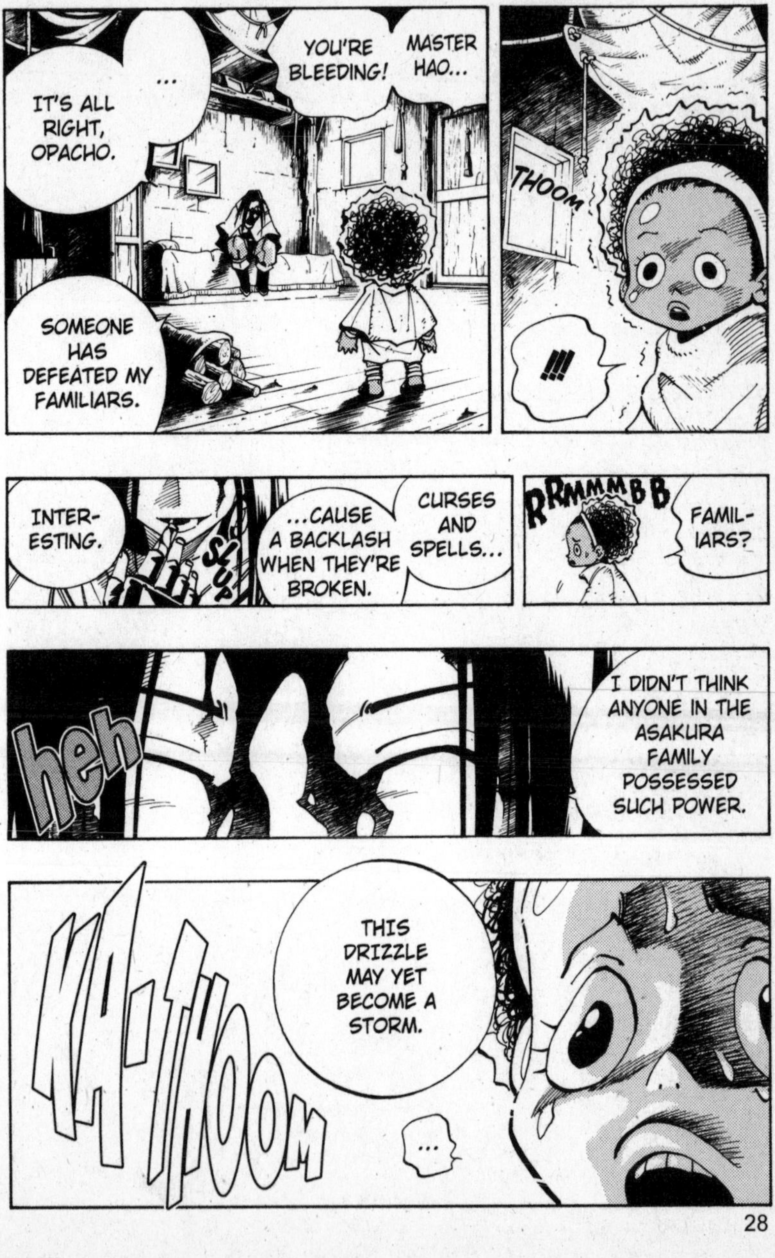
THOOM
!!!
MASTER HAO...
YOU'RE BLEEDING!
...
IT'S ALL RIGHT, OPACHO.
SOMEONE HAS DEFEATED MY FAMILIARS.
FAMILIARS?
RRMMMBB
CURSES AND SPELLS...
...CAUSE A BACKLASH WHEN THEY'RE BROKEN.
SLUP
INTERESTING.
I DIDN'T THINK ANYONE IN THE ASAKURA FAMILY POSSESSED SUCH POWER.
heh
THIS DRIZZLE MAY YET BECOME A STORM.
KA-THOOM
...

Reincarnation 91: When the Pieces Come Together

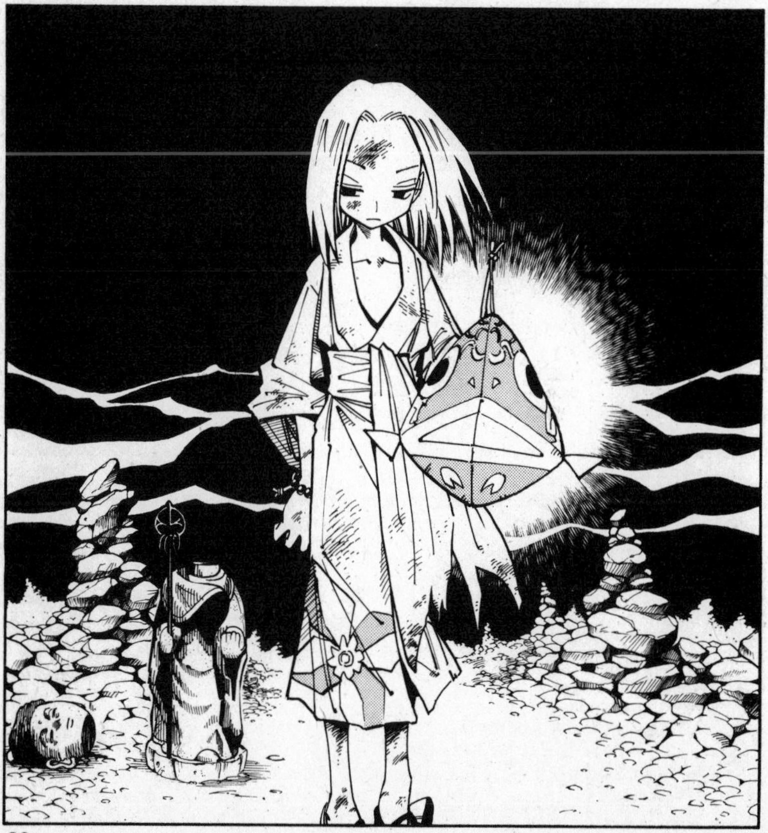

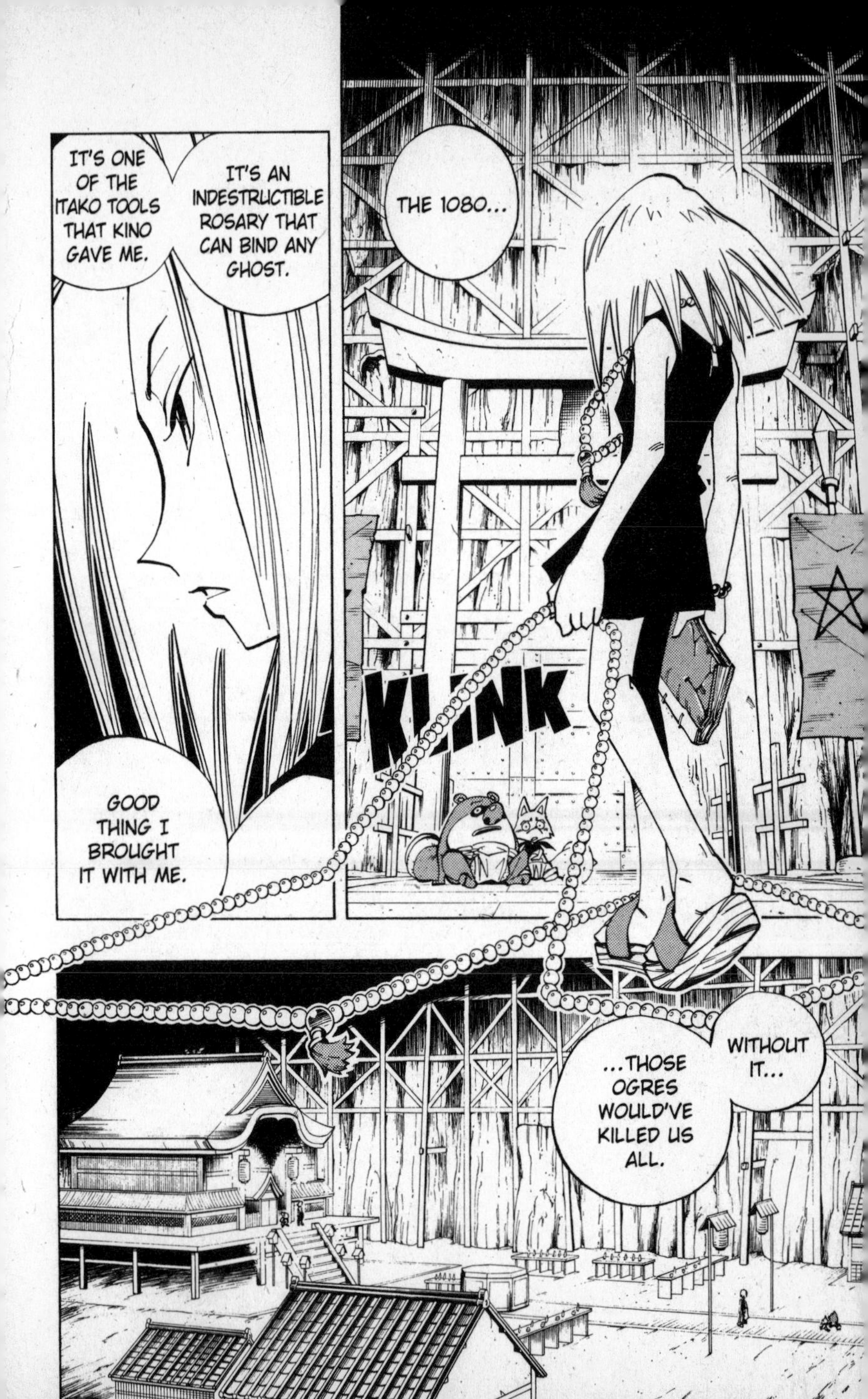
THE 1080...
KLINK
IT'S AN INDESTRUCTIBLE ROSARY THAT CAN BIND ANY GHOST.
IT'S ONE OF THE ITAKO TOOLS THAT KINO GAVE ME.
GOOD THING I BROUGHT IT WITH ME.
WITHOUT IT...
...THOSE OGRES WOULD'VE KILLED US ALL.

READ THIS WAY

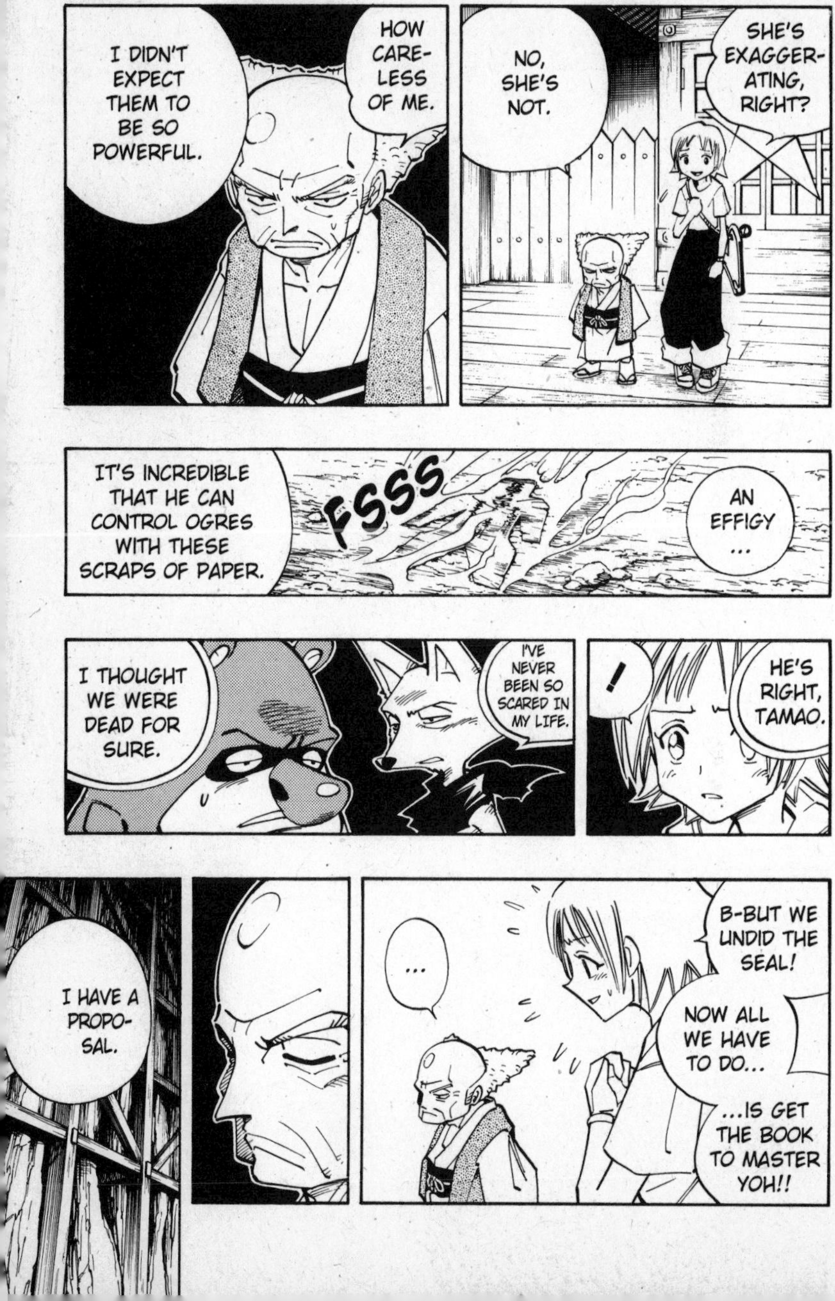
SHE'S EXAGGERATING, RIGHT?
NO, SHE'S NOT.
HOW CARELESS OF ME.
I DIDN'T EXPECT THEM TO BE SO POWERFUL.
AN EFFIGY...
FSSS
IT'S INCREDIBLE THAT HE CAN CONTROL OGRES WITH THESE SCRAPS OF PAPER.
HE'S RIGHT, TAMAO.
!
I'VE NEVER BEEN SO SCARED IN MY LIFE.
I THOUGHT WE WERE DEAD FOR SURE.
B-BUT WE UNDID THE SEAL!
NOW ALL WE HAVE TO DO...
...IS GET THE BOOK TO MASTER YOH!!
...
I HAVE A PROPOSAL.

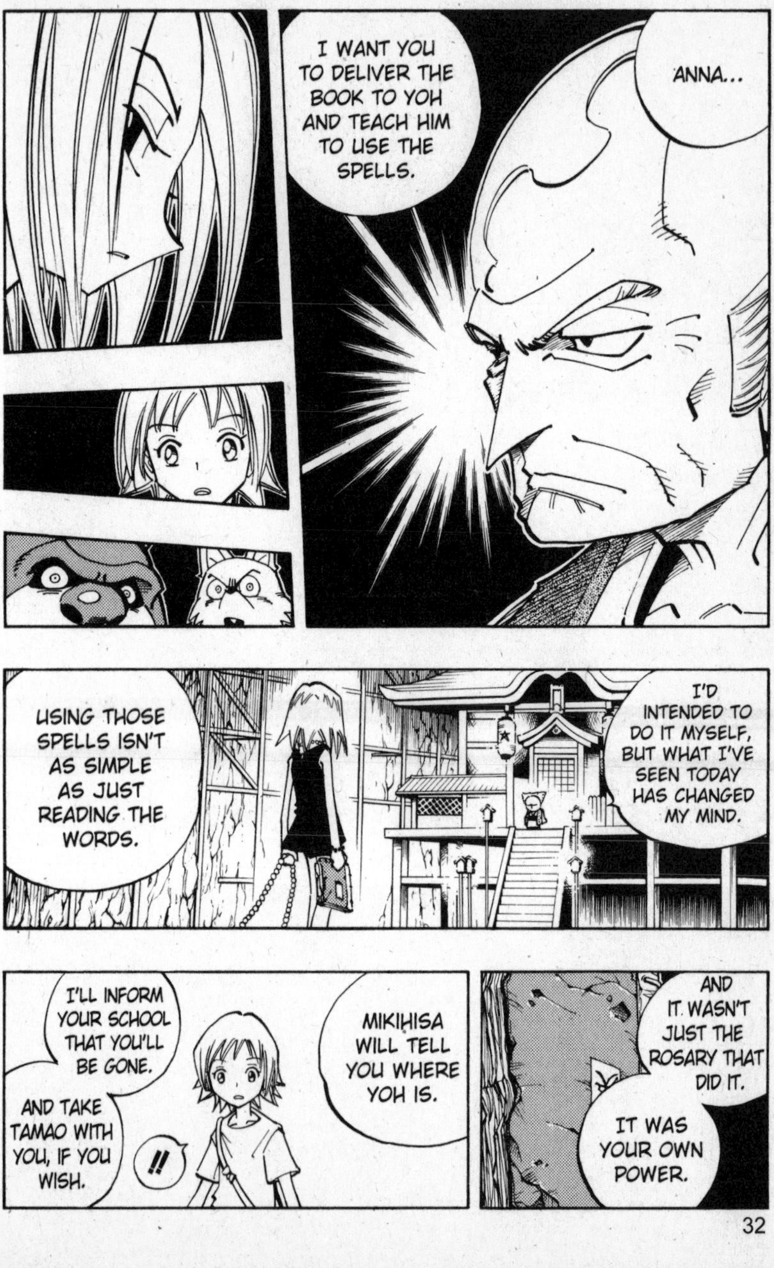
ANNA...
I WANT YOU TO DELIVER THE BOOK TO YOH AND TEACH HIM TO USE THE SPELLS.
I'D INTENDED TO DO IT MYSELF, BUT WHAT I'VE SEEN TODAY HAS CHANGED MY MIND.
USING THOSE SPELLS ISN'T AS SIMPLE AS JUST READING THE WORDS.
AND IT WASN'T JUST THE ROSARY THAT DID IT.
IT WAS YOUR OWN POWER.
MIKIHISA WILL TELL YOU WHERE YOH IS.
I'LL INFORM YOUR SCHOOL THAT YOU'LL BE GONE.
AND TAKE TAMAO WITH YOU, IF YOU WISH.
!!

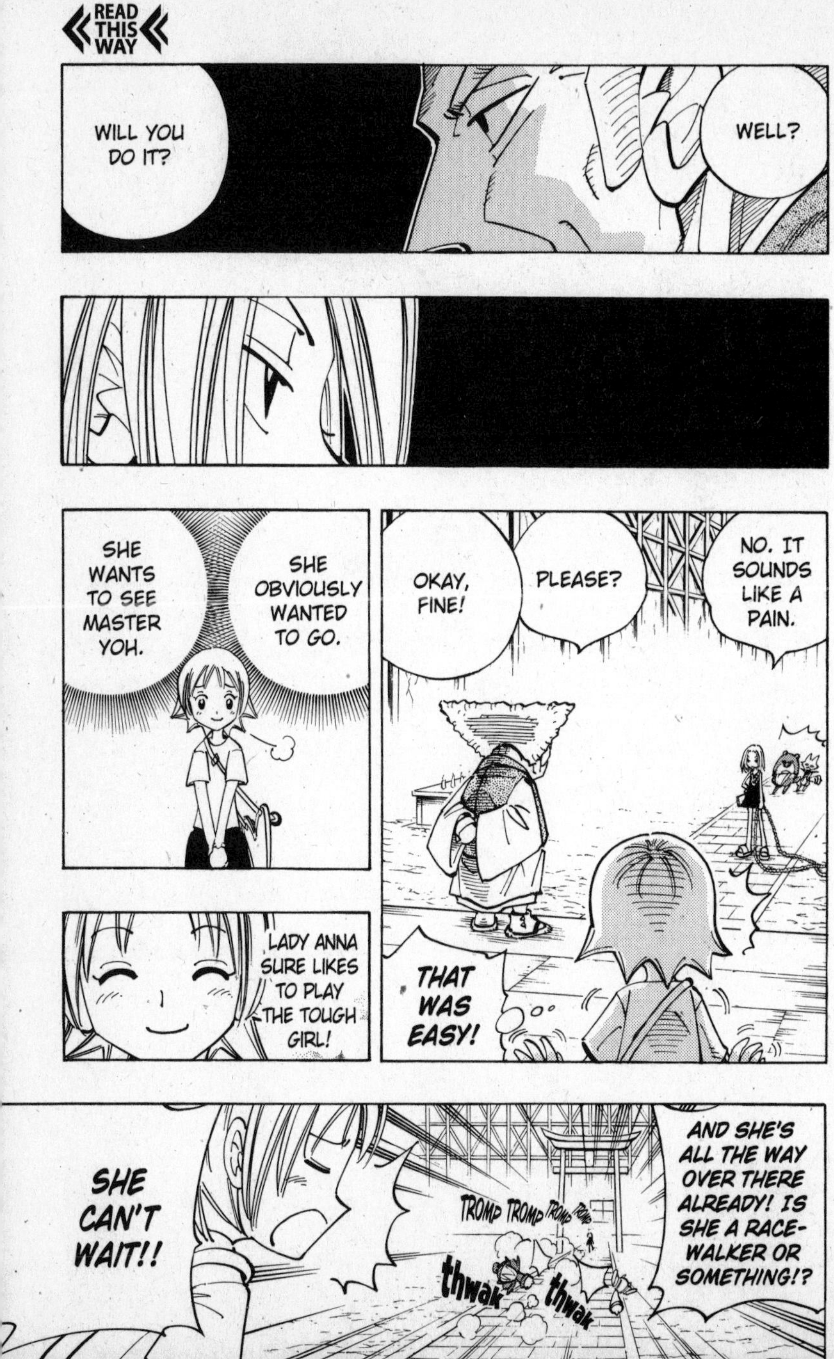
READ THIS WAY
WELL?
WILL YOU DO IT?
NO. IT SOUNDS LIKE A PAIN.
PLEASE?
OKAY, FINE!
THAT WAS EASY!
SHE OBVIOUSLY WANTED TO GO.
SHE WANTS TO SEE MASTER YOH.
LADY ANNA SURE LIKES TO PLAY THE TOUGH GIRL!
AND SHE'S ALL THE WAY OVER THERE ALREADY! IS SHE A RACE-WALKER OR SOMETHING!?
TROMP TROMP TROMP TROMP
thwak thwak
SHE CAN'T WAIT!!

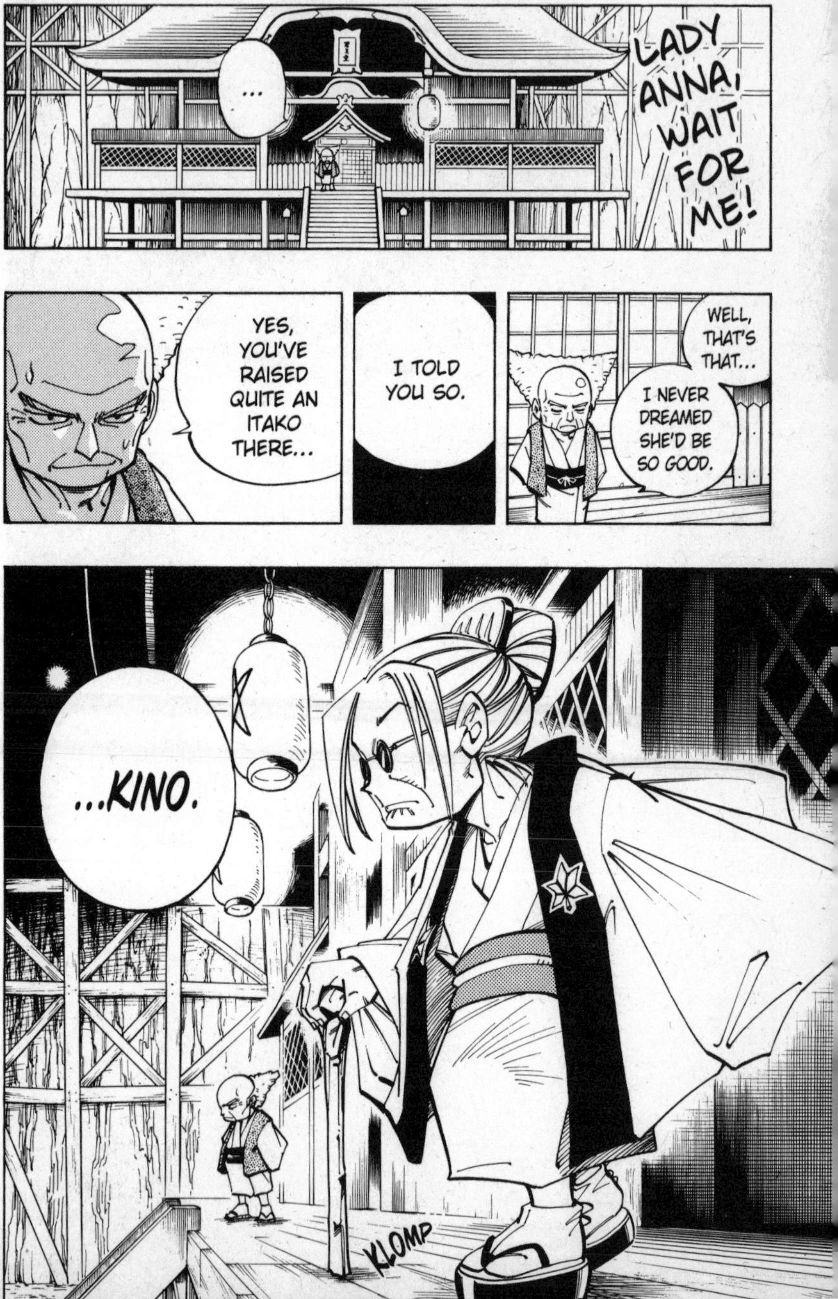
LADY ANNA, WAIT FOR ME!
...
WELL, THAT'S THAT...
I NEVER DREAMED SHE'D BE SO GOOD.
I TOLD YOU SO.
YES, YOU'VE RAISED QUITE AN ITAKO THERE...
...KINO.
KLOMP

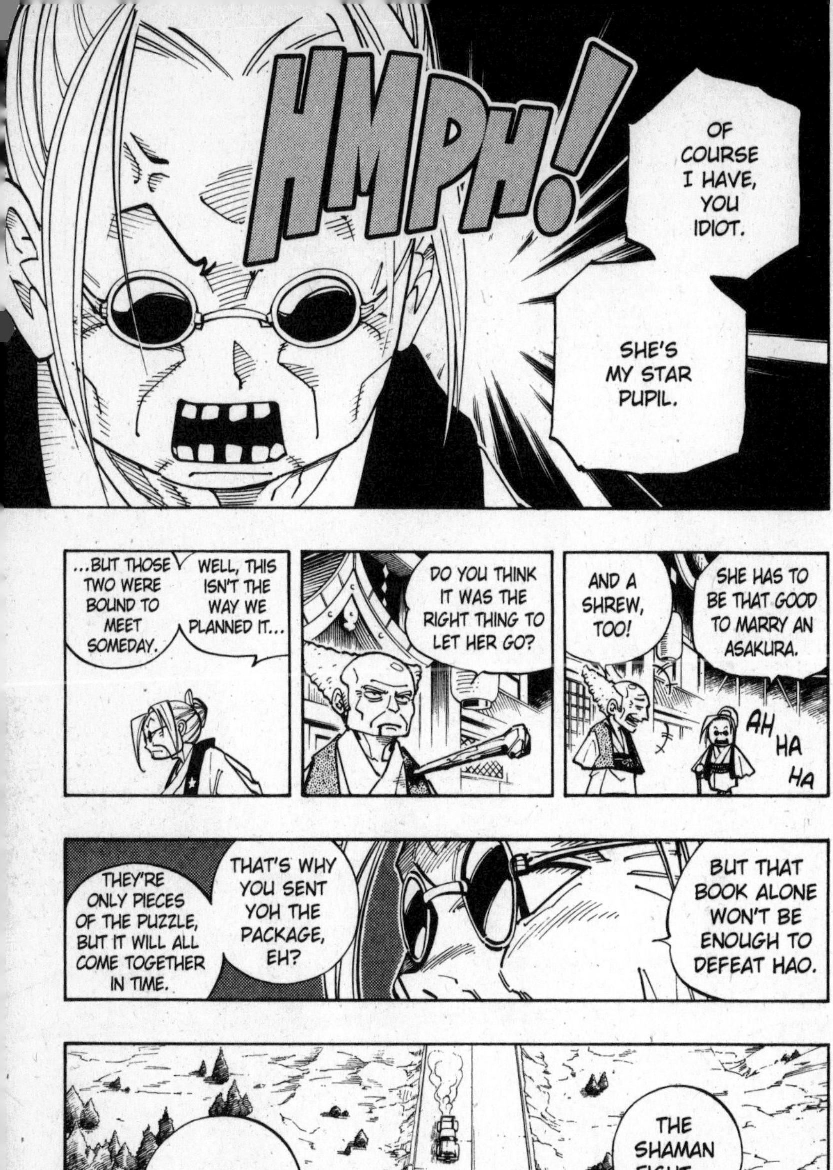
HMPH!
OF COURSE I HAVE, YOU IDIOT.
SHE'S MY STAR PUPIL.
SHE HAS TO BE THAT GOOD TO MARRY AN ASAKURA.
AND A SHREW, TOO!
AH HA HA
DO YOU THINK IT WAS THE RIGHT THING TO LET HER GO?
WELL, THIS ISN'T THE WAY WE PLANNED IT...
...BUT THOSE TWO WERE BOUND TO MEET SOMEDAY.
BUT THAT BOOK ALONE WON'T BE ENOUGH TO DEFEAT HAO.
THAT'S WHY YOU SENT YOH THE PACKAGE, EH?
THEY'RE ONLY PIECES OF THE PUZZLE, BUT IT WILL ALL COME TOGETHER IN TIME.
THE SHAMAN FIGHT...
ALL THOSE SHAMANS...

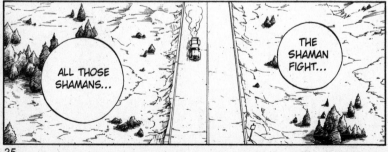

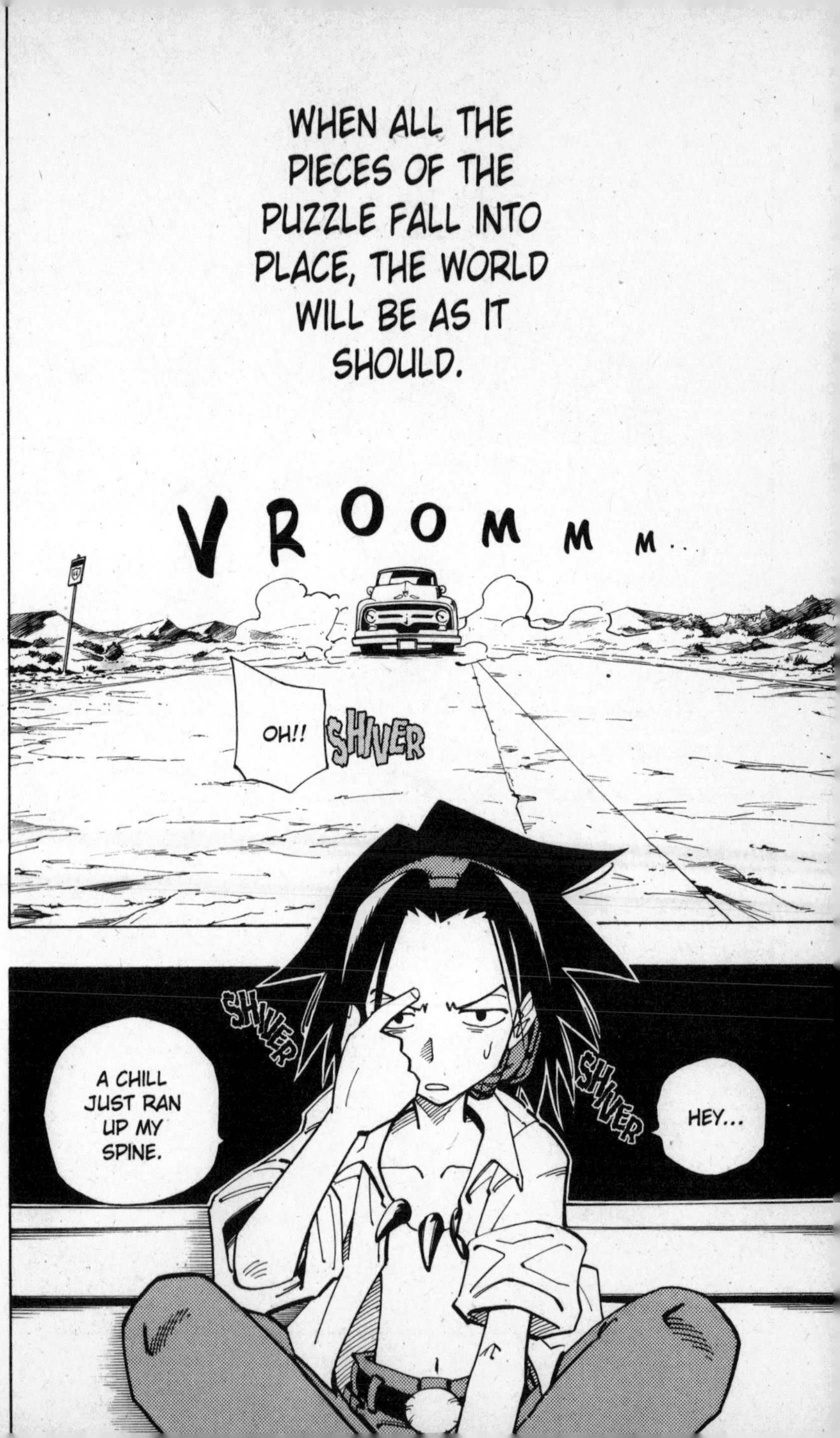
WHEN ALL THE PIECES OF THE PUZZLE FALL INTO PLACE, THE WORLD WILL BE AS IT SHOULD.
VROOMMM...
SHIVER
OH!!
SHIVER
HEY...
SHIVER
A CHILL JUST RAN UP MY SPINE.

READ THIS WAY

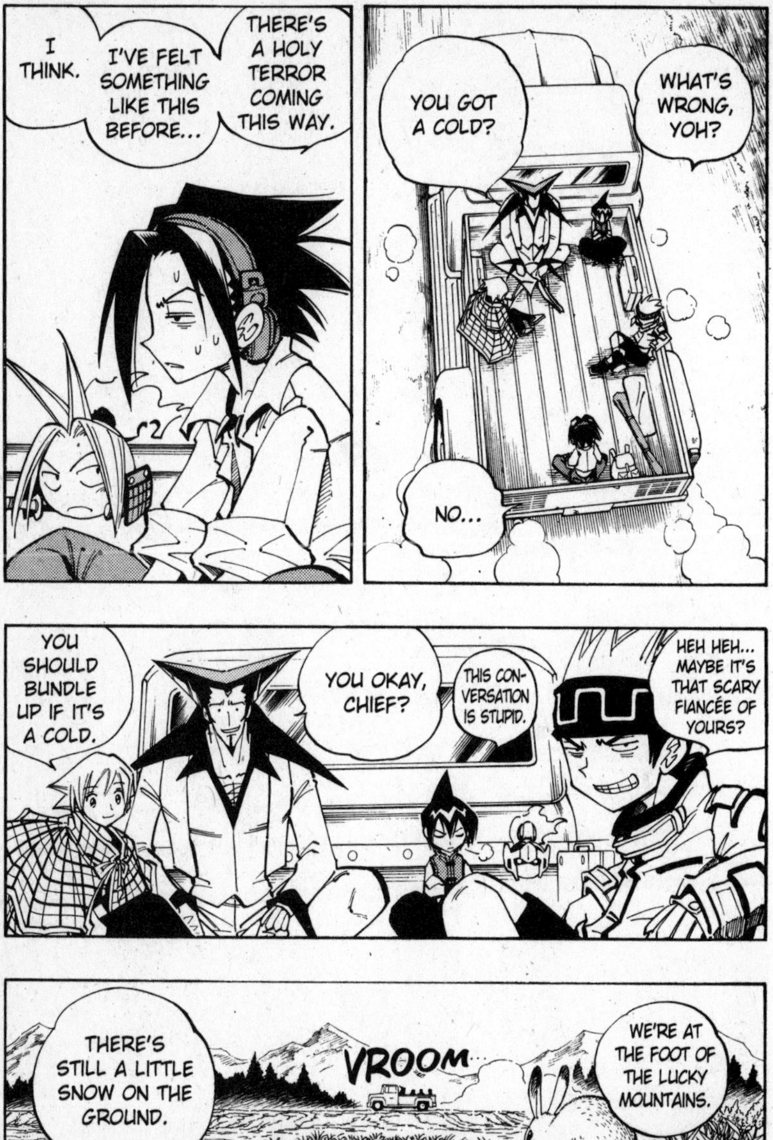
WHAT'S WRONG, YOH?
YOU GOT A COLD?
NO...
THERE'S A HOLY TERROR COMING THIS WAY.
I'VE FELT SOMETHING LIKE THIS BEFORE...
I THINK.
HEH HEH... MAYBE IT'S THAT SCARY FIANCÉE OF YOURS?
THIS CONVERSATION IS STUPID.
YOU OKAY, CHIEF?
YOU SHOULD BUNDLE UP IF IT'S A COLD.
WE'RE AT THE FOOT OF THE LUCKY MOUNTAINS.
VROOM...
THERE'S STILL A LITTLE SNOW ON THE GROUND.

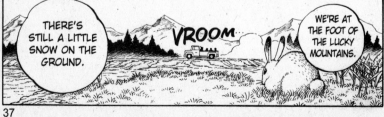

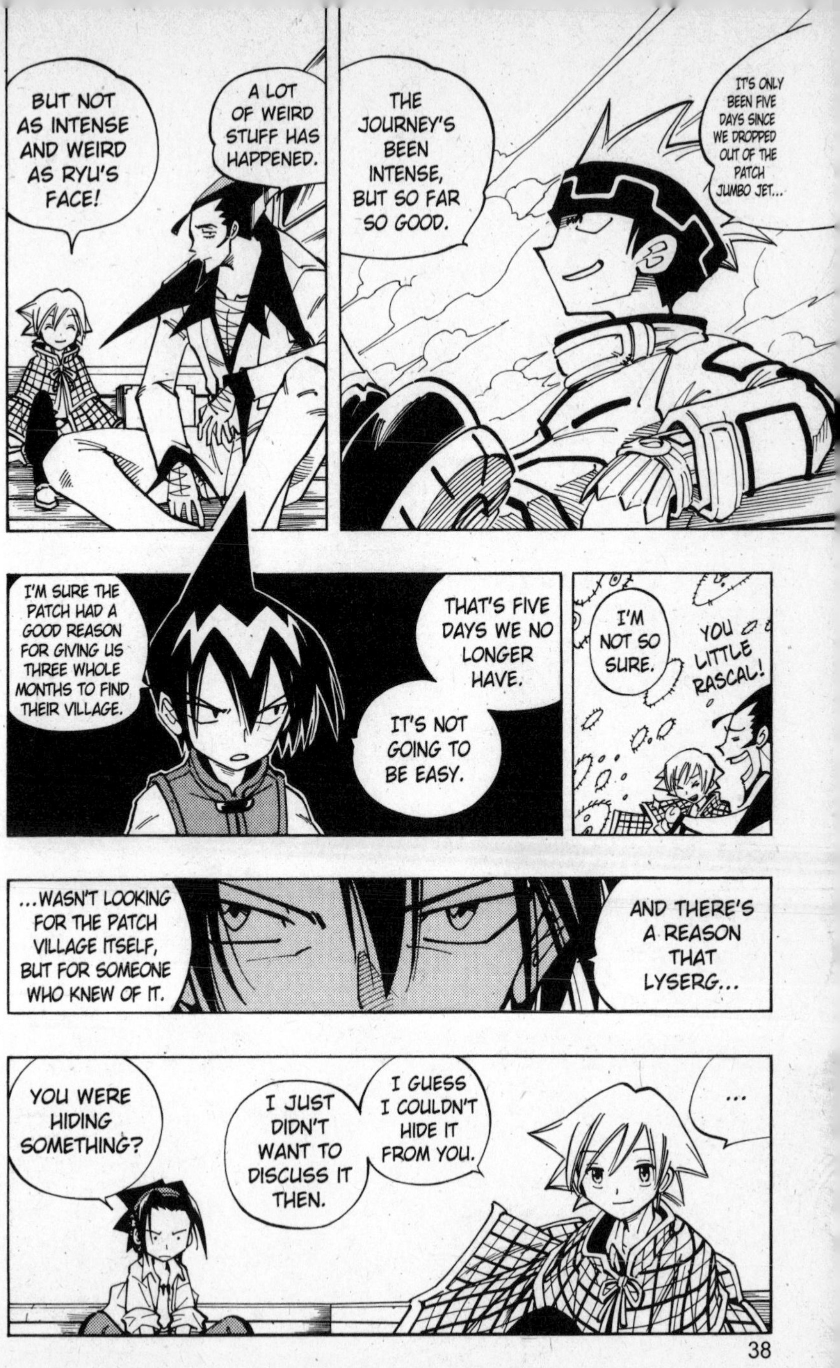
IT'S ONLY BEEN FIVE DAYS SINCE WE DROPPED OUT OF THE PATCH JUMBO JET...
THE JOURNEY'S BEEN INTENSE, BUT SO FAR SO GOOD.
A LOT OF WEIRD STUFF HAS HAPPENED.
BUT NOT AS INTENSE AND WEIRD AS RYU'S FACE!
I'M NOT SO SURE.
YOU LITTLE RASCAL!
THAT'S FIVE DAYS WE NO LONGER HAVE.
IT'S NOT GOING TO BE EASY.
I'M SURE THE PATCH HAD A GOOD REASON FOR GIVING US THREE WHOLE MONTHS TO FIND THEIR VILLAGE.
AND THERE'S A REASON THAT LYSERG...
...WASN'T LOOKING FOR THE PATCH VILLAGE ITSELF, BUT FOR SOMEONE WHO KNEW OF IT.
...
I GUESS I COULDN'T HIDE IT FROM YOU.
I JUST DIDN'T WANT TO DISCUSS IT THEN.
YOU WERE HIDING SOMETHING?

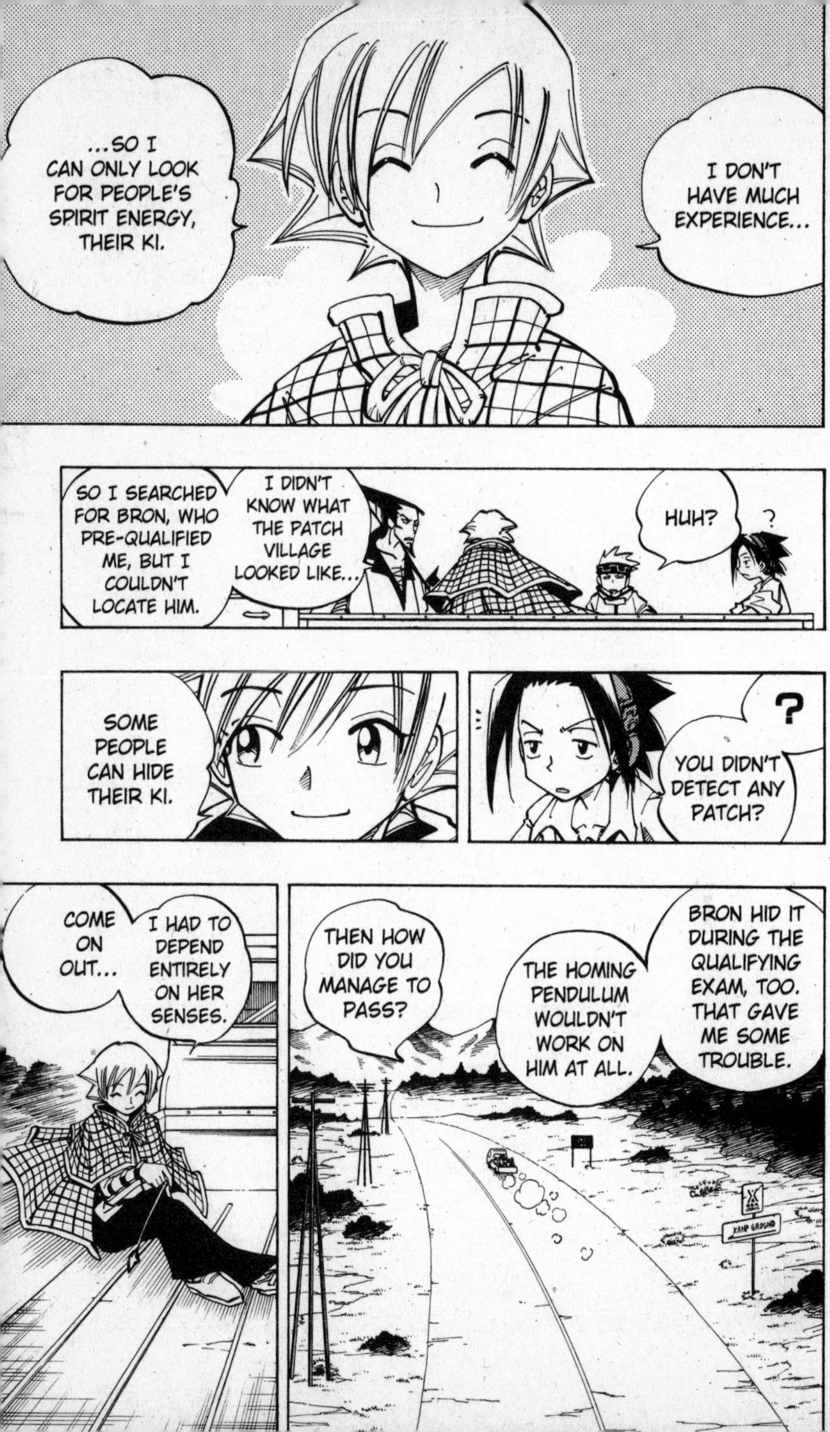
I DON'T HAVE MUCH EXPERIENCE...
...SO I CAN ONLY LOOK FOR PEOPLE'S SPIRIT ENERGY, THEIR KI.
HUH?
?
I DIDN'T KNOW WHAT THE PATCH VILLAGE LOOKED LIKE...
SO I SEARCHED FOR BRON, WHO PRE-QUALIFIED ME, BUT I COULDN'T LOCATE HIM.
?
YOU DIDN'T DETECT ANY PATCH?
SOME PEOPLE CAN HIDE THEIR KI.
BRON HID IT DURING THE QUALIFYING EXAM, TOO. THAT GAVE ME SOME TROUBLE.
THE HOMING PENDULUM WOULDN'T WORK ON HIM AT ALL.
THEN HOW DID YOU MANAGE TO PASS?
I HAD TO DEPEND ENTIRELY ON HER SENSES.
COME ON OUT...

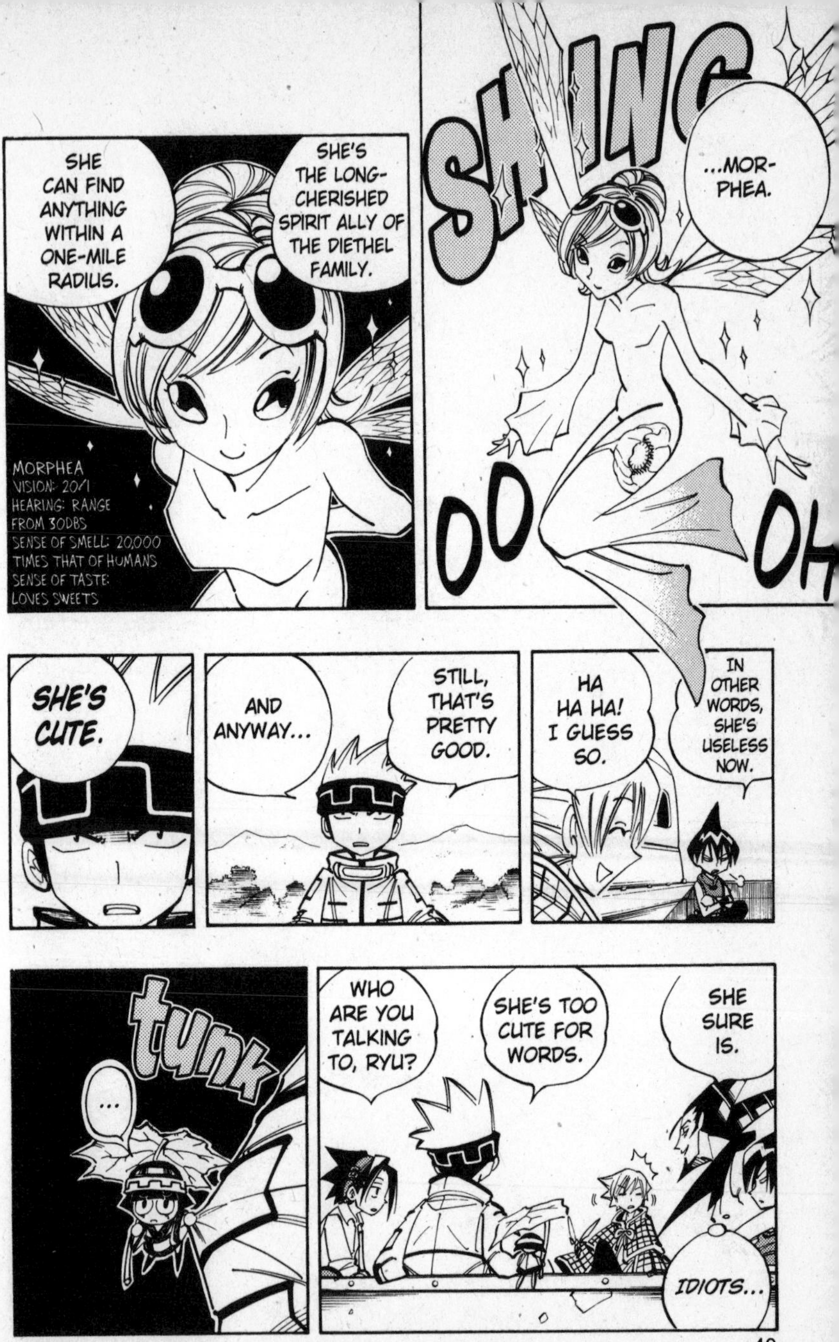
SHING
...MORPHEA.
DOOOH
SHE'S THE LONG-CHERISHED SPIRIT ALLY OF THE DIETHEL FAMILY.
SHE CAN FIND ANYTHING WITHIN A ONE-MILE RADIUS.
MORPHEA
VISION: 20/1
HEARING: RANGE FROM 30DBS
SENSE OF SMELL: 20,000 TIMES THAT OF HUMANS
SENSE OF TASTE: LOVES SWEETS
IN OTHER WORDS, SHE'S USELESS NOW.
HA HA HA! I GUESS SO.
STILL, THAT'S PRETTY GOOD.
AND ANYWAY...
SHE'S CUTE.
SHE SURE IS.
SHE'S TOO CUTE FOR WORDS.
WHO ARE YOU TALKING TO, RYU?
IDIOTS...
tunk
...

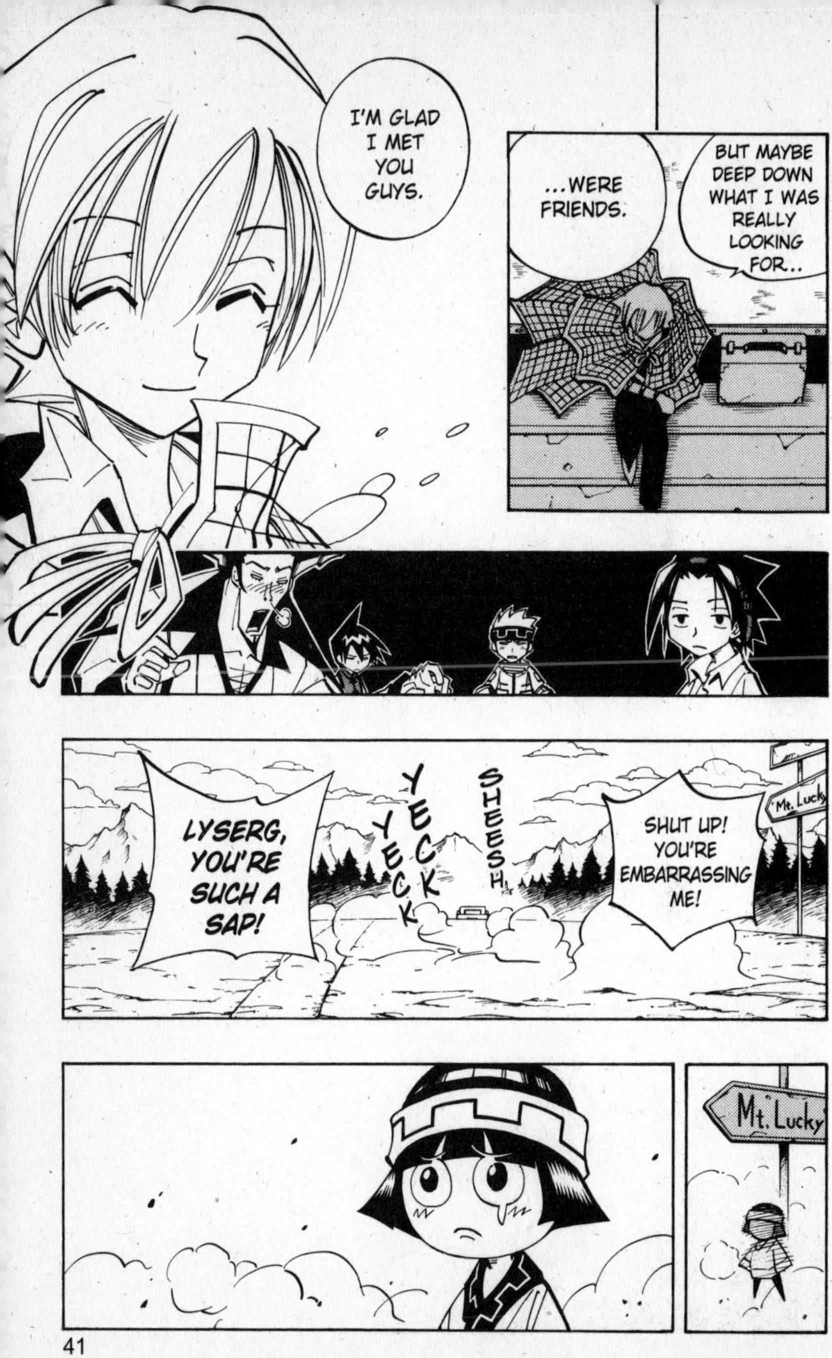
BUT MAYBE DEEP DOWN WHAT I WAS REALLY LOOKING FOR...
...WERE FRIENDS.
I'M GLAD I MET YOU GUYS.
Mt. Lucky
SHUT UP! YOU'RE EMBARRASSING ME!
SHEESH
YECK YECK
LYSERG, YOU'RE SUCH A SAP!
Mt. Lucky

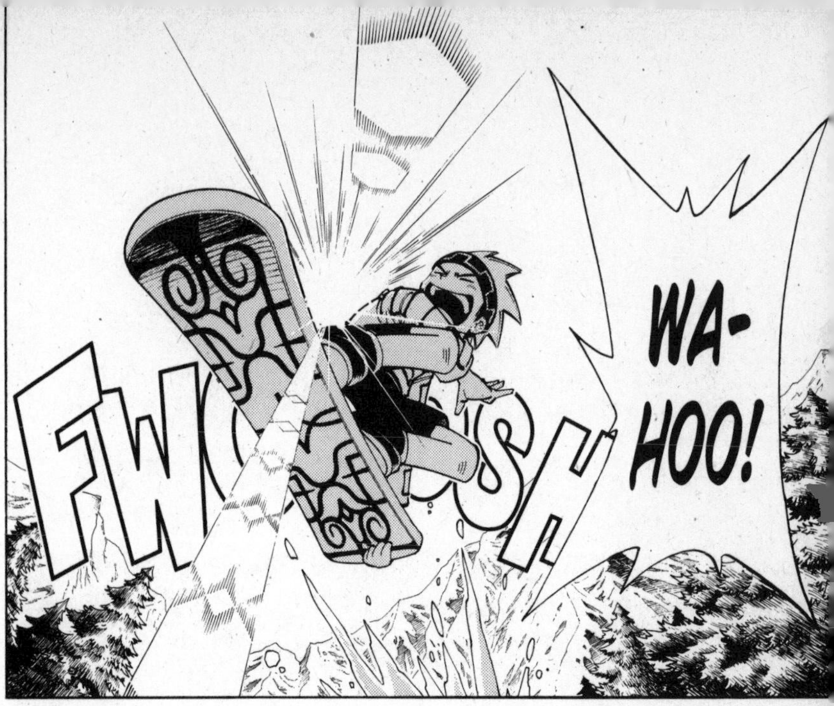
WA-HOO!
FWOOSH

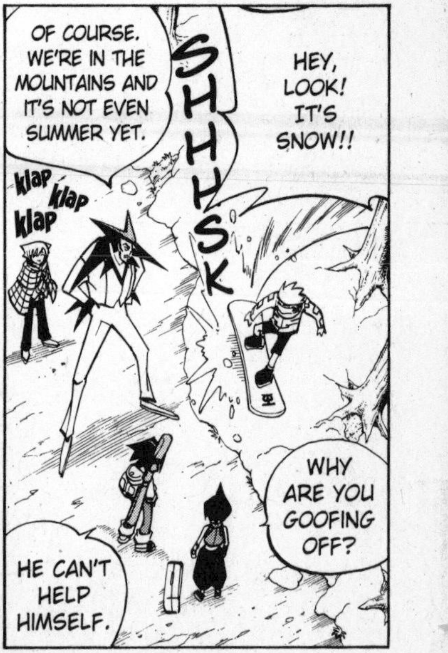
HEY, LOOK! IT'S SNOW!!
OF COURSE. WE'RE IN THE MOUNTAINS AND IT'S NOT EVEN SUMMER YET.
SHHHSK
klap klap klap
WHY ARE YOU GOOFING OFF?
HE CAN'T HELP HIMSELF.

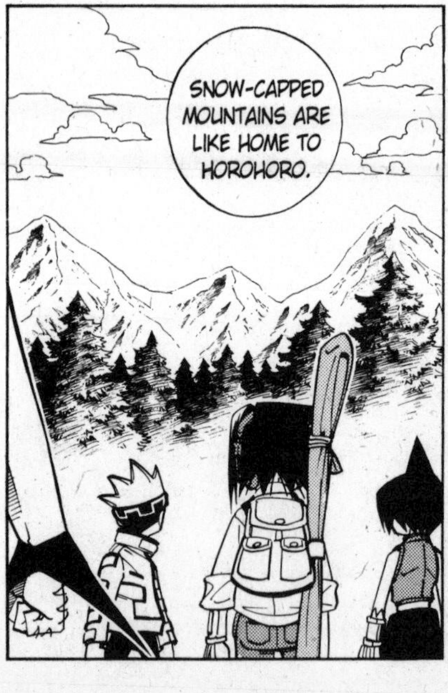
SNOW-CAPPED MOUNTAINS ARE LIKE HOME TO HOROHORO.

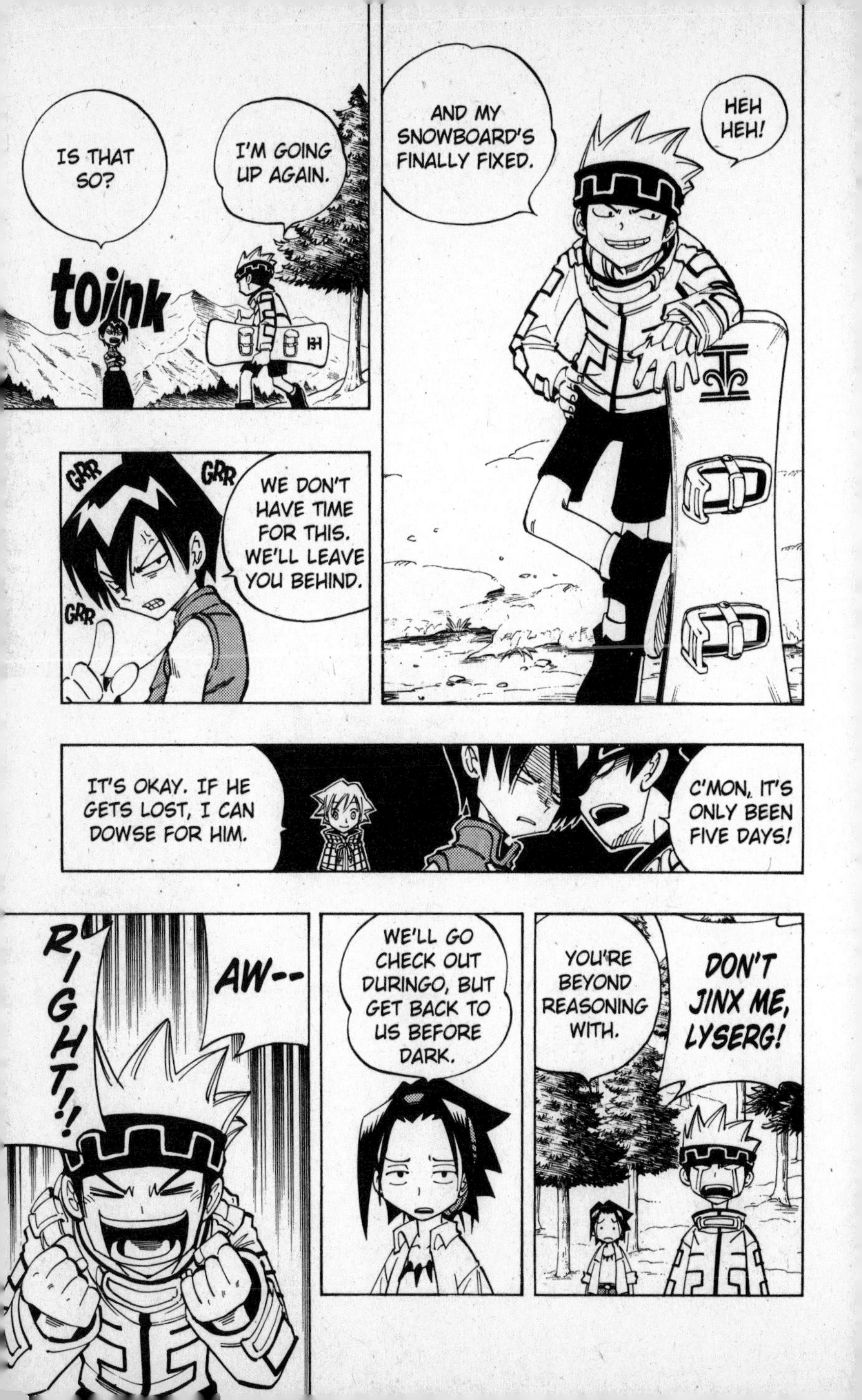
HEH HEH!
AND MY SNOWBOARD'S FINALLY FIXED.
I'M GOING UP AGAIN.
IS THAT SO?
toink
GRR GRR GRR
WE DON'T HAVE TIME FOR THIS. WE'LL LEAVE YOU BEHIND.
C'MON, IT'S ONLY BEEN FIVE DAYS!
IT'S OKAY. IF HE GETS LOST, I CAN DOWSE FOR HIM.
DON'T JINX ME, LYSERG!
YOU'RE BEYOND REASONING WITH.
WE'LL GO CHECK OUT DURINGO, BUT GET BACK TO US BEFORE DARK.
AW--
RIGHT!!

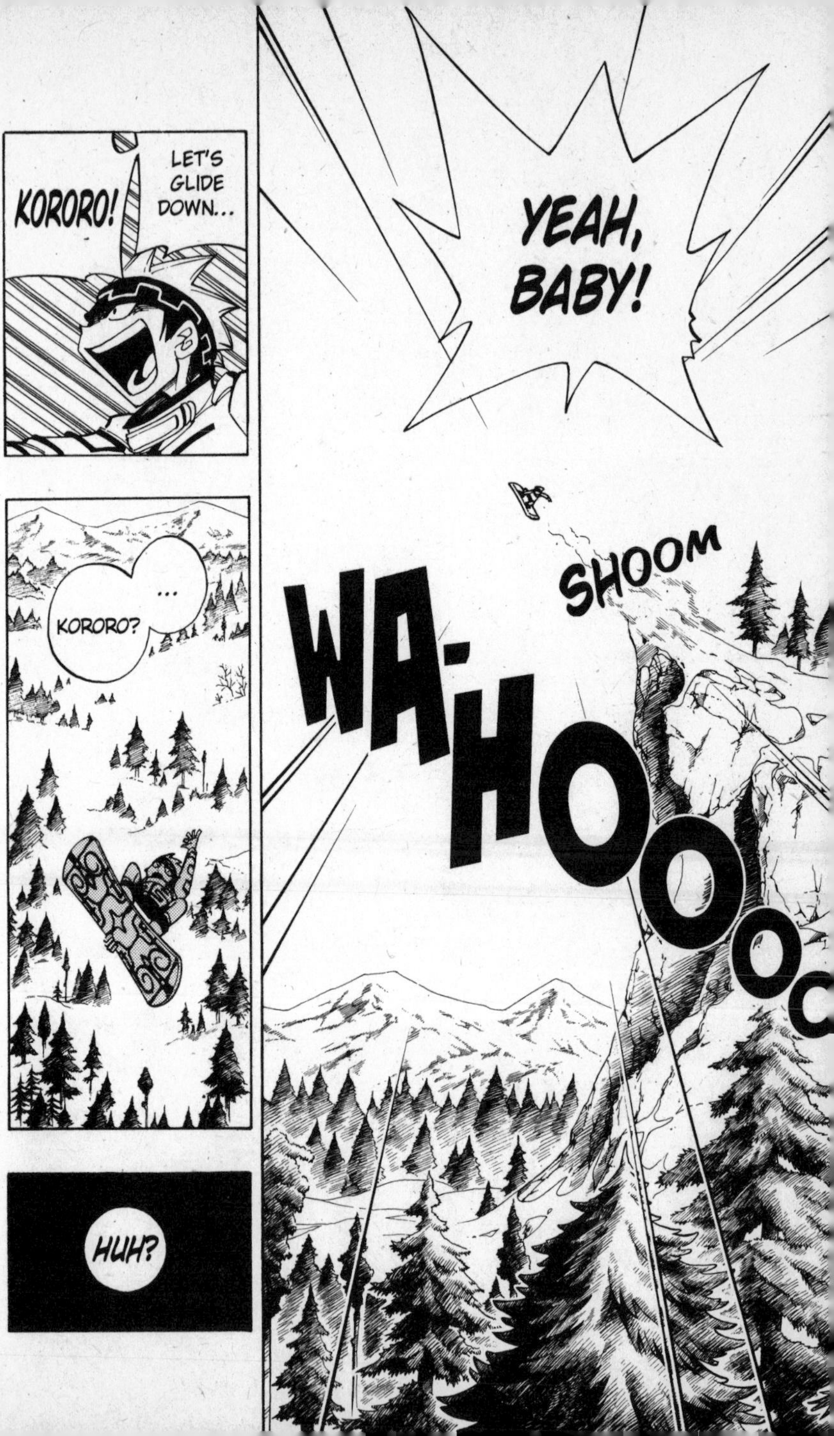
YEAH, BABY!
SHOOM
WA-HOOOOO
KORORO!
LET'S GLIDE DOWN...
...
KORORO?
HUH?

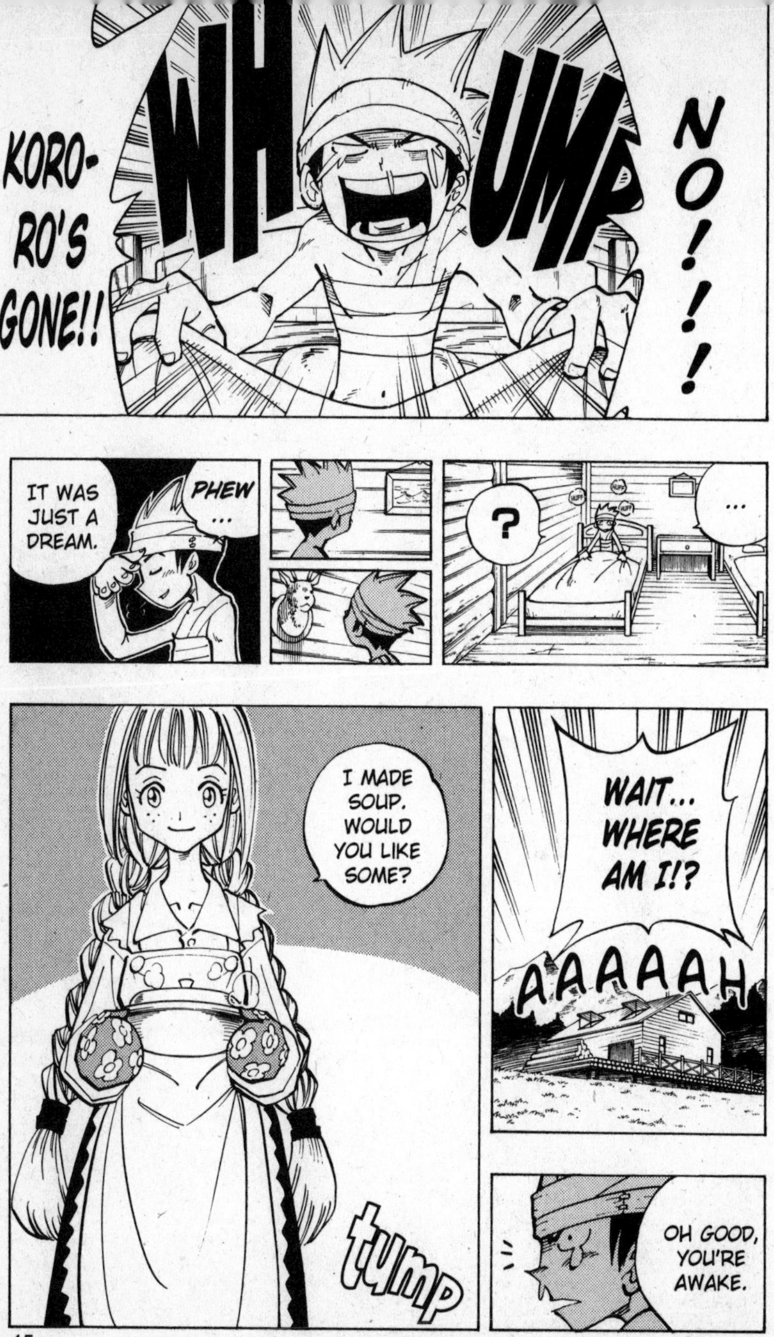
NO!!!!
WHUMP
KORORO'S GONE!!
...
HUFF
HUFF
HUFF
?
PHEW...
IT WAS JUST A DREAM.
WAIT... WHERE AM I!?
AAAAAH
OH GOOD, YOU'RE AWAKE.
I MADE SOUP. WOULD YOU LIKE SOME?
tump

SHAMAN
KING
11

*ULTRA SENJI
RYAKKETSU*

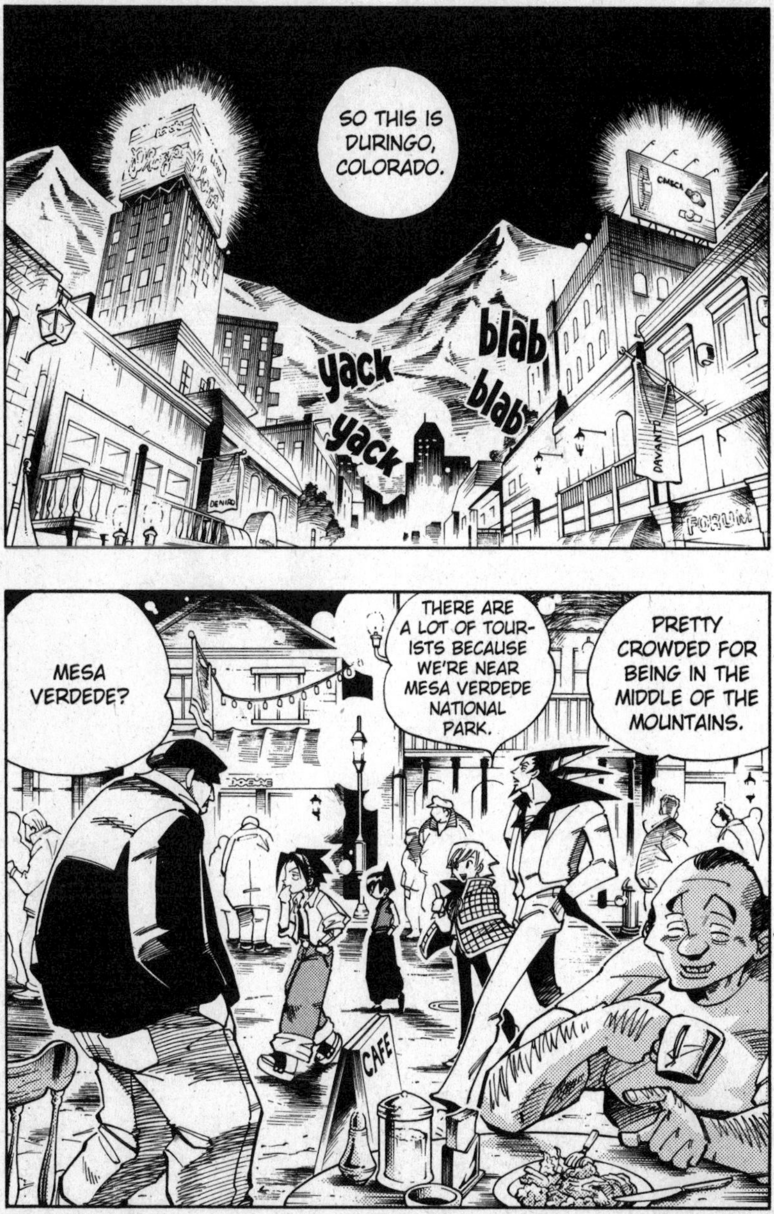
SO THIS IS DURINGO, COLORADO.
blab
blab
yack
yack
DENIRO
DAVANTI
FORUM
PRETTY CROWDED FOR BEING IN THE MIDDLE OF THE MOUNTAINS.
THERE ARE A LOT OF TOURISTS BECAUSE WE'RE NEAR MESA VERDEDE NATIONAL PARK.
MESA VERDEDE?
CAFE

Reincarnation 92: Horohoro's Stirring Tale – Week One

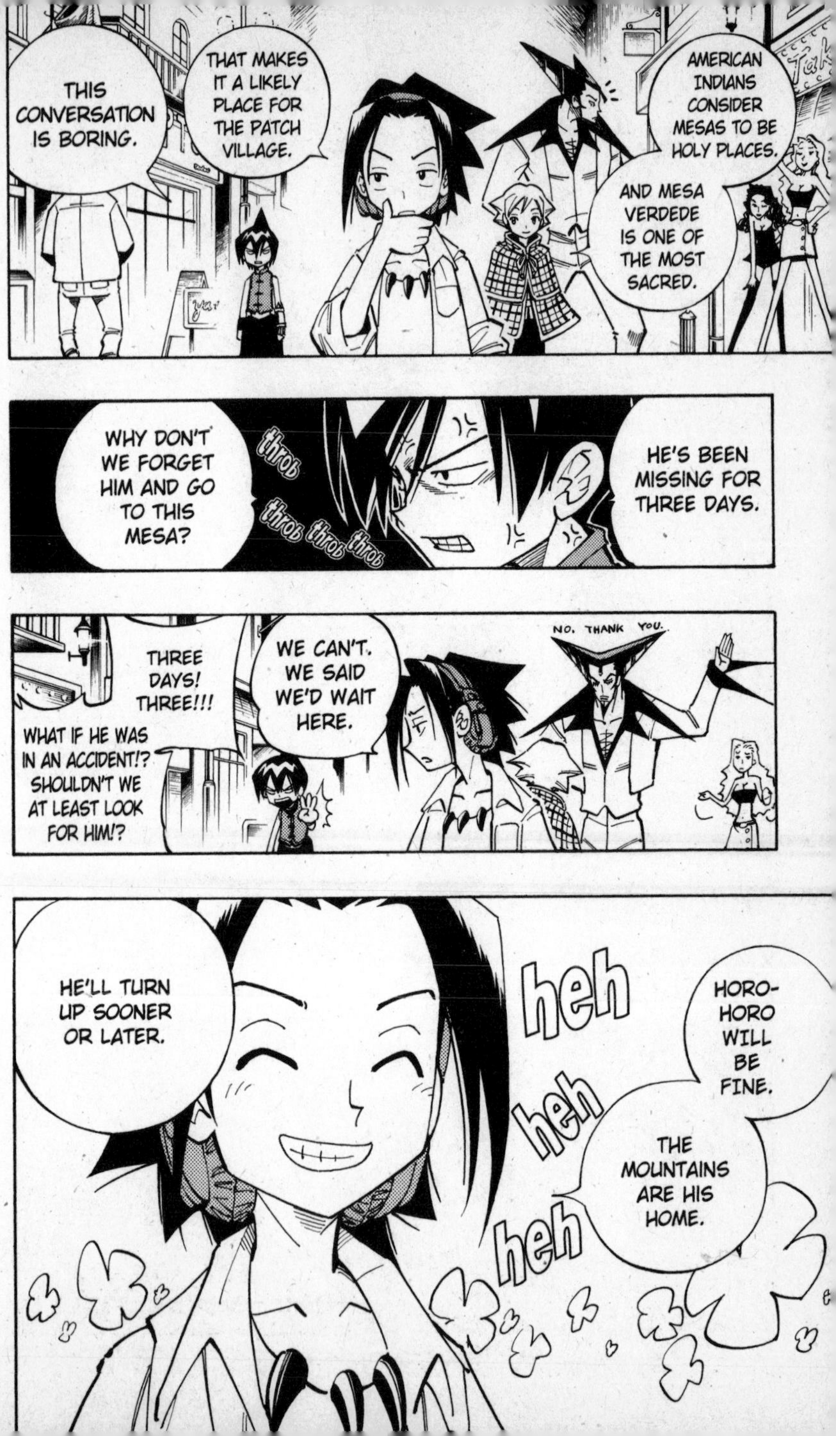
AMERICAN INDIANS CONSIDER MESAS TO BE HOLY PLACES.
AND MESA VERDEDE IS ONE OF THE MOST SACRED.
THAT MAKES IT A LIKELY PLACE FOR THE PATCH VILLAGE.
THIS CONVERSATION IS BORING.
HE'S BEEN MISSING FOR THREE DAYS.
throb
throb throb throb
WHY DON'T WE FORGET HIM AND GO TO THIS MESA?
NO. THANK YOU.
WE CAN'T. WE SAID WE'D WAIT HERE.
THREE DAYS! THREE!!!
WHAT IF HE WAS IN AN ACCIDENT!? SHOULDN'T WE AT LEAST LOOK FOR HIM!?
HORO-HORO WILL BE FINE.
THE MOUNTAINS ARE HIS HOME.
heh
heh
heh
HE'LL TURN UP SOONER OR LATER.

Reincarnation 92: Horohoro's Stirring Tale–Week One

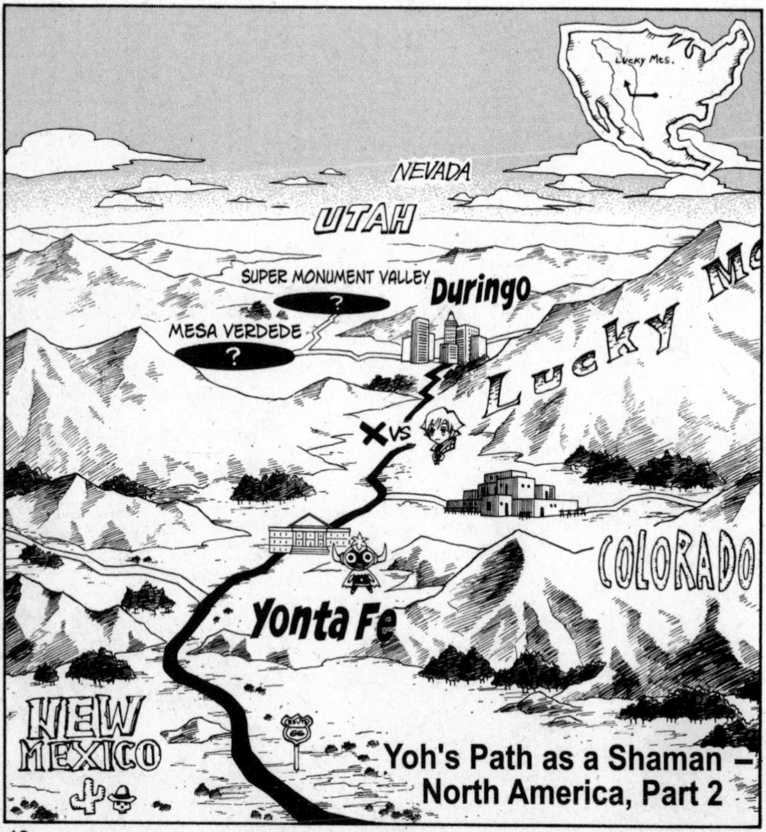
Lucky Mts.
NEVADA
UTAH
SUPER MONUMENT VALLEY
?
Duringo
MESA VERDEDE
?
Lucky
VS
COLORADO
Yonta Fe
NEW MEXICO
Yoh's Path as a Shaman – North America, Part 2

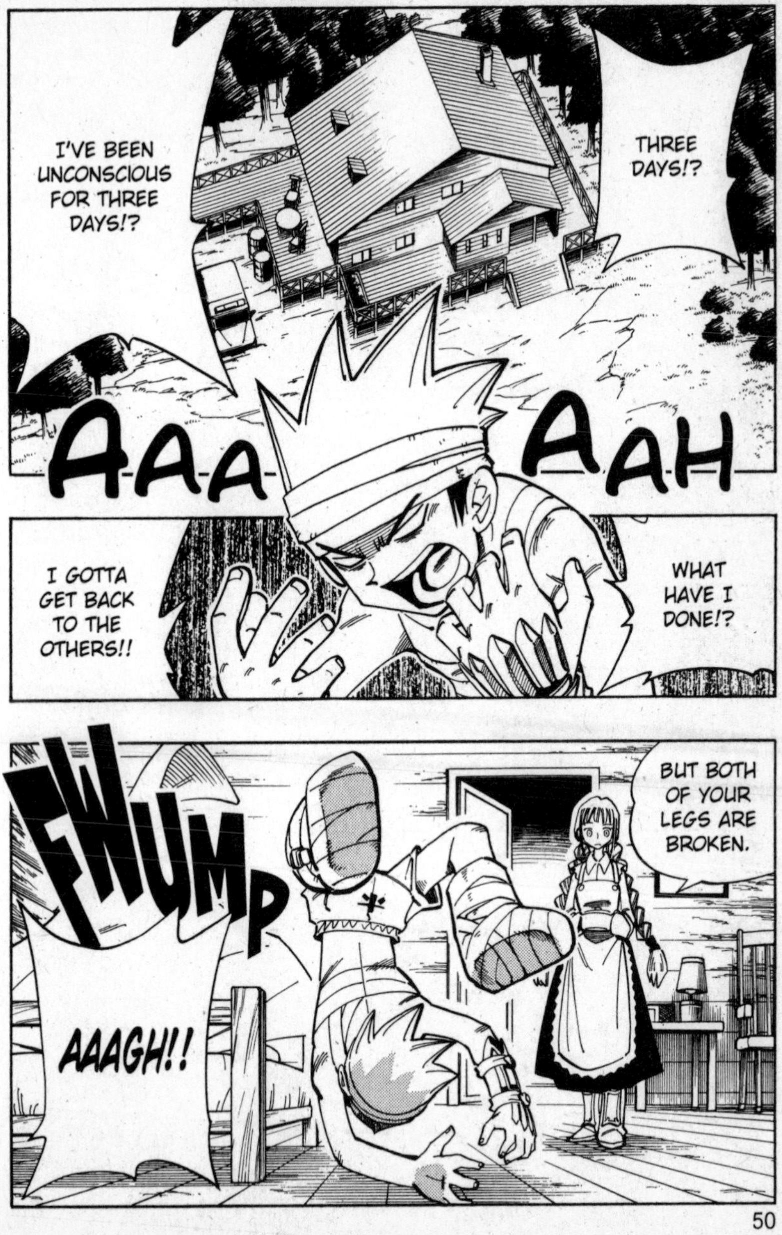
THREE DAYS!?
I'VE BEEN UNCONSCIOUS FOR THREE DAYS!?
AAAAAH
WHAT HAVE I DONE!?
I GOTTA GET BACK TO THE OTHERS!!
BUT BOTH OF YOUR LEGS ARE BROKEN.
FWUMP
AAAGH!!

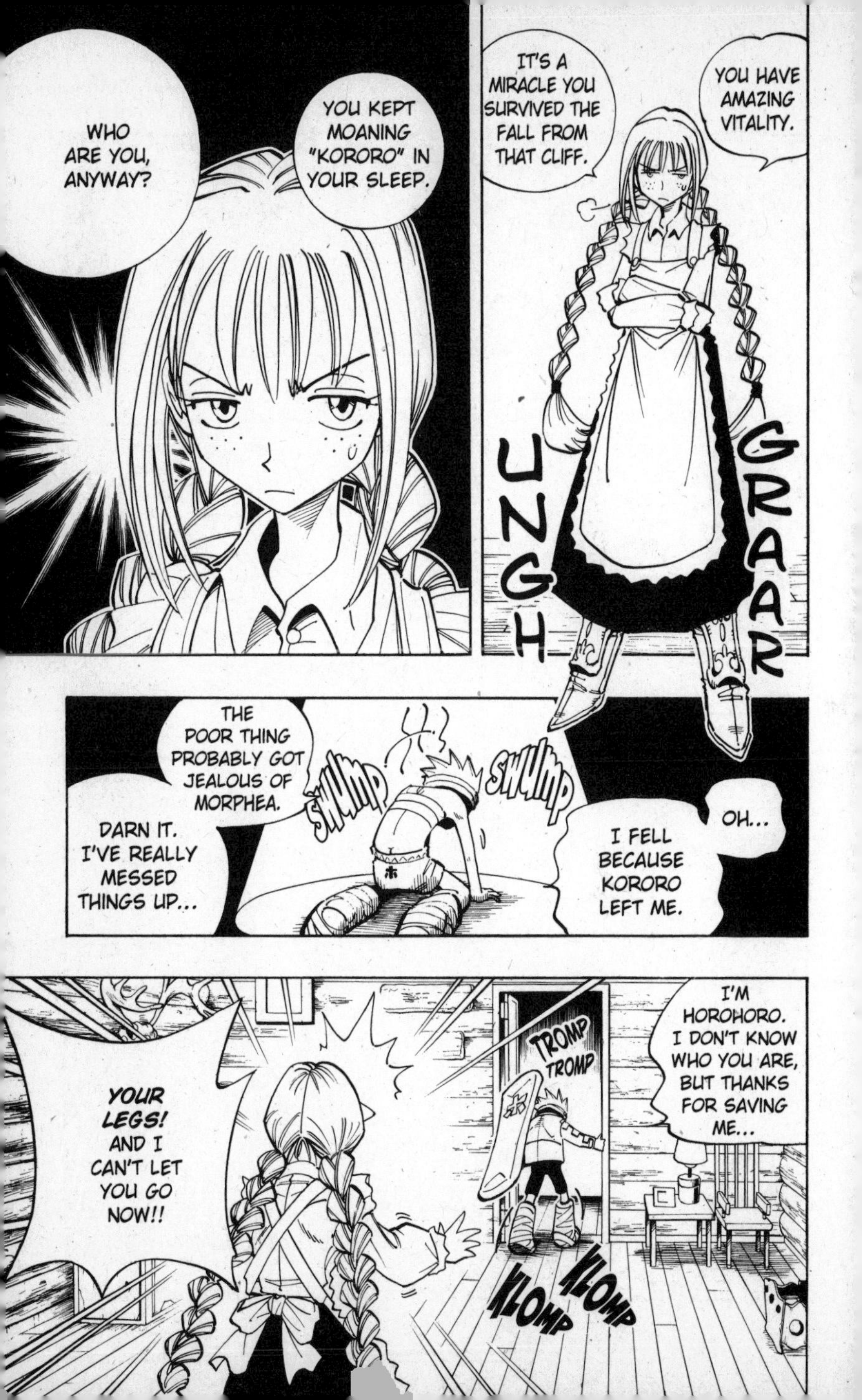
YOU HAVE AMAZING VITALITY.
IT'S A MIRACLE YOU SURVIVED THE FALL FROM THAT CLIFF.
GRAAR
UNGH
YOU KEPT MOANING "KORORO" IN YOUR SLEEP.
WHO ARE YOU, ANYWAY?
OH...
I FELL BECAUSE KORORO LEFT ME.
SHUMP
SHUMP
THE POOR THING PROBABLY GOT JEALOUS OF MORPHEA.
DARN IT. I'VE REALLY MESSED THINGS UP...
I'M HOROHORO. I DON'T KNOW WHO YOU ARE, BUT THANKS FOR SAVING ME...
TROMP TROMP
KLOMP KLOMP
YOUR LEGS! AND I CAN'T LET YOU GO NOW!!

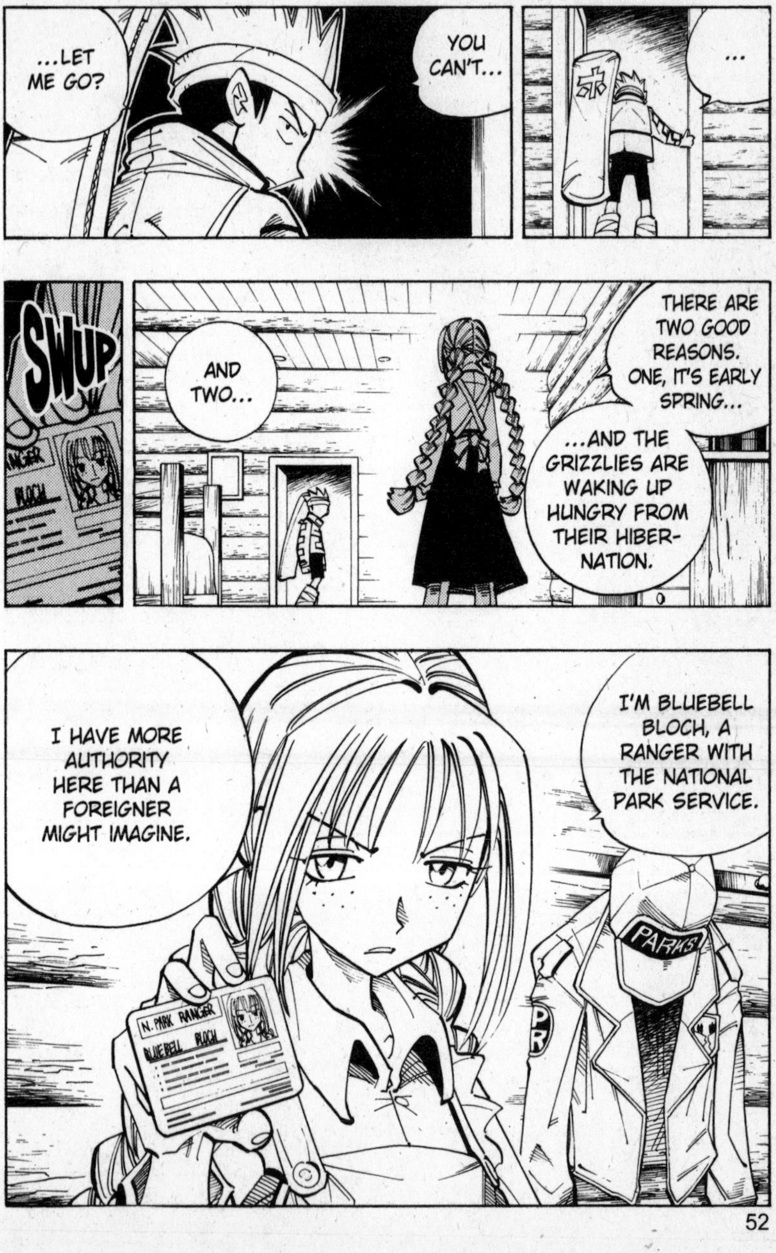
...
YOU CAN'T...
...LET ME GO?
THERE ARE TWO GOOD REASONS. ONE, IT'S EARLY SPRING...
...AND THE GRIZZLIES ARE WAKING UP HUNGRY FROM THEIR HIBER-NATION.
AND TWO...
SWUP
I'M BLUEBELL BLOCH, A RANGER WITH THE NATIONAL PARK SERVICE.
I HAVE MORE AUTHORITY HERE THAN A FOREIGNER MIGHT IMAGINE.
PARKS
PR
N. PARK RANGER
BLUEBELL BLOCH

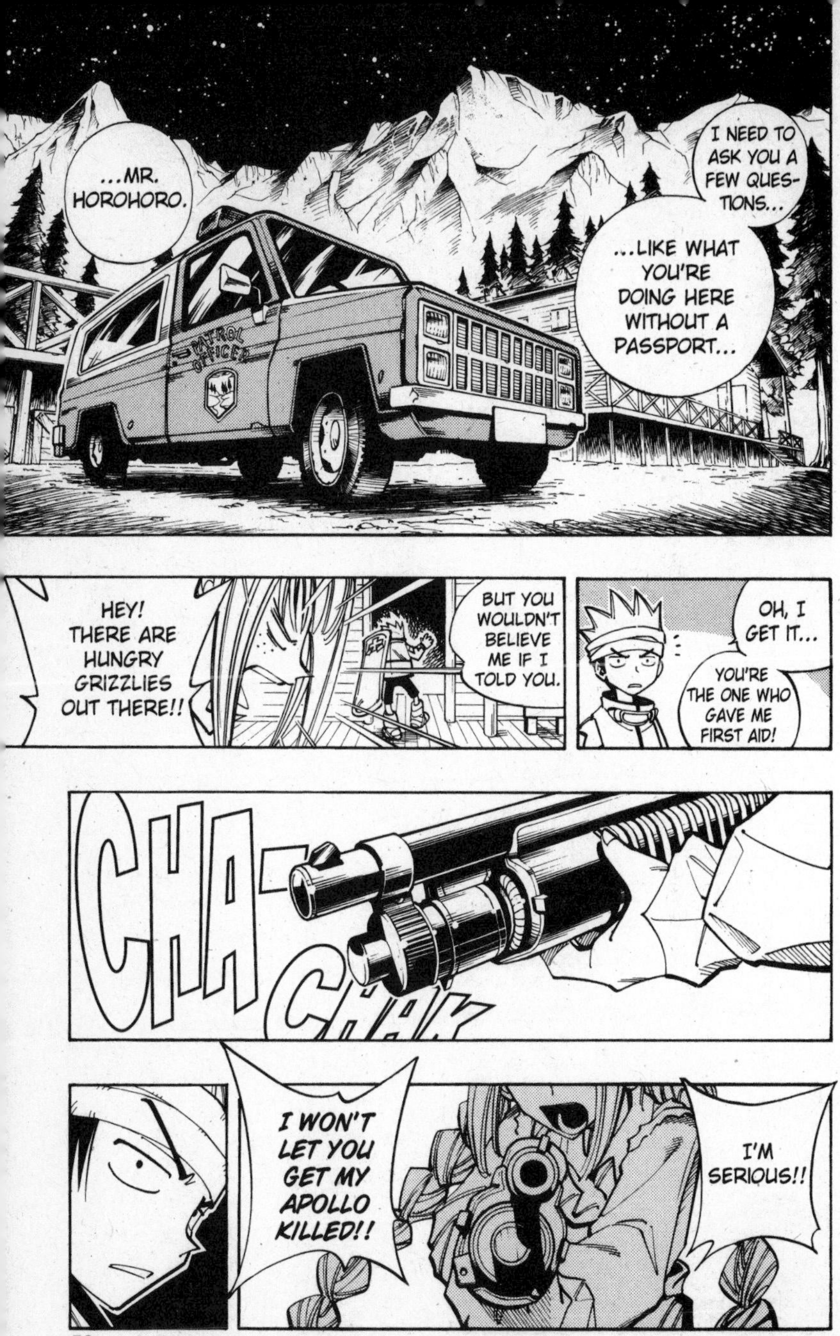
I NEED TO ASK YOU A FEW QUES-TIONS...
...LIKE WHAT YOU'RE DOING HERE WITHOUT A PASSPORT...
...MR. HOROHORO.
OH, I GET IT...
YOU'RE THE ONE WHO GAVE ME FIRST AID!
BUT YOU WOULDN'T BELIEVE ME IF I TOLD YOU.
HEY! THERE ARE HUNGRY GRIZZLIES OUT THERE!!
CHA-CHAK
I'M SERIOUS!!
I WON'T LET YOU GET MY APOLLO KILLED!!

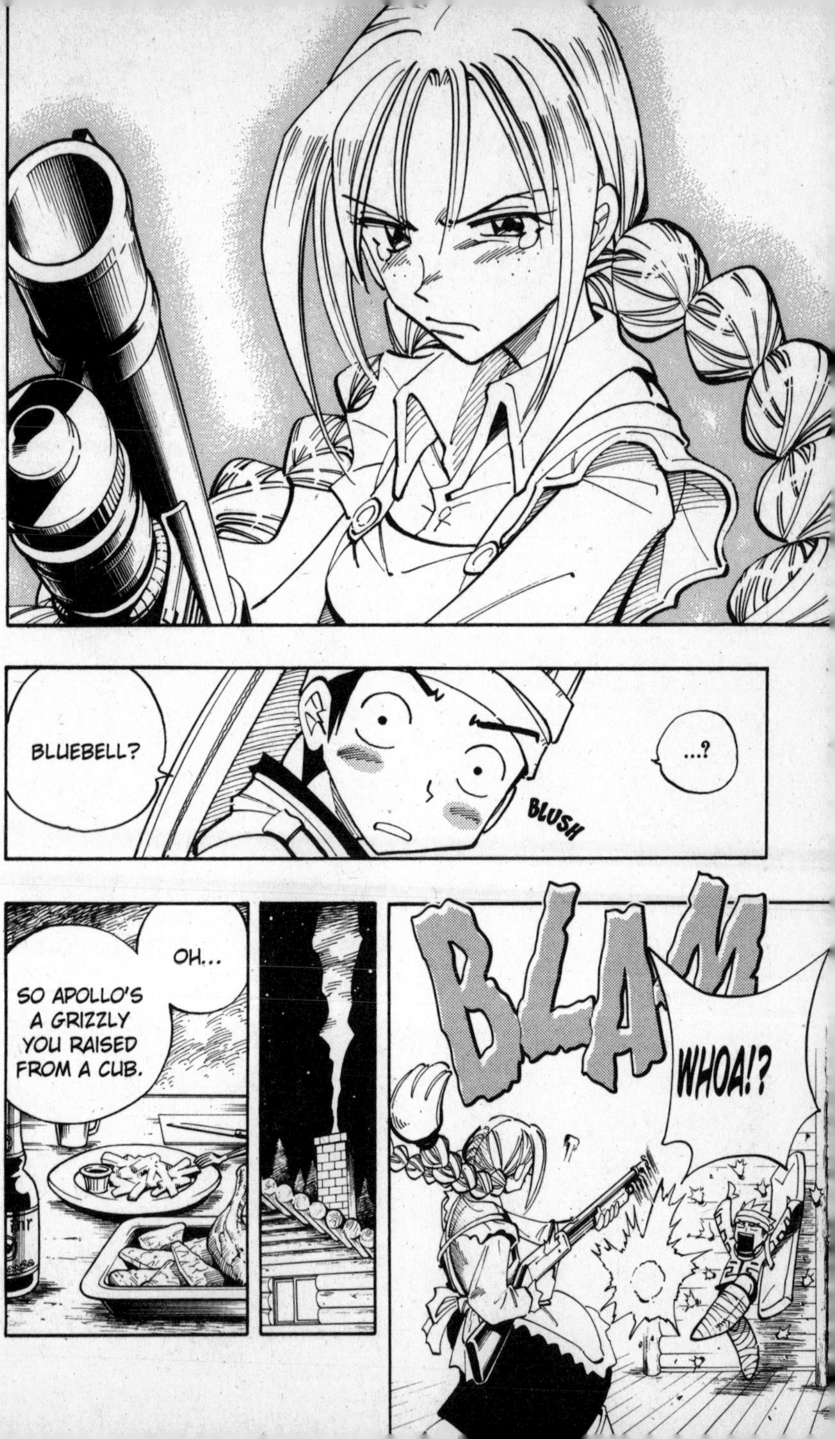
...?
BLUSH
BLUEBELL?
BLAM
WHOA!?
OH...
SO APOLLO'S A GRIZZLY YOU RAISED FROM A CUB.

READ THIS WAY

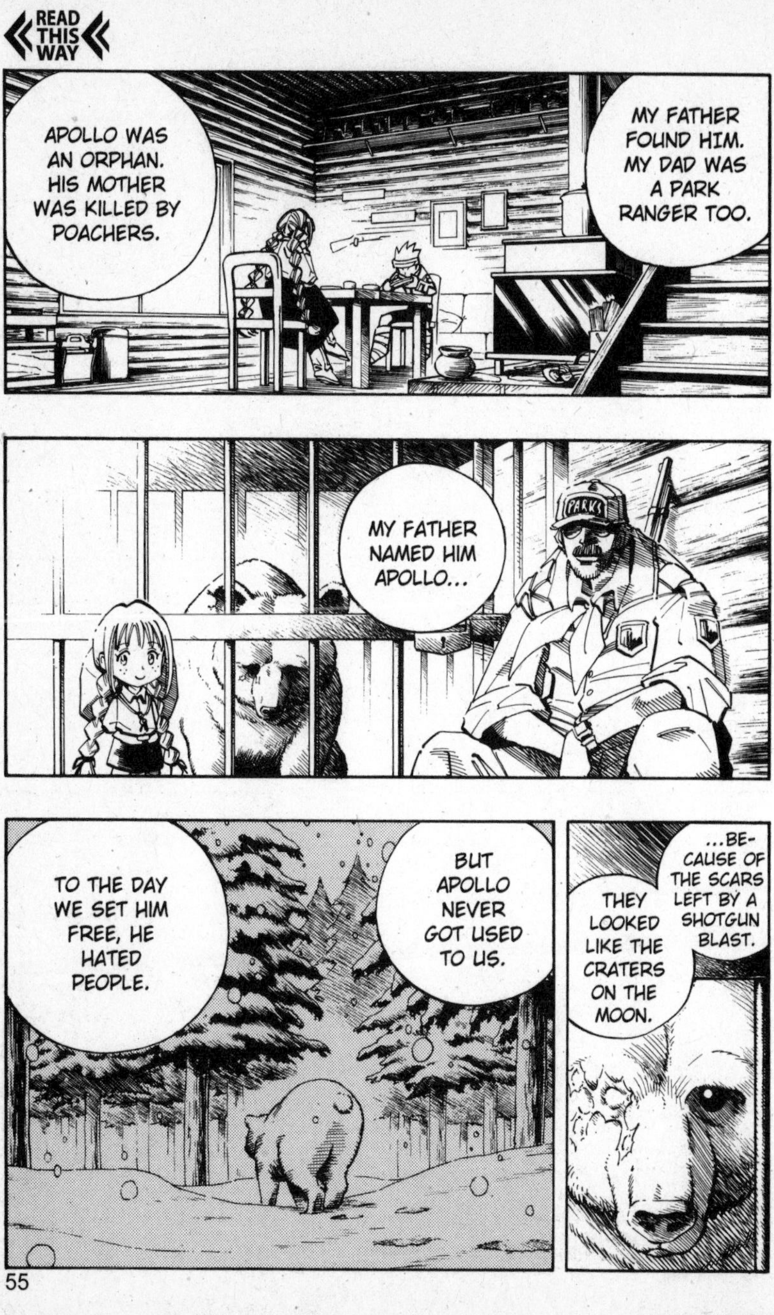

APOLLO WAS AN ORPHAN. HIS MOTHER WAS KILLED BY POACHERS.
MY FATHER FOUND HIM. MY DAD WAS A PARK RANGER TOO.
MY FATHER NAMED HIM APOLLO...
PARKS
...BE-CAUSE OF THE SCARS LEFT BY A SHOTGUN BLAST.
THEY LOOKED LIKE THE CRATERS ON THE MOON.
BUT APOLLO NEVER GOT USED TO US.
TO THE DAY WE SET HIM FREE, HE HATED PEOPLE.

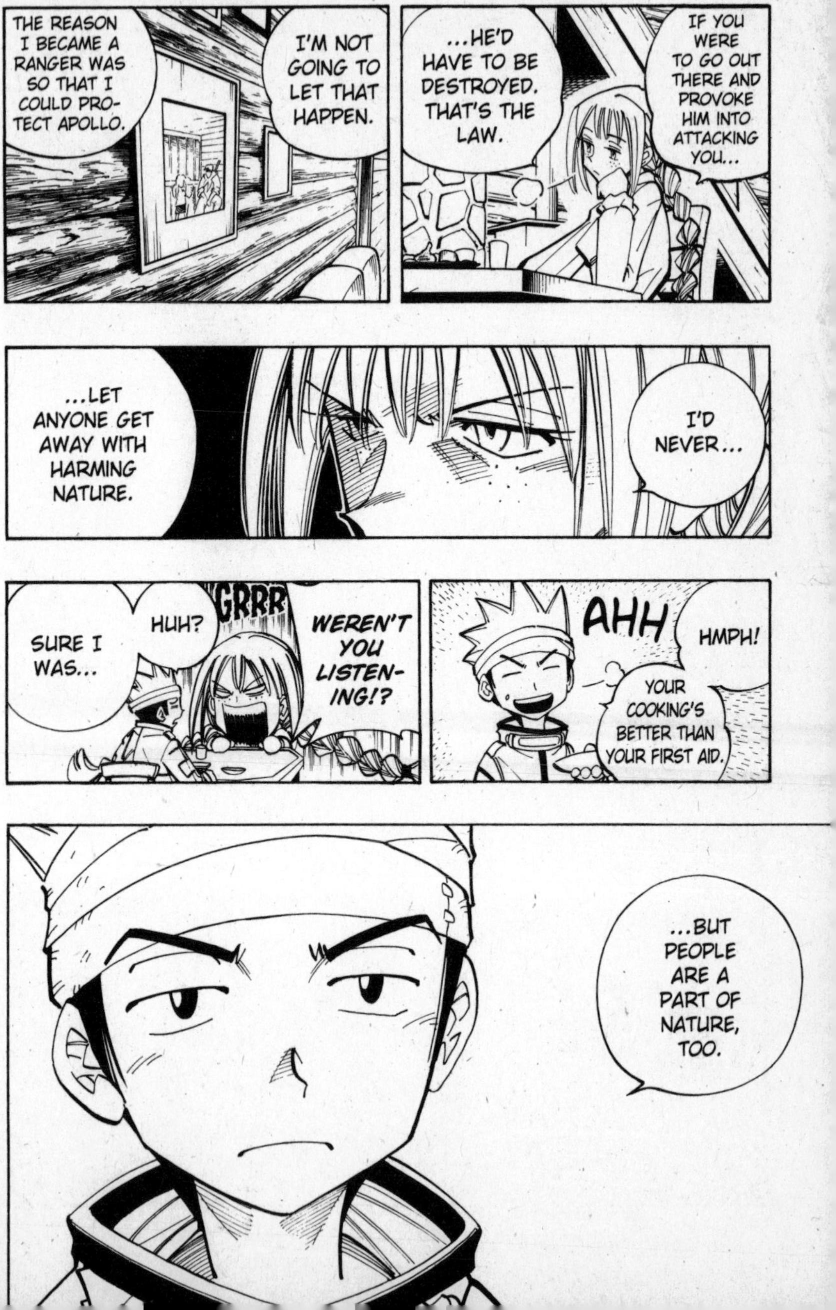
IF YOU WERE TO GO OUT THERE AND PROVOKE HIM INTO ATTACKING YOU...
...HE'D HAVE TO BE DESTROYED. THAT'S THE LAW.
I'M NOT GOING TO LET THAT HAPPEN.
THE REASON I BECAME A RANGER WAS SO THAT I COULD PROTECT APOLLO.
I'D NEVER...
...LET ANYONE GET AWAY WITH HARMING NATURE.
AHH
HMPH!
YOUR COOKING'S BETTER THAN YOUR FIRST AID.
WEREN'T YOU LISTENING!?
GRRR
HUH?
SURE I WAS...
...BUT PEOPLE ARE A PART OF NATURE, TOO.

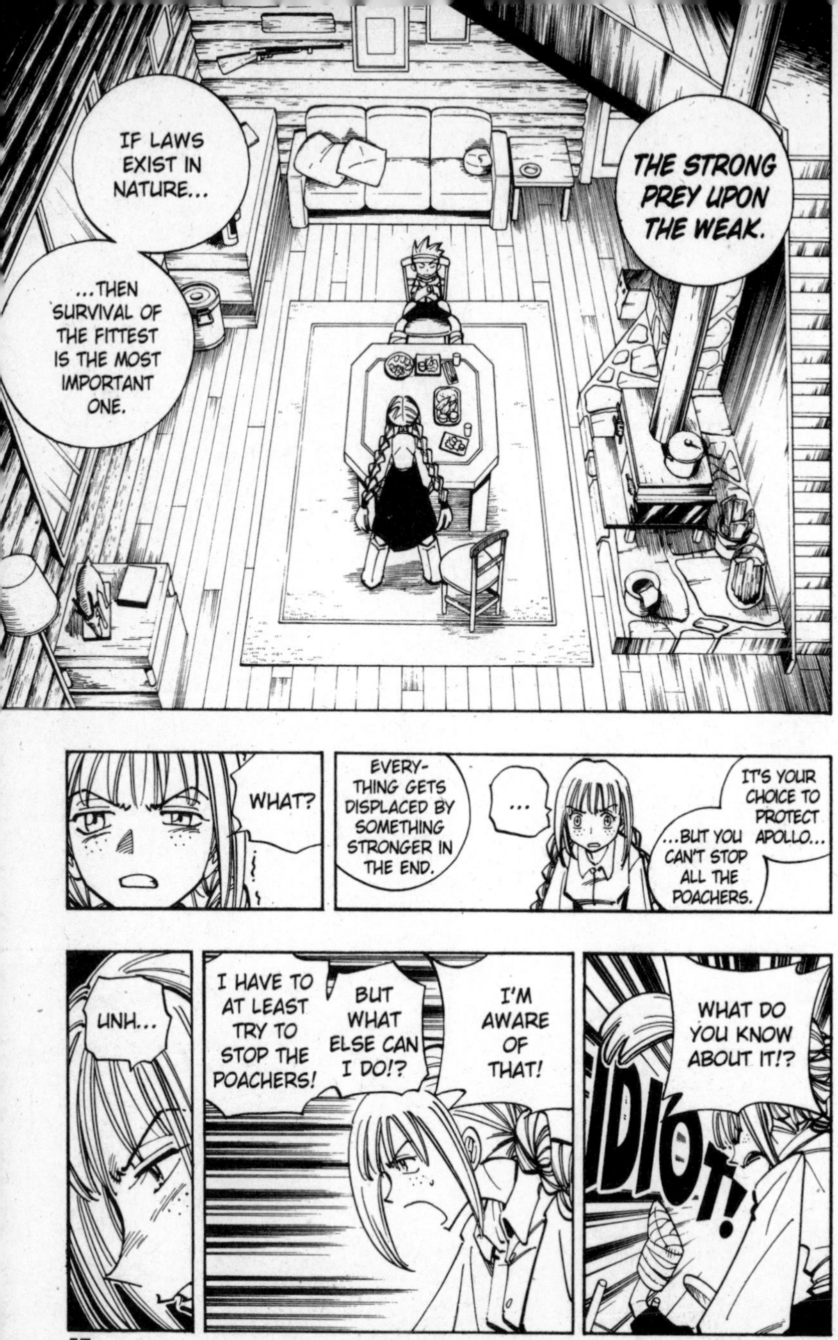
THE STRONG PREY UPON THE WEAK.
IF LAWS EXIST IN NATURE...
...THEN SURVIVAL OF THE FITTEST IS THE MOST IMPORTANT ONE.
IT'S YOUR CHOICE TO PROTECT APOLLO...
...BUT YOU CAN'T STOP ALL THE POACHERS.
...
EVERY-THING GETS DISPLACED BY SOMETHING STRONGER IN THE END.
WHAT?
WHAT DO YOU KNOW ABOUT IT!?
IDIOT!
I'M AWARE OF THAT!
BUT WHAT ELSE CAN I DO!?
I HAVE TO AT LEAST TRY TO STOP THE POACHERS!
UNH...

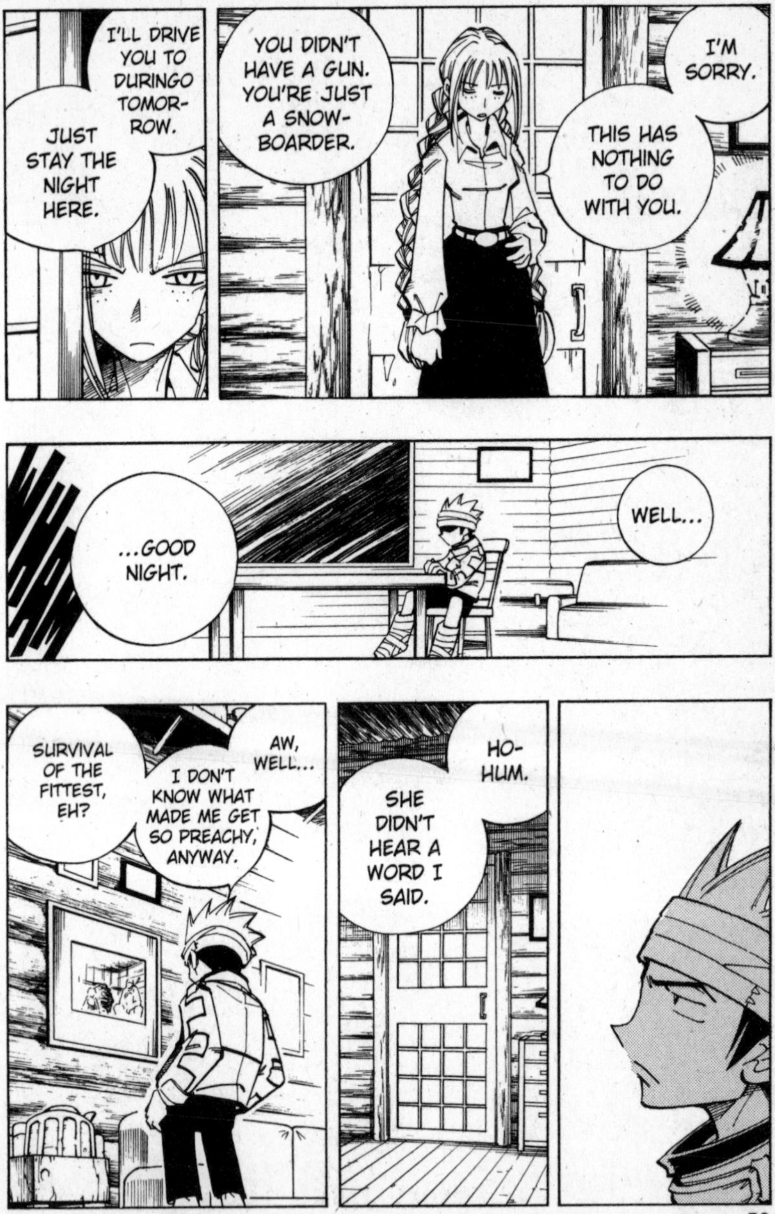

I'M SORRY.
THIS HAS NOTHING TO DO WITH YOU.
YOU DIDN'T HAVE A GUN. YOU'RE JUST A SNOW-BOARDER.
I'LL DRIVE YOU TO DURINGO TOMOR-ROW.
JUST STAY THE NIGHT HERE.
WELL...
...GOOD NIGHT.
HO-HUM.
SHE DIDN'T HEAR A WORD I SAID.
AW, WELL...
I DON'T KNOW WHAT MADE ME GET SO PREACHY, ANYWAY.
SURVIVAL OF THE FITTEST, EH?

READ THIS WAY

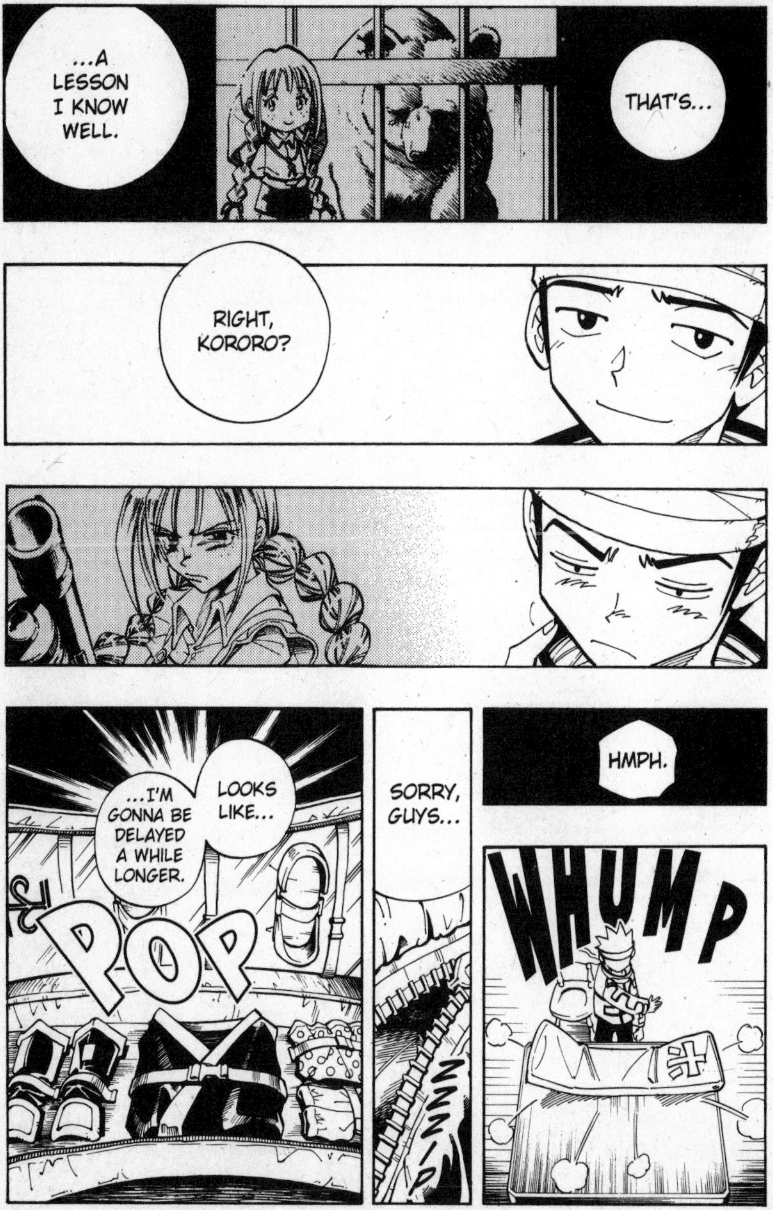
THAT'S...
...A LESSON I KNOW WELL.
RIGHT, KORORO?
HMPH.
WHUMP
SORRY, GUYS...
ZZZIP
LOOKS LIKE...
...I'M GONNA BE DELAYED A WHILE LONGER.
POP

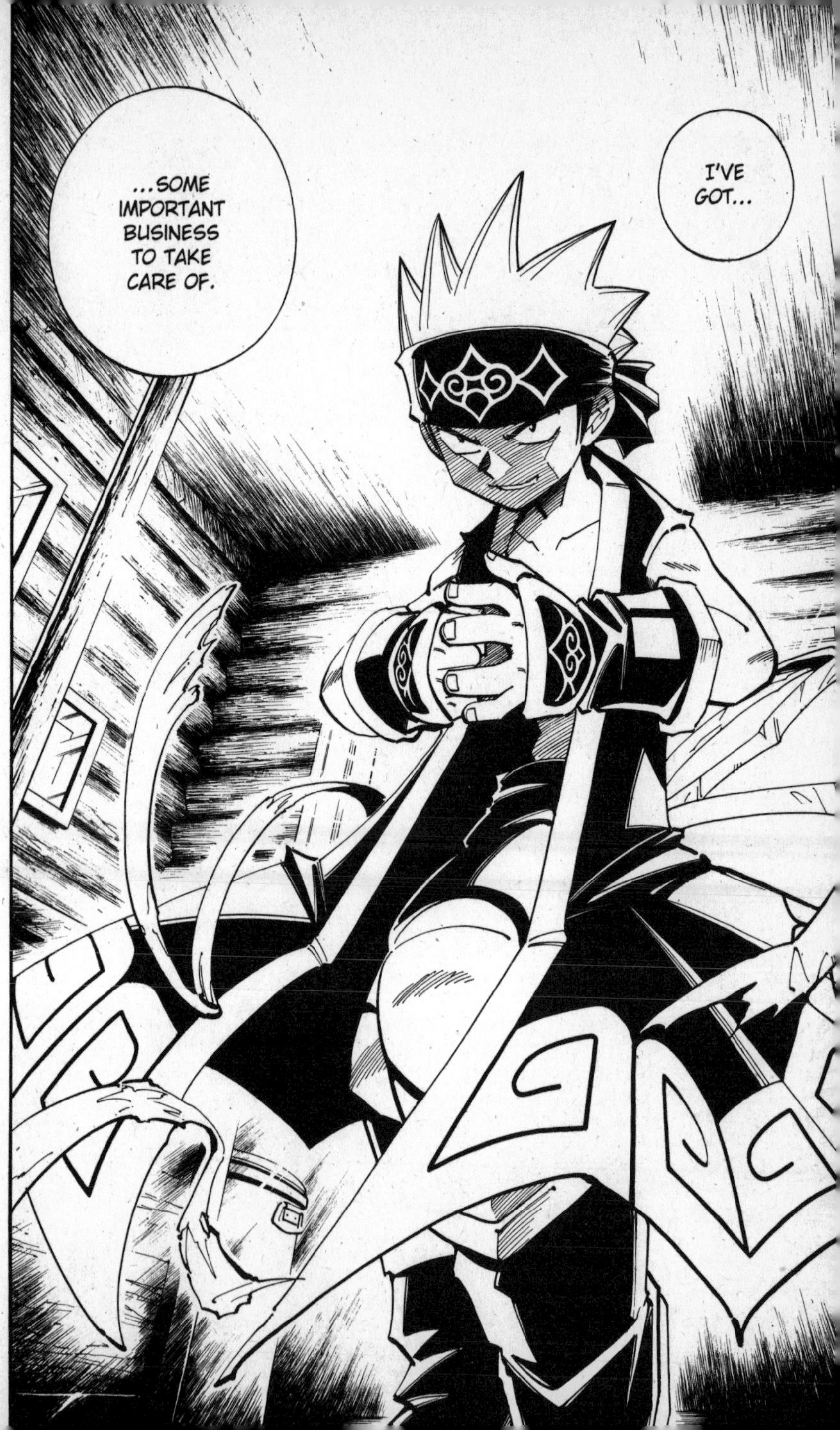
I'VE GOT...
...SOME IMPORTANT BUSINESS TO TAKE CARE OF.

READ THIS WAY

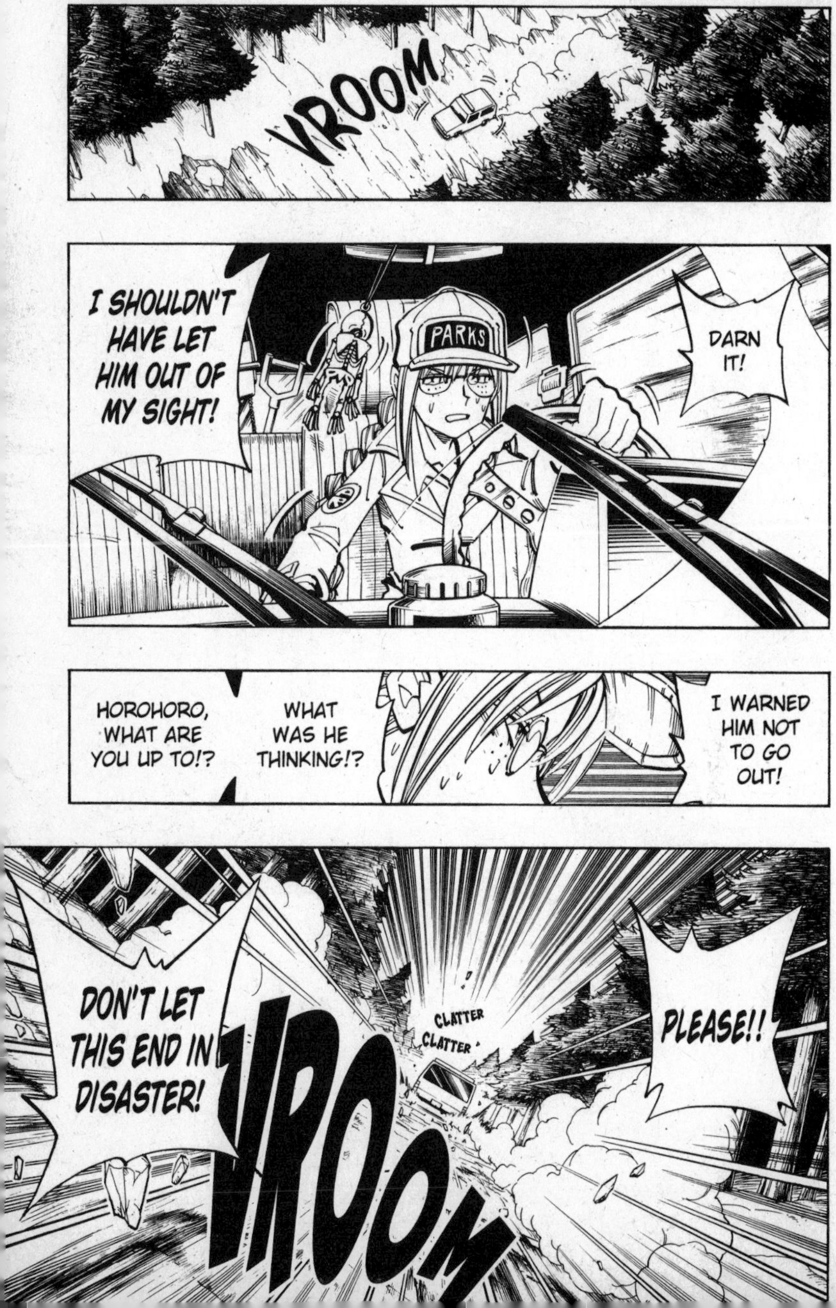
VROOM
DARN IT!
I SHOULDN'T HAVE LET HIM OUT OF MY SIGHT!
PARKS
I WARNED HIM NOT TO GO OUT!
WHAT WAS HE THINKING!?
HOROHORO, WHAT ARE YOU UP TO!?
PLEASE!!
CLATTER
CLATTER
DON'T LET THIS END IN DISASTER!
VROOM

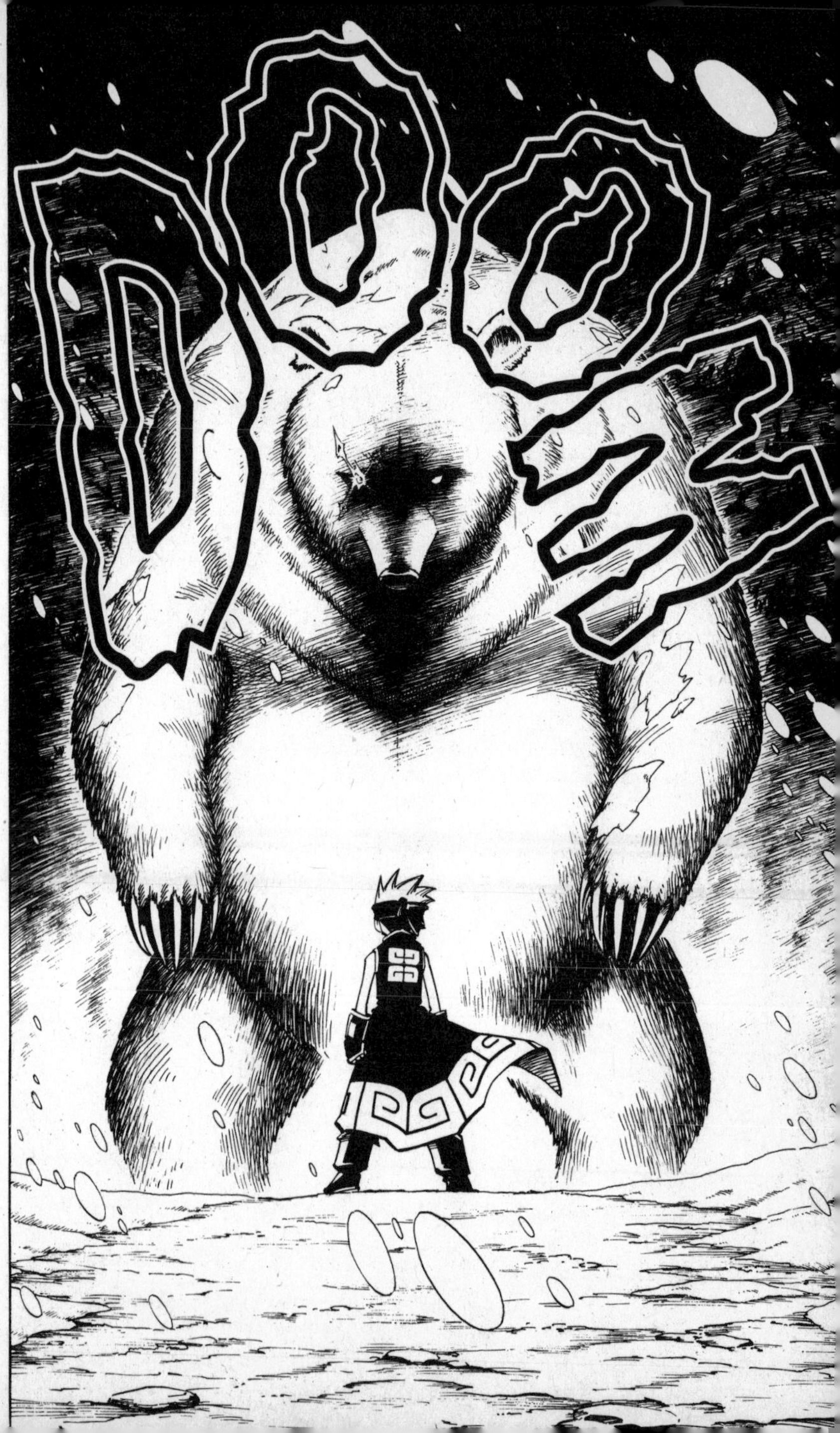
DOOM

READ THIS WAY

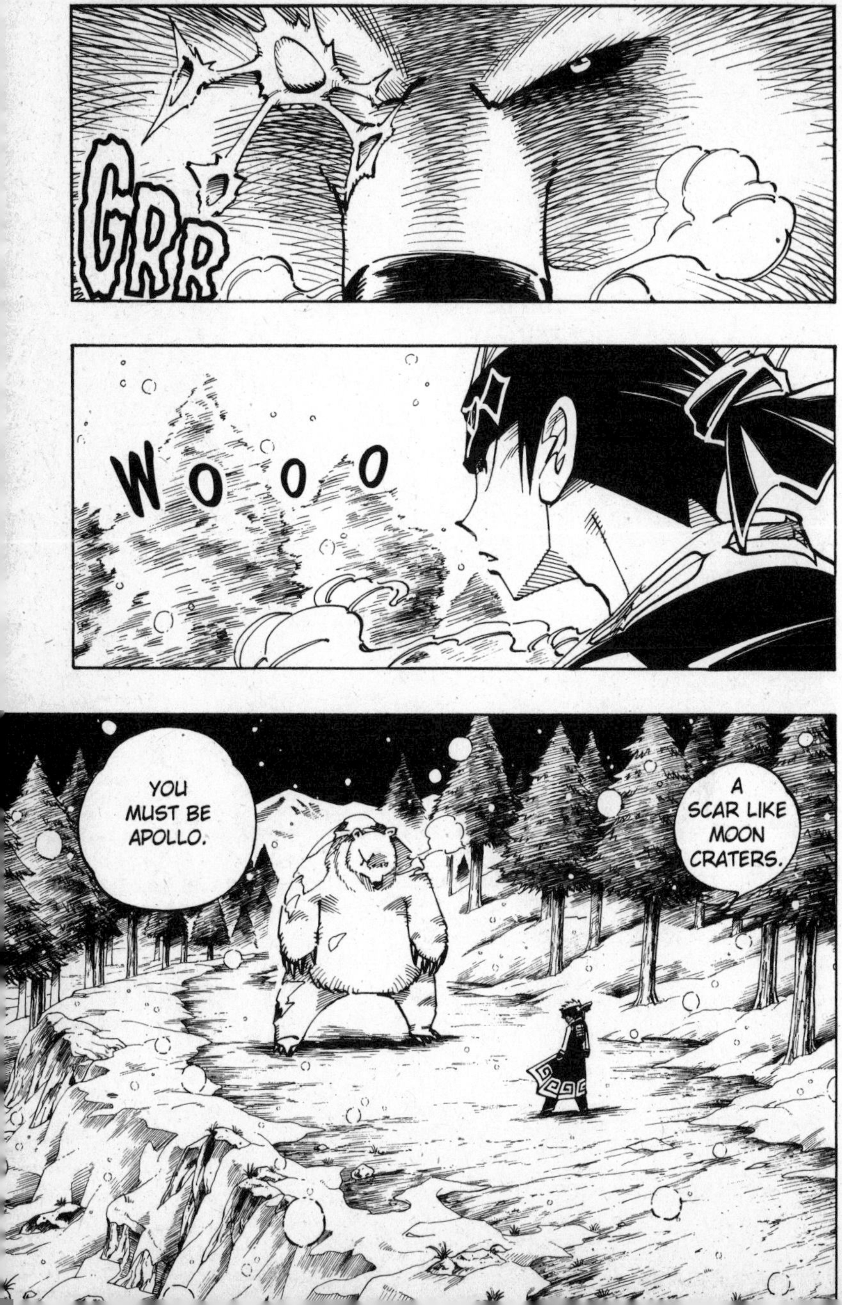
GRR
WOOO
A SCAR LIKE MOON CRATERS.
YOU MUST BE APOLLO.

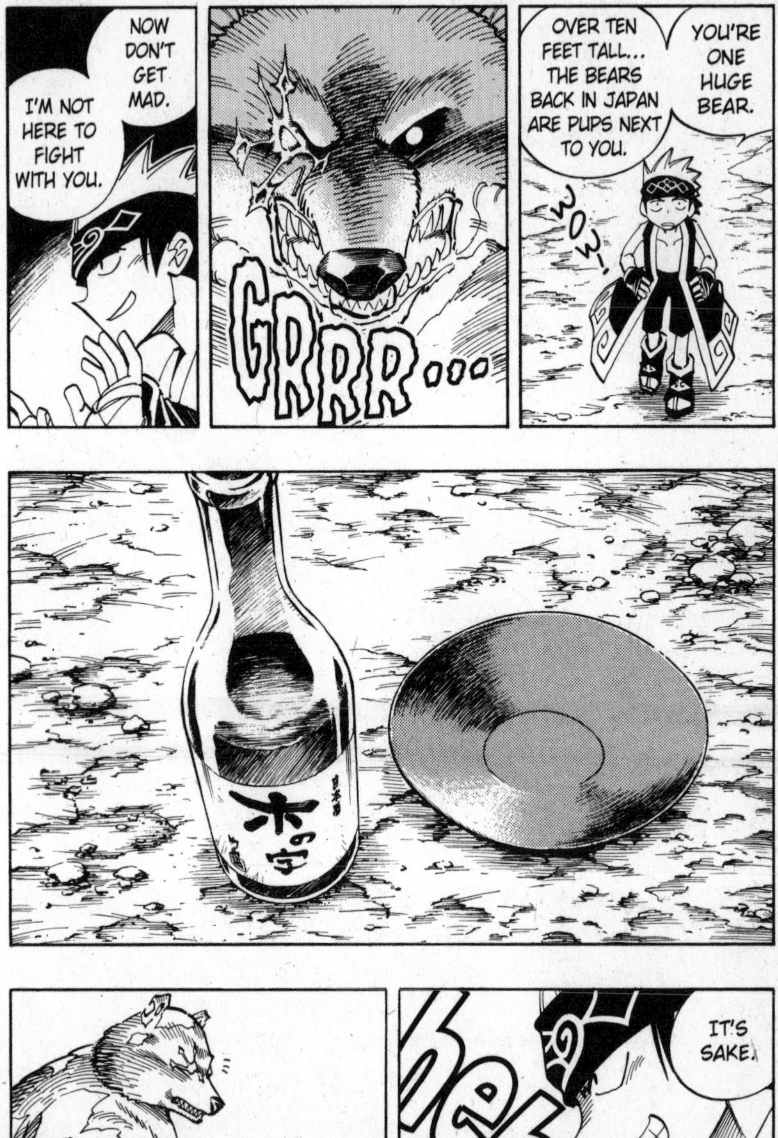
YOU'RE ONE HUGE BEAR.
OVER TEN FEET TALL... THE BEARS BACK IN JAPAN ARE PUPS NEXT TO YOU.
WOW!
GRRR...
NOW DON'T GET MAD.
I'M NOT HERE TO FIGHT WITH YOU.
IT'S SAKE.
heh

READ THIS WAY

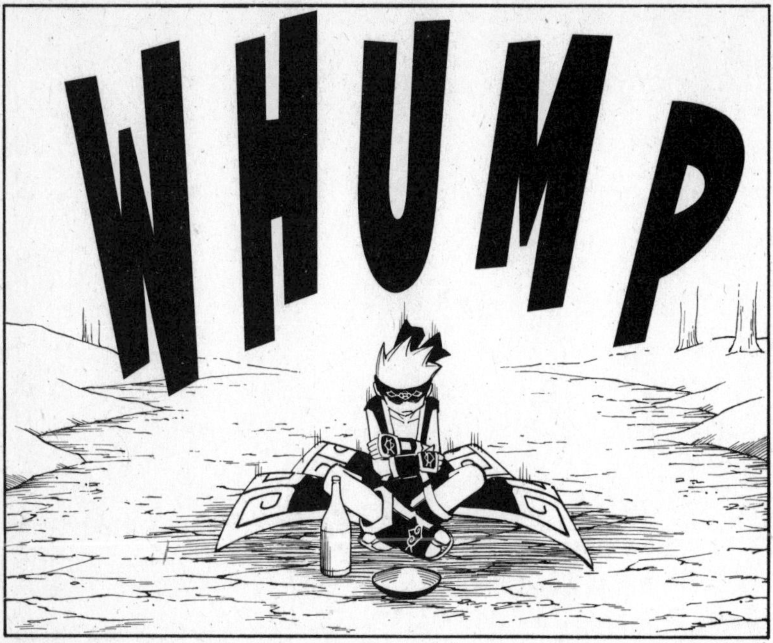
WHUMP

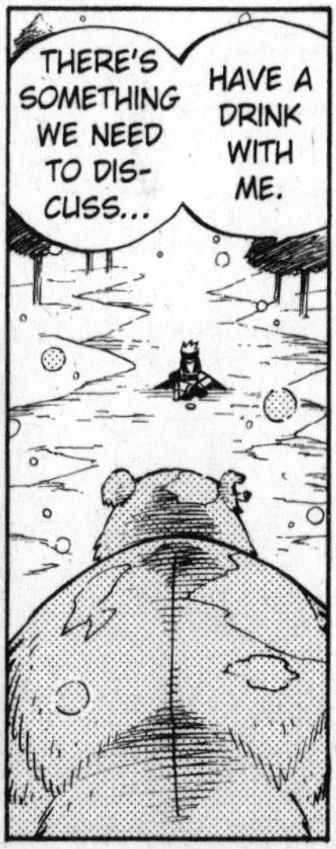
HAVE A DRINK WITH ME.
THERE'S SOMETHING WE NEED TO DIS-CUSS...

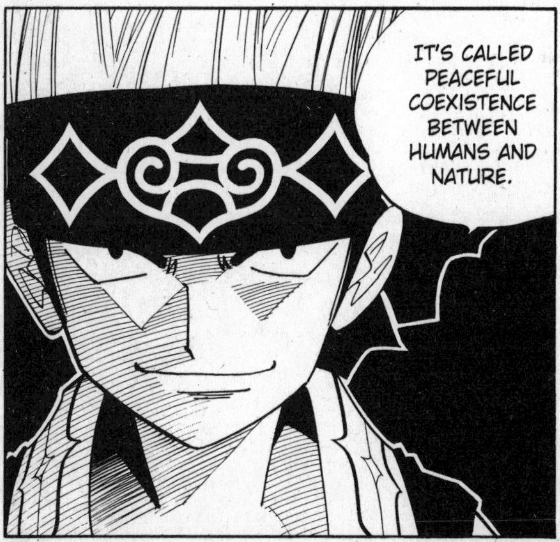
IT'S CALLED PEACEFUL COEXISTENCE BETWEEN HUMANS AND NATURE.

SHAMAN KING CHARACTER FILE No.48

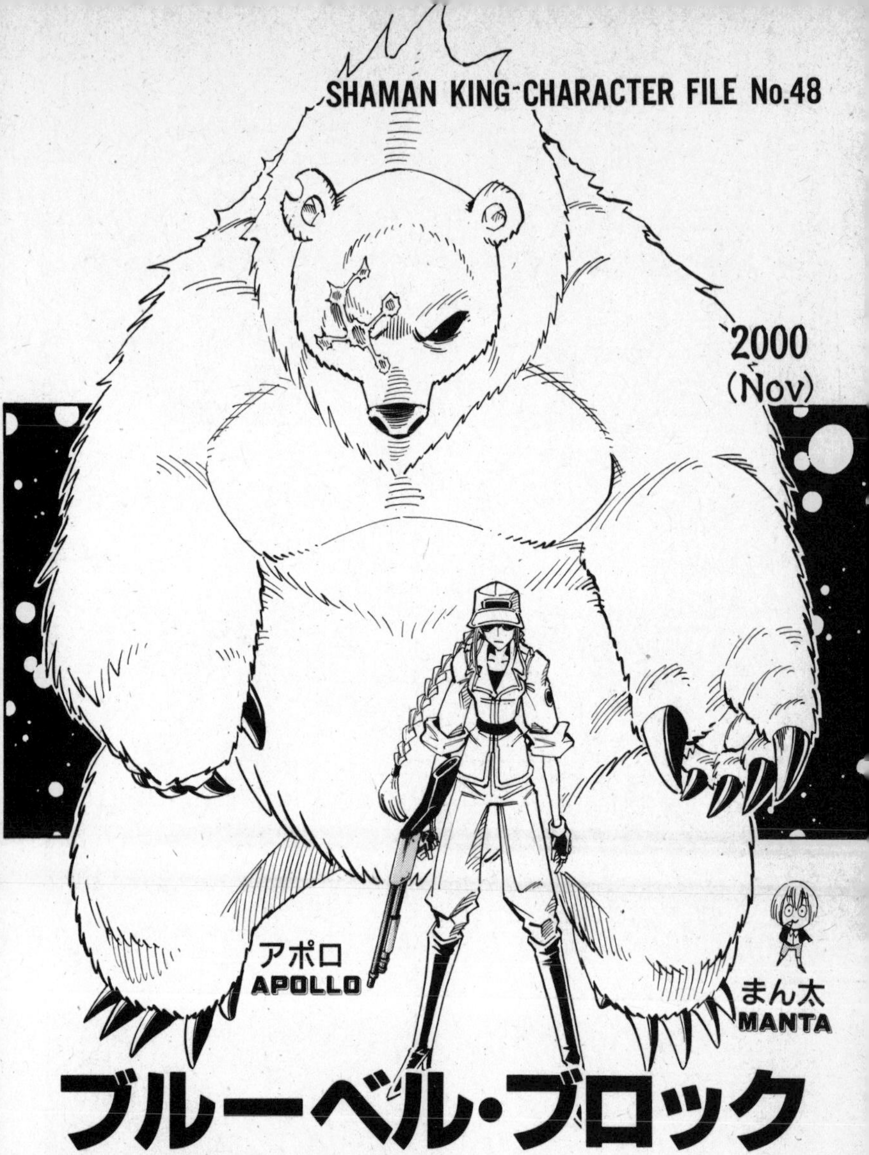
2000
(Nov)
アポロ
APOLLO
まん太
MANTA

ブルーベル・ブロック

BLUEBELL BLOCH

BORN: DECEMBER 3
SIGN: SAGITTARIUS
BLOOD TYPE: A
AGE: 22

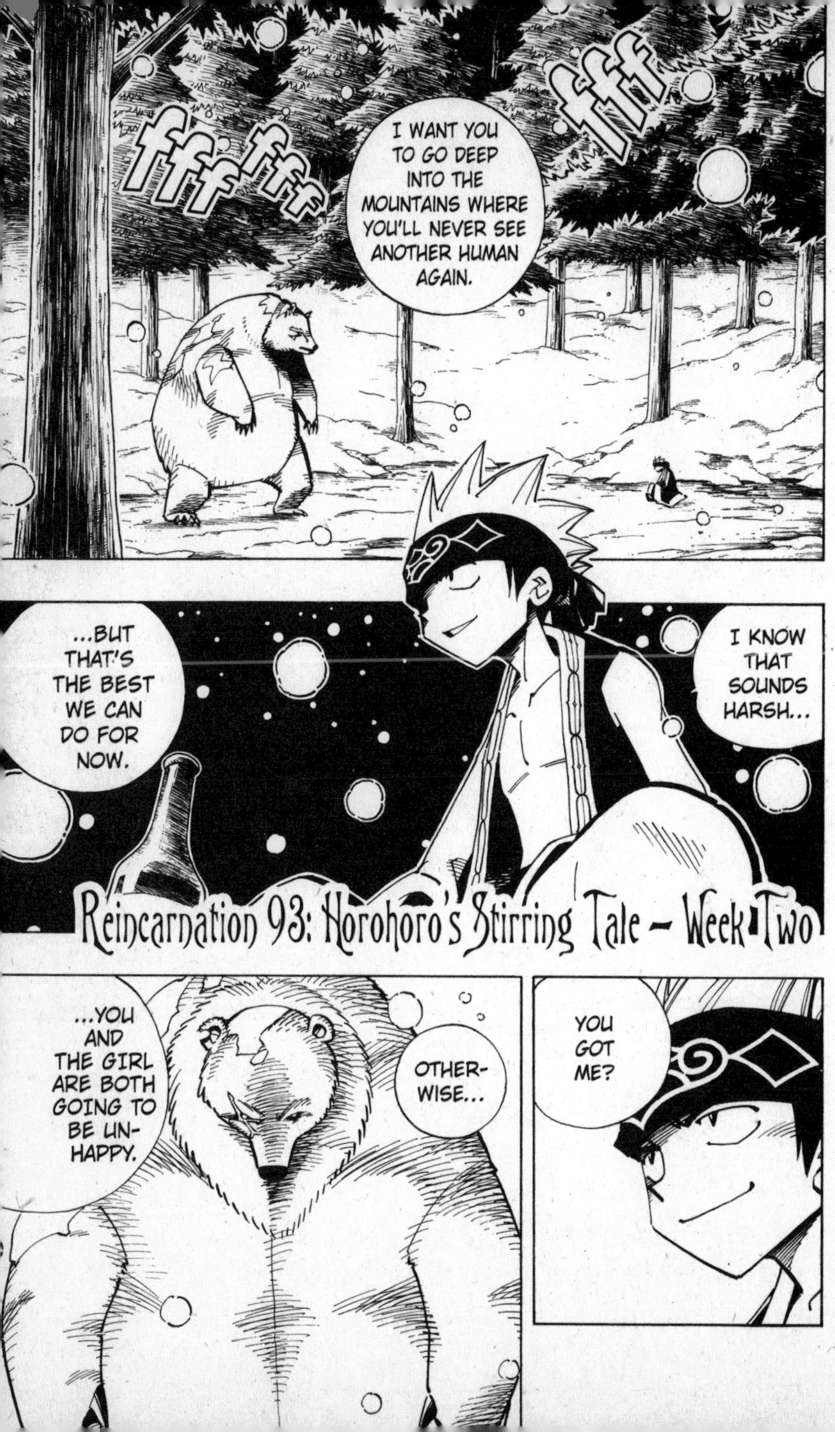
ffff
I WANT YOU TO GO DEEP INTO THE MOUNTAINS WHERE YOU'LL NEVER SEE ANOTHER HUMAN AGAIN.
ffffff
I KNOW THAT SOUNDS HARSH...
...BUT THAT'S THE BEST WE CAN DO FOR NOW.
Reincarnation 93: Horohoro's Stirring Tale – Week Two
YOU GOT ME?
OTHER-WISE...
...YOU AND THE GIRL ARE BOTH GOING TO BE UN-HAPPY.

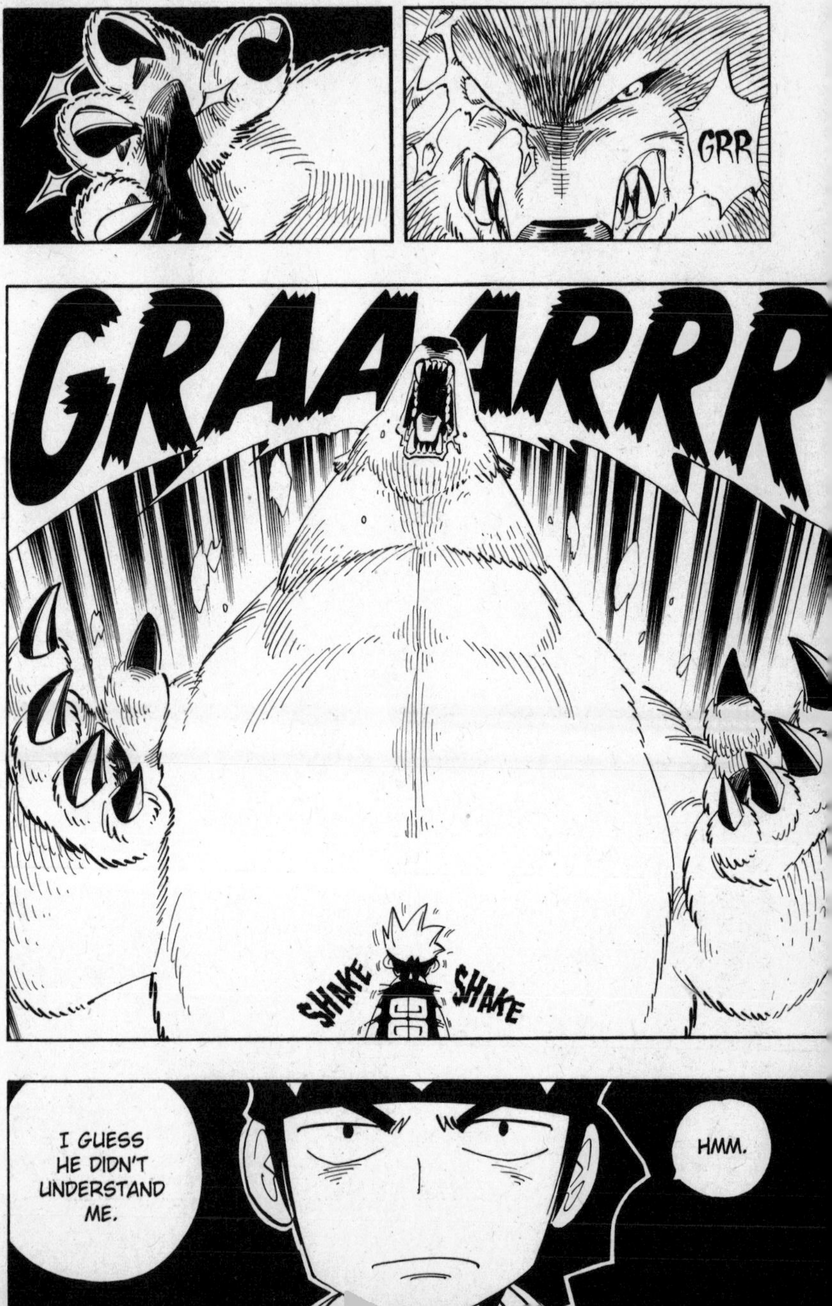
GRR
GRAAARRR
SHAKE
SHAKE
HMM.
I GUESS HE DIDN'T UNDERSTAND ME.

Reincarnation 93: Horohoro's Stirring Tale – Week Two

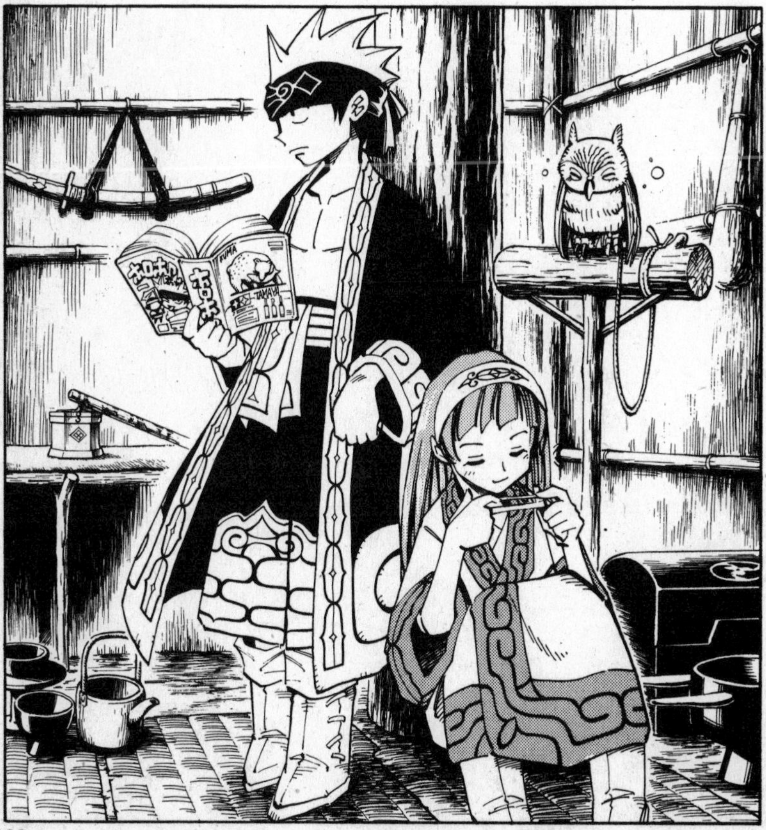

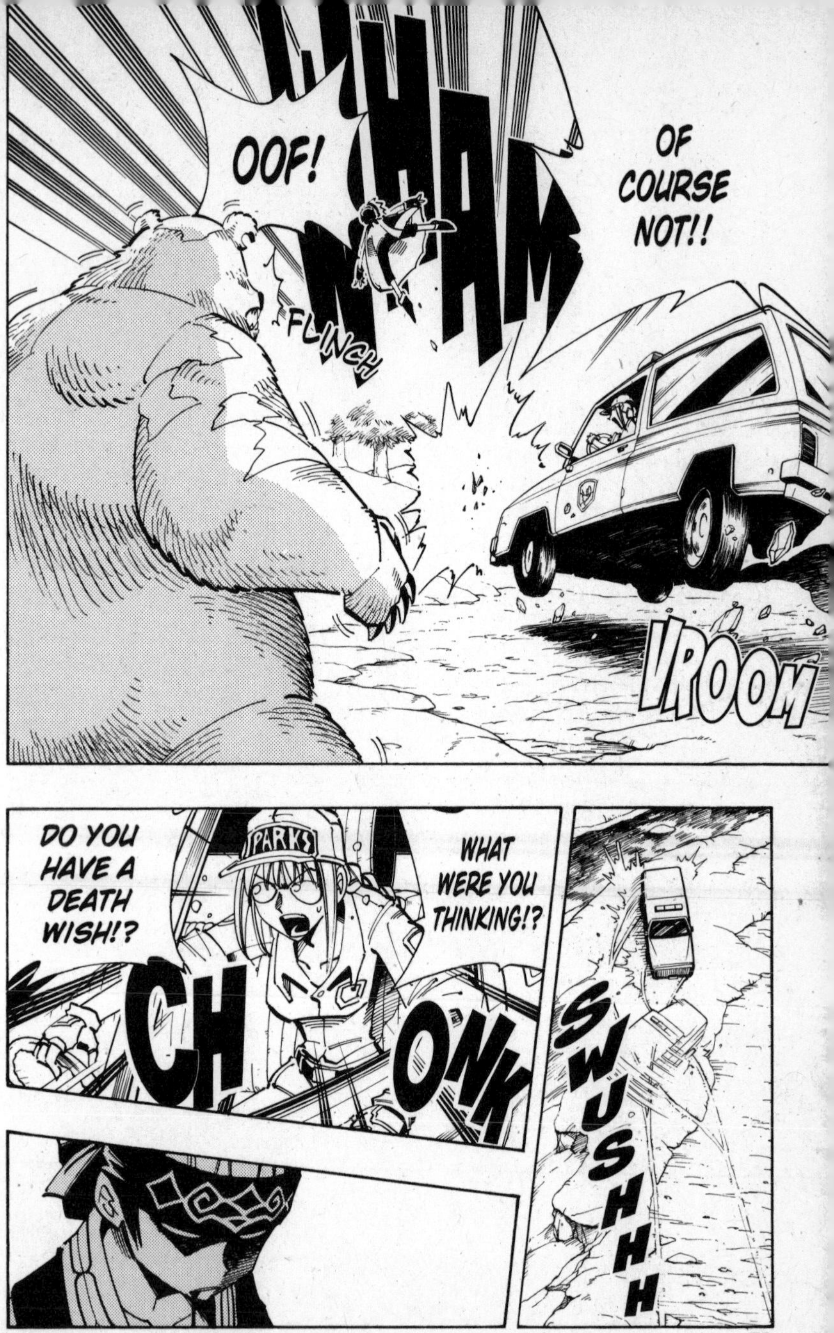
OF COURSE NOT!!
WHAM
OOF!
FLINCH
VROOM
SWUSHHH
WHAT WERE YOU THINKING!?
DO YOU HAVE A DEATH WISH!?
CHONK

READ THIS WAY

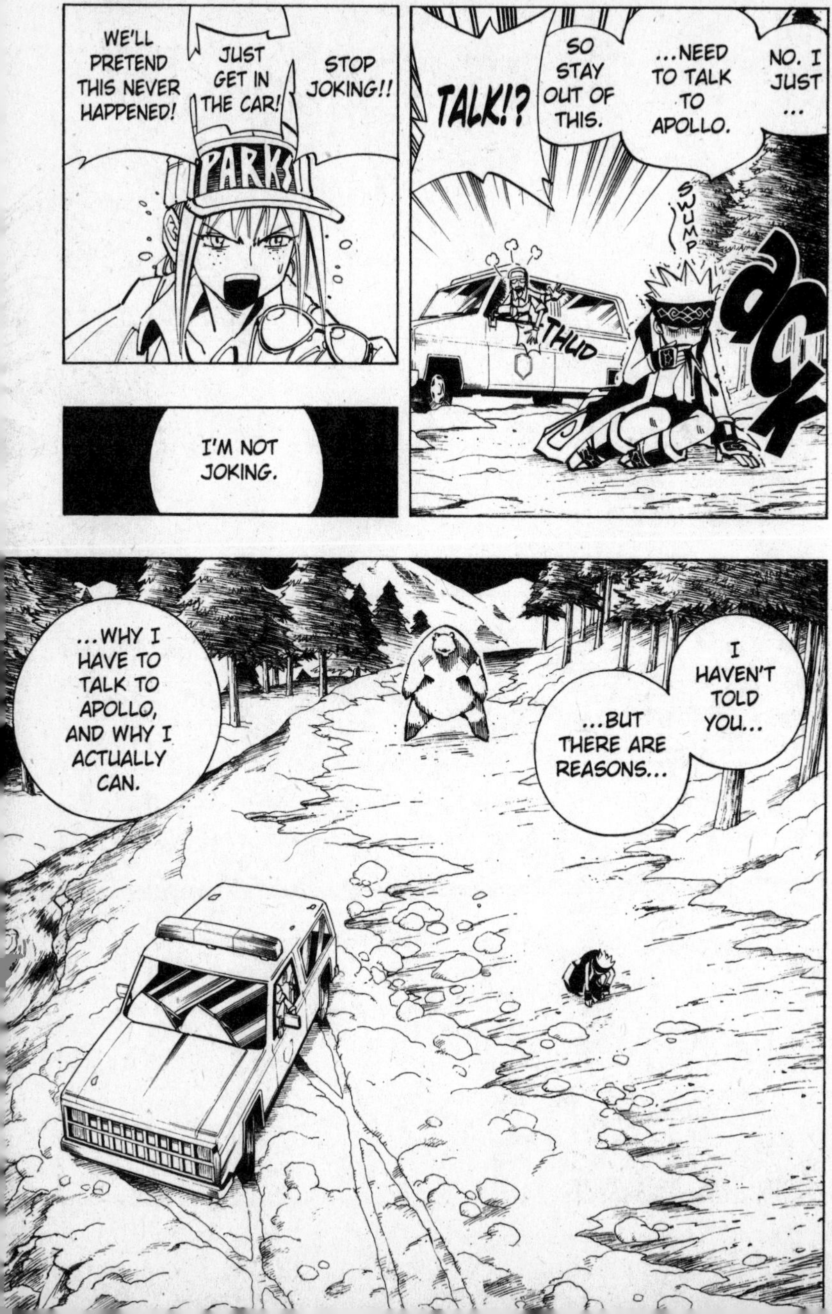
NO. I JUST ...
...NEED TO TALK TO APOLLO.
SO STAY OUT OF THIS.
TALK!?
SWUMP
THUD
ACK
STOP JOKING!!
JUST GET IN THE CAR!
WE'LL PRETEND THIS NEVER HAPPENED!
I'M NOT JOKING.
I HAVEN'T TOLD YOU...
...BUT THERE ARE REASONS...
...WHY I HAVE TO TALK TO APOLLO, AND WHY I ACTUALLY CAN.

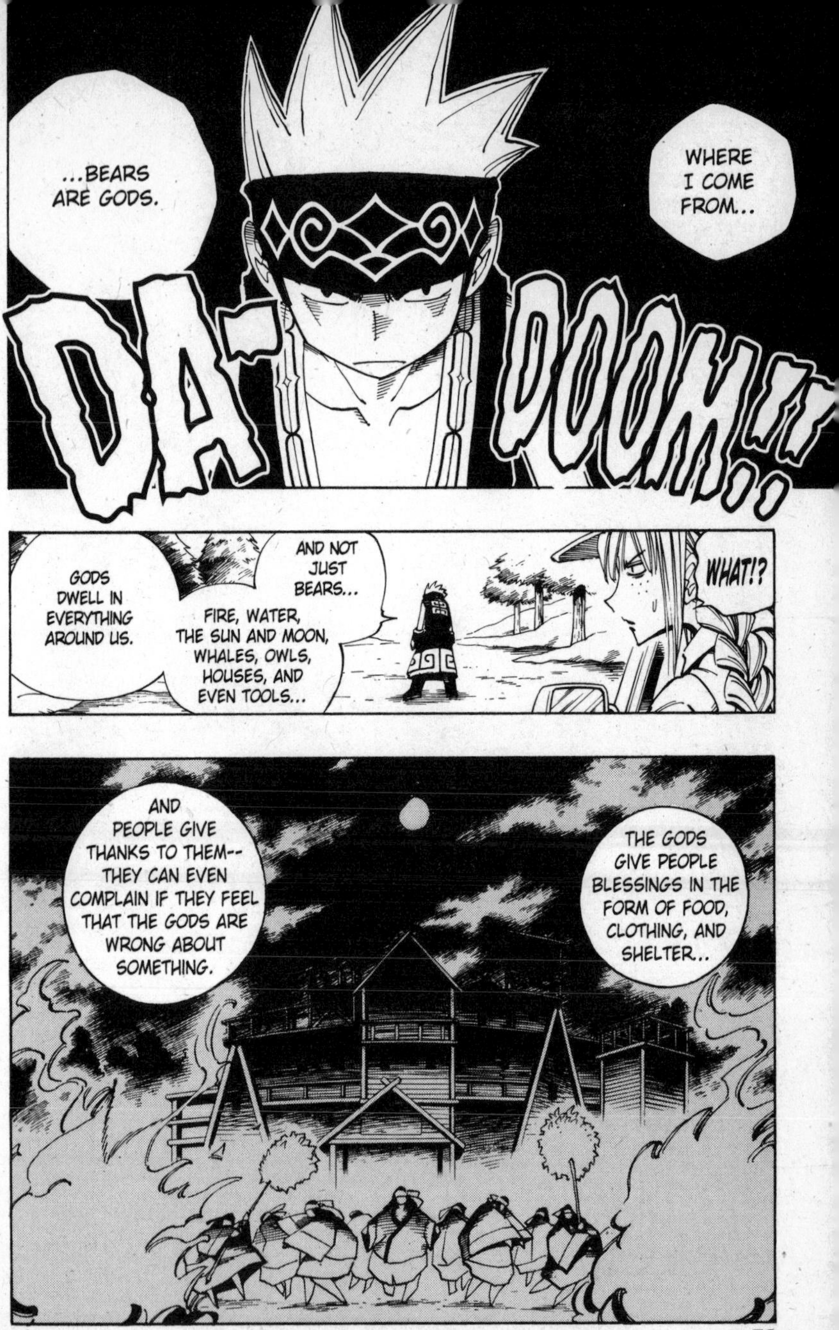
WHERE I COME FROM...
...BEARS ARE GODS.
DA-DOOM!!
WHAT!?
AND NOT JUST BEARS...
FIRE, WATER, THE SUN AND MOON, WHALES, OWLS, HOUSES, AND EVEN TOOLS...
GODS DWELL IN EVERYTHING AROUND US.
THE GODS GIVE PEOPLE BLESSINGS IN THE FORM OF FOOD, CLOTHING, AND SHELTER...
AND PEOPLE GIVE THANKS TO THEM-- THEY CAN EVEN COMPLAIN IF THEY FEEL THAT THE GODS ARE WRONG ABOUT SOMETHING.

READ THIS WAY

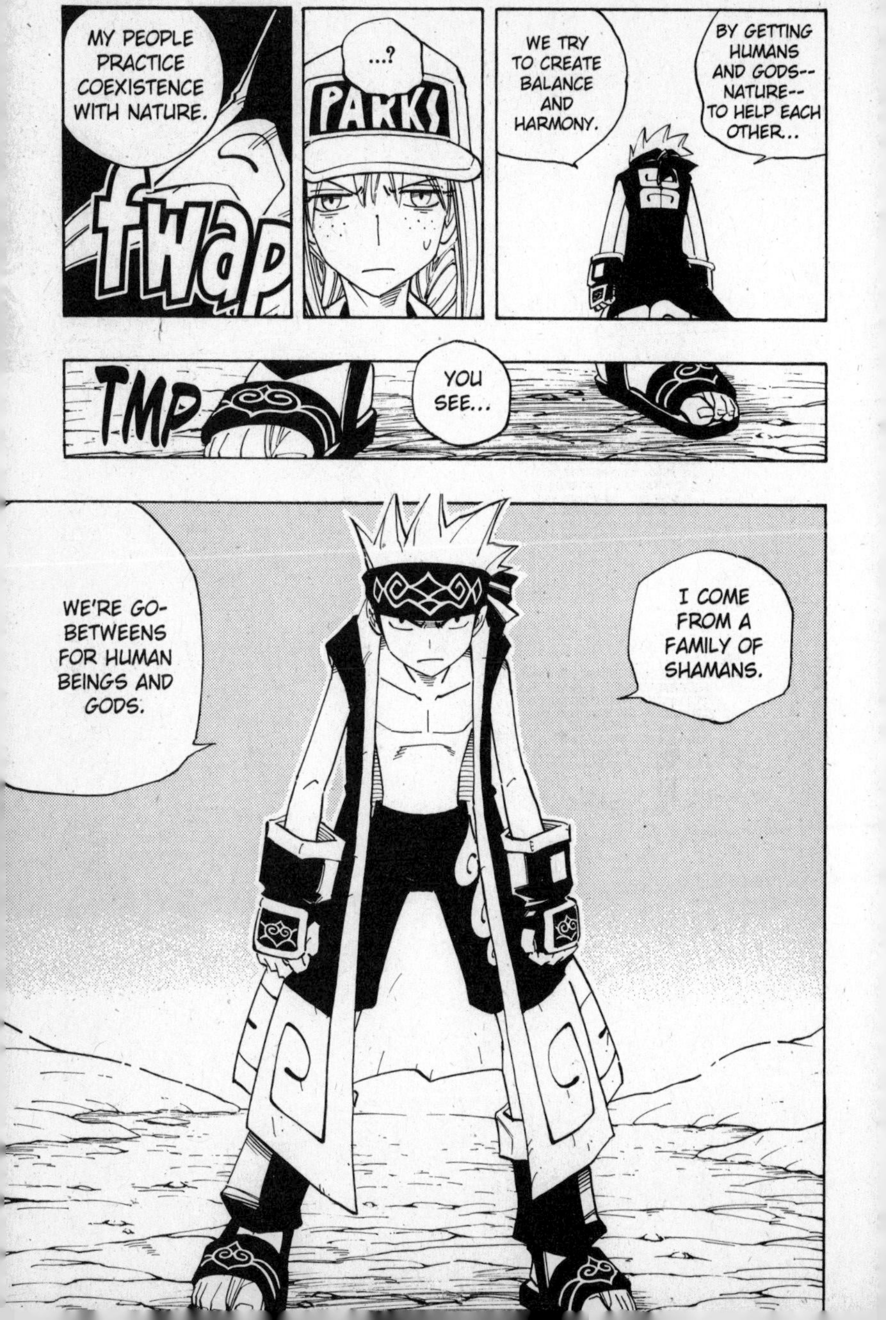
BY GETTING HUMANS AND GODS-- NATURE-- TO HELP EACH OTHER...
WE TRY TO CREATE BALANCE AND HARMONY.
PARKS
...?
MY PEOPLE PRACTICE COEXISTENCE WITH NATURE.
fwap
YOU SEE...
TMP
I COME FROM A FAMILY OF SHAMANS.
WE'RE GO-BETWEENS FOR HUMAN BEINGS AND GODS.

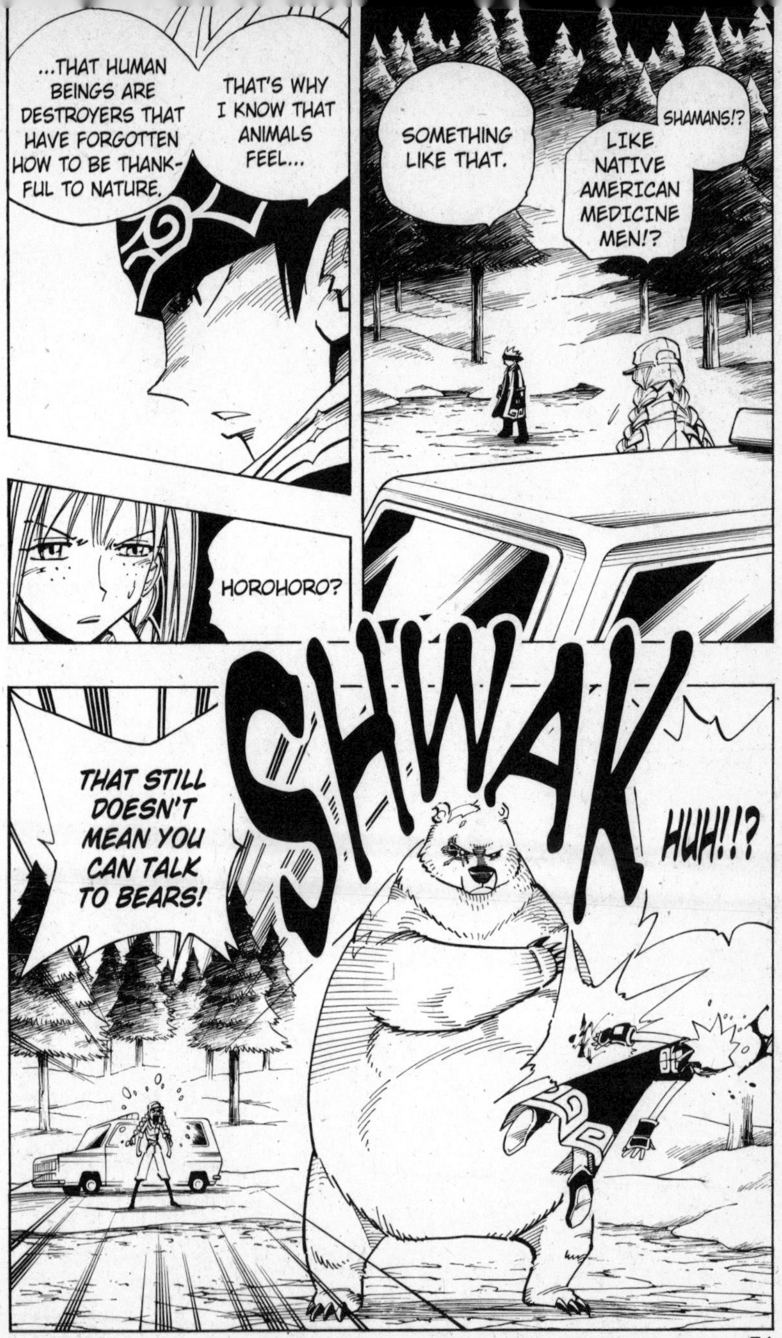
SHAMANS!?
LIKE NATIVE AMERICAN MEDICINE MEN!?
SOMETHING LIKE THAT.
THAT'S WHY I KNOW THAT ANIMALS FEEL...
...THAT HUMAN BEINGS ARE DESTROYERS THAT HAVE FORGOTTEN HOW TO BE THANK-FUL TO NATURE.
HOROHORO?
HUH!!?
SHWAK
THAT STILL DOESN'T MEAN YOU CAN TALK TO BEARS!

READ THIS WAY

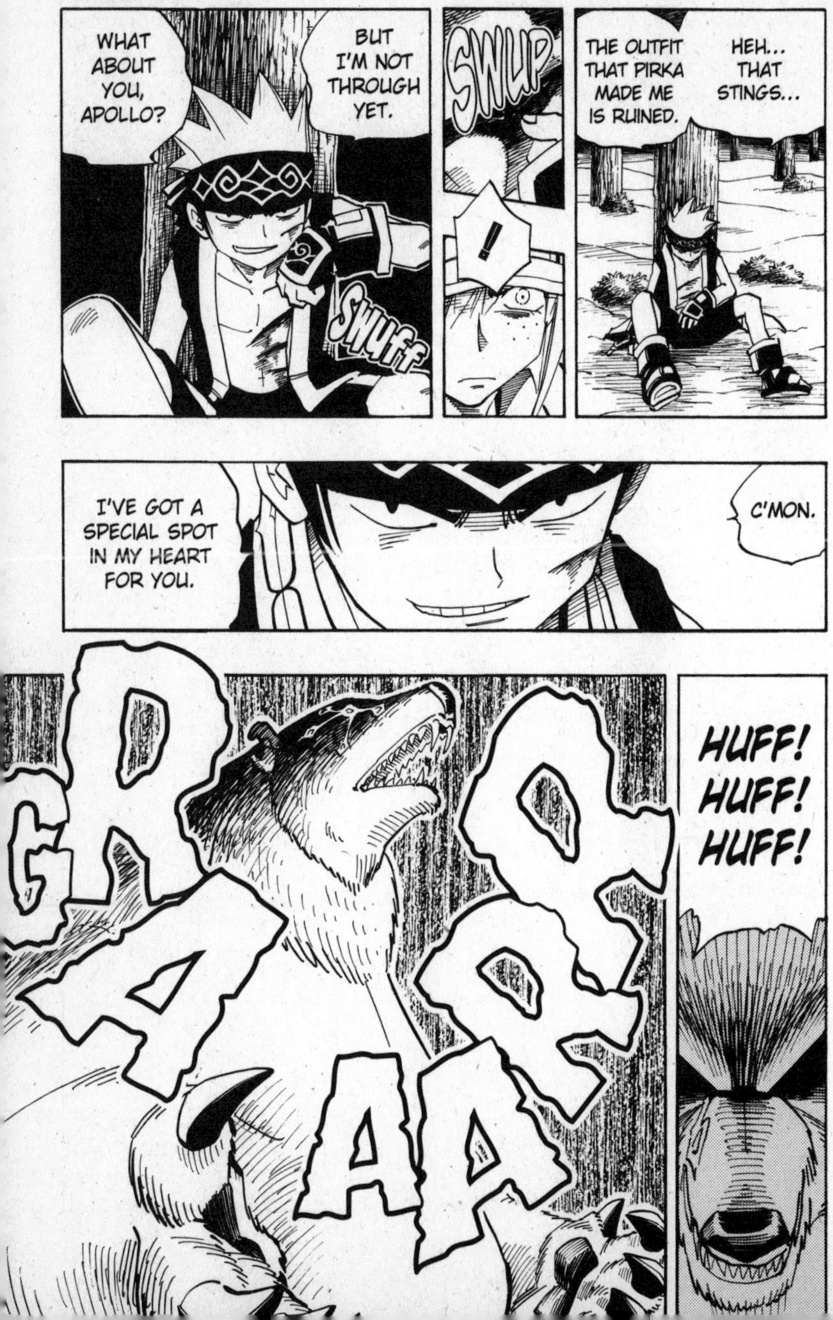
HEH... THAT STINGS...
THE OUTFIT THAT PIRKA MADE ME IS RUINED.
SWUP
!
BUT I'M NOT THROUGH YET.
WHAT ABOUT YOU, APOLLO?
SWUFF
C'MON.
I'VE GOT A SPECIAL SPOT IN MY HEART FOR YOU.
HUFF! HUFF! HUFF!
GRAAAR

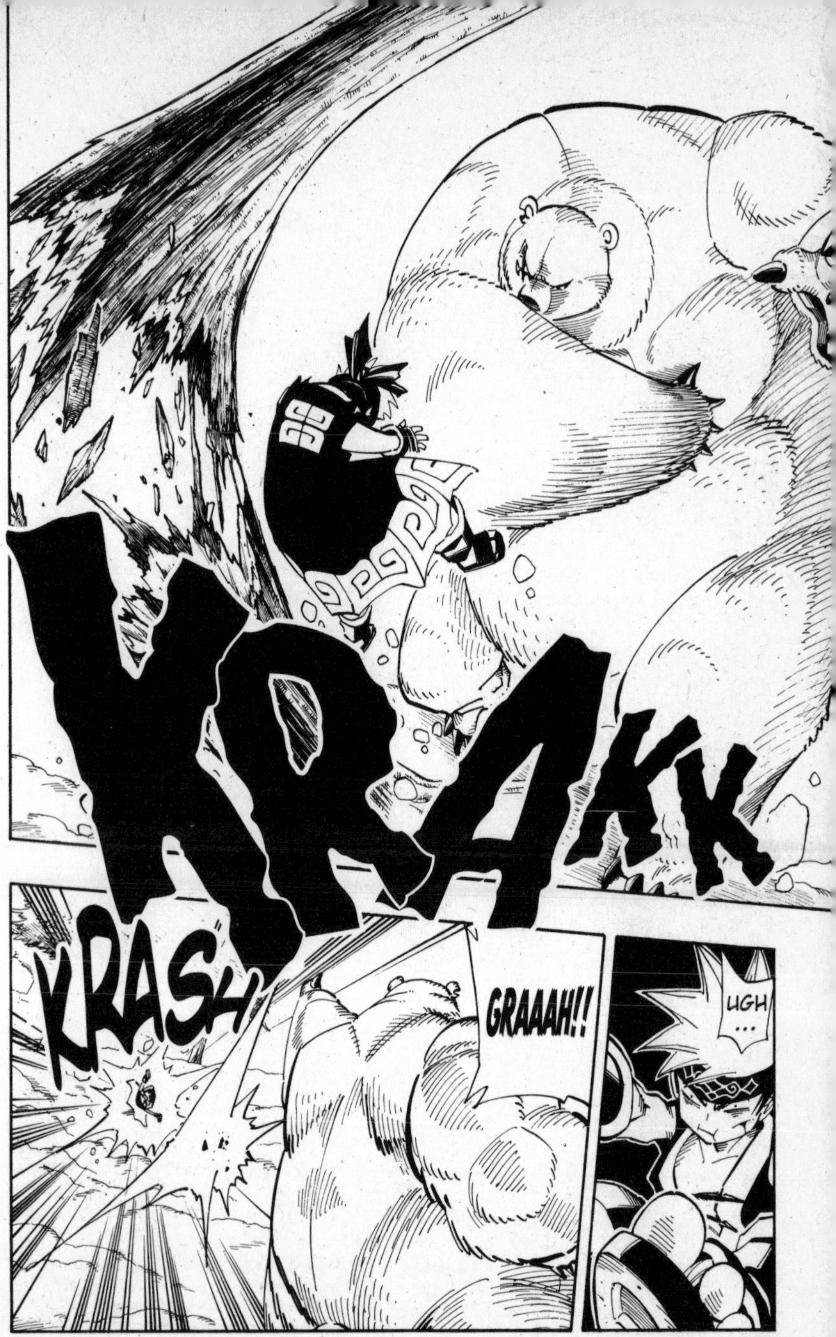
KRAKK
UGH ...
GRAAAH!!
KRASH

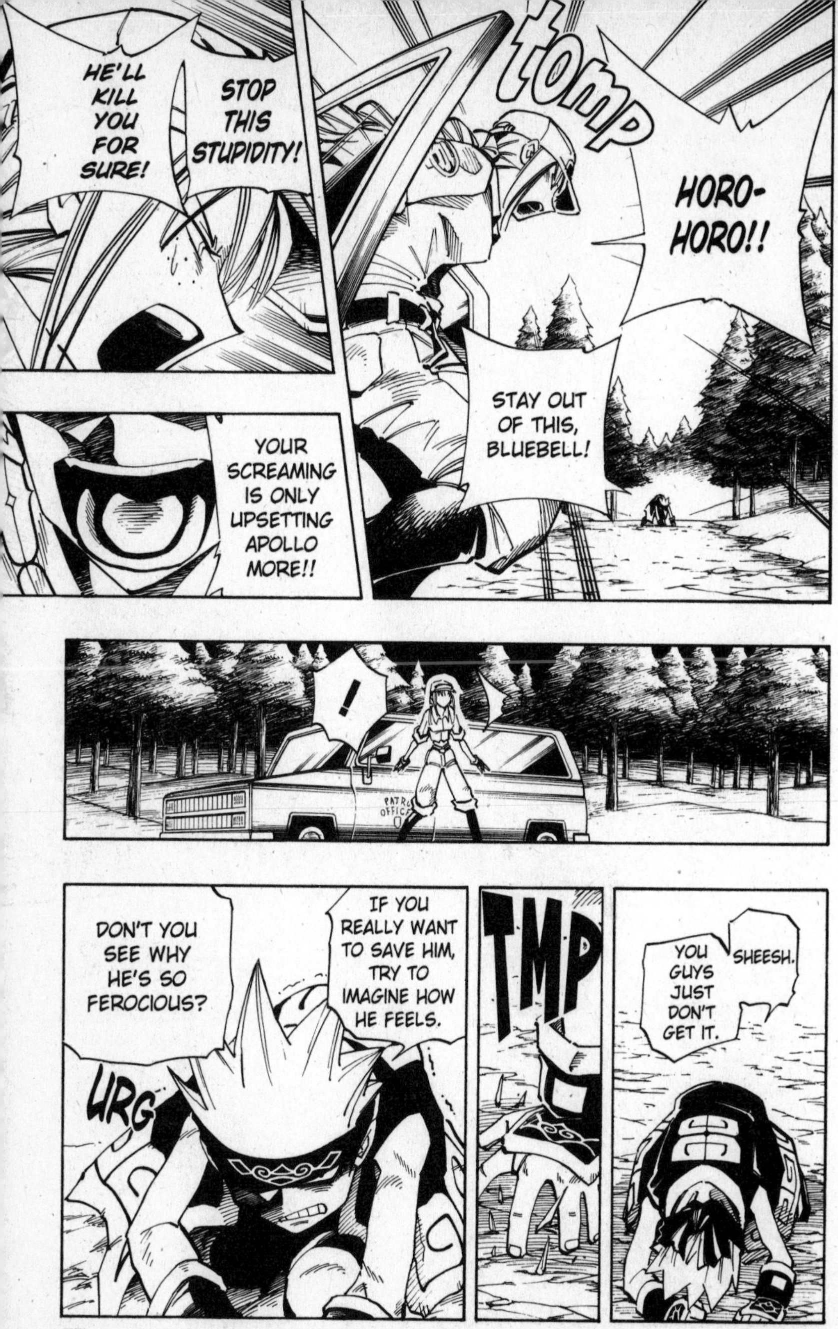

tomp
HORO-HORO!!
STAY OUT OF THIS, BLUEBELL!
STOP THIS STUPIDITY!
HE'LL KILL YOU FOR SURE!
YOUR SCREAMING IS ONLY UPSETTING APOLLO MORE!!
!
SHEESH.
YOU GUYS JUST DON'T GET IT.
TMP
IF YOU REALLY WANT TO SAVE HIM, TRY TO IMAGINE HOW HE FEELS.
DON'T YOU SEE WHY HE'S SO FEROCIOUS?
URG

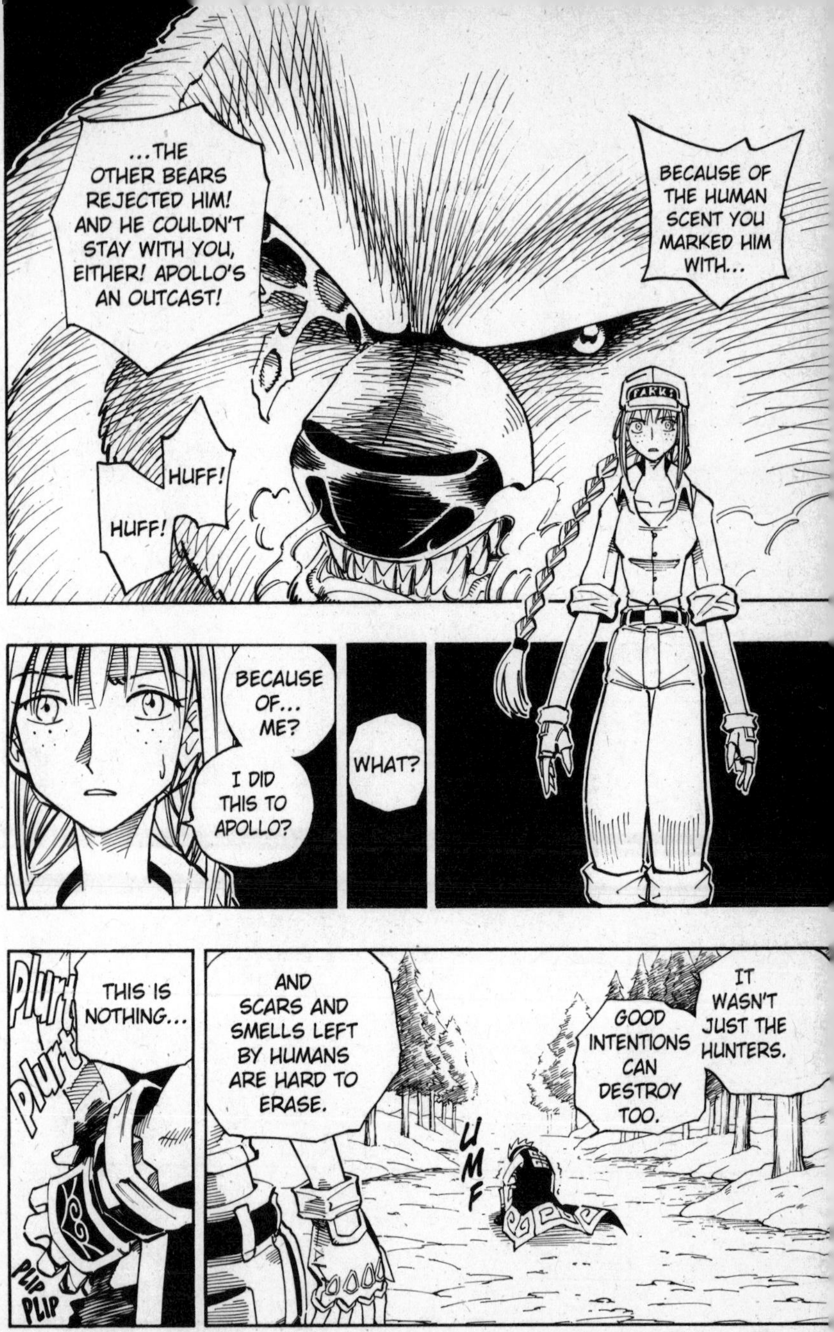
BECAUSE OF THE HUMAN SCENT YOU MARKED HIM WITH...
...THE OTHER BEARS REJECTED HIM! AND HE COULDN'T STAY WITH YOU, EITHER! APOLLO'S AN OUTCAST!
HUFF!
HUFF!
WHAT?
BECAUSE OF... ME?
I DID THIS TO APOLLO?
IT WASN'T JUST THE HUNTERS.
GOOD INTENTIONS CAN DESTROY TOO.
AND SCARS AND SMELLS LEFT BY HUMANS ARE HARD TO ERASE.
UMF
THIS IS NOTHING...
Plurt
Plurt
PLIP
PLIP

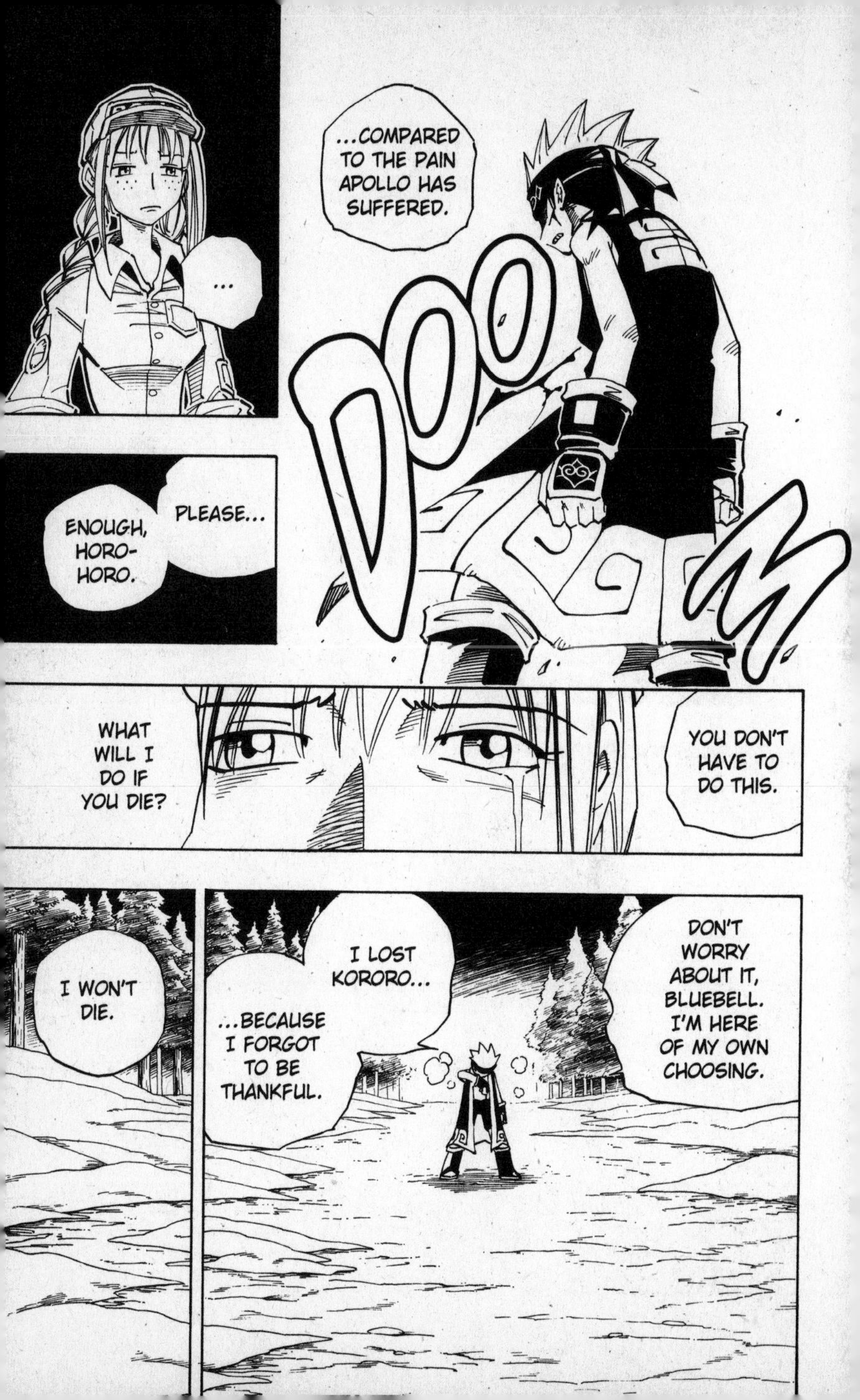
...COMPARED TO THE PAIN APOLLO HAS SUFFERED.
DOOOM
...
PLEASE...
ENOUGH, HORO-HORO.
YOU DON'T HAVE TO DO THIS.
WHAT WILL I DO IF YOU DIE?
DON'T WORRY ABOUT IT, BLUEBELL. I'M HERE OF MY OWN CHOOSING.
I LOST KORORO...
...BECAUSE I FORGOT TO BE THANKFUL.
I WON'T DIE.

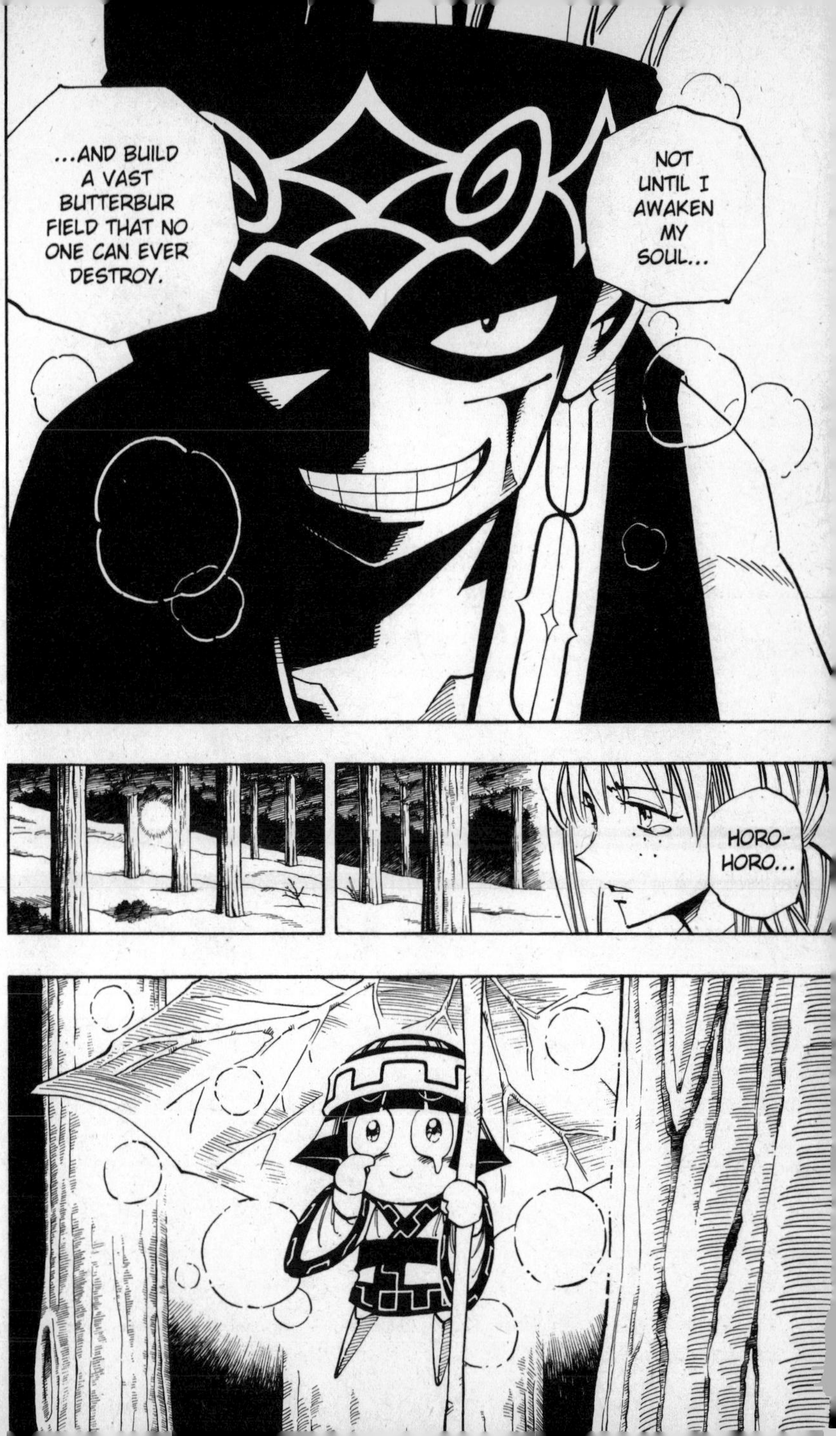
NOT UNTIL I AWAKEN MY SOUL...
...AND BUILD A VAST BUTTERBUR FIELD THAT NO ONE CAN EVER DESTROY.
HORO-HORO...

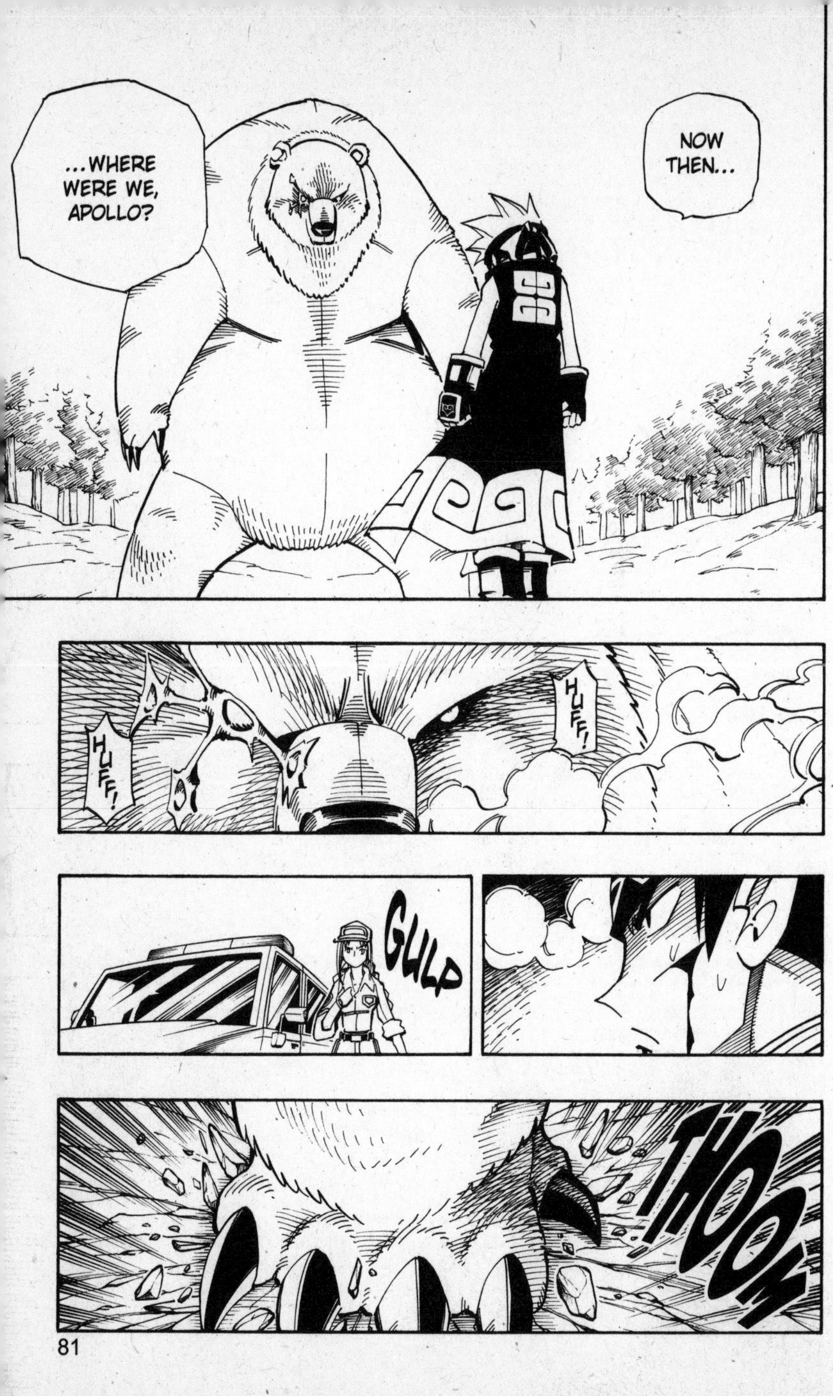
NOW THEN...
...WHERE WERE WE, APOLLO?
HUFF!
HUFF!
GULP
THOOM

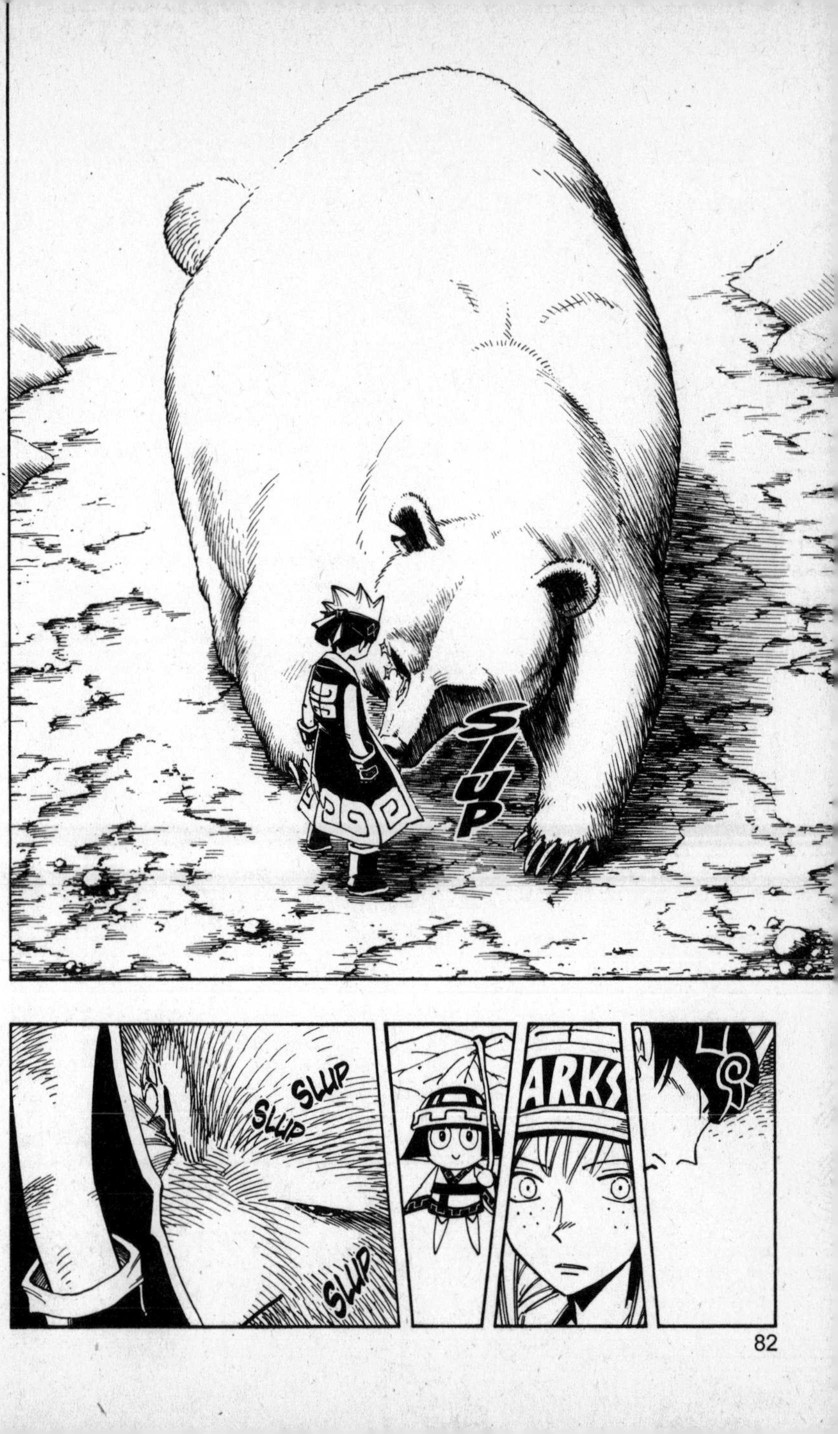
SLUP
ARKS
SLUP
SLUP
SLUP

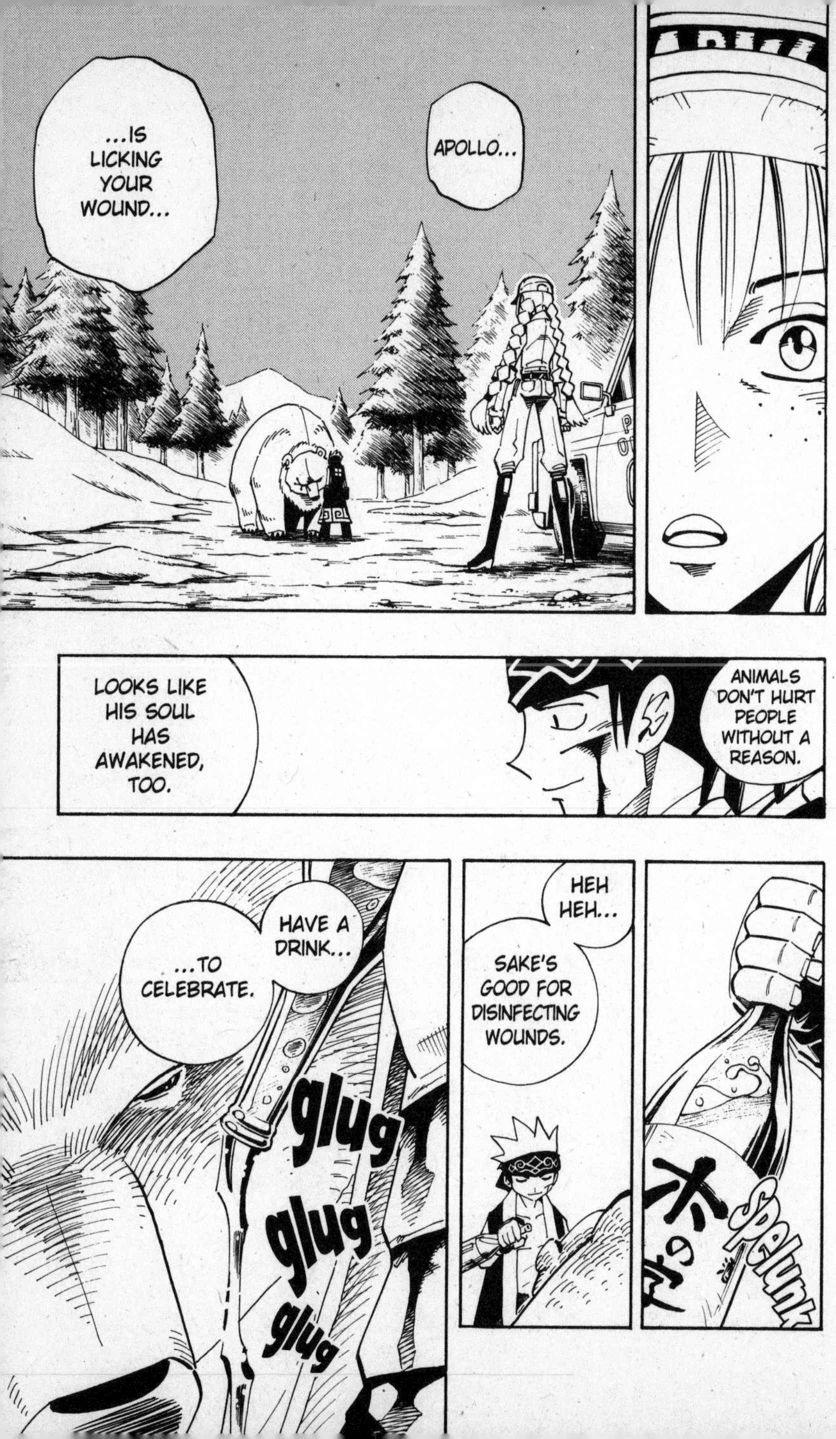
APOLLO...
...IS LICKING YOUR WOUND...
ANIMALS DON'T HURT PEOPLE WITHOUT A REASON.
LOOKS LIKE HIS SOUL HAS AWAKENED, TOO.
Spelunk
HEH HEH...
SAKE'S GOOD FOR DISINFECTING WOUNDS.
HAVE A DRINK...
...TO CELEBRATE.
glug
glug
glug

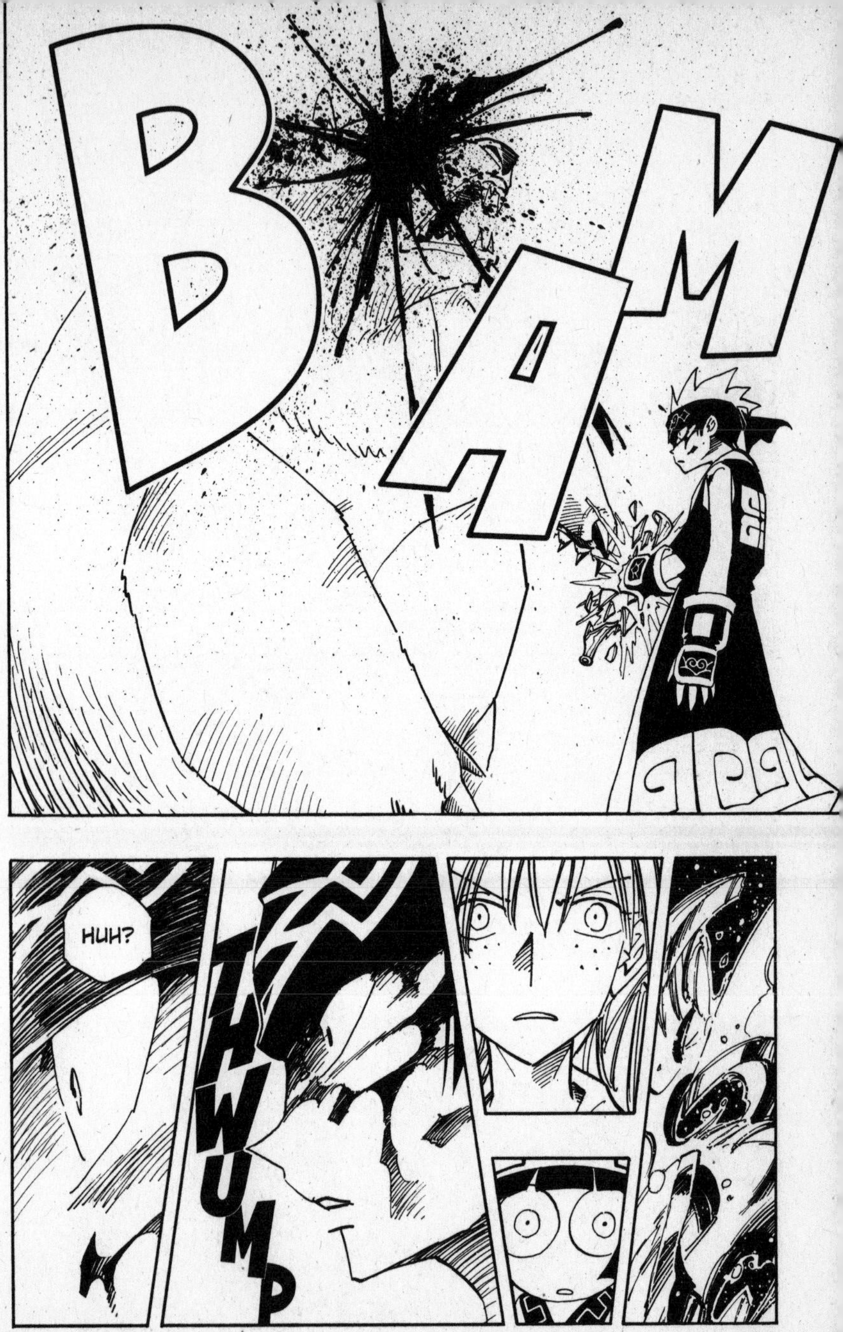
BAM
THWUMP
HUH?

READ THIS WAY

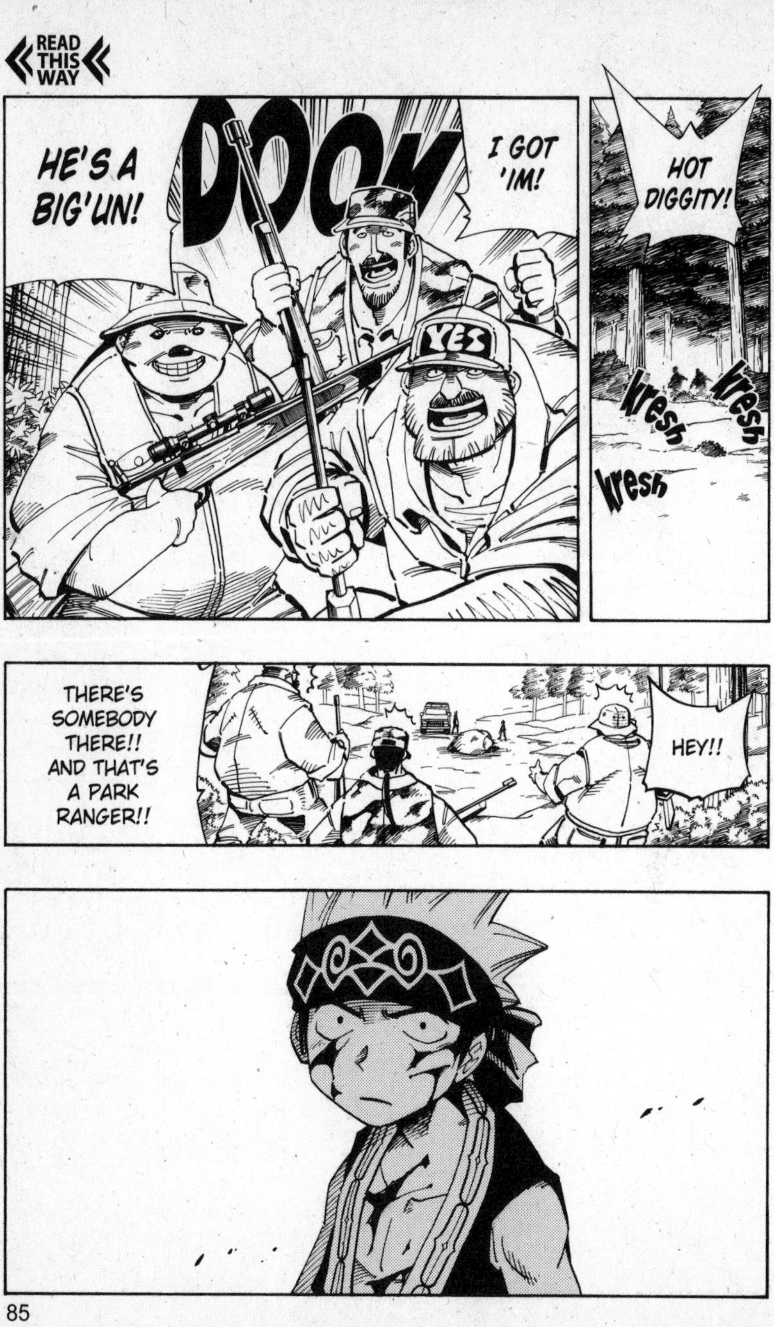

HOT DIGGITY!
kresh
kresh
kresh
I GOT 'IM!
DOOM
HE'S A BIG'UN!
HEY!!
THERE'S SOMEBODY THERE!! AND THAT'S A PARK RANGER!!

SHAMAN KING
11

IKUPASUY

Reincarnation 94: Horohoro's Stirring Tale – Week Three

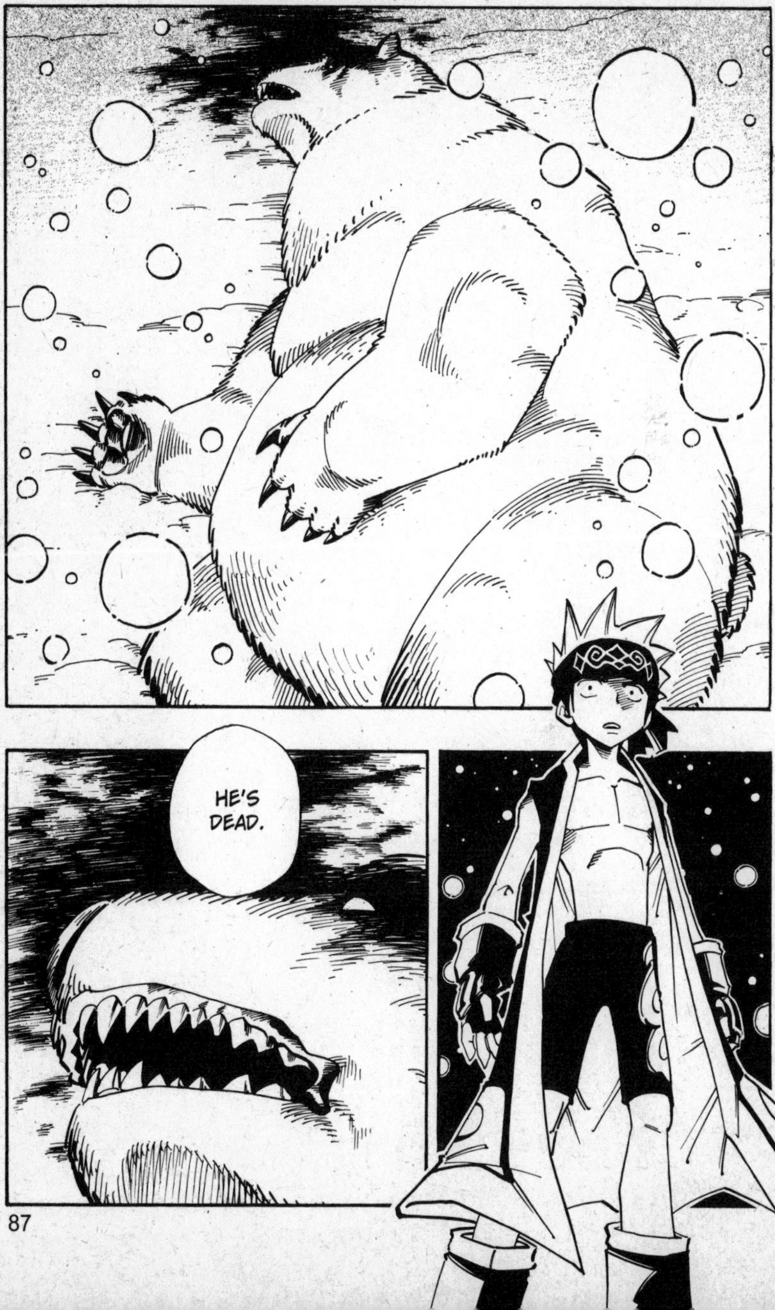
HE'S DEAD.

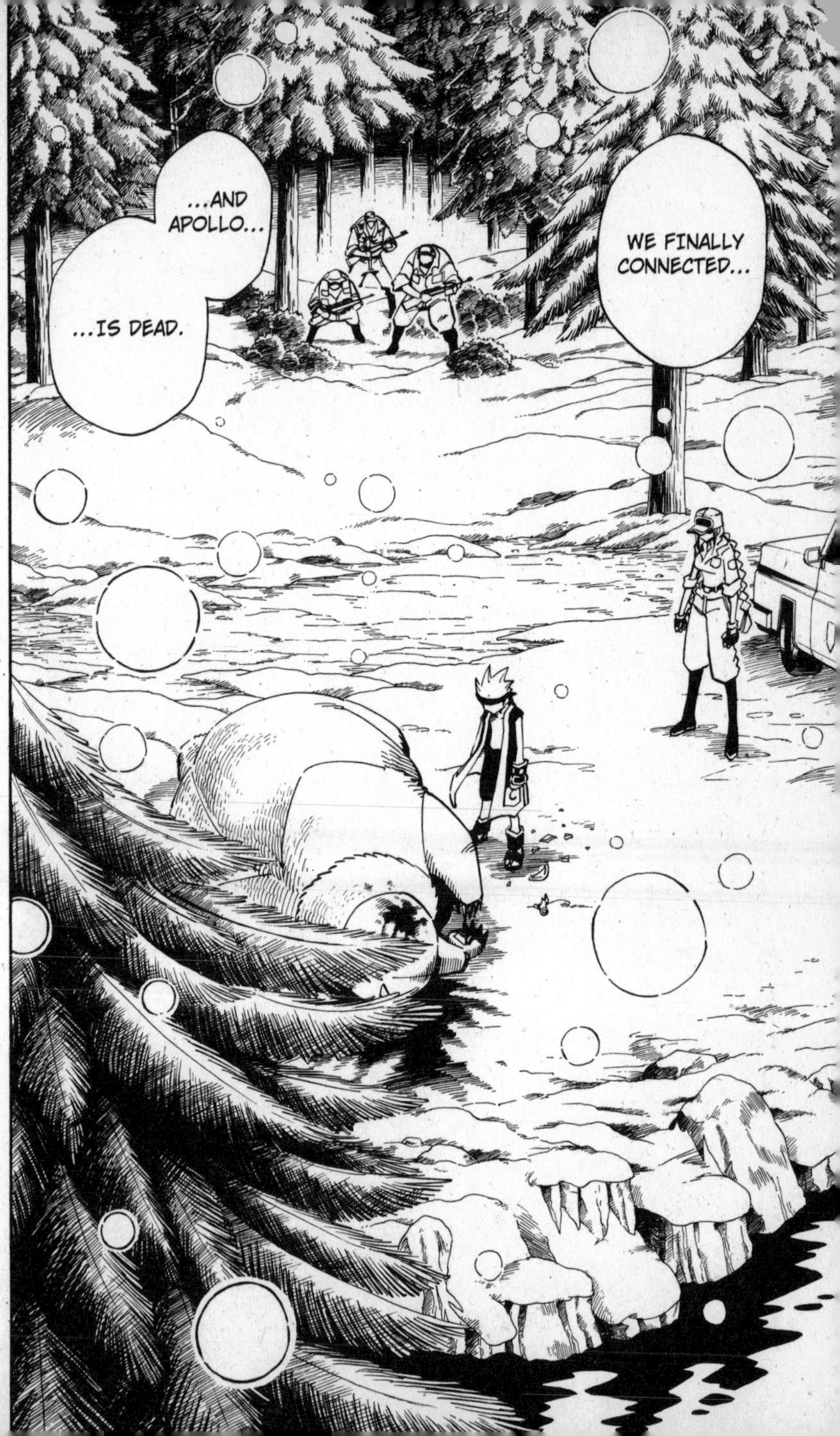
WE FINALLY CONNECTED...
...AND APOLLO...
...IS DEAD.

Reincarnation 94: Horohoro's Stirring Tale~ Week Three

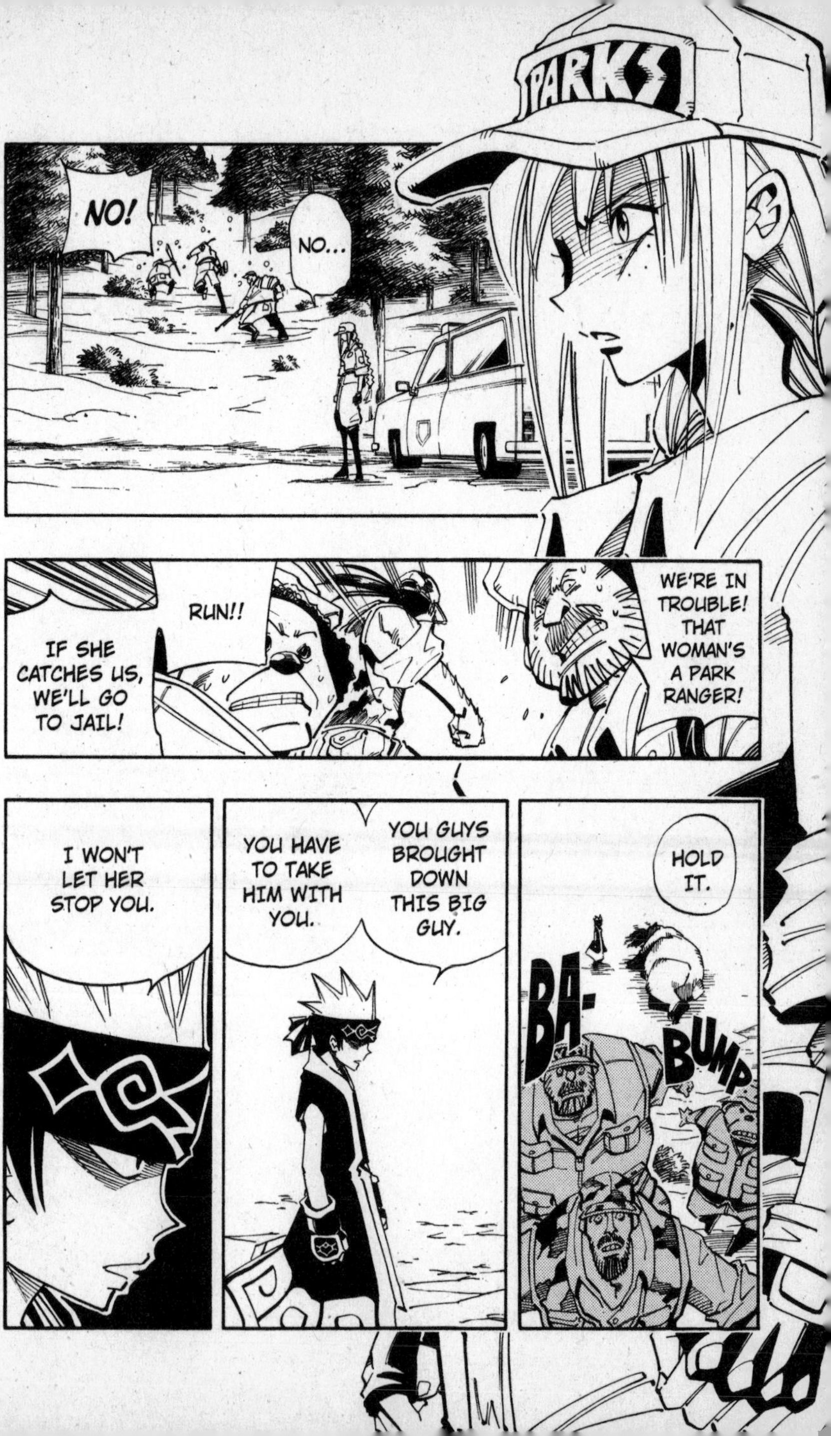
PARKS
NO...
NO!
WE'RE IN TROUBLE! THAT WOMAN'S A PARK RANGER!
RUN!!
IF SHE CATCHES US, WE'LL GO TO JAIL!
HOLD IT.
BA-BUMP
YOU GUYS BROUGHT DOWN THIS BIG GUY.
YOU HAVE TO TAKE HIM WITH YOU.
I WON'T LET HER STOP YOU.

READ THIS WAY

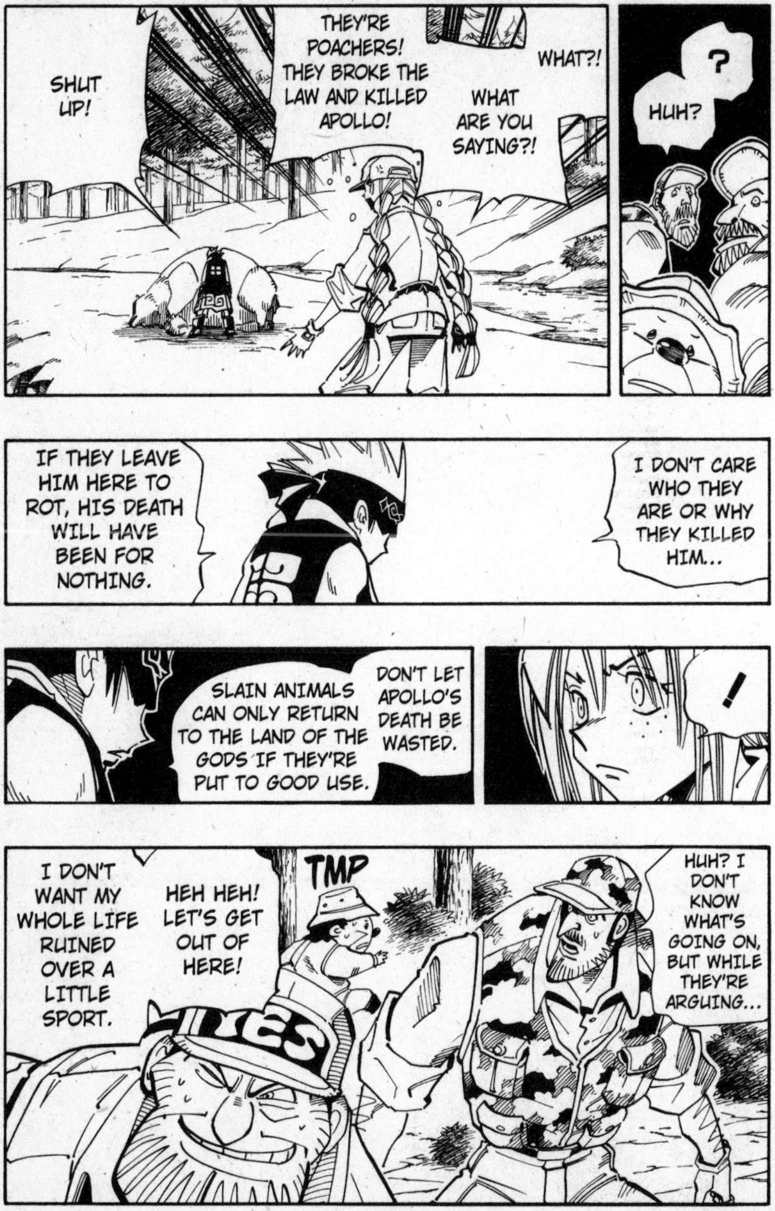
?
HUH?
WHAT?!
WHAT ARE YOU SAYING?!
THEY'RE POACHERS! THEY BROKE THE LAW AND KILLED APOLLO!
SHUT UP!
I DON'T CARE WHO THEY ARE OR WHY THEY KILLED HIM...
IF THEY LEAVE HIM HERE TO ROT, HIS DEATH WILL HAVE BEEN FOR NOTHING.
!
DON'T LET APOLLO'S DEATH BE WASTED.
SLAIN ANIMALS CAN ONLY RETURN TO THE LAND OF THE GODS IF THEY'RE PUT TO GOOD USE.
HUH? I DON'T KNOW WHAT'S GOING ON, BUT WHILE THEY'RE ARGUING...
TMP
HEH HEH! LET'S GET OUT OF HERE!
I DON'T WANT MY WHOLE LIFE RUINED OVER A LITTLE SPORT.

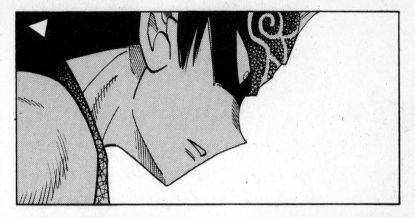

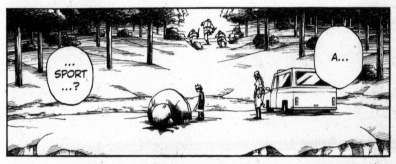

A...
... SPORT ...?
OF COURSE! WHAT DID YOU THINK THEY WERE DOING?!
IF EVERYONE WERE LIKE YOU, MY JOB WOULDN'T BE NECESSARY.
CHAK
FREEZE!!

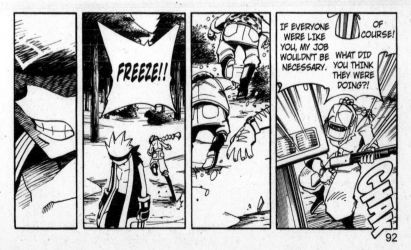

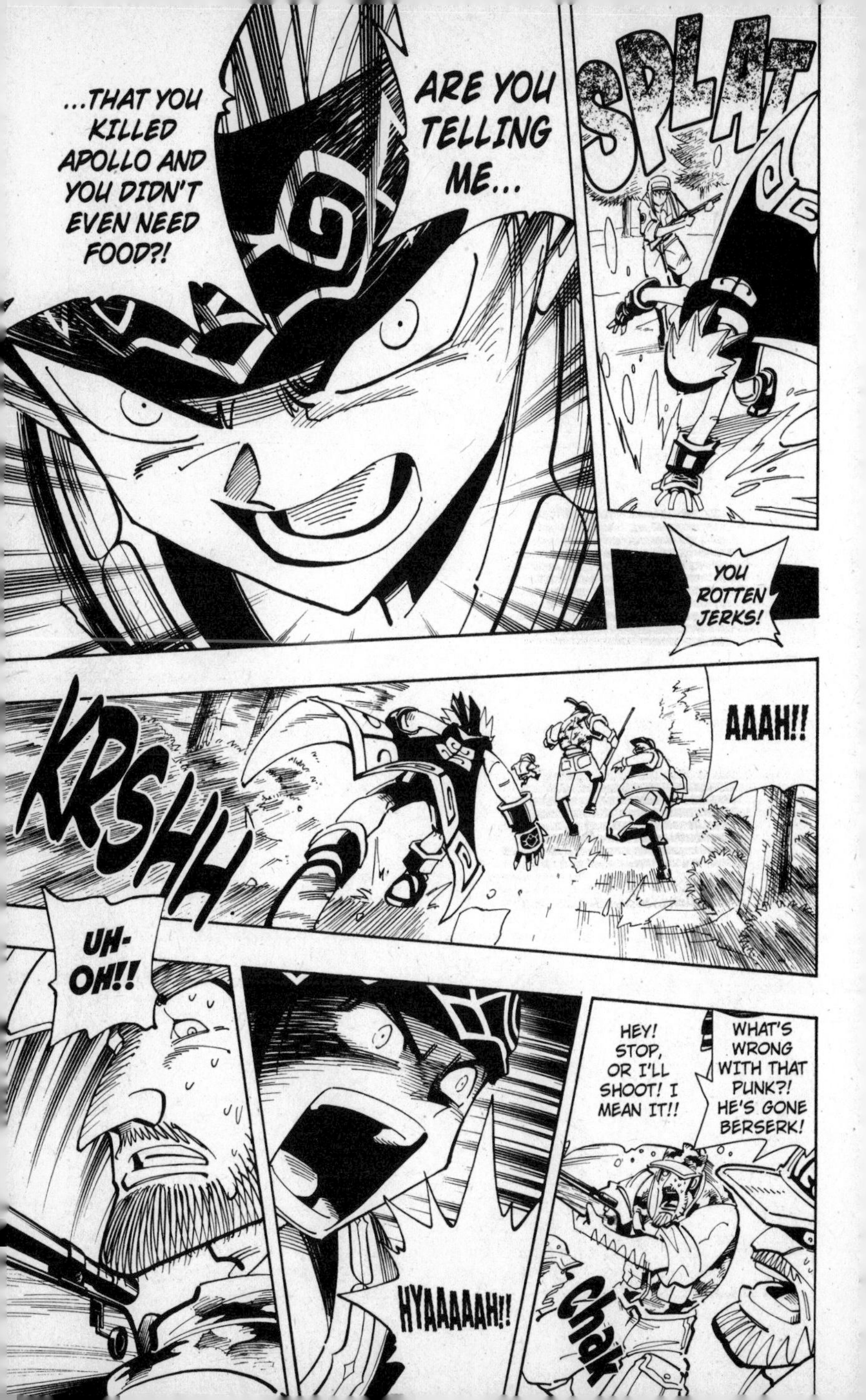
SPLAT
YOU ROTTEN JERKS!
ARE YOU TELLING ME...
...THAT YOU KILLED APOLLO AND YOU DIDN'T EVEN NEED FOOD?!
AAAH!!
KRSHH
WHAT'S WRONG WITH THAT PUNK?! HE'S GONE BERSERK!
HEY! STOP, OR I'LL SHOOT! I MEAN IT!!
Chak
HYAAAAAH!!
UH-OH!!

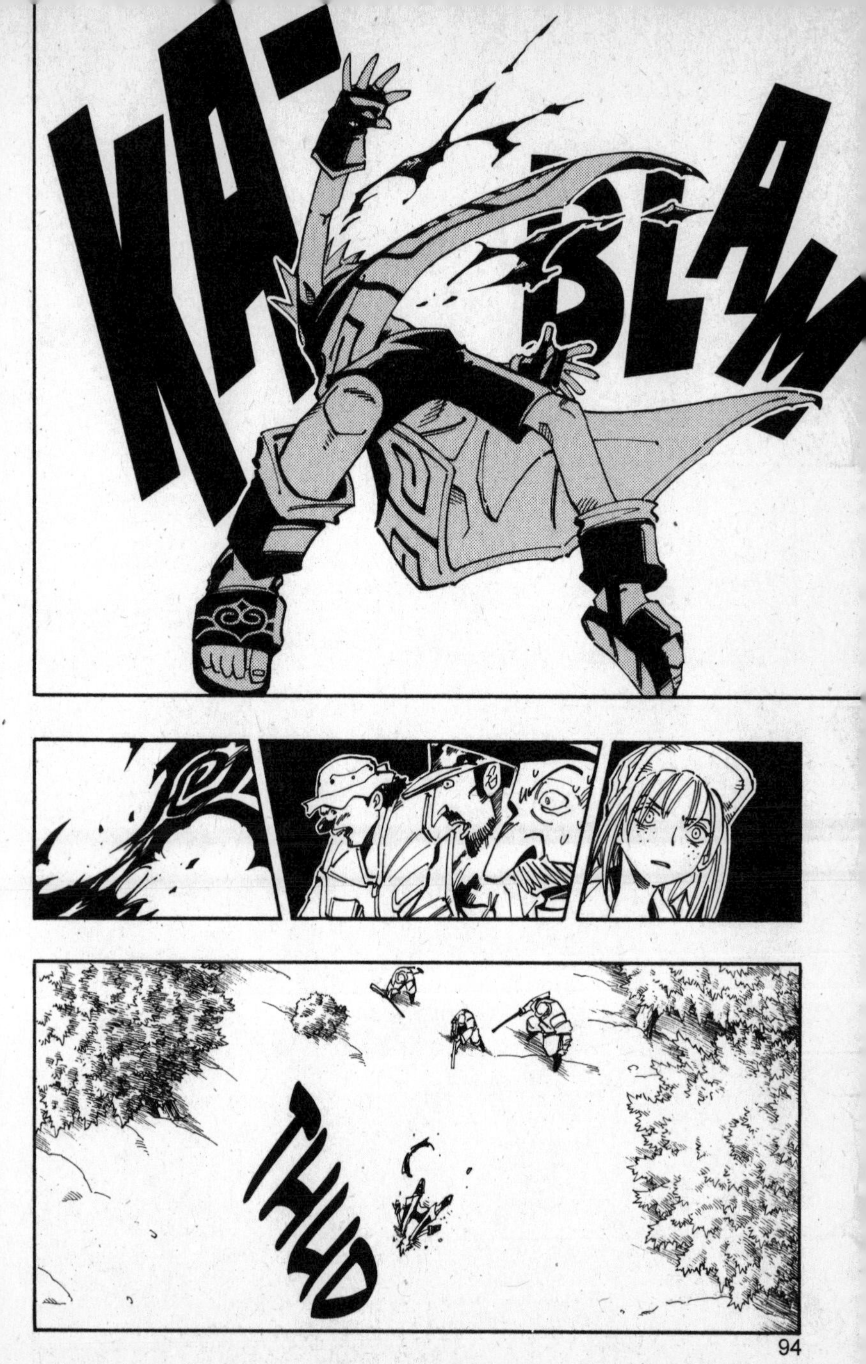
KA-BLAM
THUD

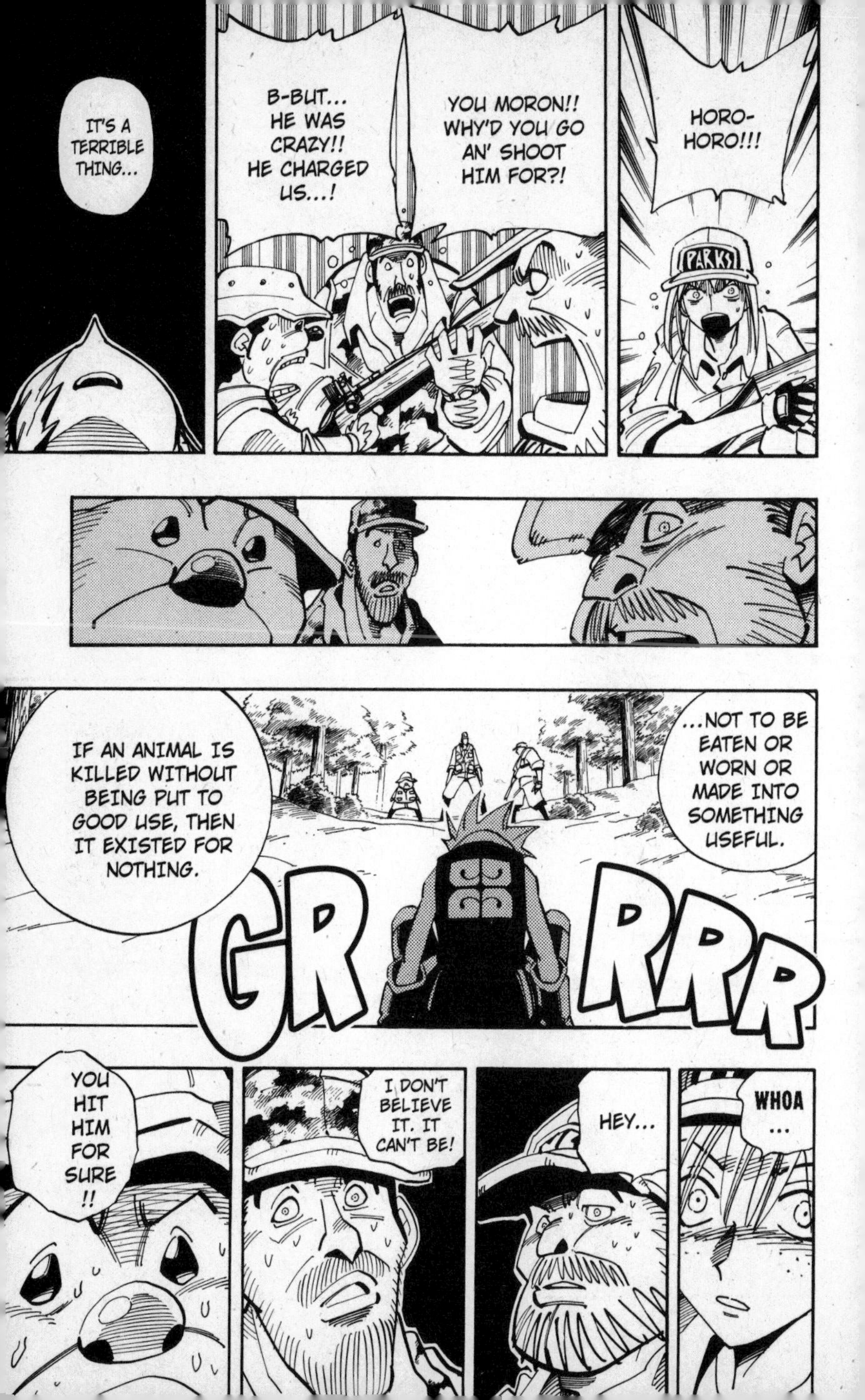
HORO-HORO!!!
YOU MORON!! WHY'D YOU GO AN' SHOOT HIM FOR?!
B-BUT... HE WAS CRAZY!! HE CHARGED US...!
IT'S A TERRIBLE THING...
IF AN ANIMAL IS KILLED WITHOUT BEING PUT TO GOOD USE, THEN IT EXISTED FOR NOTHING.
...NOT TO BE EATEN OR WORN OR MADE INTO SOMETHING USEFUL.
GRRRR
WHOA...
HEY...
I DON'T BELIEVE IT. IT CAN'T BE!
YOU HIT HIM FOR SURE!!

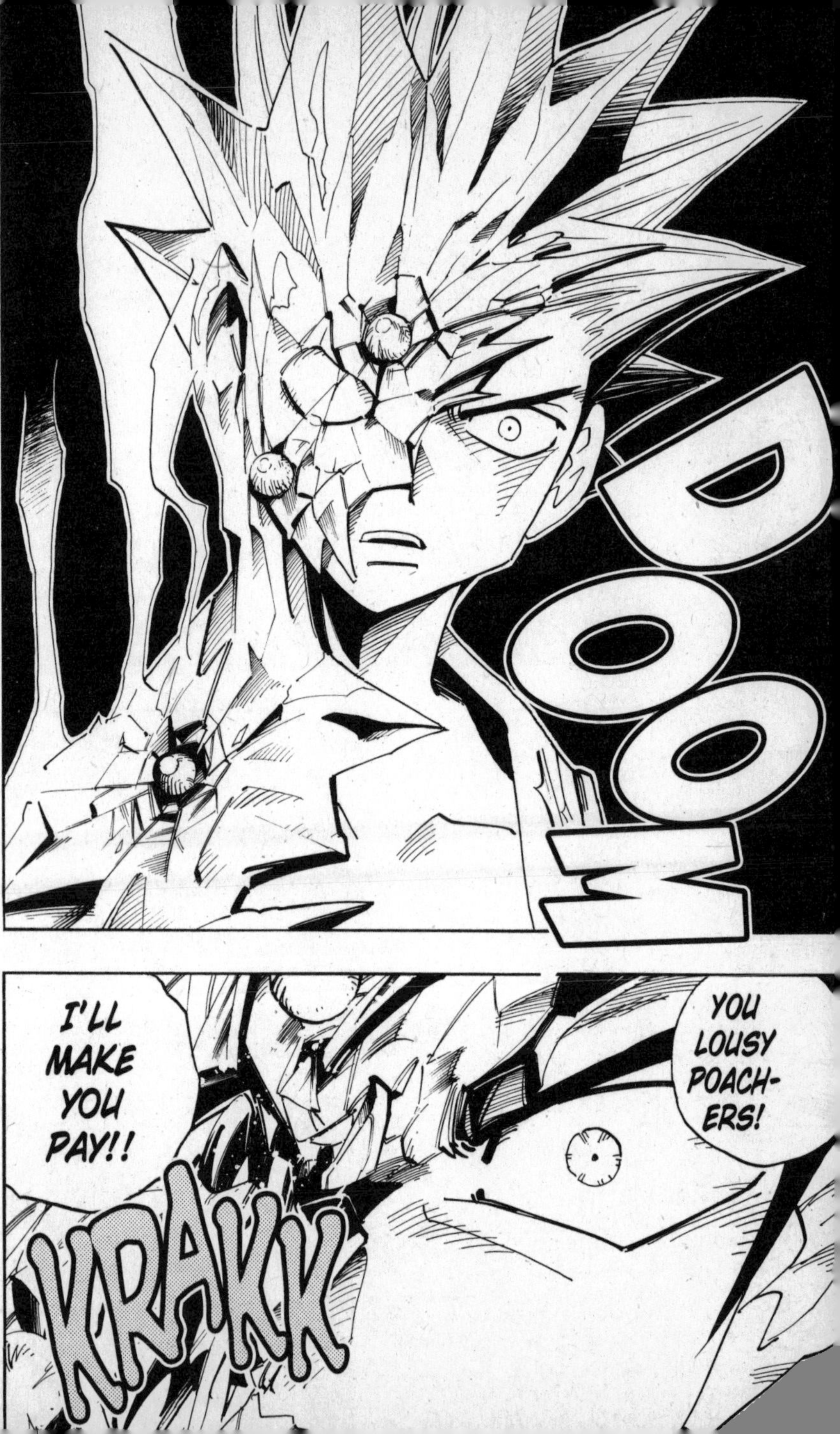
DOOOM
YOU LOUSY POACH-ERS!
I'LL MAKE YOU PAY!!
KRAKK

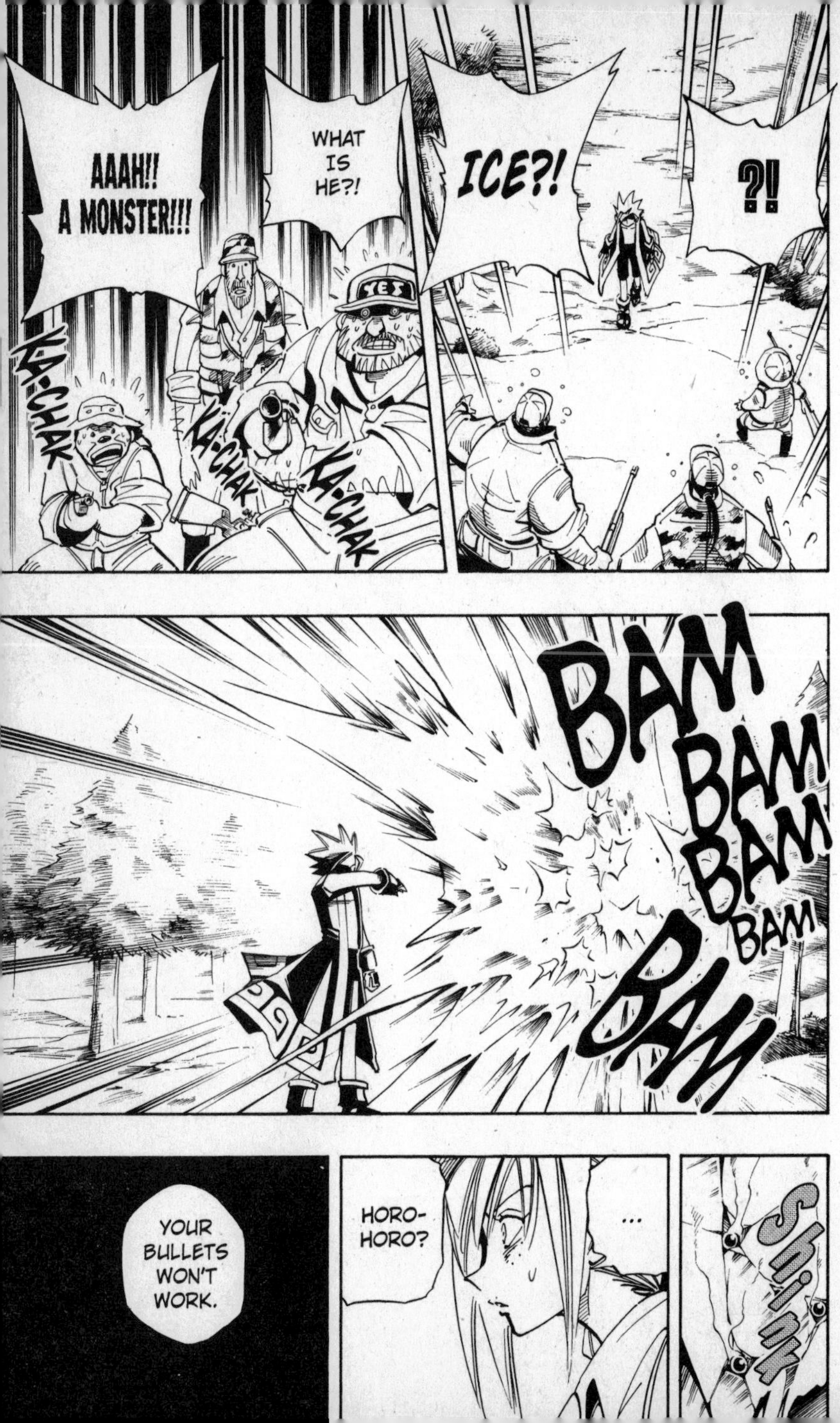
?!
ICE?!
WHAT IS HE?!
AAAH!! A MONSTER!!!
KA-CHAK
KA-CHAK
KA-CHAK
BAM
BAM
BAM
BAM
BAM
Shiiink
...
HORO-HORO?
YOUR BULLETS WON'T WORK.

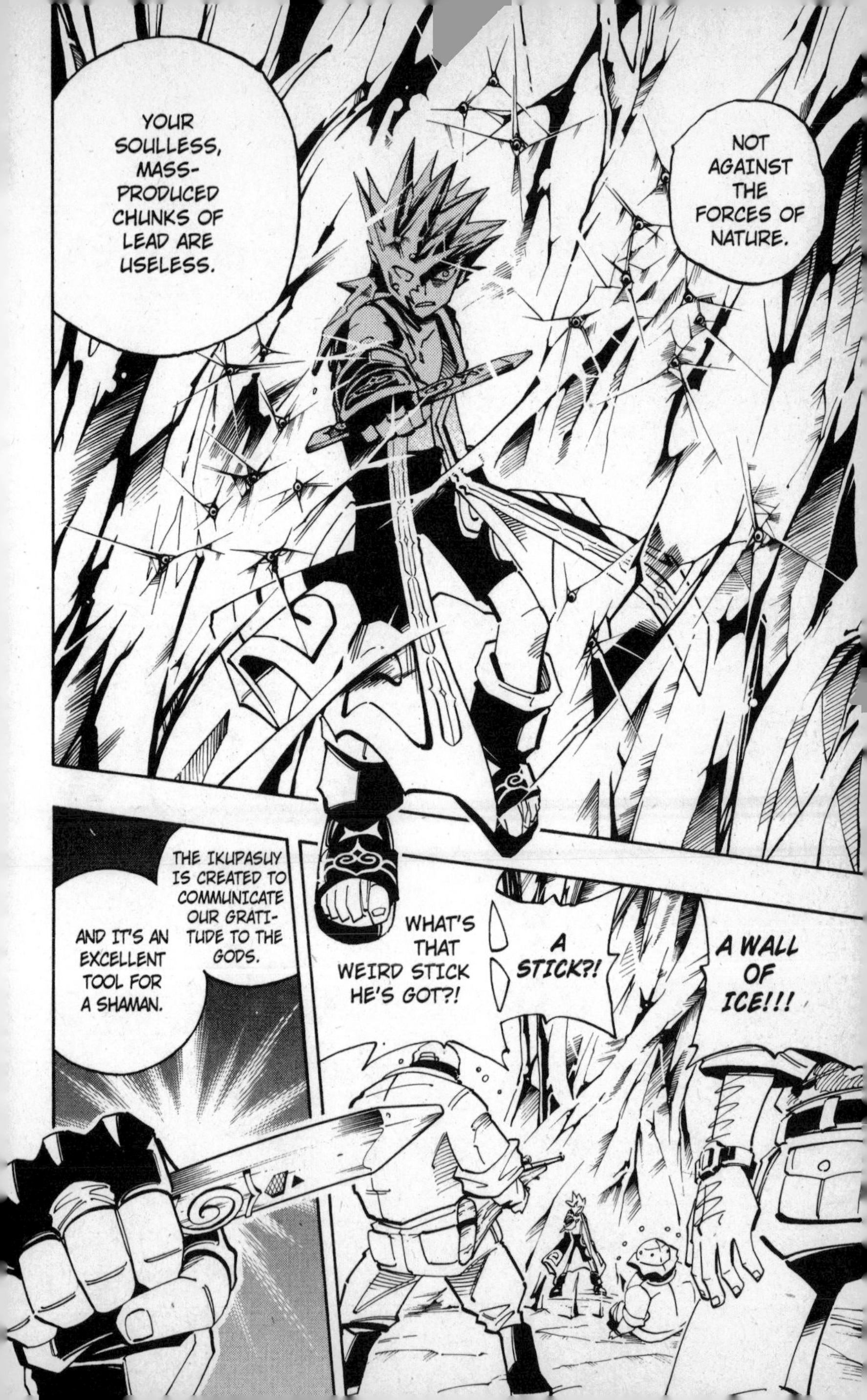
YOUR SOULLESS, MASS-PRODUCED CHUNKS OF LEAD ARE USELESS.
NOT AGAINST THE FORCES OF NATURE.
A WALL OF ICE!!!
A STICK?!
WHAT'S THAT WEIRD STICK HE'S GOT?!
THE IKUPASUY IS CREATED TO COMMUNICATE OUR GRATITUDE TO THE GODS.
AND IT'S AN EXCELLENT TOOL FOR A SHAMAN.

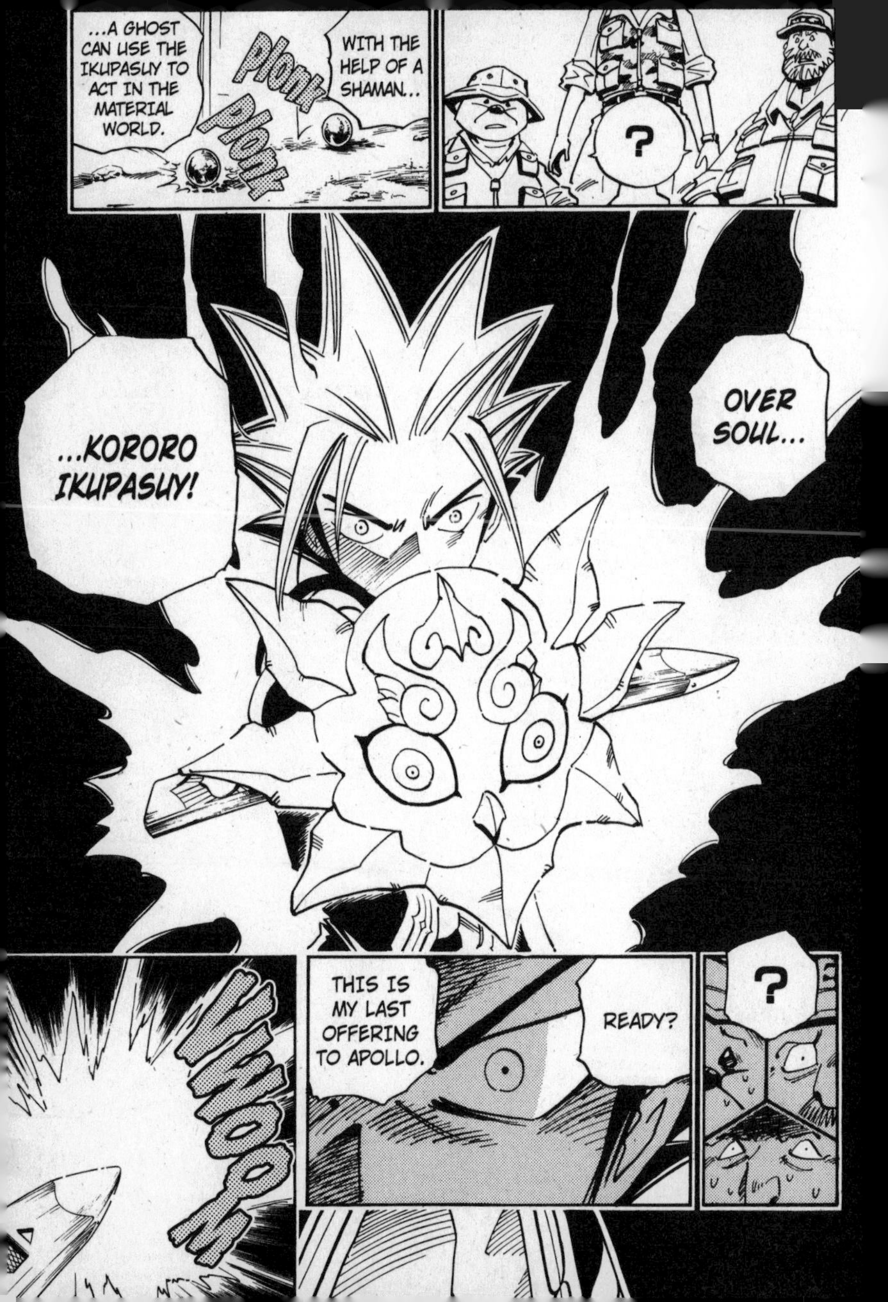
?
WITH THE HELP OF A SHAMAN...
...A GHOST CAN USE THE IKUPASUY TO ACT IN THE MATERIAL WORLD.
PLONK
PLONK
OVER SOUL...
...KORORO IKUPASUY!
?
THIS IS MY LAST OFFERING TO APOLLO.
READY?
WHOOM

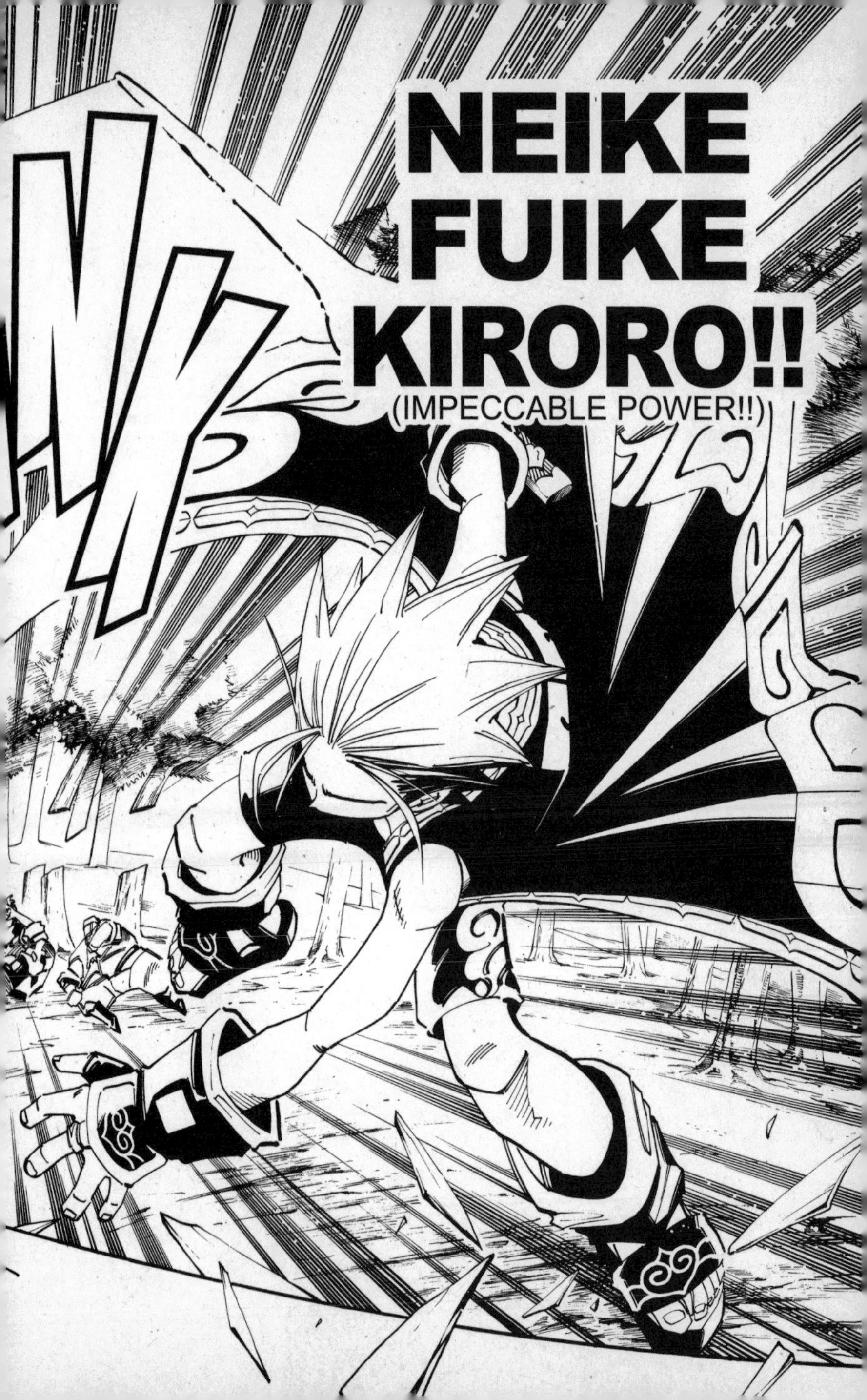
NEIKE FUIKE KIRORO!!
(IMPECCABLE POWER!!)

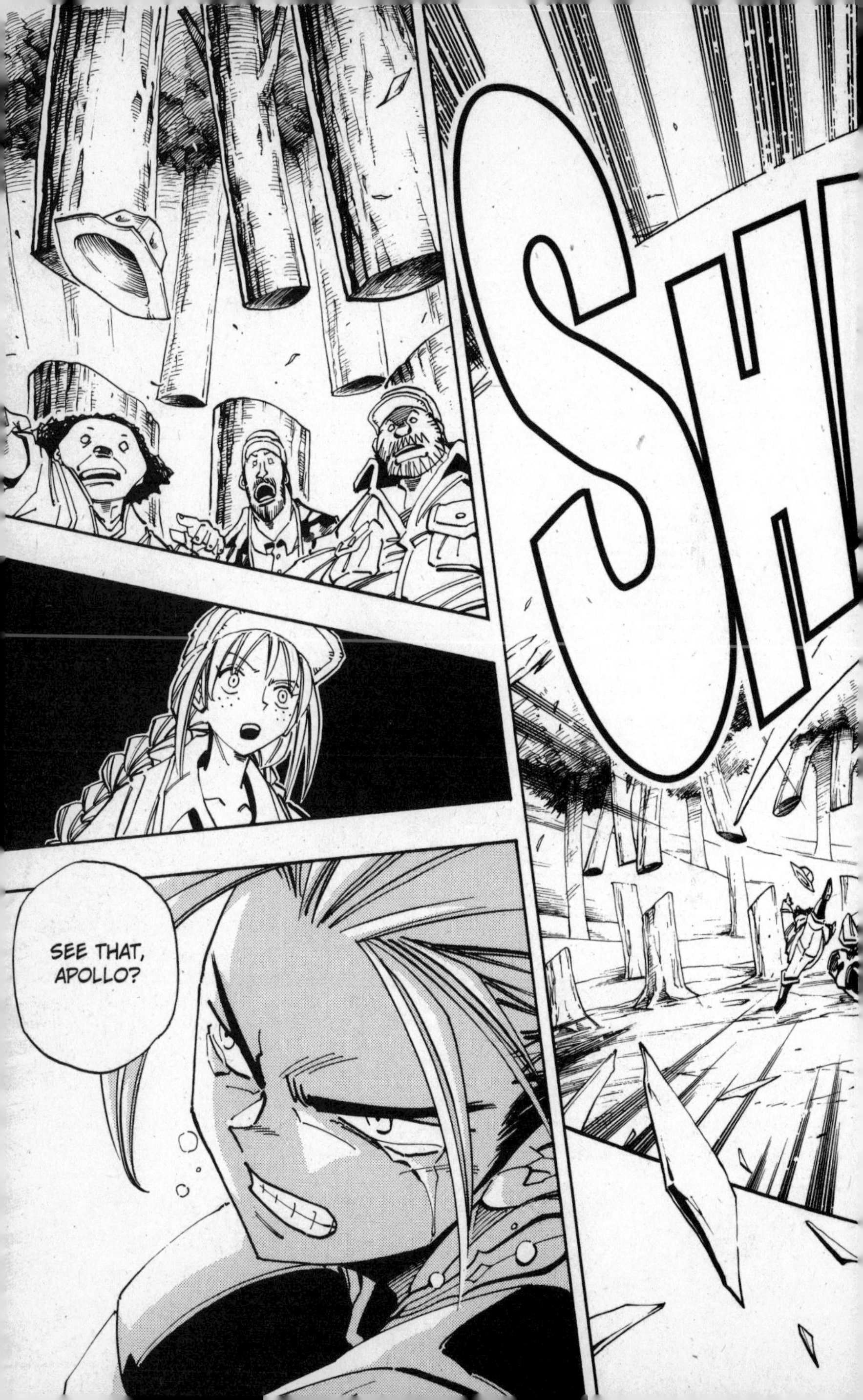
SHH
SEE THAT, APOLLO?

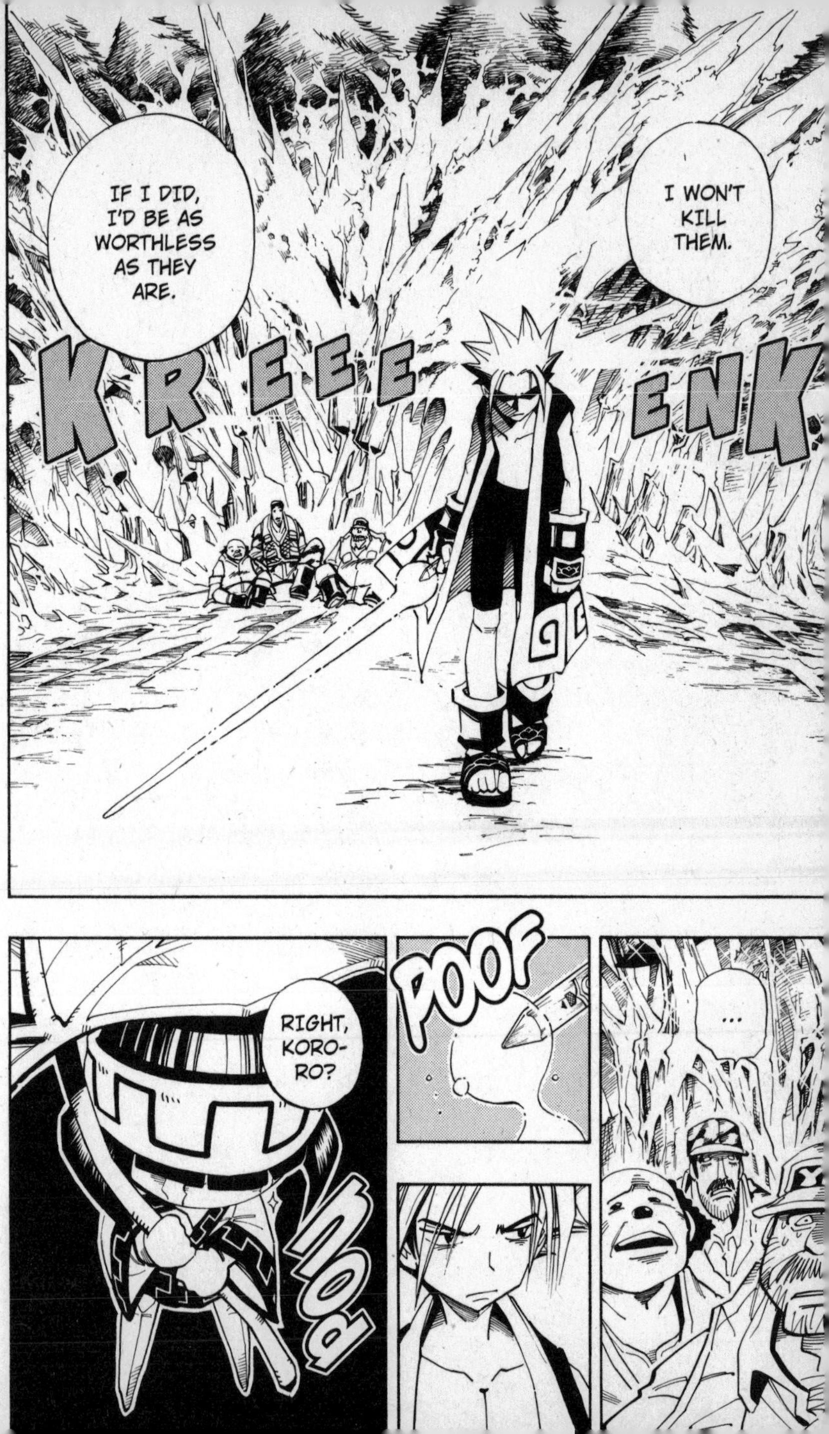
I WON'T KILL THEM.
IF I DID, I'D BE AS WORTHLESS AS THEY ARE.
KREEEENK
...
POOF
RIGHT, KORO-RO?
POOF

READ THIS WAY

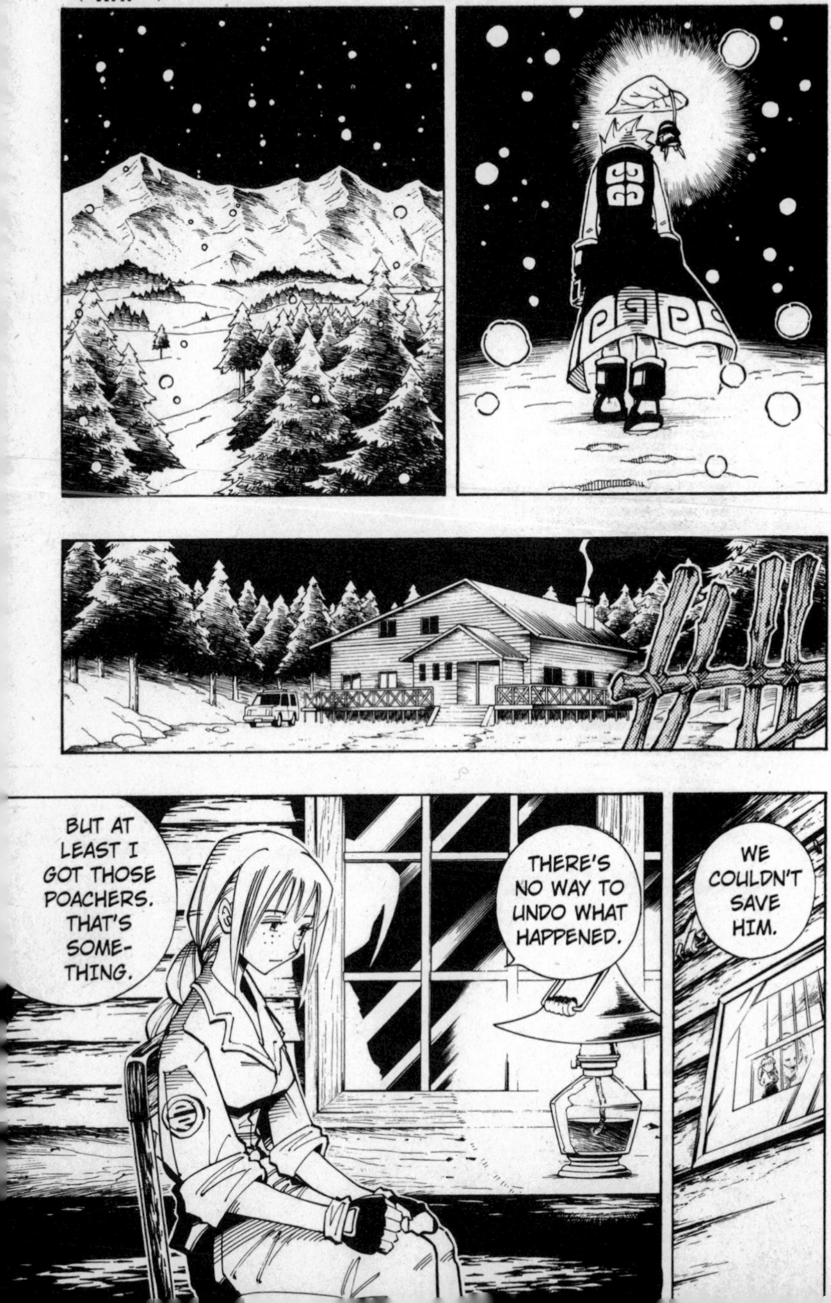
WE COULDN'T SAVE HIM.
THERE'S NO WAY TO UNDO WHAT HAPPENED.
BUT AT LEAST I GOT THOSE POACHERS. THAT'S SOME-THING.

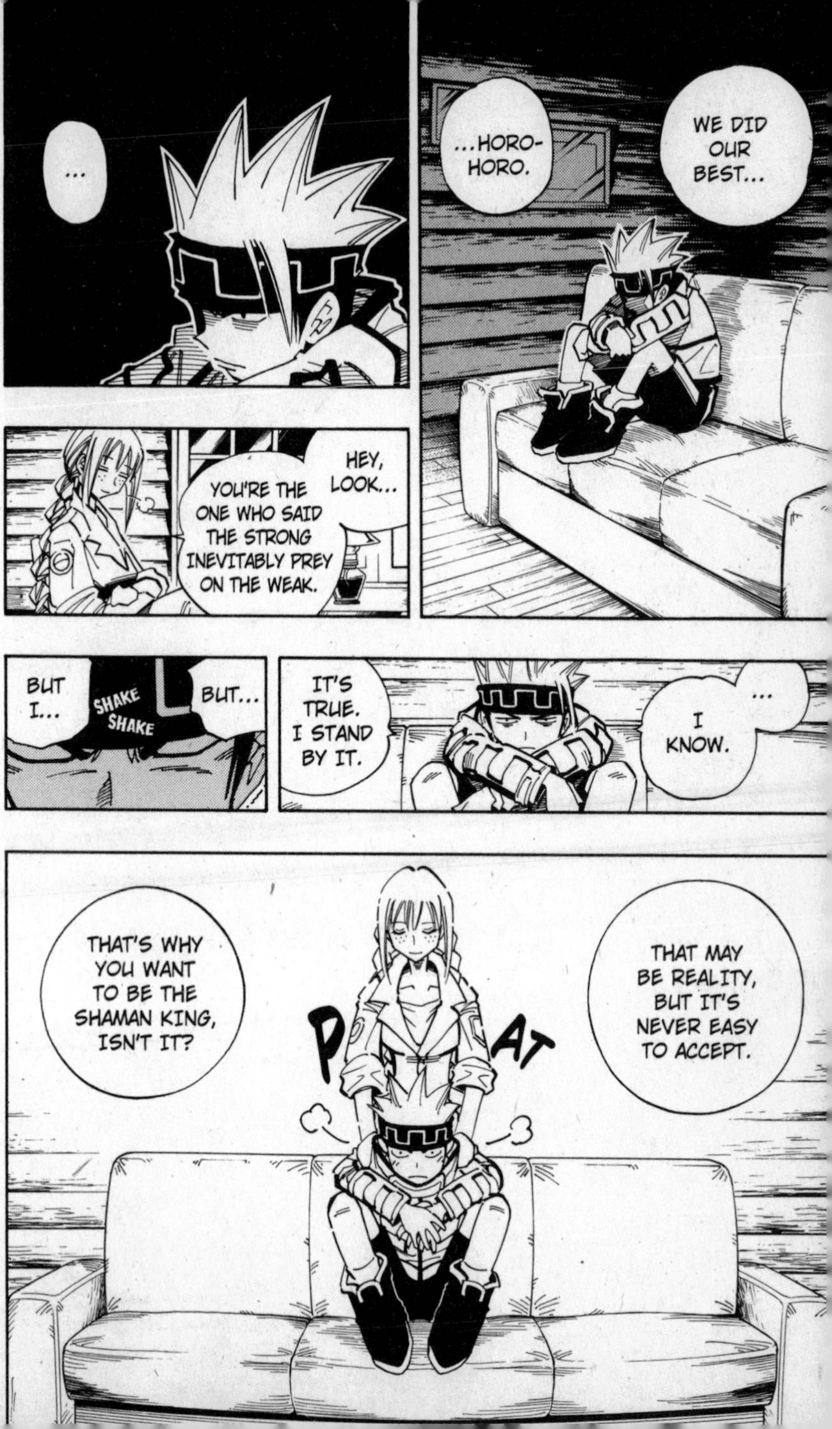
WE DID OUR BEST...
...HORO-HORO.
...
HEY, LOOK...
YOU'RE THE ONE WHO SAID THE STRONG INEVITABLY PREY ON THE WEAK.
...
I KNOW.
IT'S TRUE. I STAND BY IT.
BUT...
SHAKE SHAKE
BUT I...
THAT MAY BE REALITY, BUT IT'S NEVER EASY TO ACCEPT.
PAT
THAT'S WHY YOU WANT TO BE THE SHAMAN KING, ISN'T IT?

READ THIS WAY

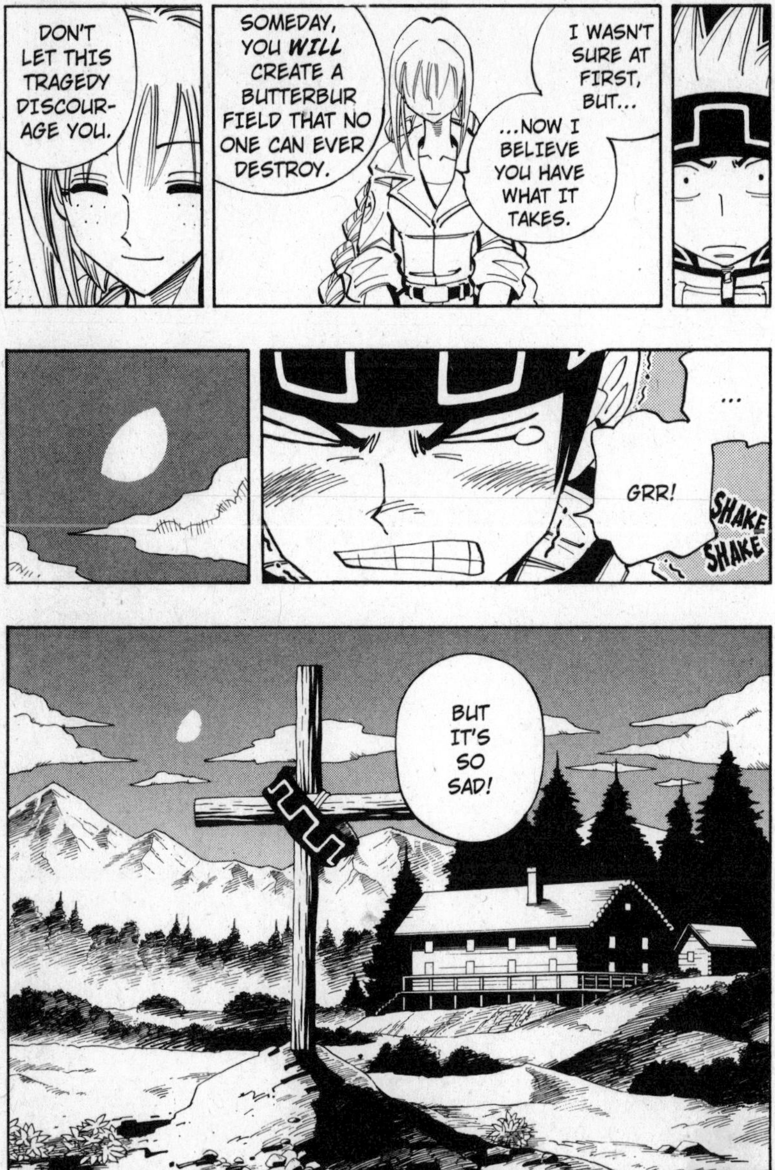
I WASN'T SURE AT FIRST, BUT...
...NOW I BELIEVE YOU HAVE WHAT IT TAKES.
SOMEDAY, YOU **WILL** CREATE A BUTTERBUR FIELD THAT NO ONE CAN EVER DESTROY.
DON'T LET THIS TRAGEDY DISCOUR-AGE YOU.
...
GRR!
SHAKE SHAKE
BUT IT'S SO SAD!

SHAMAN KING CHARACTER FILE No.49

Mr.リトル・レイク

LITTLE LAKE

2000
(Nov)

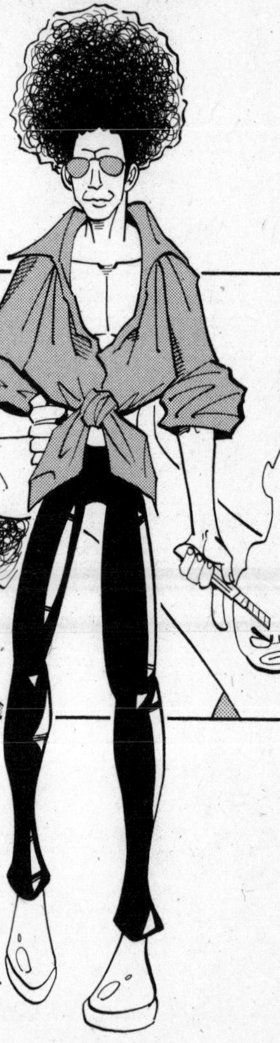

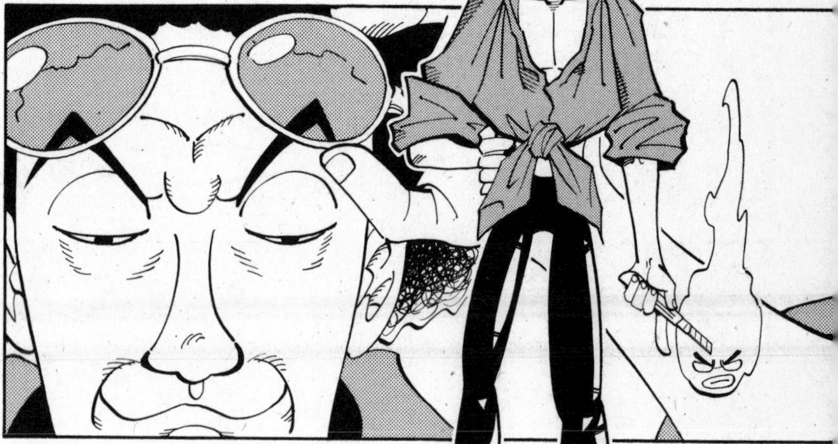

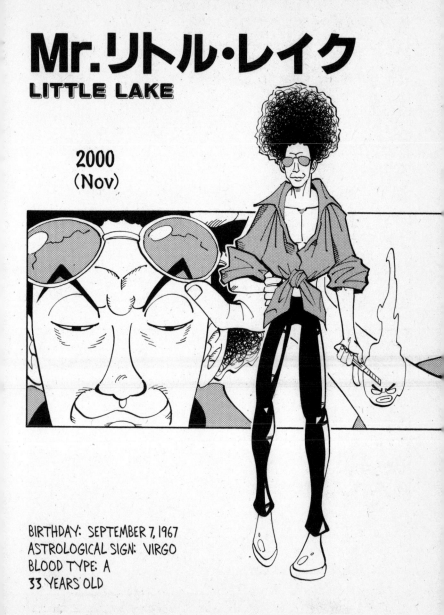

BIRTHDAY: SEPTEMBER 7, 1967
ASTROLOGICAL SIGN: VIRGO
BLOOD TYPE: A
33 YEARS OLD

Reincarnation 95:

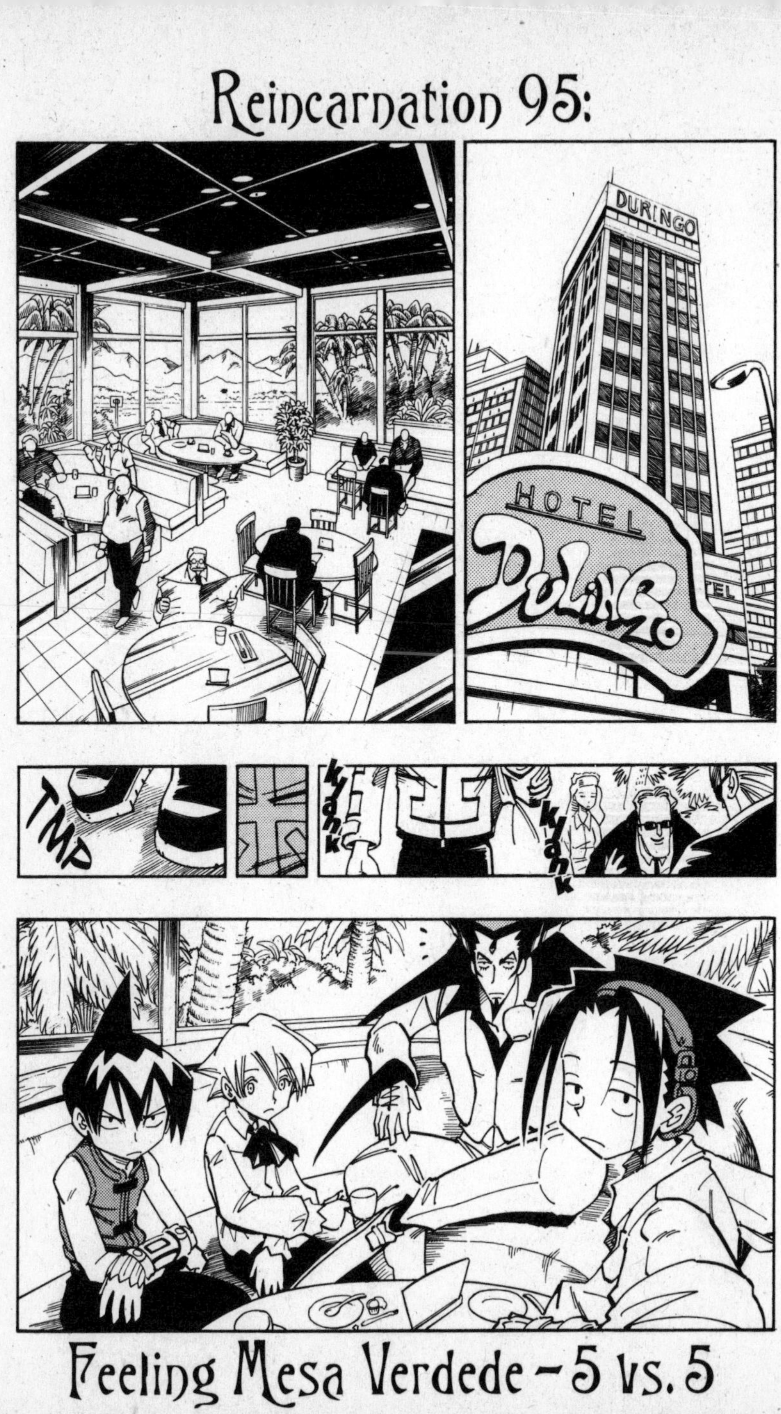
DURINGO
HOTEL
klank
klank
TMP

Feeling Mesa Verdede – 5 vs. 5

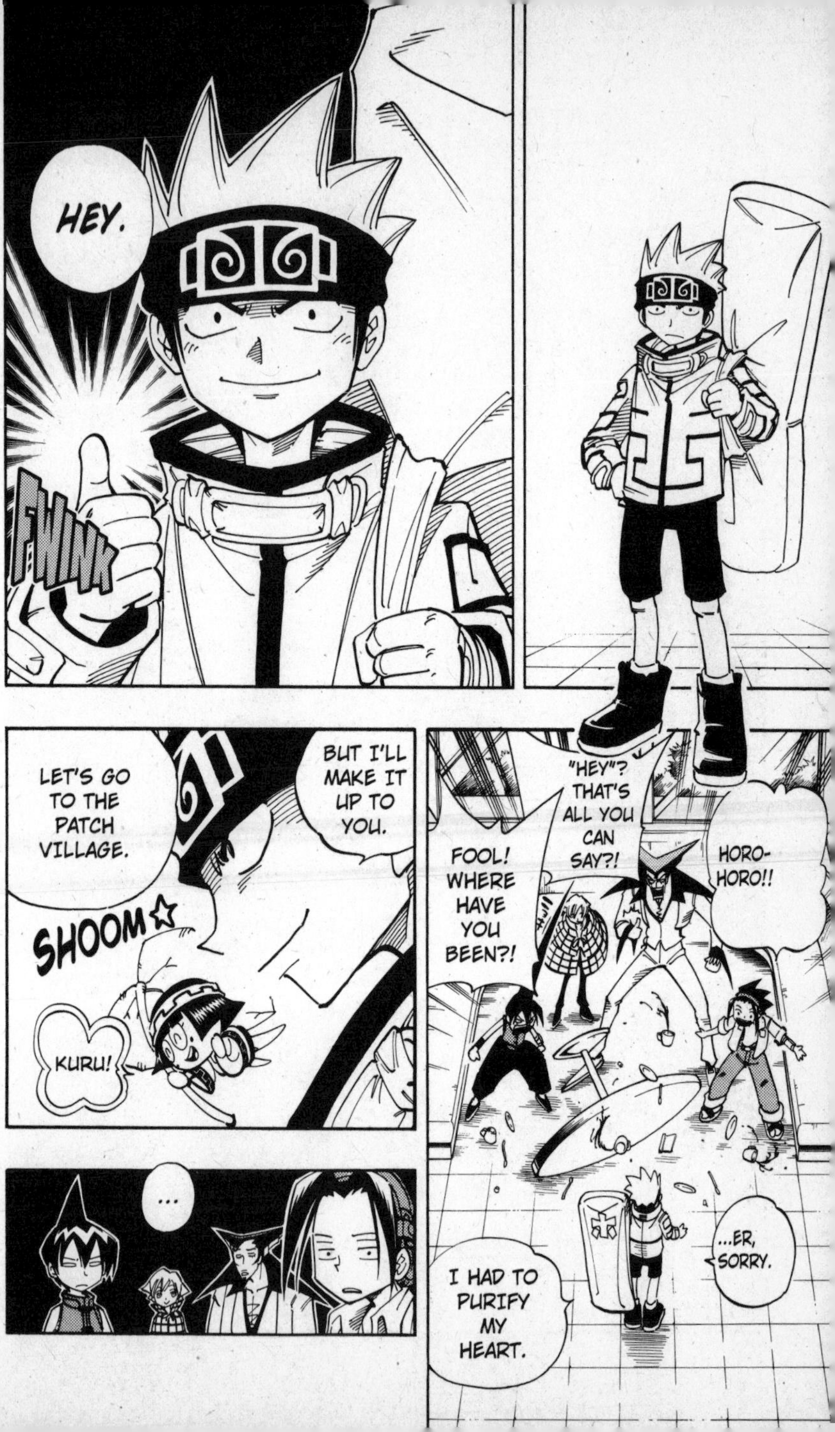
HEY.
FWINK
HORO-HORO!!
"HEY"? THAT'S ALL YOU CAN SAY?!
FOOL! WHERE HAVE YOU BEEN?!
...ER, SORRY.
I HAD TO PURIFY MY HEART.
BUT I'LL MAKE IT UP TO YOU.
LET'S GO TO THE PATCH VILLAGE.
SHOOM☆
KURU!
...

Reincarnation 95:
Feeling
Mesa Verdede ~
5 vs. 5

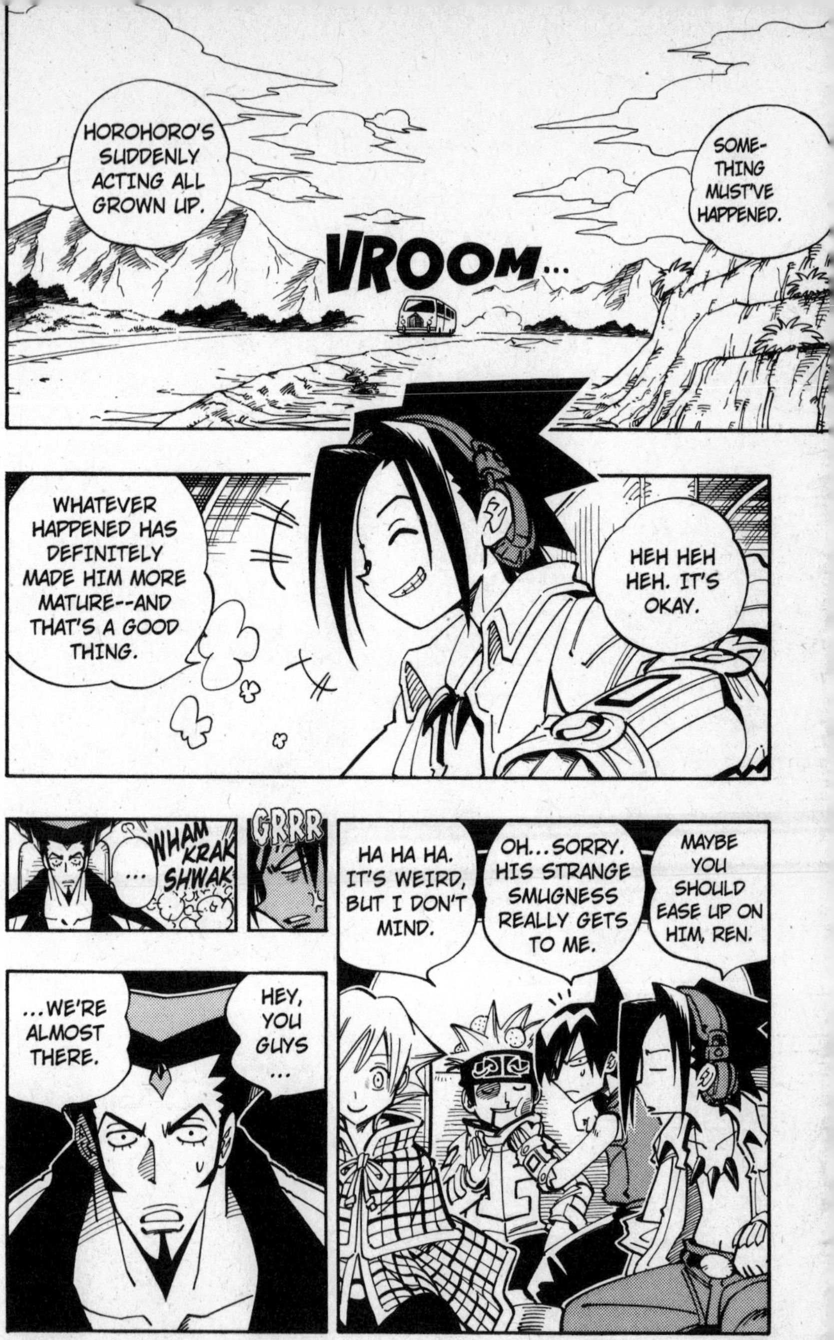
SOME-THING MUST'VE HAPPENED.
HOROHORO'S SUDDENLY ACTING ALL GROWN UP.
VROOM...
HEH HEH HEH. IT'S OKAY.
WHATEVER HAPPENED HAS DEFINITELY MADE HIM MORE MATURE--AND THAT'S A GOOD THING.
MAYBE YOU SHOULD EASE UP ON HIM, REN.
OH...SORRY. HIS STRANGE SMUGNESS REALLY GETS TO ME.
HA HA HA. IT'S WEIRD, BUT I DON'T MIND.
GRRR
WHAM
KRAK
SHWAK
...
HEY, YOU GUYS ...
...WE'RE ALMOST THERE.

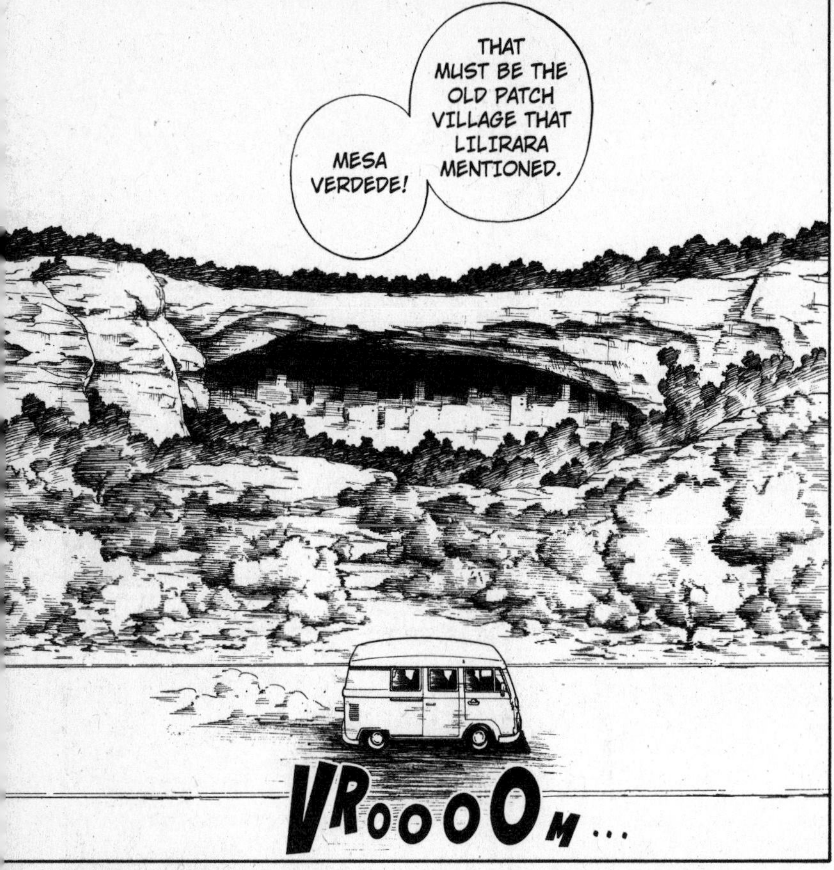
THAT MUST BE THE OLD PATCH VILLAGE THAT LILIRARA MENTIONED.
MESA VERDEDE!
VROOOOM...

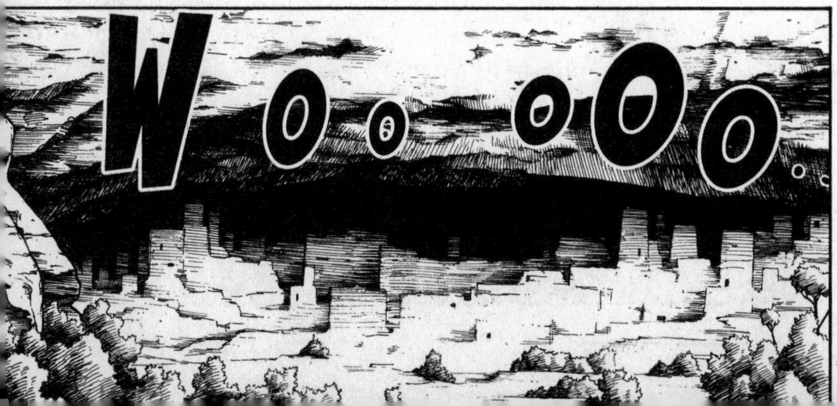
WOOOOOO..

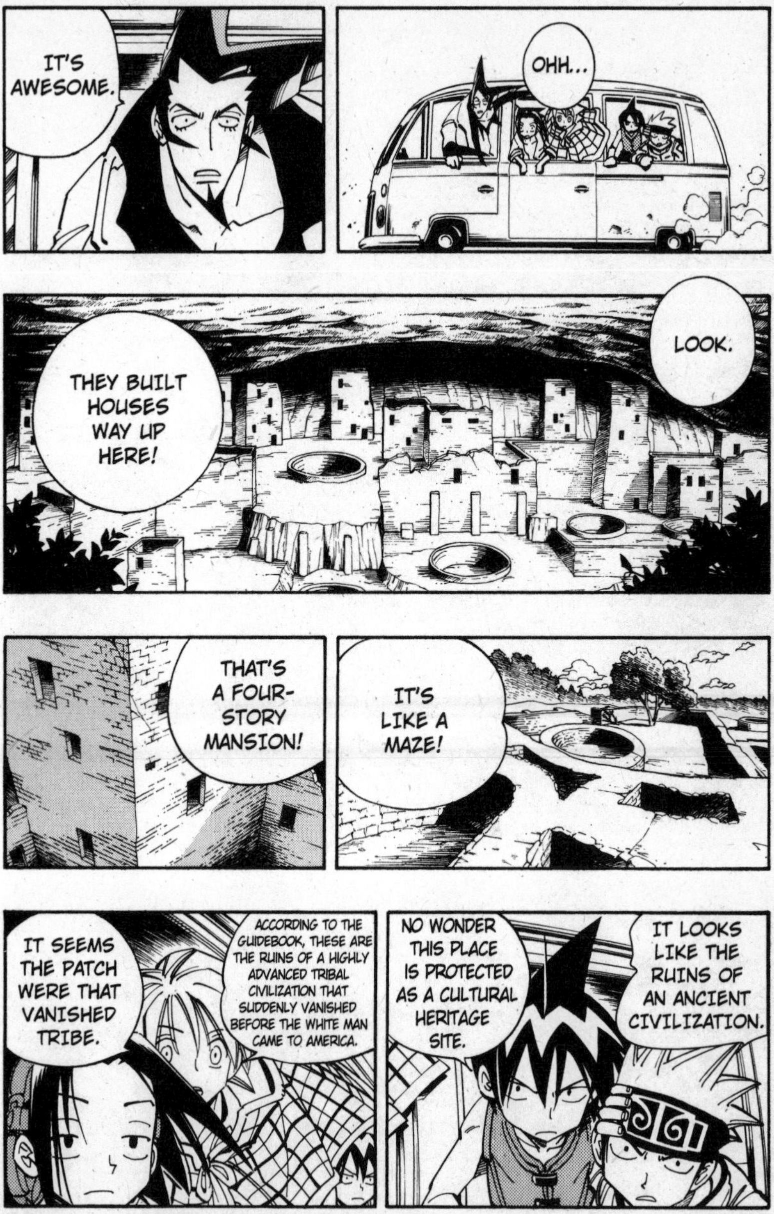
OHH...
IT'S AWESOME.
LOOK.
THEY BUILT HOUSES WAY UP HERE!
IT'S LIKE A MAZE!
THAT'S A FOUR-STORY MANSION!
IT LOOKS LIKE THE RUINS OF AN ANCIENT CIVILIZATION.
NO WONDER THIS PLACE IS PROTECTED AS A CULTURAL HERITAGE SITE.
ACCORDING TO THE GUIDEBOOK, THESE ARE THE RUINS OF A HIGHLY ADVANCED TRIBAL CIVILIZATION THAT SUDDENLY VANISHED BEFORE THE WHITE MAN CAME TO AMERICA.
IT SEEMS THE PATCH WERE THAT VANISHED TRIBE.

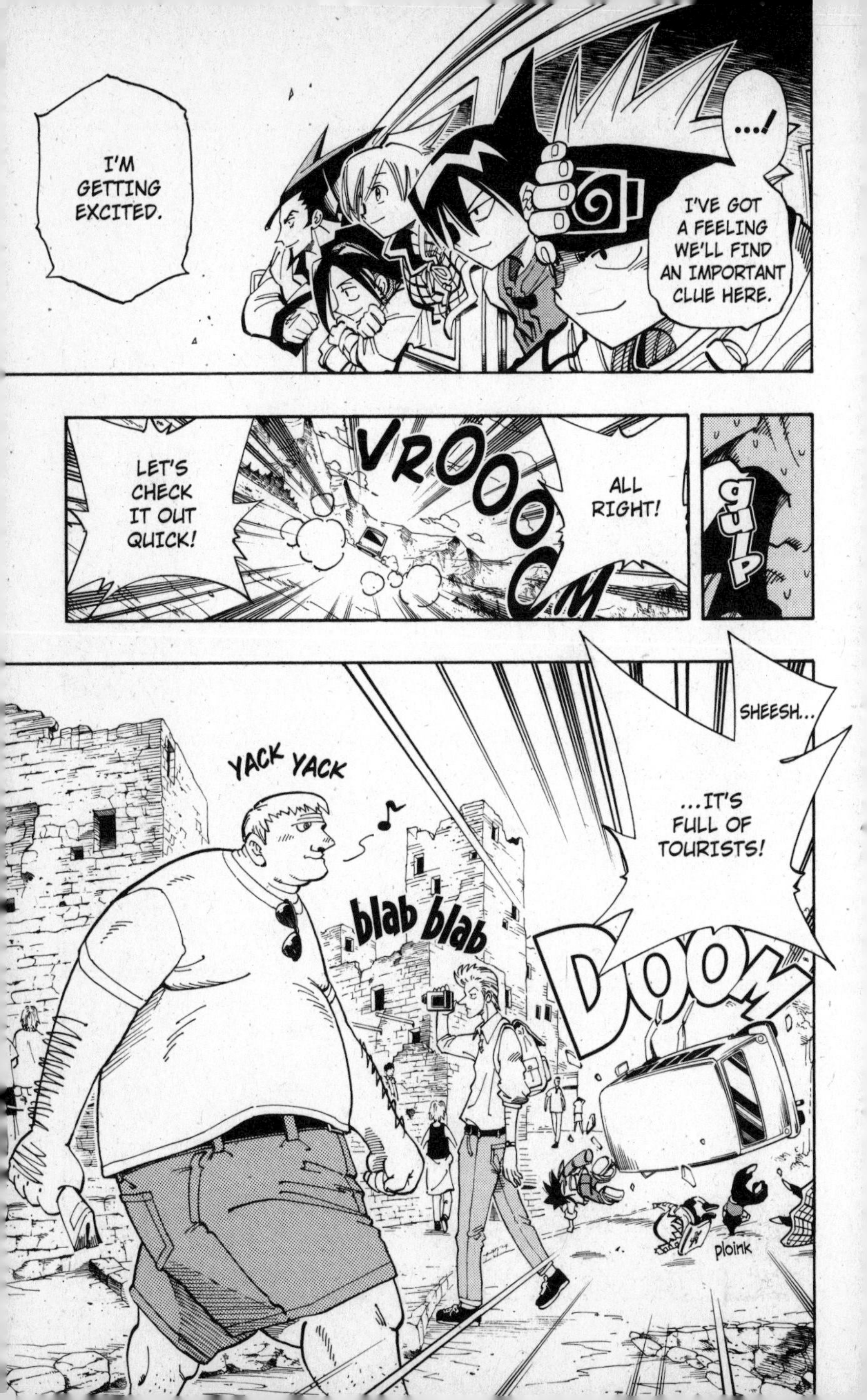
...!
I'VE GOT A FEELING WE'LL FIND AN IMPORTANT CLUE HERE.
I'M GETTING EXCITED.
gulp
ALL RIGHT!
VROOOOOM
LET'S CHECK IT OUT QUICK!
SHEESH...
...IT'S FULL OF TOURISTS!
DOOM
YACK YACK
blab blab
ploink

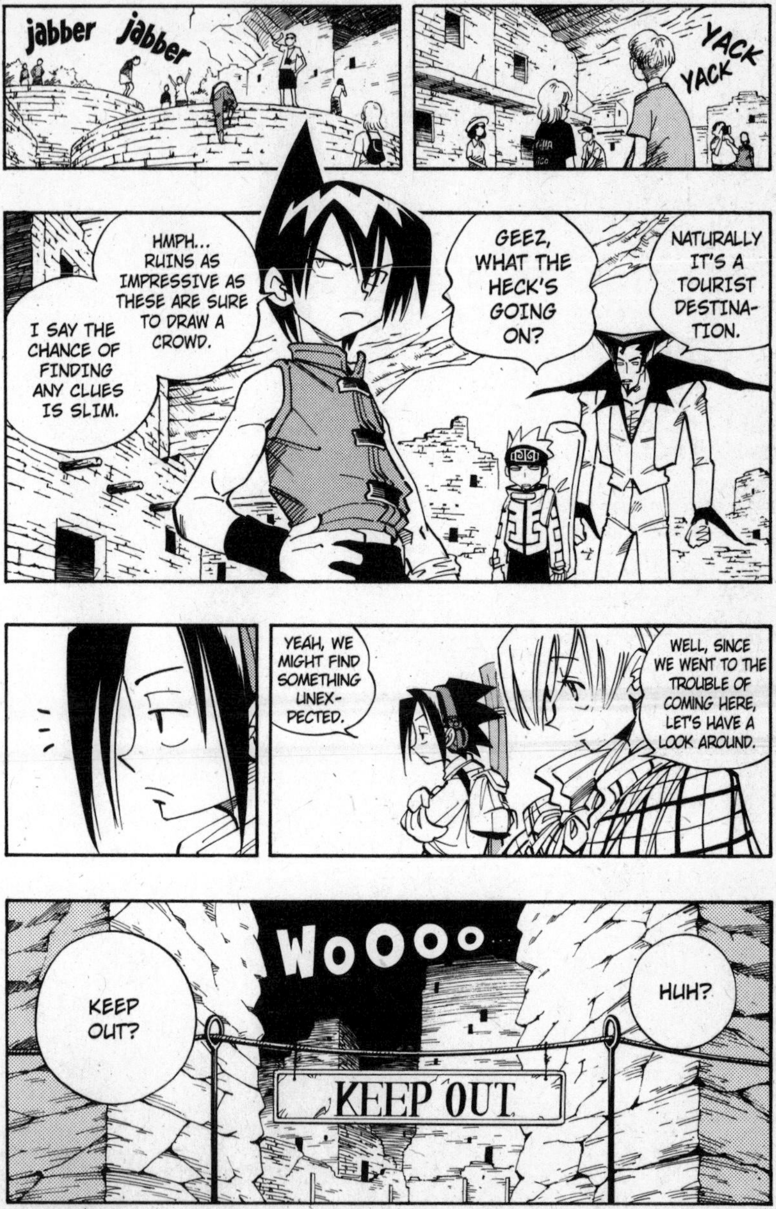
YACK
YACK
jabber
jabber
NATURALLY IT'S A TOURIST DESTINA-TION.
GEEZ, WHAT THE HECK'S GOING ON?
HMPH... RUINS AS IMPRESSIVE AS THESE ARE SURE TO DRAW A CROWD.
I SAY THE CHANCE OF FINDING ANY CLUES IS SLIM.
WELL, SINCE WE WENT TO THE TROUBLE OF COMING HERE, LET'S HAVE A LOOK AROUND.
YEAH, WE MIGHT FIND SOMETHING UNEX-PECTED.
HUH?
WOOOO...
KEEP OUT?
KEEP OUT

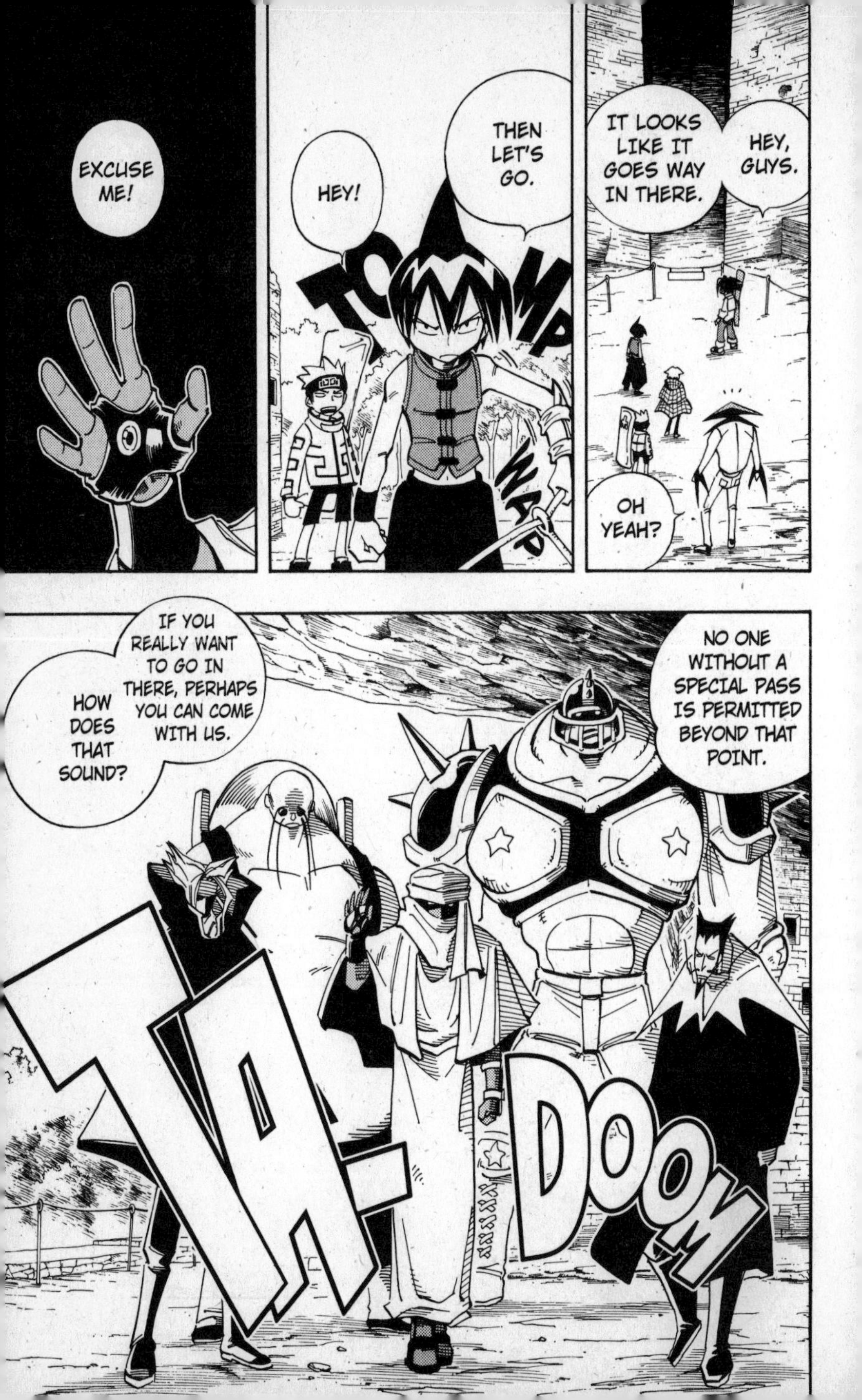
HEY, GUYS.
IT LOOKS LIKE IT GOES WAY IN THERE.
OH YEAH?
THEN LET'S GO.
WAP
HEY!
EXCUSE ME!
NO ONE WITHOUT A SPECIAL PASS IS PERMITTED BEYOND THAT POINT.
IF YOU REALLY WANT TO GO IN THERE, PERHAPS YOU CAN COME WITH US.
HOW DOES THAT SOUND?
TA-DOOOM

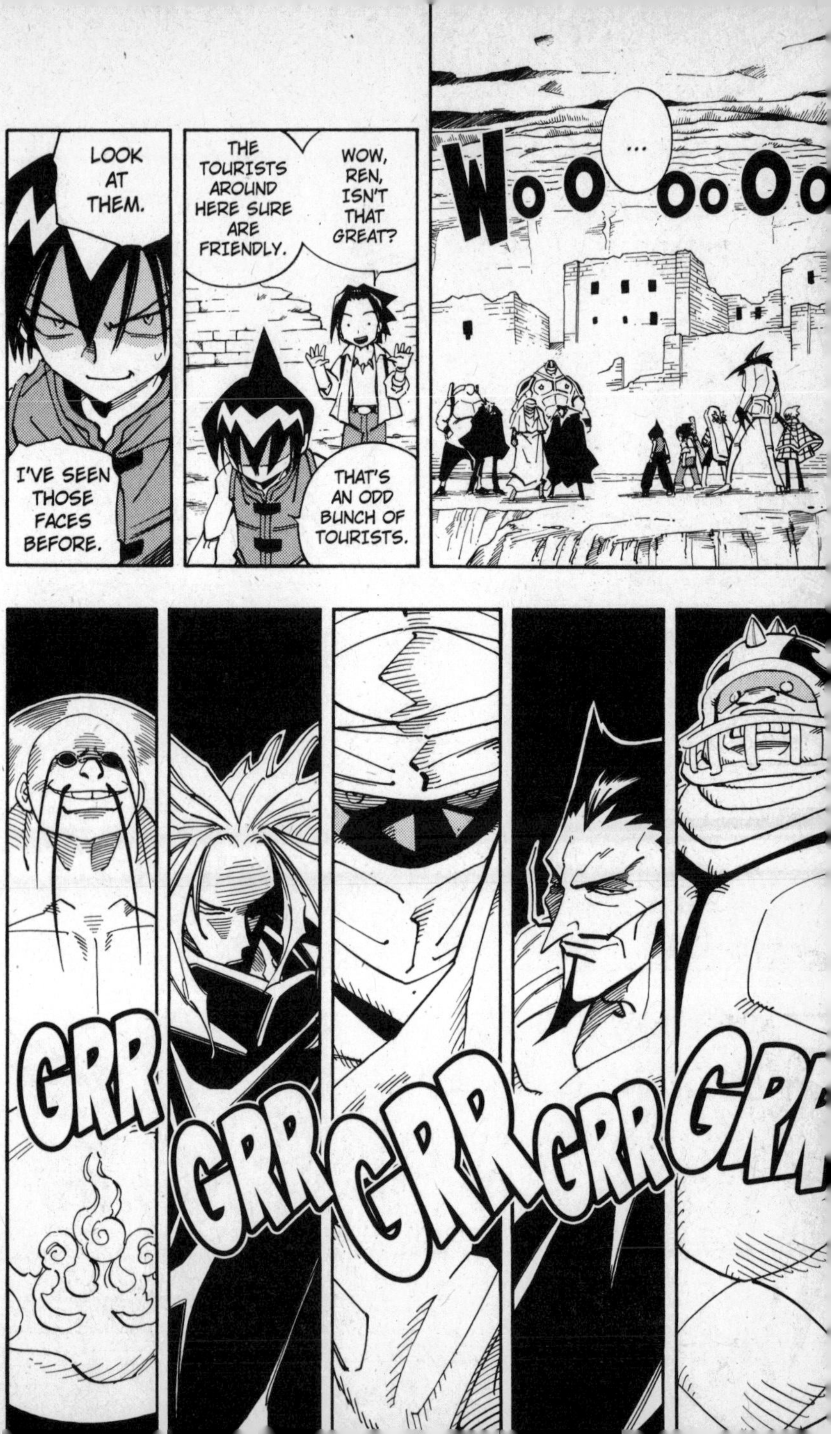
WOOOOOOO
...
WOW, REN, ISN'T THAT GREAT?
THE TOURISTS AROUND HERE SURE ARE FRIENDLY.
THAT'S AN ODD BUNCH OF TOURISTS.
LOOK AT THEM.
I'VE SEEN THOSE FACES BEFORE.
GRR
GRR
GRR
GRR
GRR

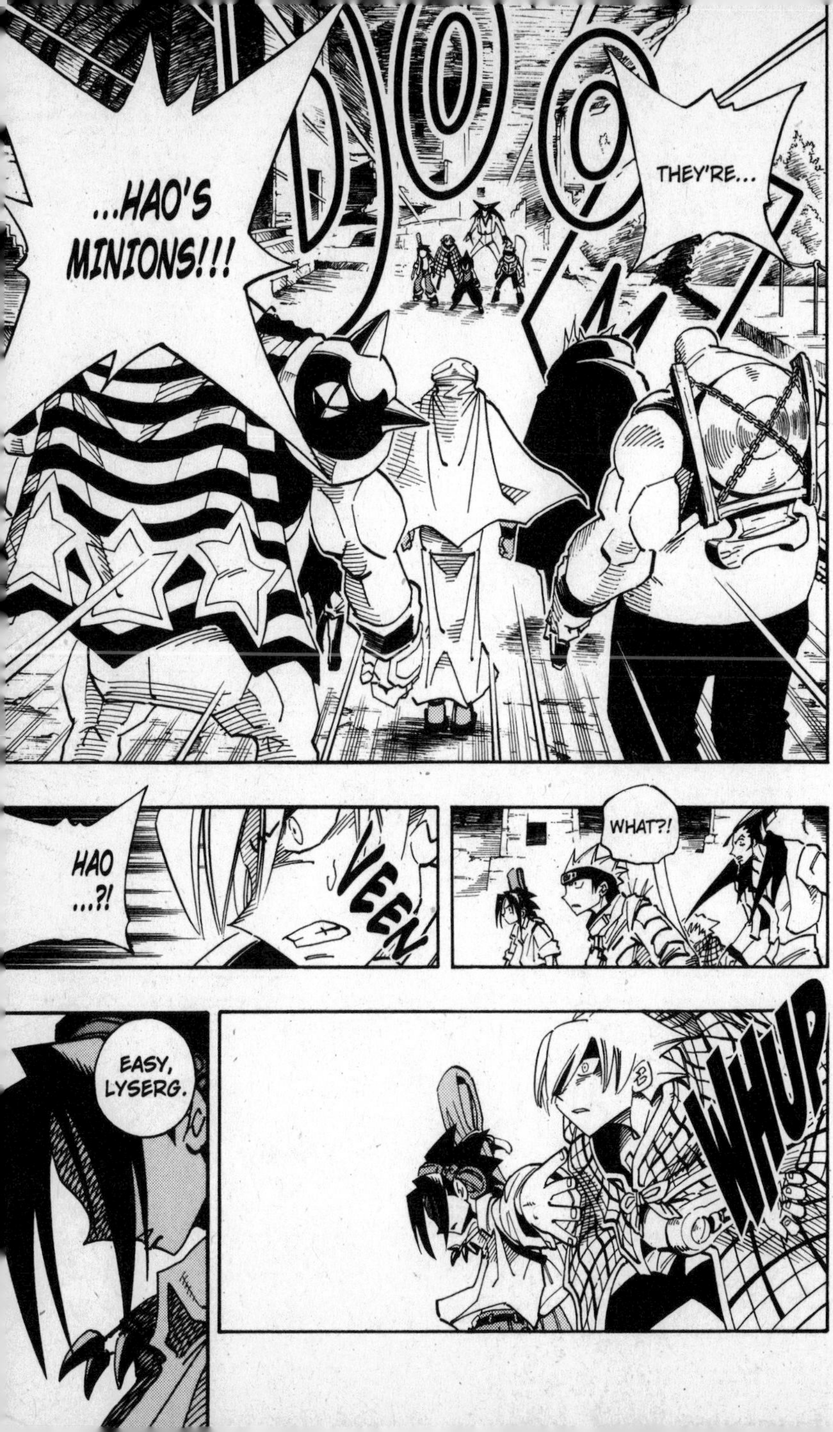
THEY'RE...
...HAO'S MINIONS!!!
WHAT?!
HAO ...?!
VEEN
WHUP
EASY, LYSERG.

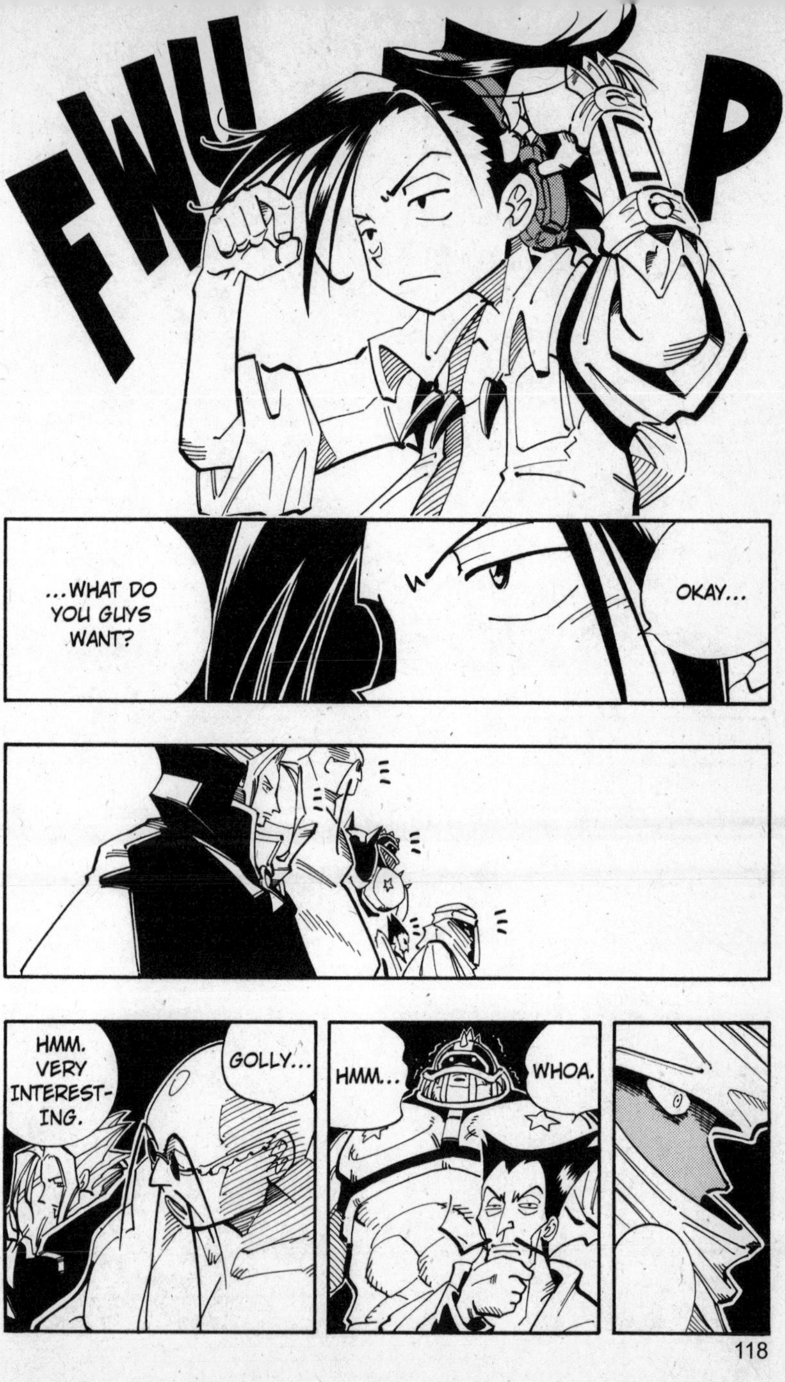
FWUP
OKAY...
...WHAT DO YOU GUYS WANT?
WHOA.
HMM...
GOLLY...
HMM. VERY INTERESTING.

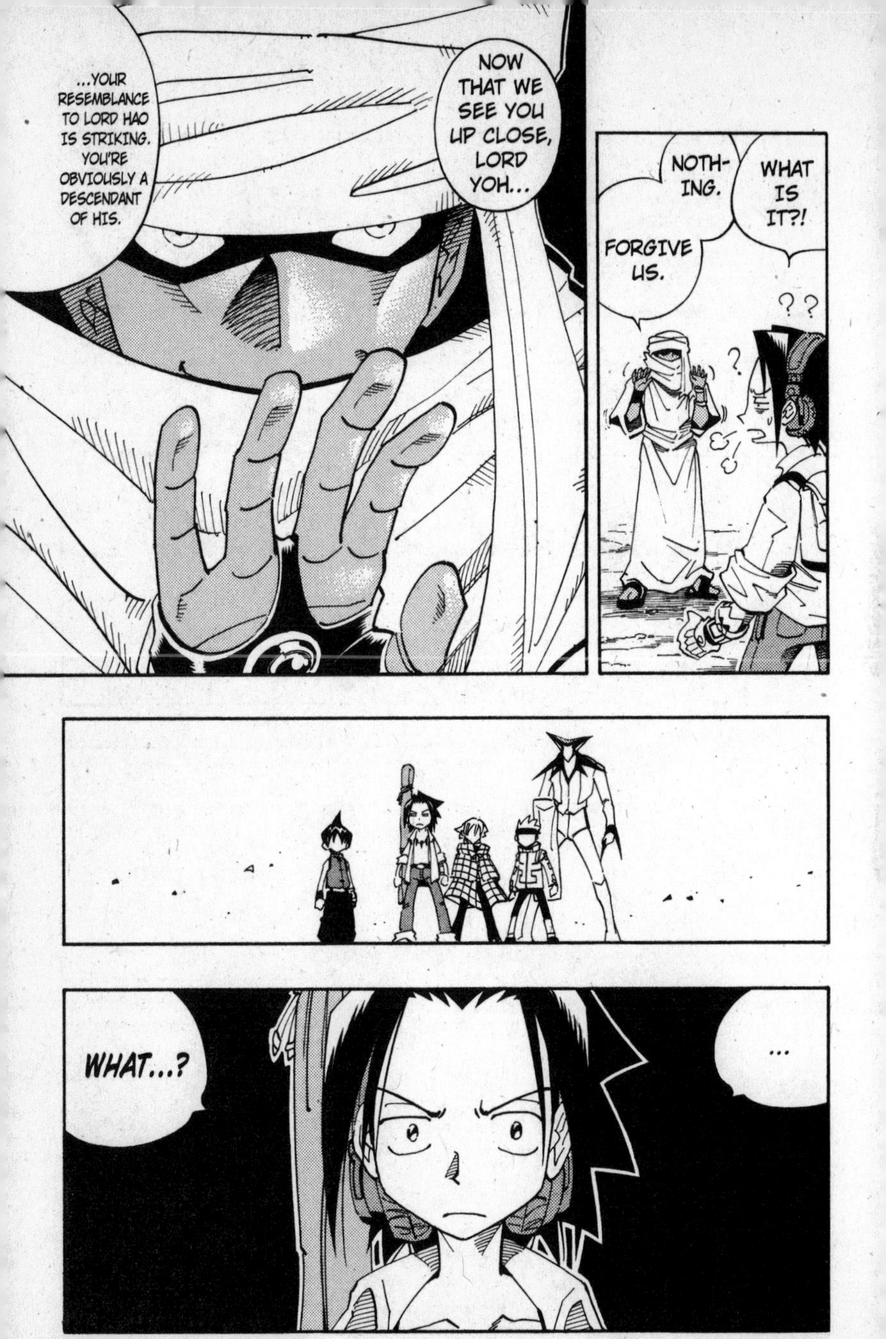
WHAT IS IT?!
NOTH-ING.
FORGIVE US.
NOW THAT WE SEE YOU UP CLOSE, LORD YOH...
...YOUR RESEMBLANCE TO LORD HAO IS STRIKING. YOU'RE OBVIOUSLY A DESCENDANT OF HIS.
...
WHAT...?

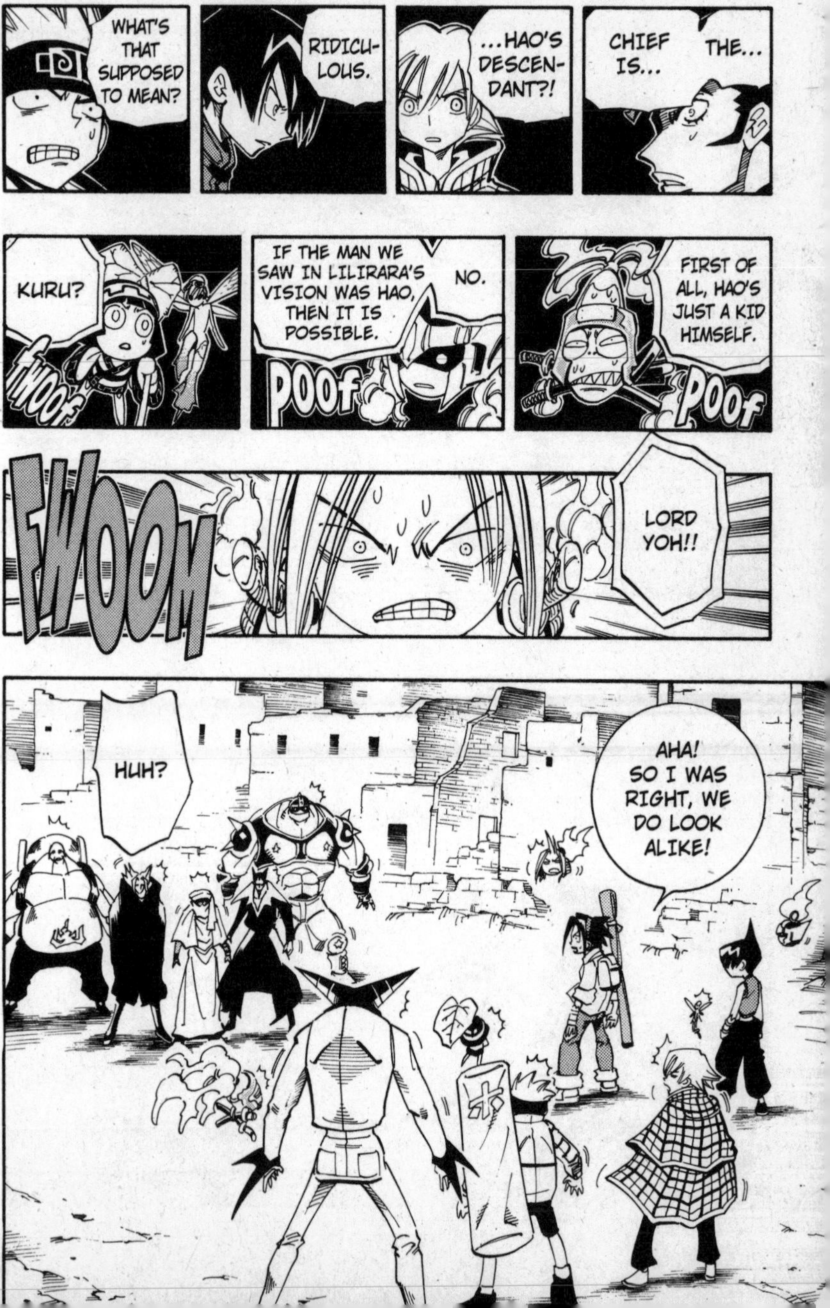
THE...
CHIEF IS...
...HAO'S DESCEN-DANT?!
RIDICU-LOUS.
WHAT'S THAT SUPPOSED TO MEAN?
FIRST OF ALL, HAO'S JUST A KID HIMSELF.
POOF
NO.
IF THE MAN WE SAW IN LILIRARA'S VISION WAS HAO, THEN IT IS POSSIBLE.
POOF
KURU?
FWOOF
LORD YOH!!
FWOOM
AHA! SO I WAS RIGHT, WE DO LOOK ALIKE!
HUH?

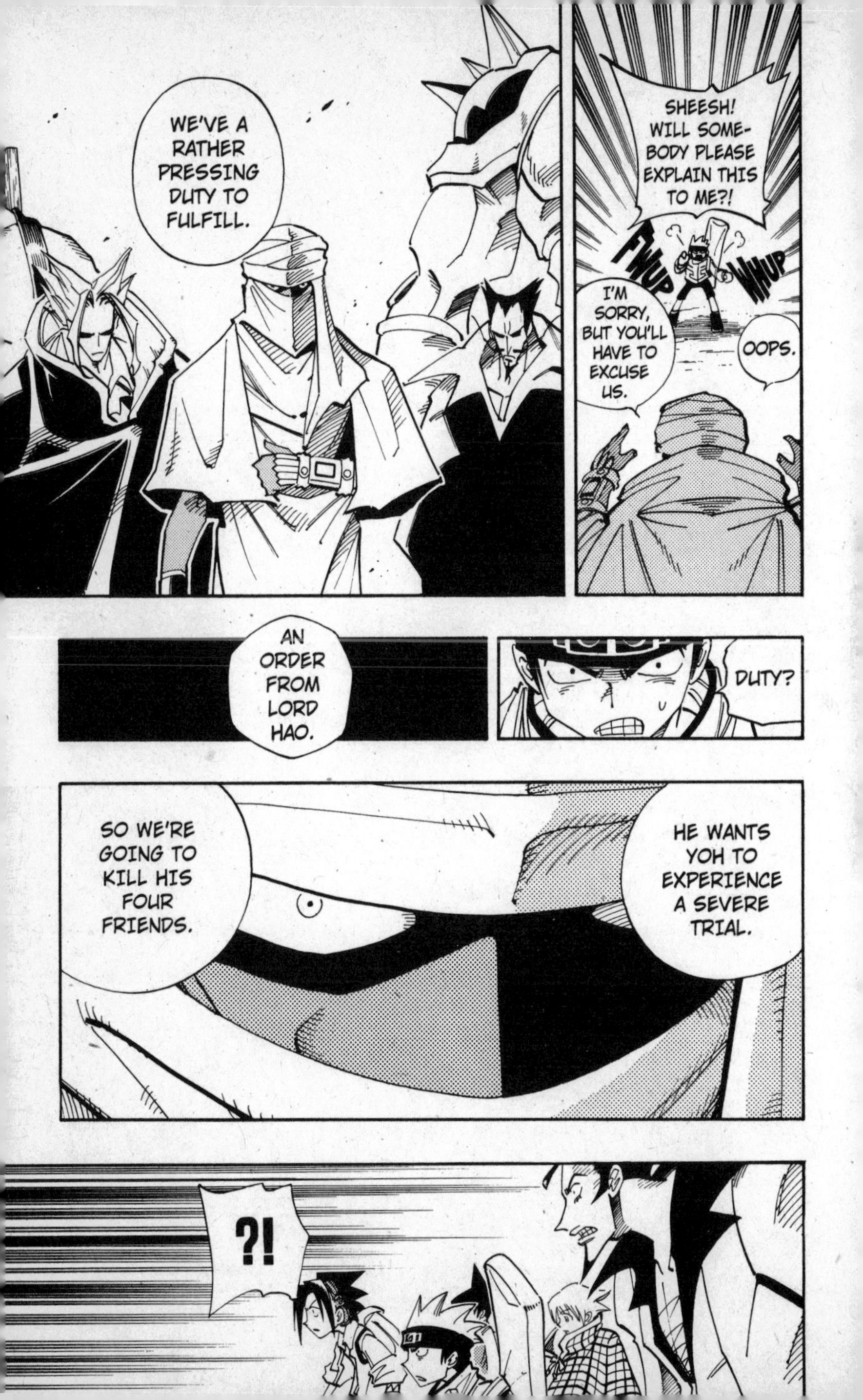
SHEESH! WILL SOMEBODY PLEASE EXPLAIN THIS TO ME?!
FWUP
WHUP
I'M SORRY, BUT YOU'LL HAVE TO EXCUSE US.
OOPS.
WE'VE A RATHER PRESSING DUTY TO FULFILL.
DUTY?
AN ORDER FROM LORD HAO.
HE WANTS YOH TO EXPERIENCE A SEVERE TRIAL.
SO WE'RE GOING TO KILL HIS FOUR FRIENDS.
?!

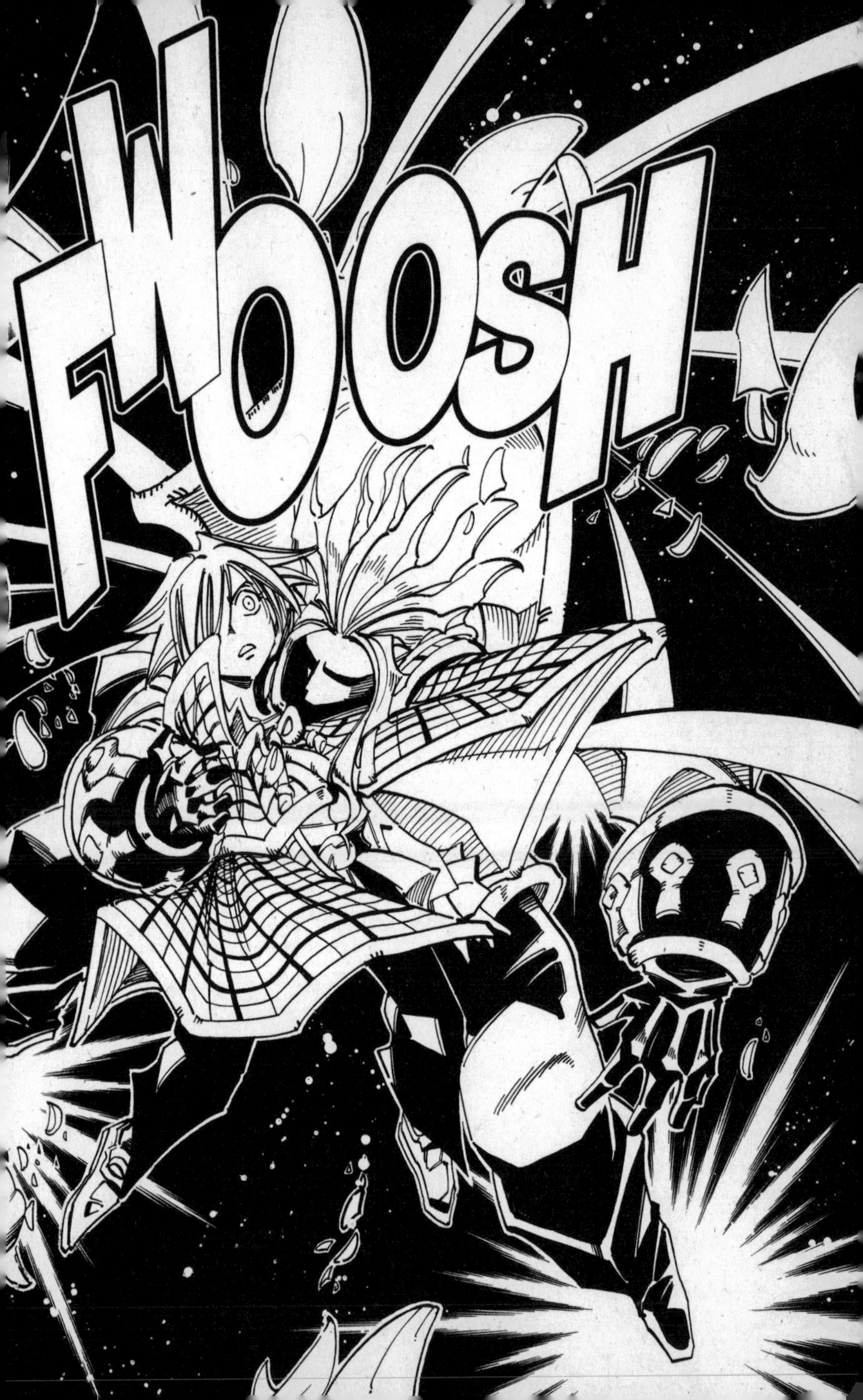
FWOOSH

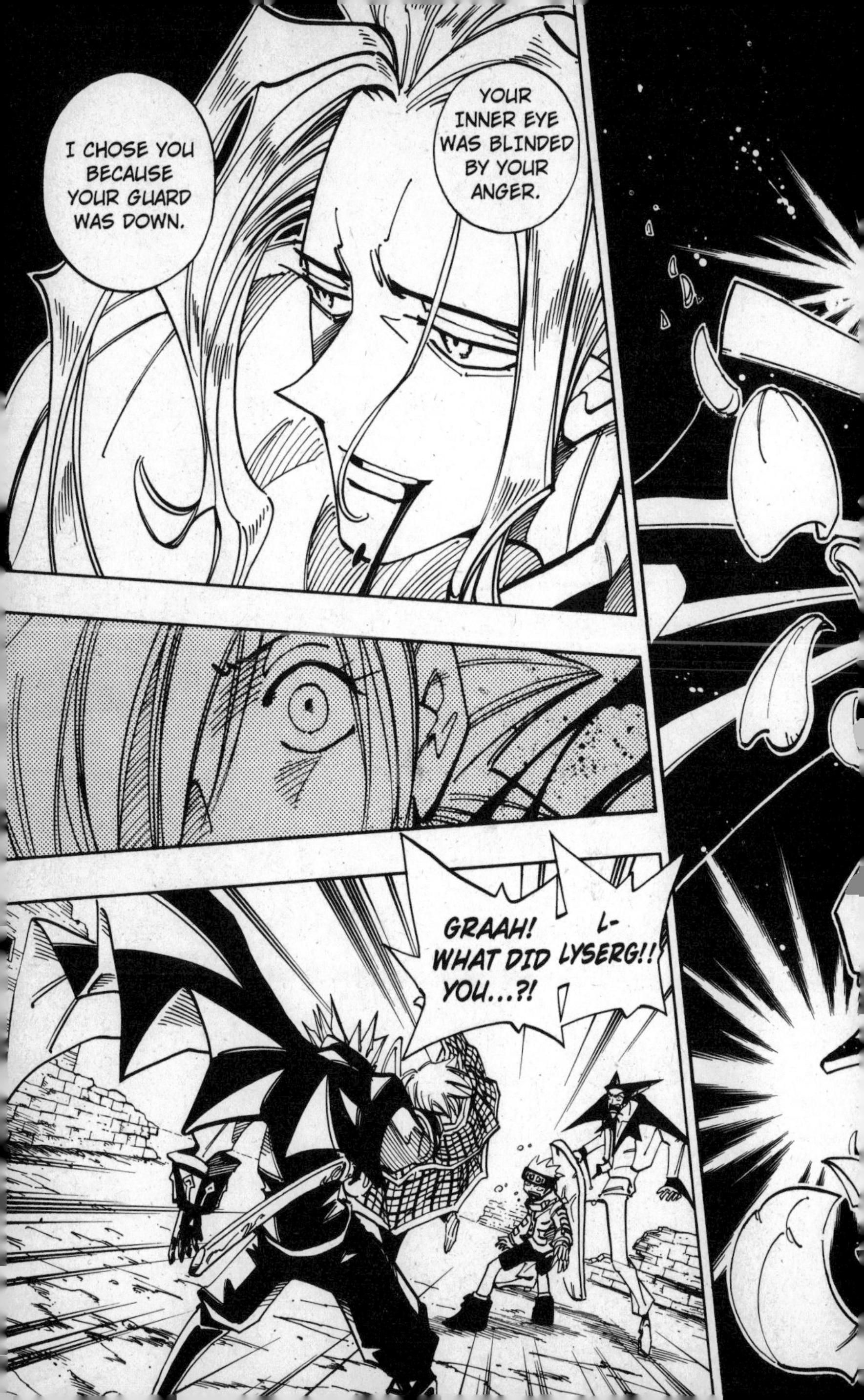
YOUR INNER EYE WAS BLINDED BY YOUR ANGER.
I CHOSE YOU BECAUSE YOUR GUARD WAS DOWN.
L- LYSERG!!
GRAAH! WHAT DID YOU...?!

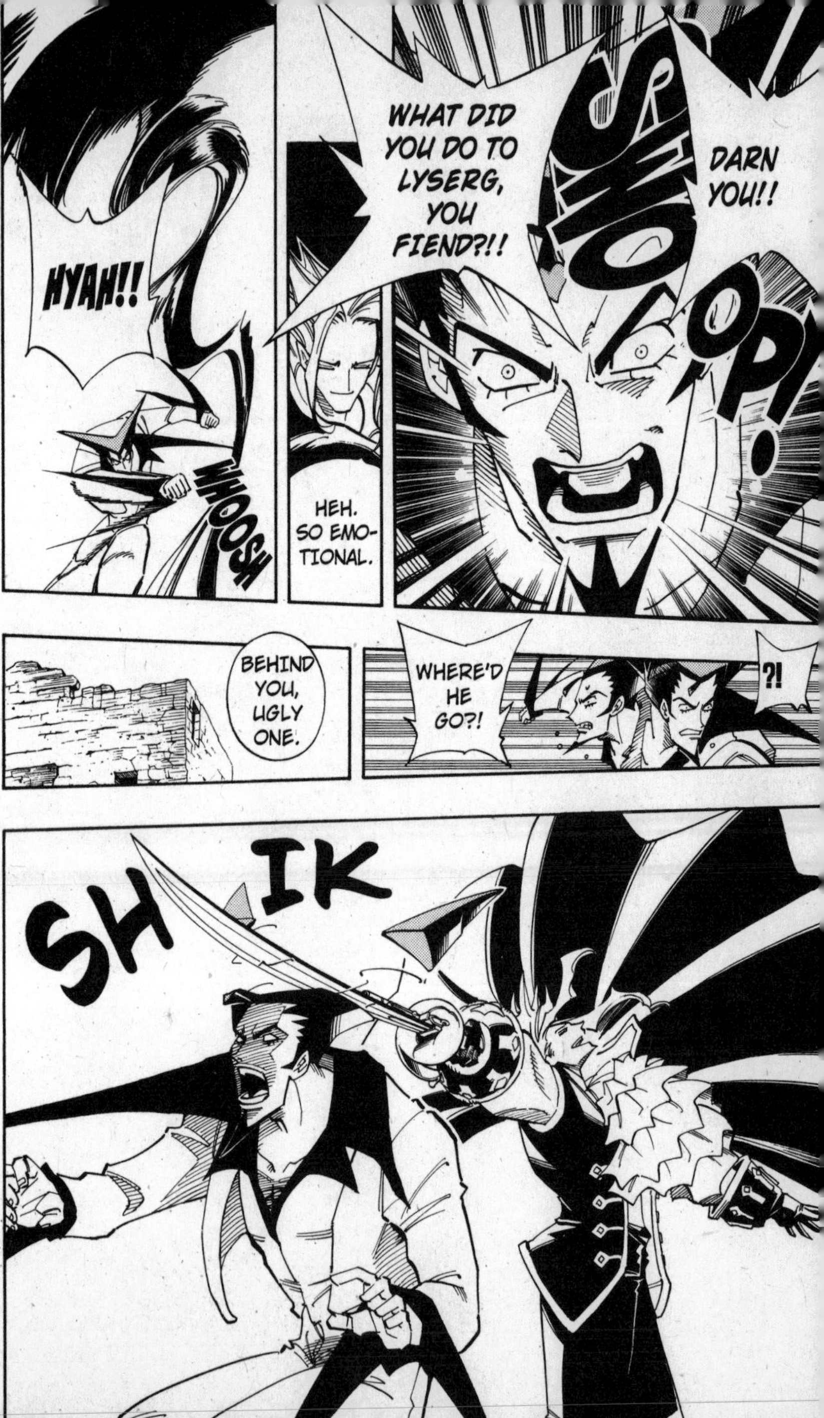
DARN YOU!!
WHAT DID YOU DO TO LYSERG, YOU FIEND?!!
SHOOP!
HEH. SO EMOTIONAL.
HYAH!!
WHOOSH
?!
WHERE'D HE GO?!
BEHIND YOU, UGLY ONE.
SHIK

READ THIS WAY

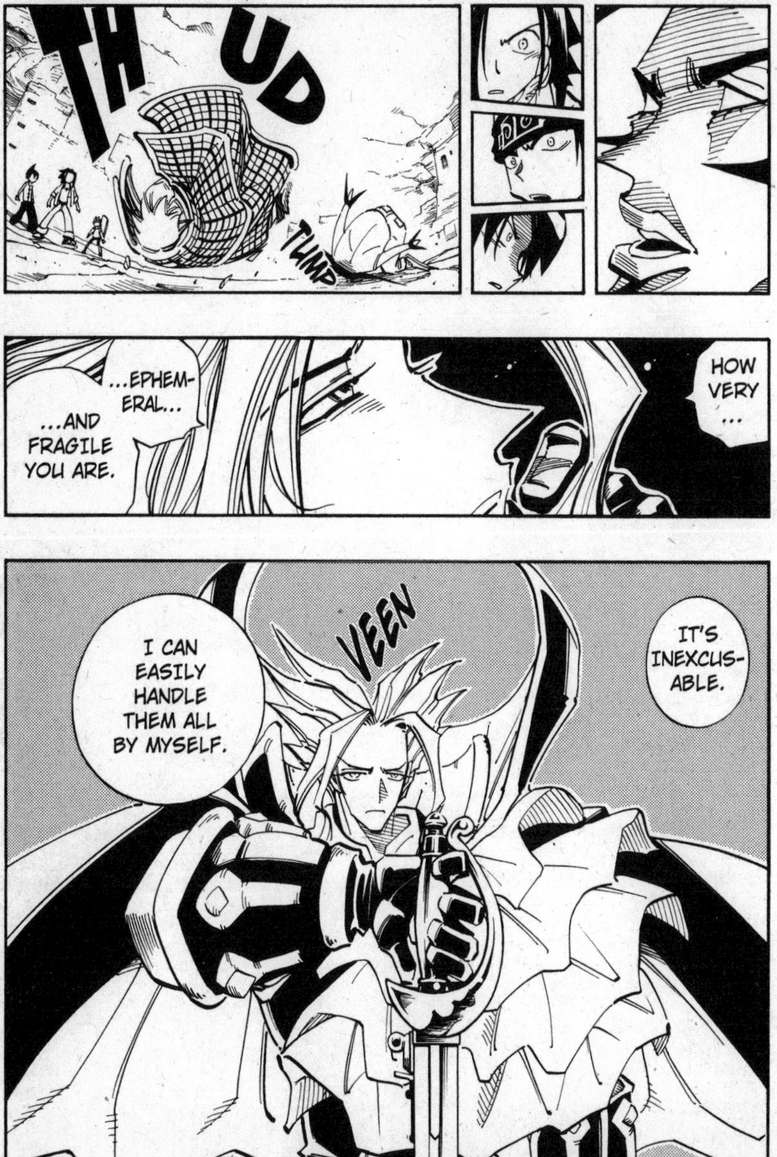
TH UD
TUMP
HOW VERY...
...EPHEM-ERAL...
...AND FRAGILE YOU ARE.
IT'S INEXCUS-ABLE.
VEEN
I CAN EASILY HANDLE THEM ALL BY MYSELF.

SHAMAN KING
11

EDITING TOOLS

Reincarnation 96: Blood and Pompadours

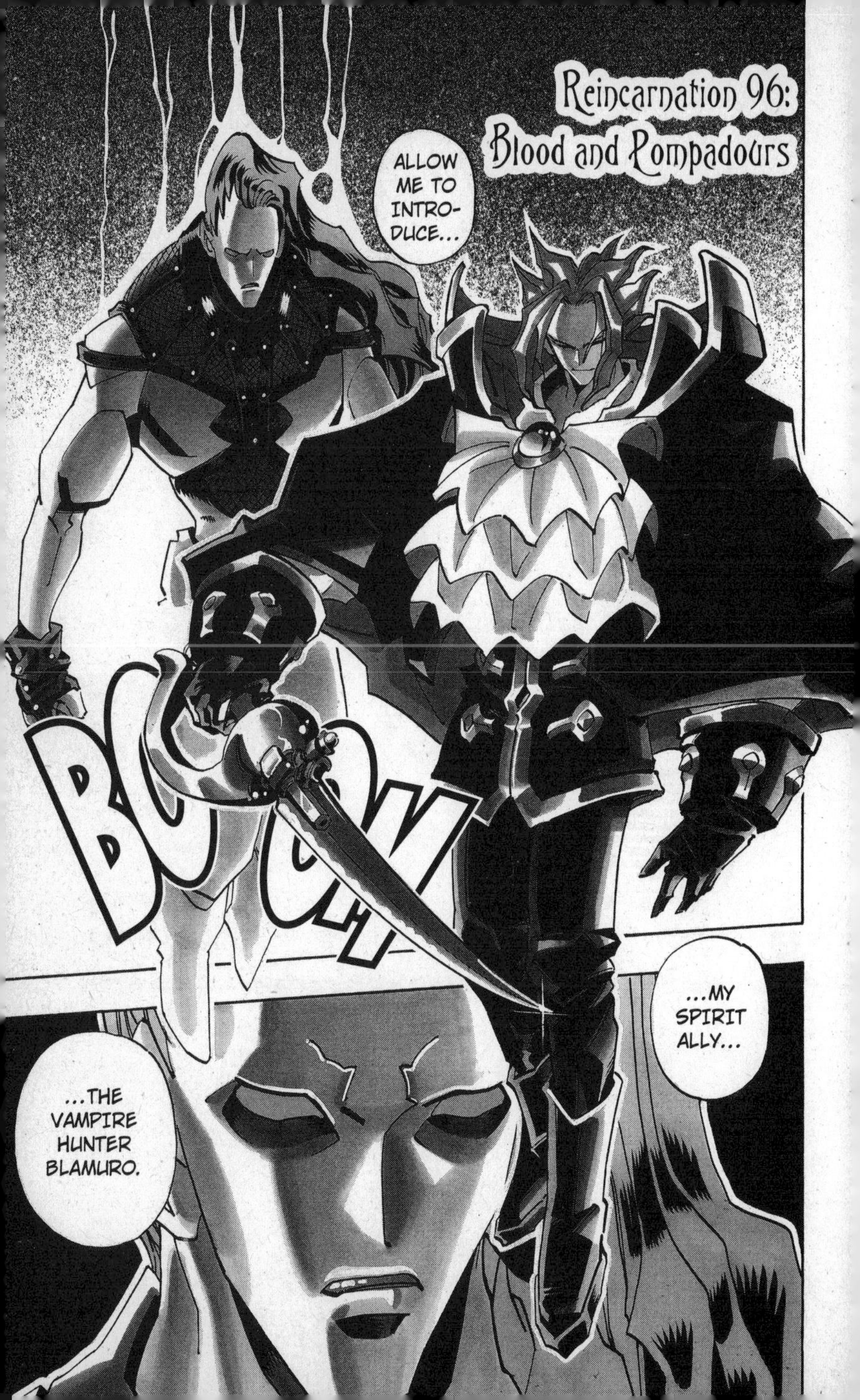
ALLOW ME TO INTRO-DUCE...
...MY SPIRIT ALLY...
...THE VAMPIRE HUNTER BLAMURO.

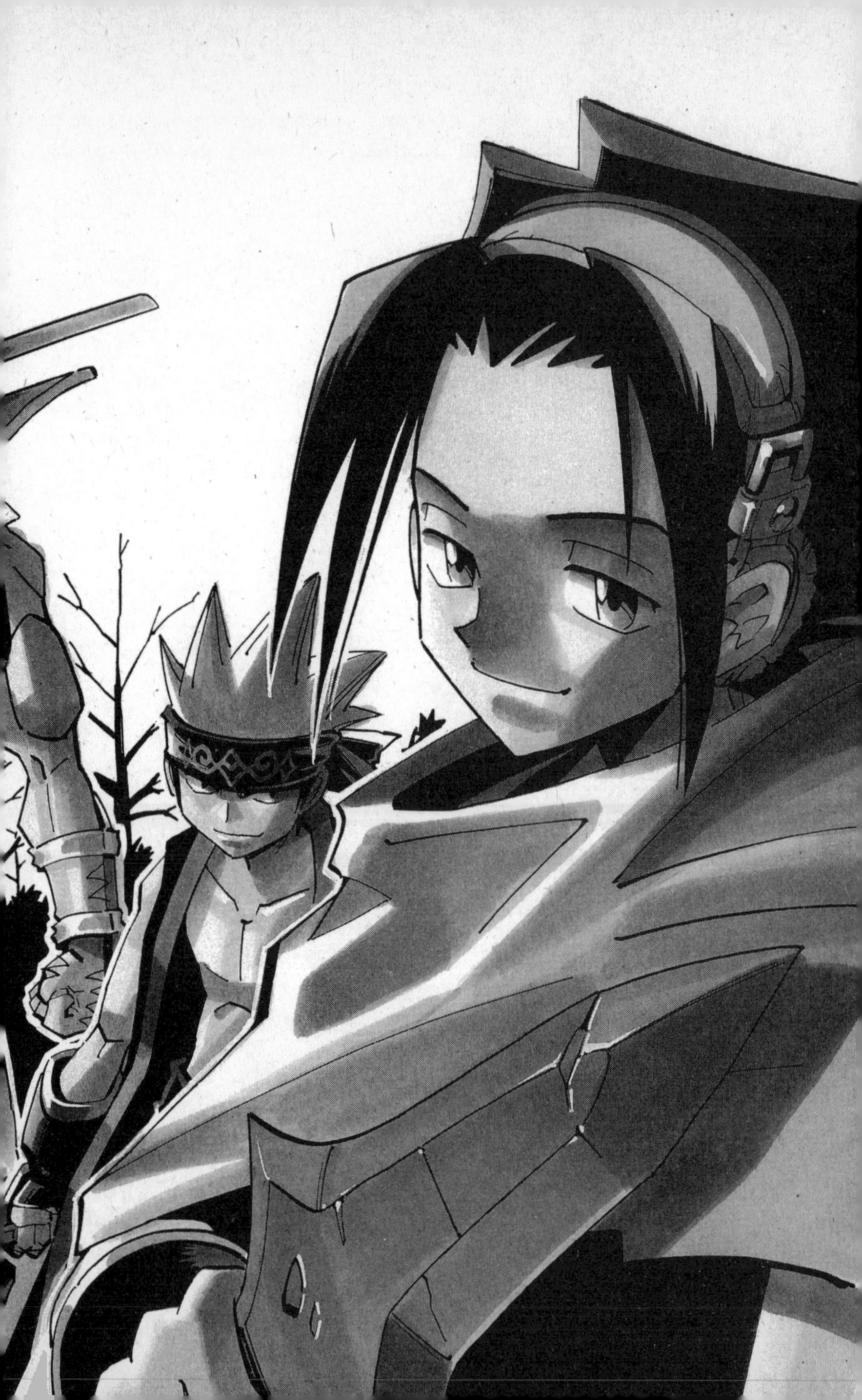

Reincarnation 96:
Blood and Pompadours

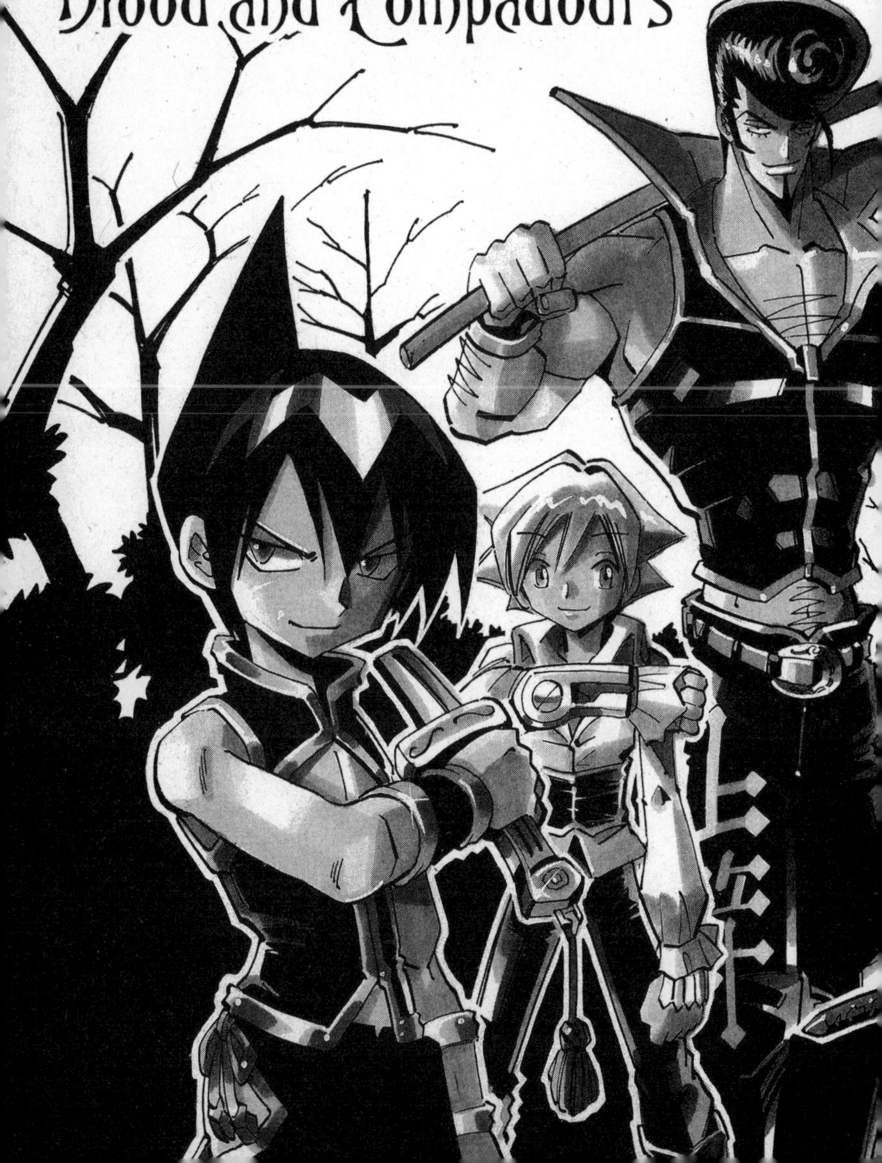

Shaman King™

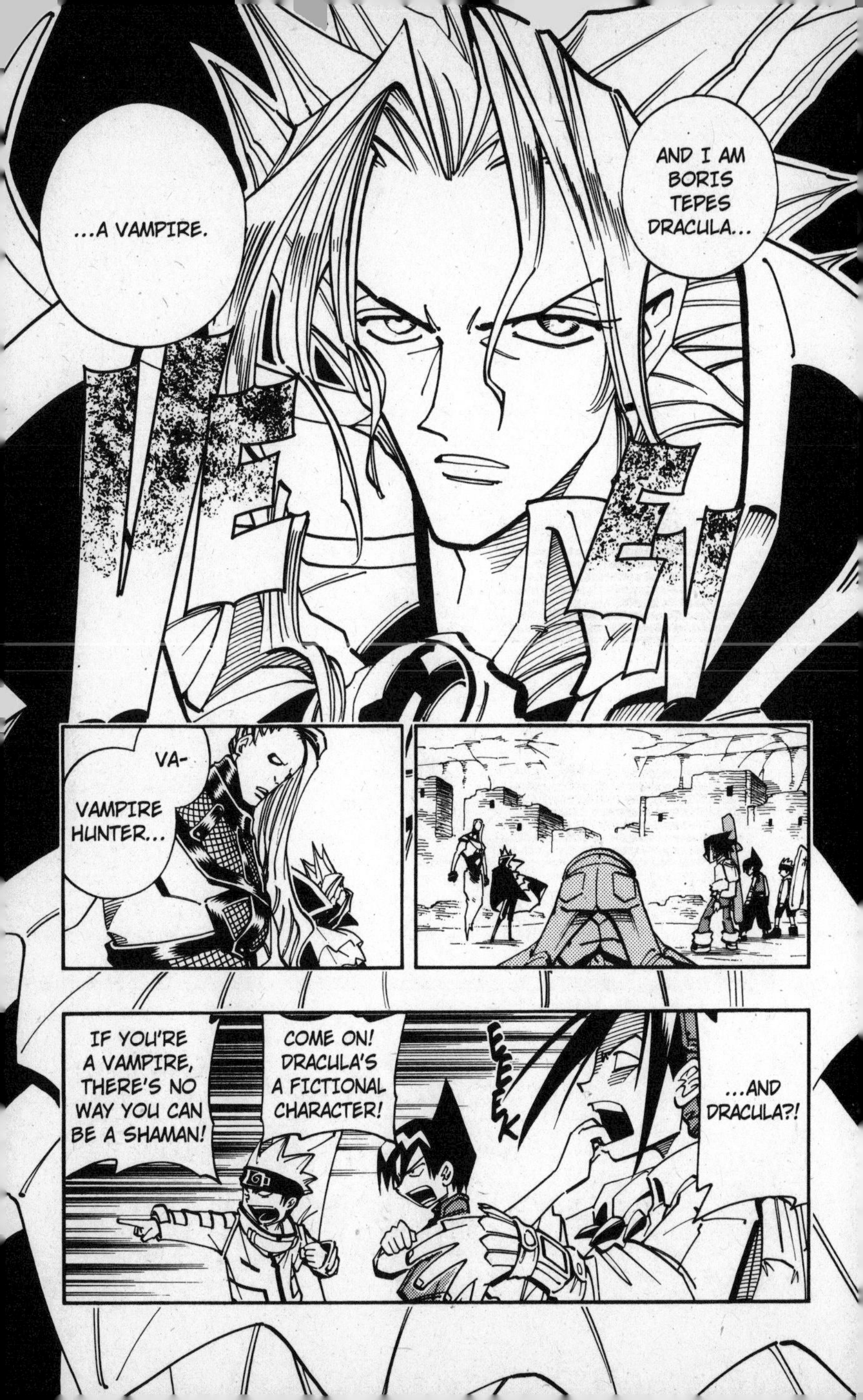
AND I AM BORIS TEPES DRACULA...
...A VAMPIRE.
VA-
VAMPIRE HUNTER...
...AND DRACULA?!
COME ON! DRACULA'S A FICTIONAL CHARACTER!
IF YOU'RE A VAMPIRE, THERE'S NO WAY YOU CAN BE A SHAMAN!

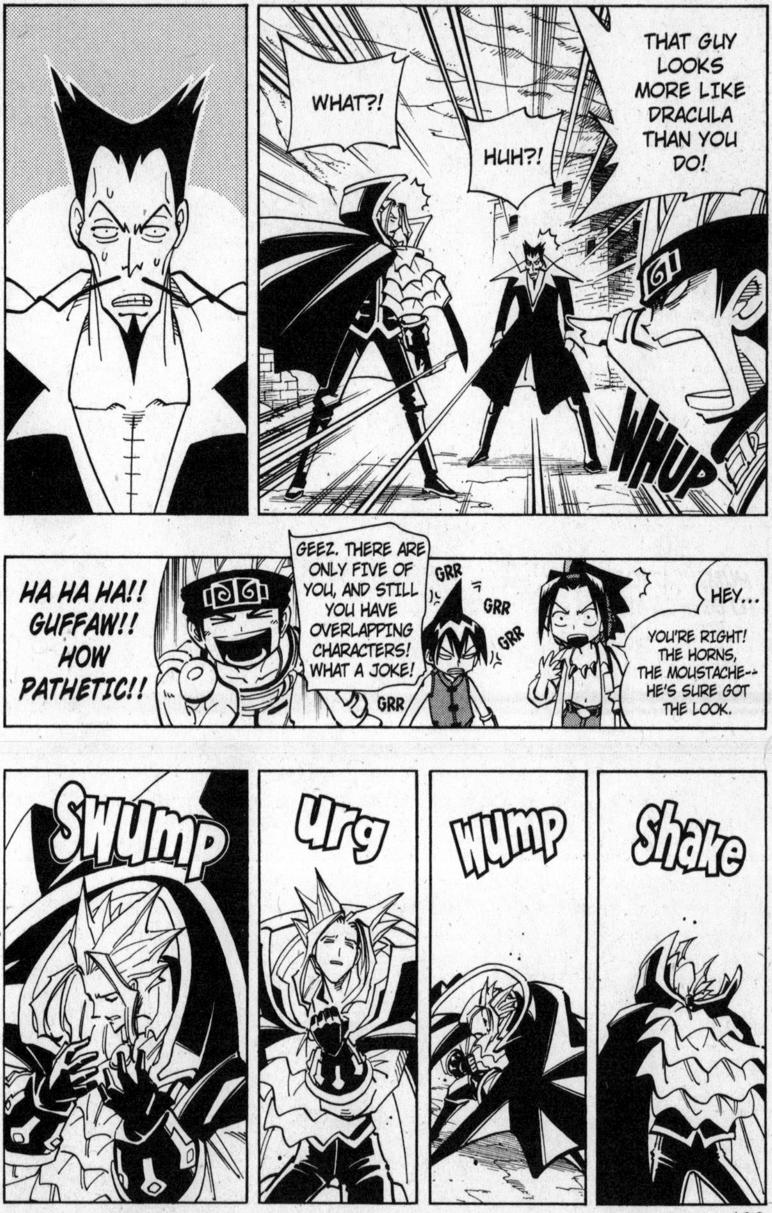
THAT GUY LOOKS MORE LIKE DRACULA THAN YOU DO!
HUH?!
WHAT?!
WHUP
HEY...
YOU'RE RIGHT! THE HORNS, THE MOUSTACHE-- HE'S SURE GOT THE LOOK.
GRR
GRR
GRR
GEEZ. THERE ARE ONLY FIVE OF YOU, AND STILL YOU HAVE OVERLAPPING CHARACTERS! WHAT A JOKE!
GRR
HA HA HA!! GUFFAW!! HOW PATHETIC!!
Shake
Wump
urg
Swump

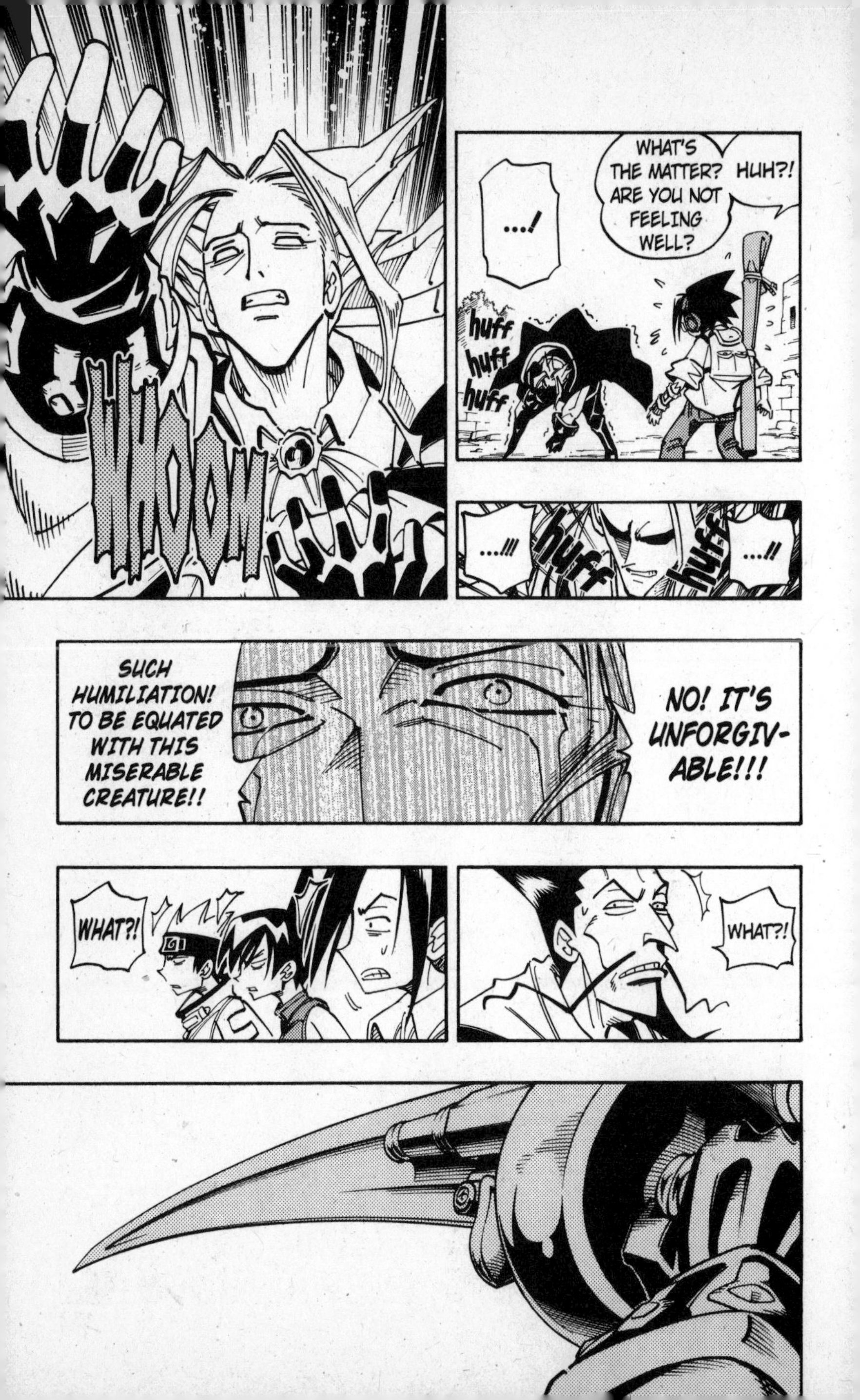
HUH?!
WHAT'S THE MATTER? ARE YOU NOT FEELING WELL?
...!
huff huff huff
...!!
huff
huff
...!!!
WHOOM
NO! IT'S UNFORGIV-ABLE!!!
SUCH HUMILIATION! TO BE EQUATED WITH THIS MISERABLE CREATURE!!
WHAT?!
WHAT?!

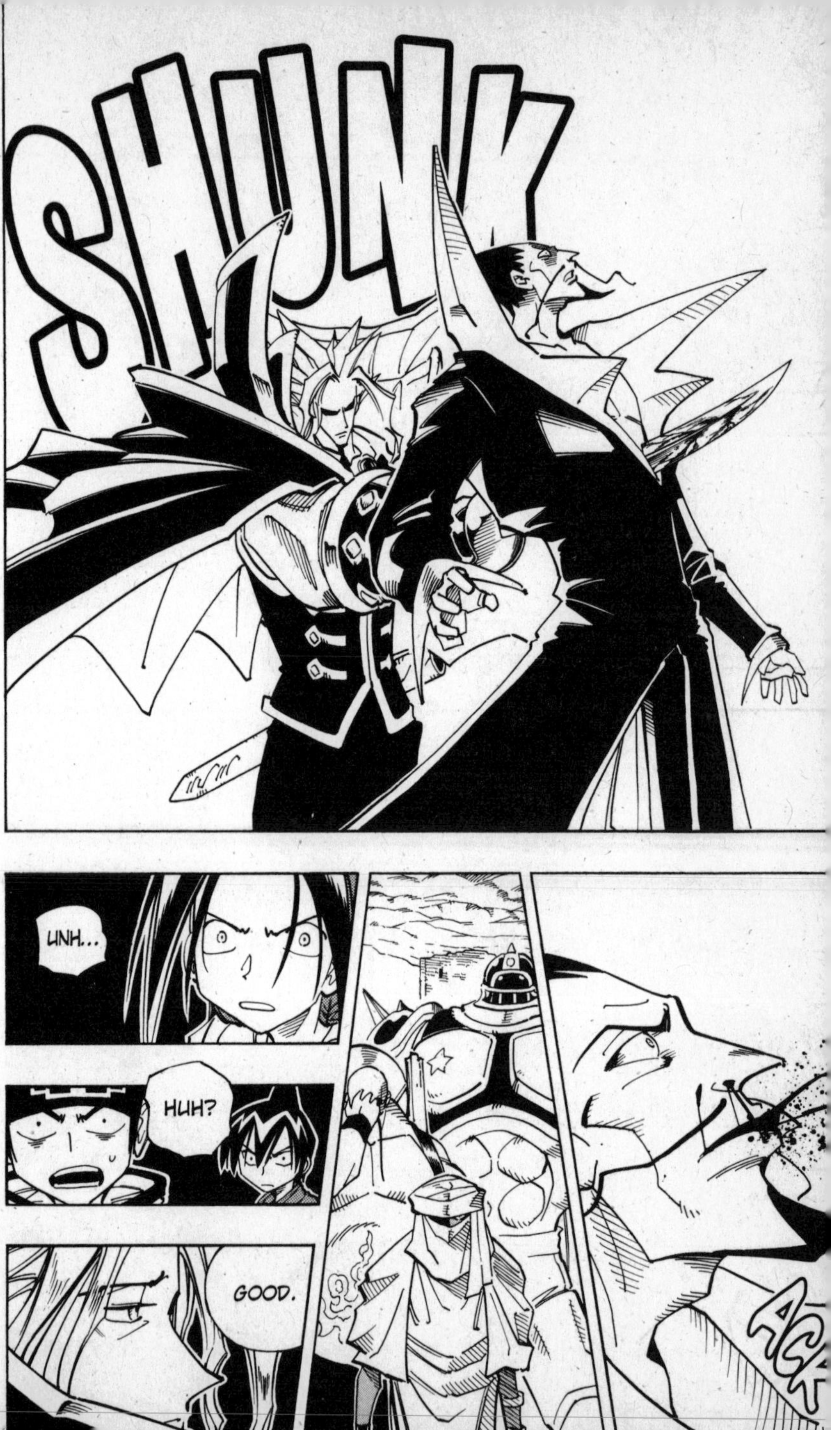
SHUNK
ACK
UNH...
HUH?
GOOD.

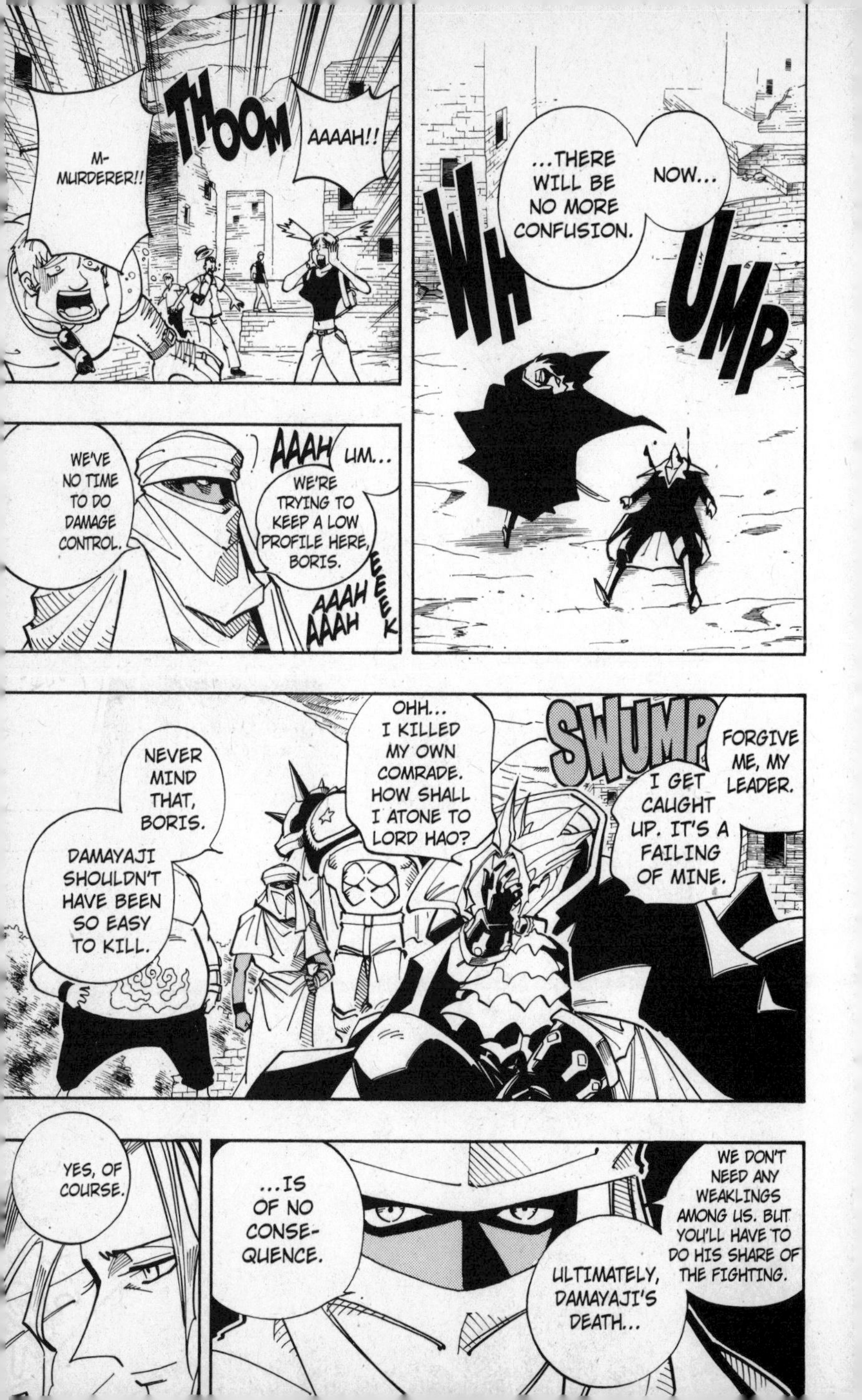
NOW...
...THERE WILL BE NO MORE CONFUSION.
WHUMP
THOOM
AAAAH!!
M-MURDERER!!
AAAH
UM... WE'RE TRYING TO KEEP A LOW PROFILE HERE, BORIS.
WE'VE NO TIME TO DO DAMAGE CONTROL.
EEEEK
AAAH AAAH
FORGIVE ME, MY LEADER.
I GET CAUGHT UP. IT'S A FAILING OF MINE.
SWUMP
OHH... I KILLED MY OWN COMRADE. HOW SHALL I ATONE TO LORD HAO?
NEVER MIND THAT, BORIS.
DAMAYAJI SHOULDN'T HAVE BEEN SO EASY TO KILL.
ULTIMATELY, DAMAYAJI'S DEATH...
...IS OF NO CONSEQUENCE.
WE DON'T NEED ANY WEAKLINGS AMONG US. BUT YOU'LL HAVE TO DO HIS SHARE OF THE FIGHTING.
YES, OF COURSE.

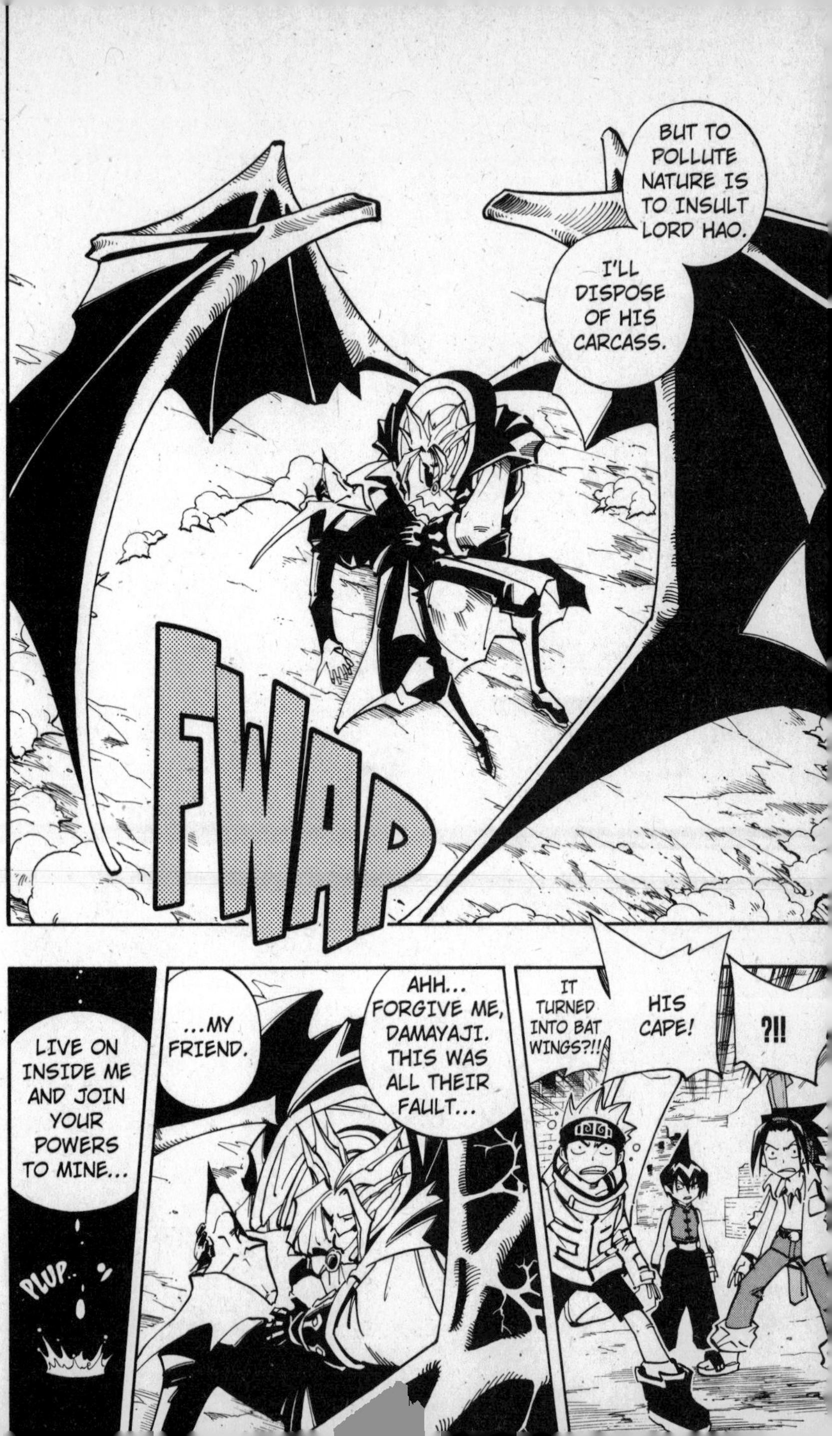
BUT TO POLLUTE NATURE IS TO INSULT LORD HAO.
I'LL DISPOSE OF HIS CARCASS.
FWAP
?!!
HIS CAPE!
IT TURNED INTO BAT WINGS?!!
AHH... FORGIVE ME, DAMAYAJI. THIS WAS ALL THEIR FAULT...
...MY FRIEND.
LIVE ON INSIDE ME AND JOIN YOUR POWERS TO MINE...
PLUP..

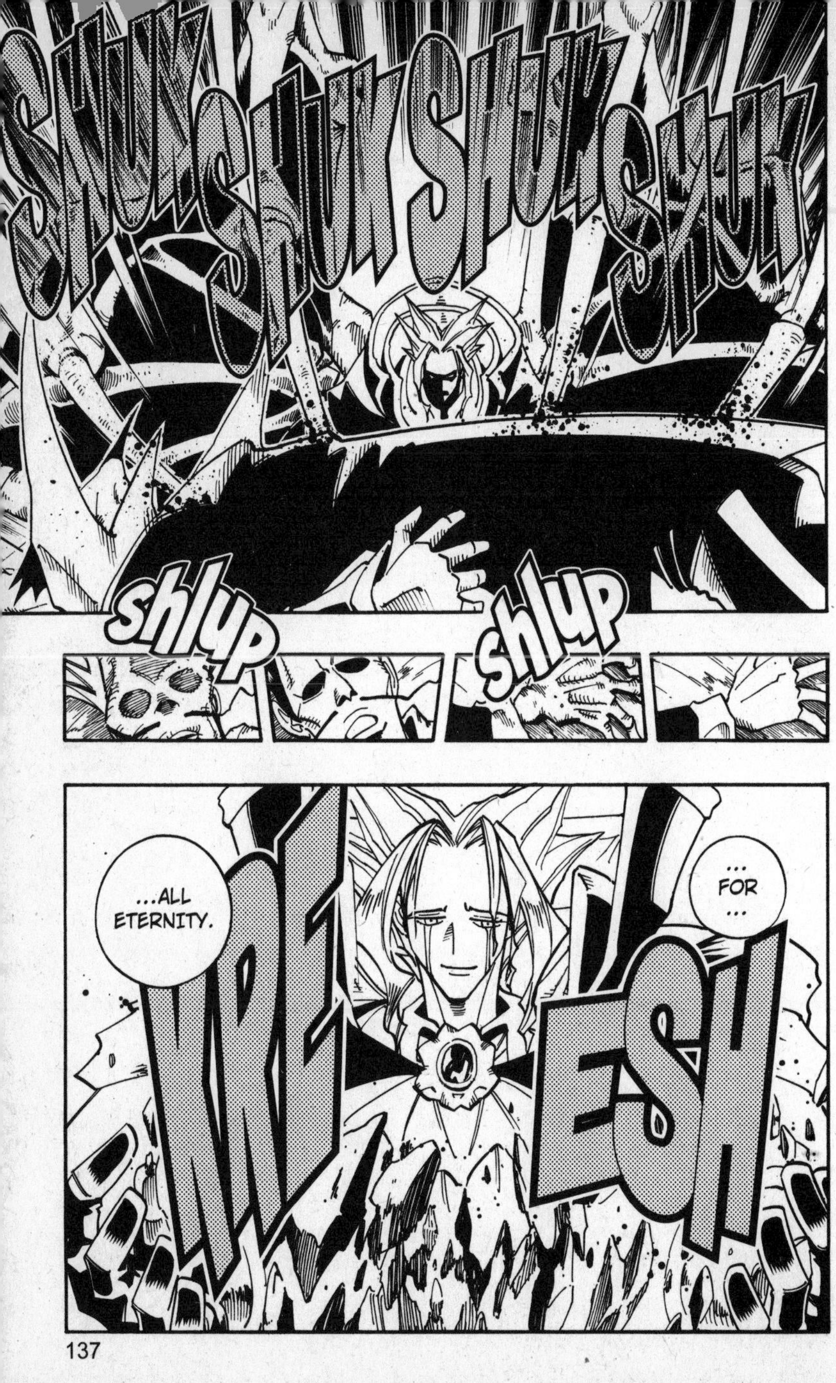
SHUNK SHUNK SHUNK SHUNK
shlup
shlup
...FOR...
...ALL ETERNITY.

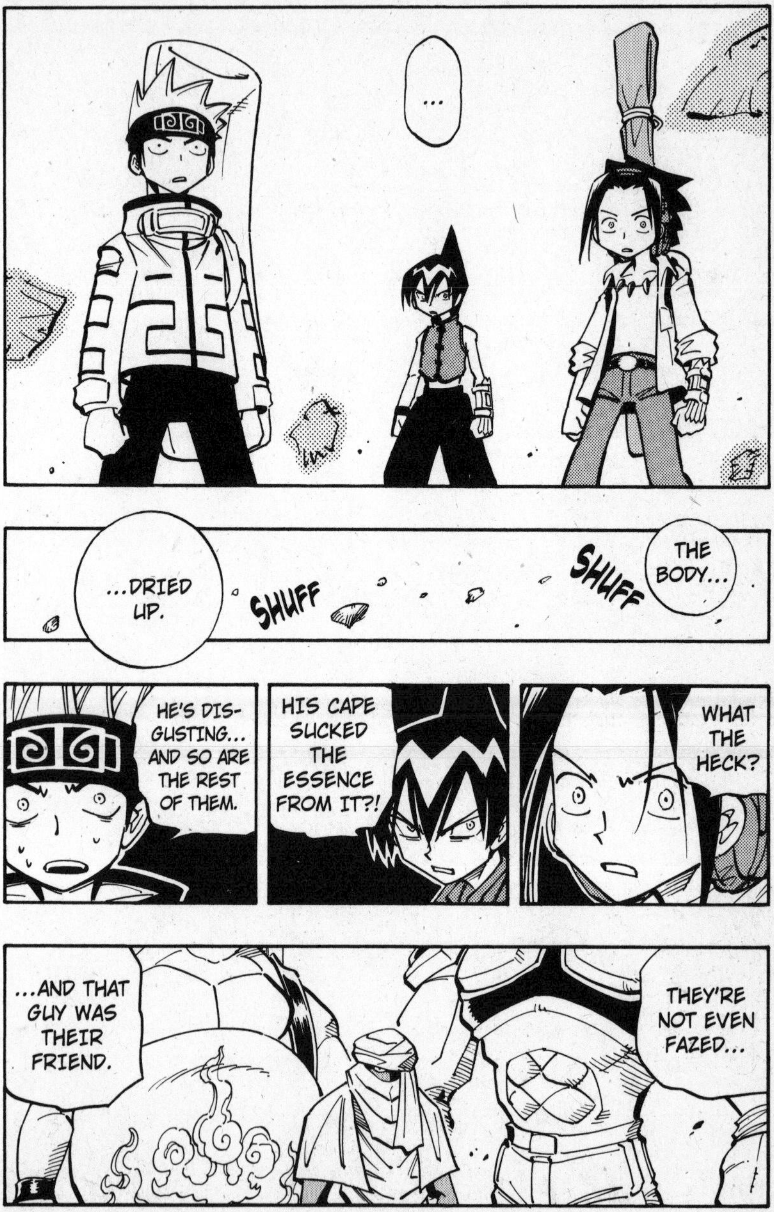
...
THE BODY...
SHUFF
SHUFF
...DRIED UP.
WHAT THE HECK?
HIS CAPE SUCKED THE ESSENCE FROM IT?!
HE'S DIS-GUSTING... AND SO ARE THE REST OF THEM.
THEY'RE NOT EVEN FAZED...
...AND THAT GUY WAS THEIR FRIEND.

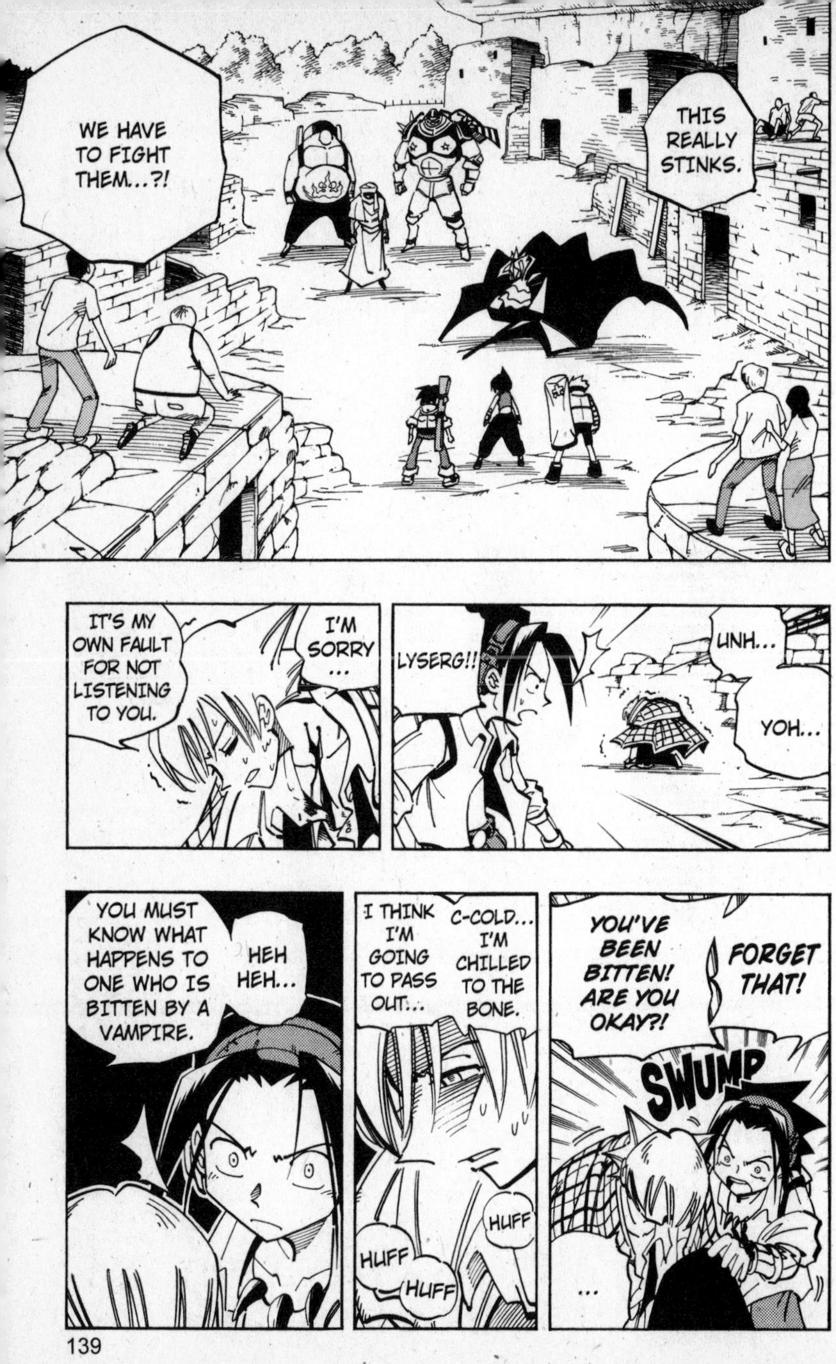
THIS REALLY STINKS.
WE HAVE TO FIGHT THEM...?!
UNH...
YOH...
LYSERG!!
I'M SORRY...
IT'S MY OWN FAULT FOR NOT LISTENING TO YOU.
FORGET THAT!
YOU'VE BEEN BITTEN! ARE YOU OKAY?!
SWUMP
...
C-COLD... I'M CHILLED TO THE BONE.
I THINK I'M GOING TO PASS OUT...
HUFF
HUFF
HUFF
HEH HEH...
YOU MUST KNOW WHAT HAPPENS TO ONE WHO IS BITTEN BY A VAMPIRE.

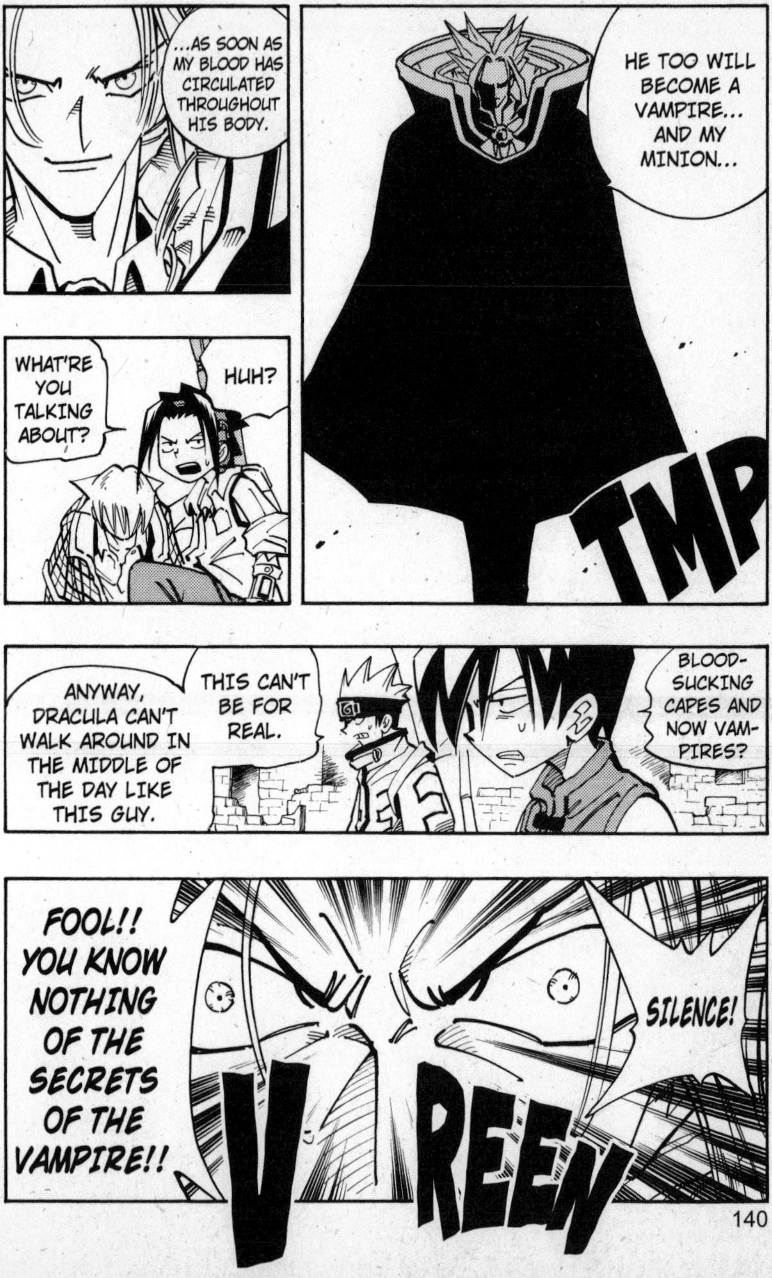
HE TOO WILL BECOME A VAMPIRE... AND MY MINION...
TMP
...AS SOON AS MY BLOOD HAS CIRCULATED THROUGHOUT HIS BODY.
HUH?
WHAT'RE YOU TALKING ABOUT?
BLOOD-SUCKING CAPES AND NOW VAM-PIRES?
THIS CAN'T BE FOR REAL.
ANYWAY, DRACULA CAN'T WALK AROUND IN THE MIDDLE OF THE DAY LIKE THIS GUY.
SILENCE!
FOOL!! YOU KNOW NOTHING OF THE SECRETS OF THE VAMPIRE!!
VREEN

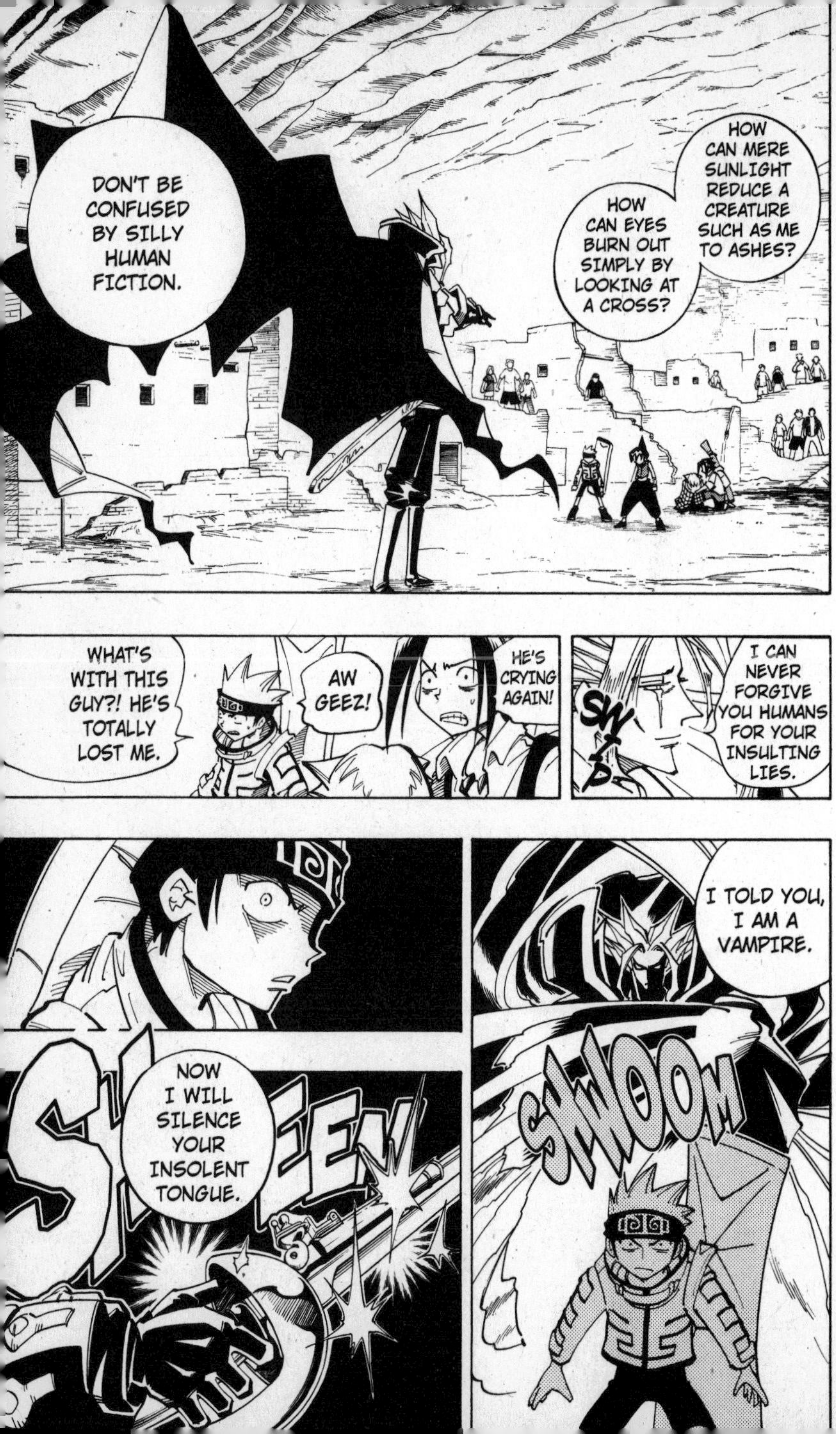
HOW CAN MERE SUNLIGHT REDUCE A CREATURE SUCH AS ME TO ASHES?
HOW CAN EYES BURN OUT SIMPLY BY LOOKING AT A CROSS?
DON'T BE CONFUSED BY SILLY HUMAN FICTION.
SWIP
I CAN NEVER FORGIVE YOU HUMANS FOR YOUR INSULTING LIES.
HE'S CRYING AGAIN!
AW GEEZ!
WHAT'S WITH THIS GUY?! HE'S TOTALLY LOST ME.
I TOLD YOU, I AM A VAMPIRE.
SHWOOM
NOW I WILL SILENCE YOUR INSOLENT TONGUE.

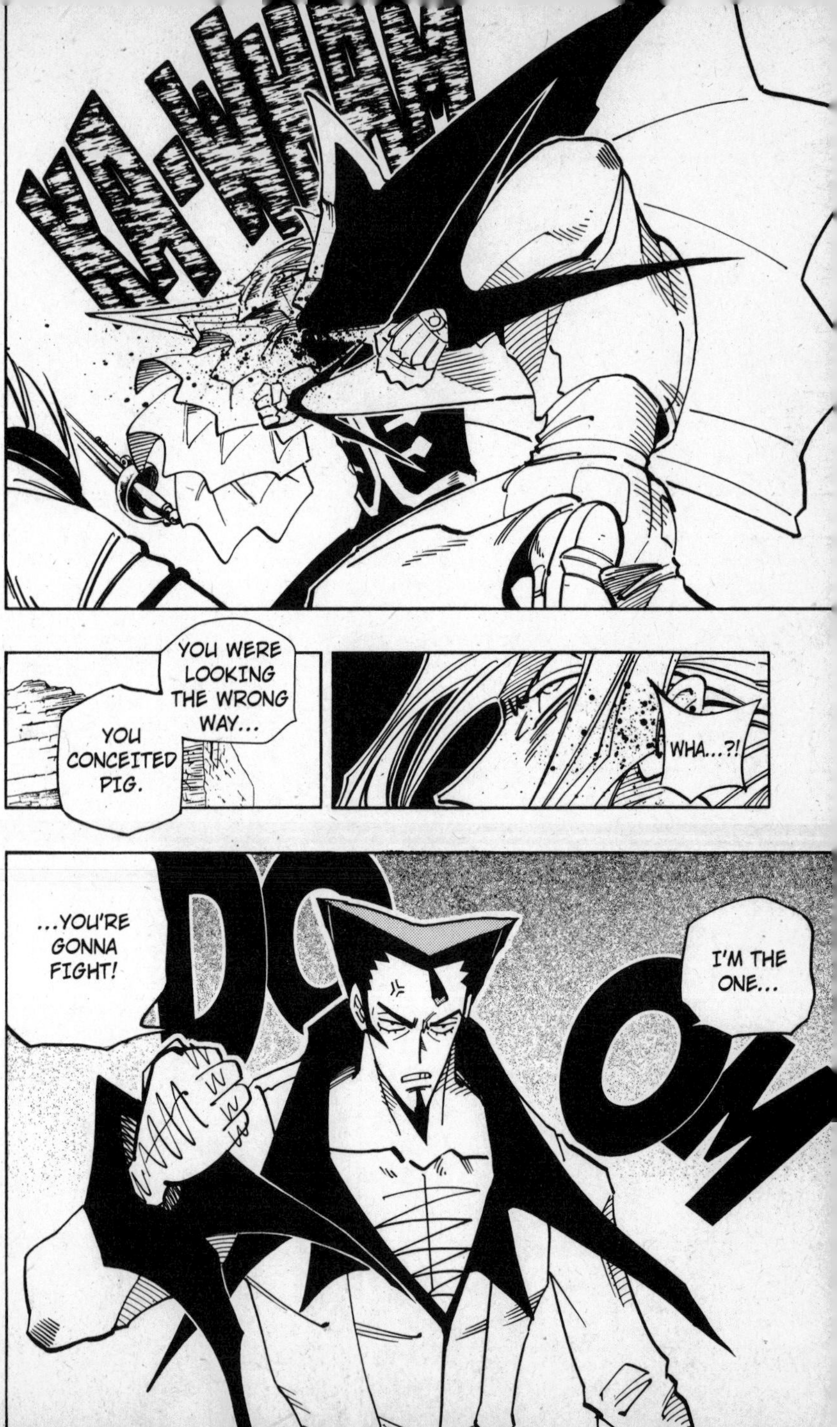
KA-WHOM
WHA...?!
YOU WERE LOOKING THE WRONG WAY...
YOU CONCEITED PIG.
I'M THE ONE...
DOOM
...YOU'RE GONNA FIGHT!

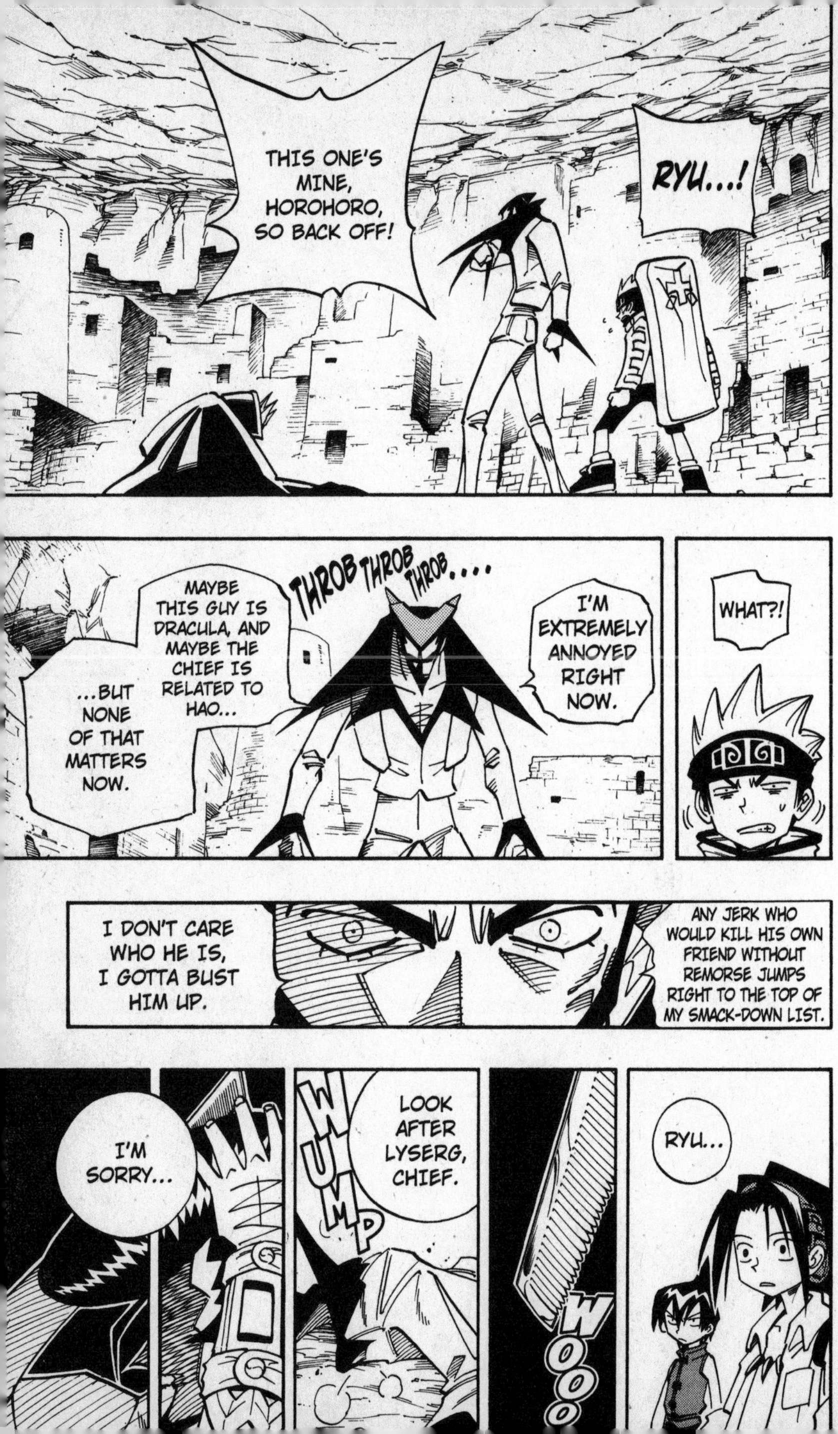
RYU...!
THIS ONE'S MINE, HOROHORO, SO BACK OFF!
WHAT?!
I'M EXTREMELY ANNOYED RIGHT NOW.
THROB THROB THROB....
MAYBE THIS GUY IS DRACULA, AND MAYBE THE CHIEF IS RELATED TO HAO...
...BUT NONE OF THAT MATTERS NOW.
ANY JERK WHO WOULD KILL HIS OWN FRIEND WITHOUT REMORSE JUMPS RIGHT TO THE TOP OF MY SMACK-DOWN LIST.
I DON'T CARE WHO HE IS, I GOTTA BUST HIM UP.
RYU...
WOOO
LOOK AFTER LYSERG, CHIEF.
WHUMP
I'M SORRY...

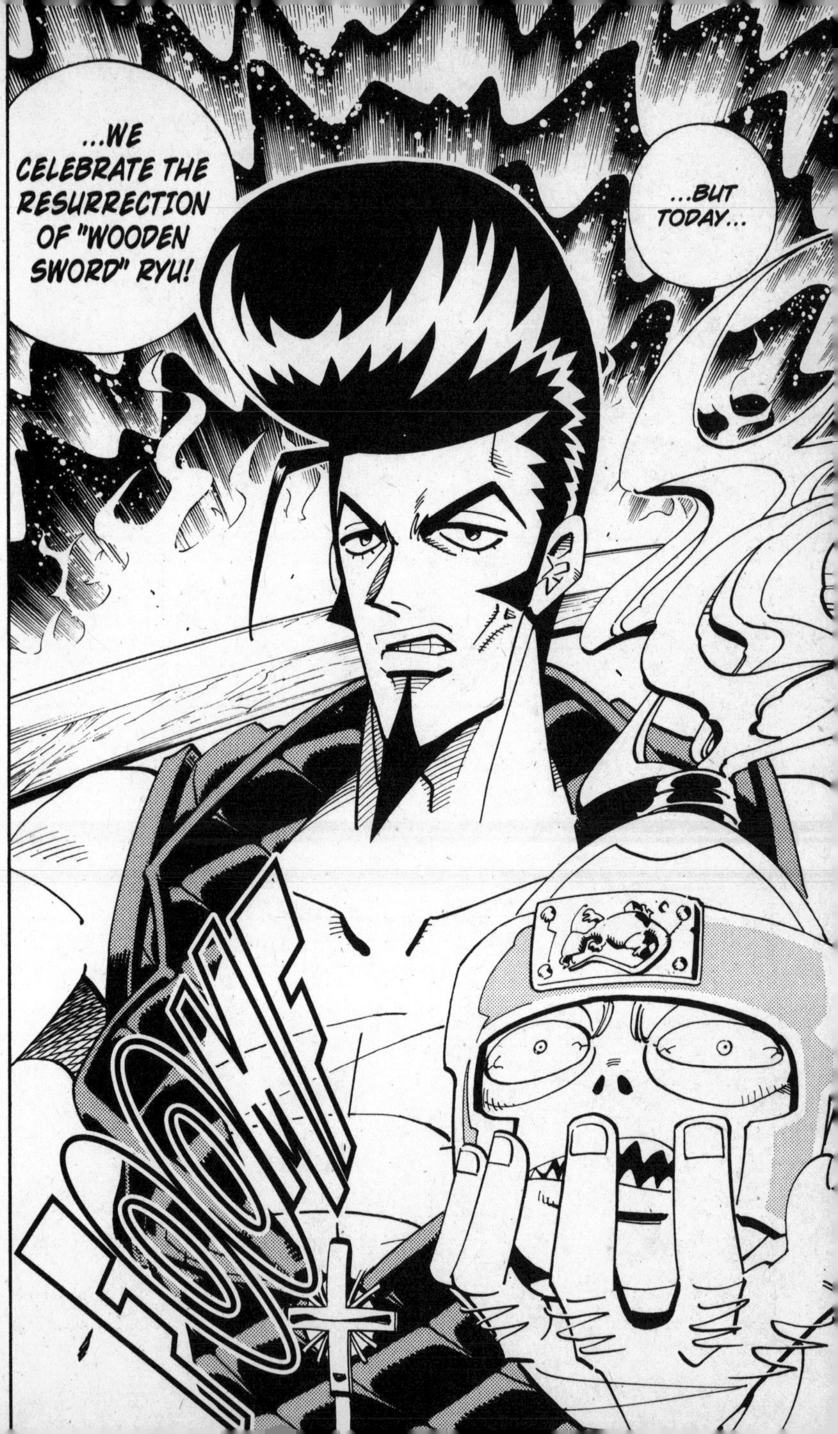
...BUT TODAY...
...WE CELEBRATE THE RESURRECTION OF "WOODEN SWORD" RYU!

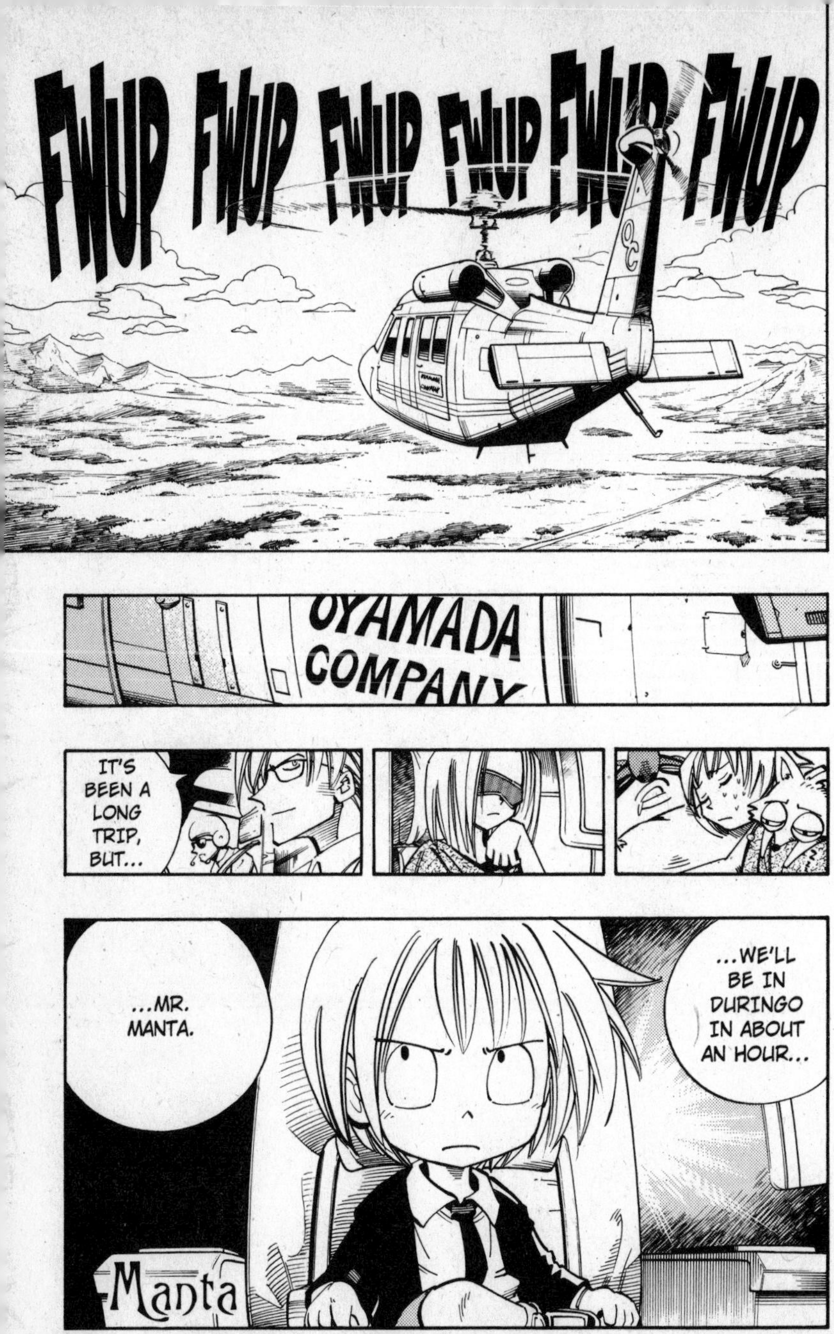
FWUP FWUP FWUP FWUP FWUP FWUP
OYAMADA COMPANY
IT'S BEEN A LONG TRIP, BUT...
...WE'LL BE IN DURINGO IN ABOUT AN HOUR...
...MR. MANTA.
Manta

SHAMAN KING CHARACTER FILE No.50

グリーン・ガラム

GREEN GARAM

2000
(Nov)

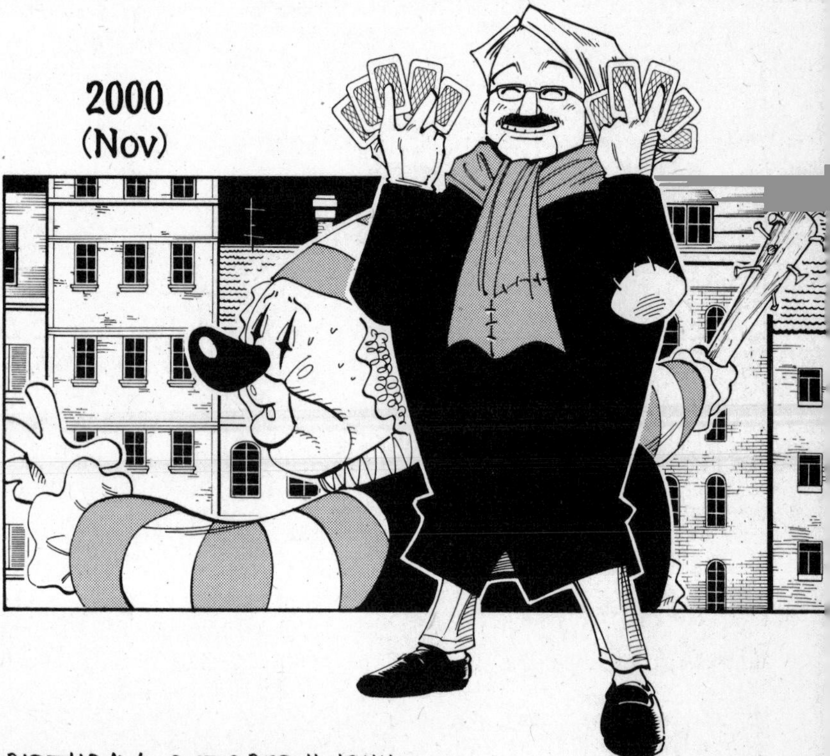

BIRTHDAY: OCTOBER 11, 1944
ASTROLOGICAL SIGN: LIBRA
BLOOD TYPE: B
56 YEARS OLD

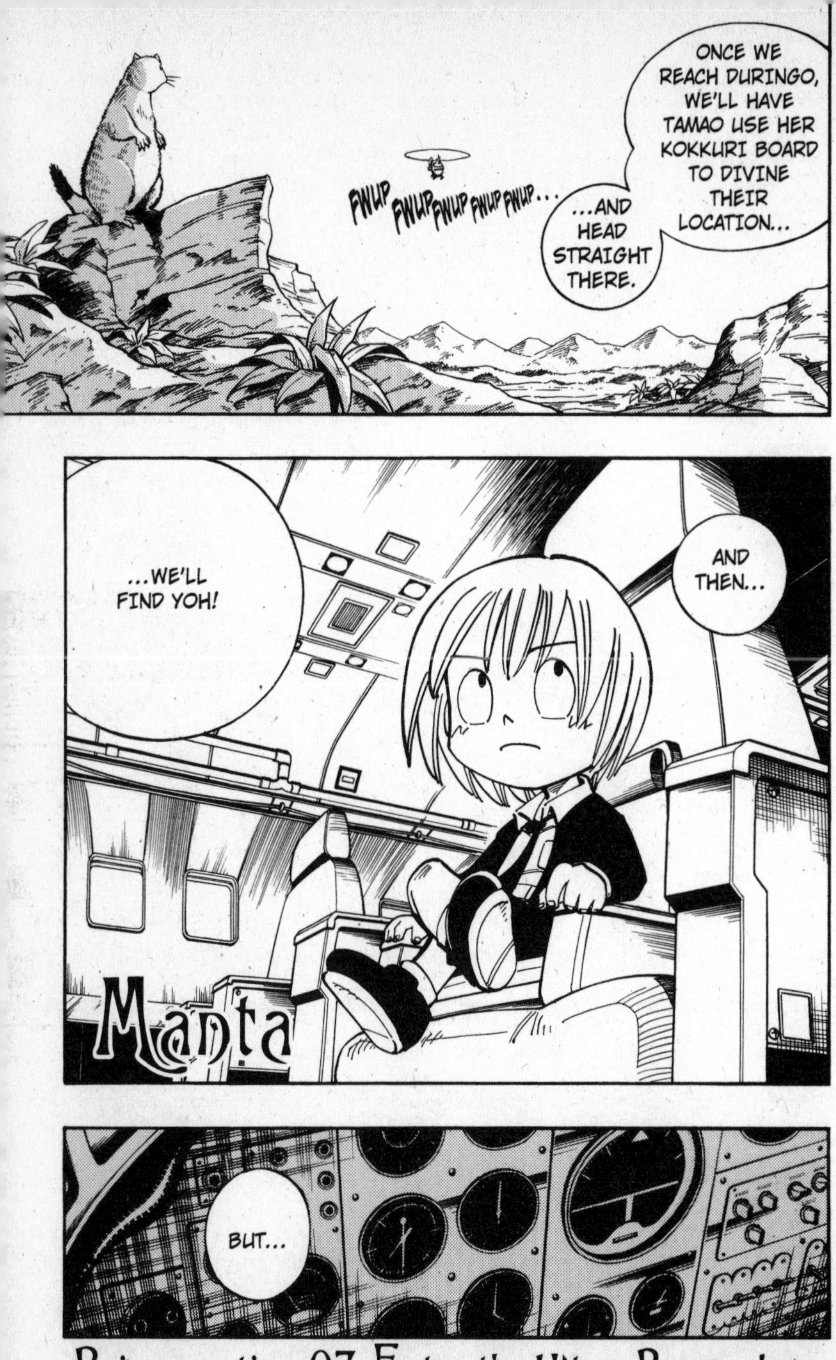
ONCE WE REACH DURINGO, WE'LL HAVE TAMAO USE HER KOKKURI BOARD TO DIVINE THEIR LOCATION...
...AND HEAD STRAIGHT THERE.
FWUP FWUP FWUP FWUP FWUP...
AND THEN...
...WE'LL FIND YOH!
Manta
BUT...

Reincarnation 97: Enter the Ultra-Pompadour

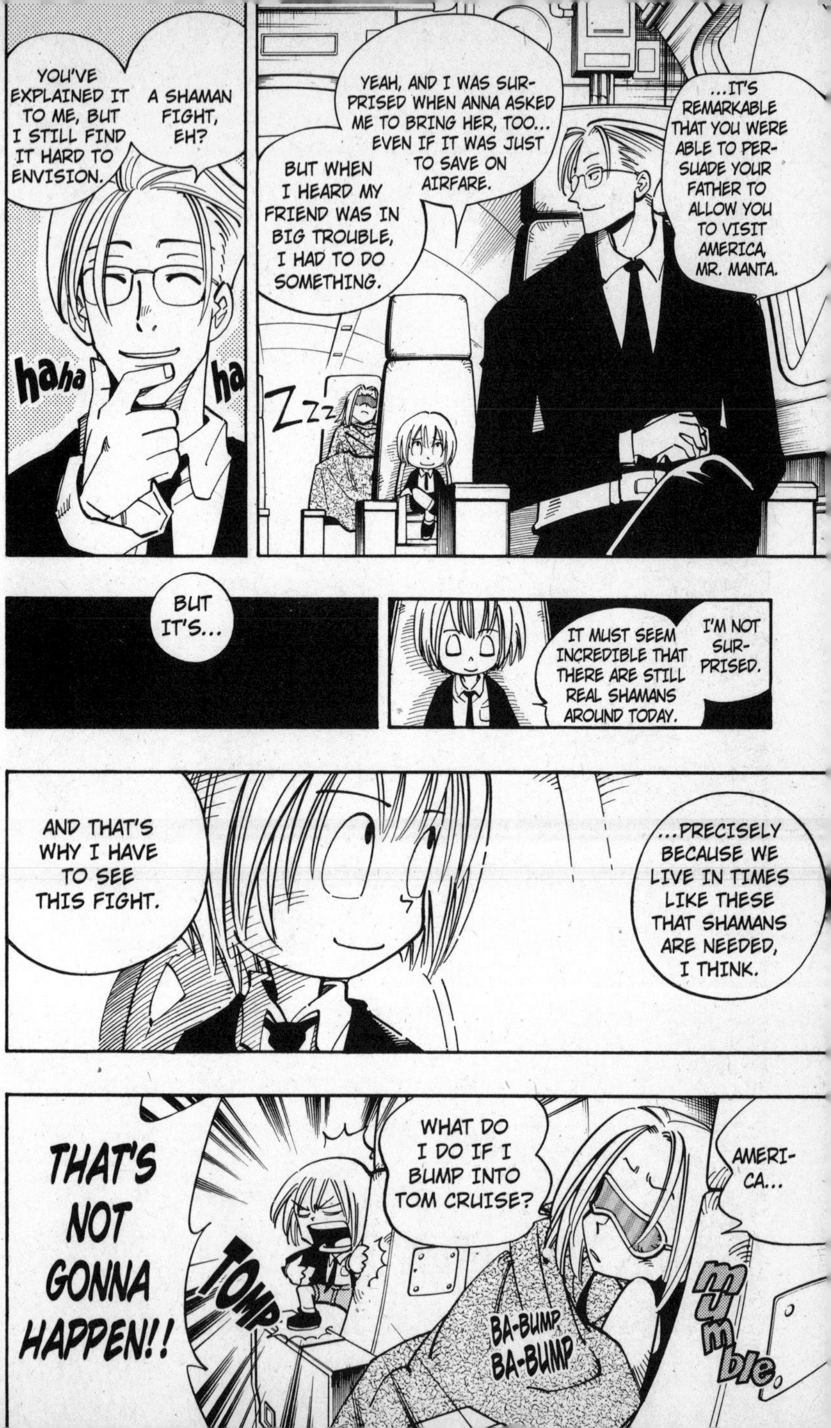
...IT'S REMARKABLE THAT YOU WERE ABLE TO PERSUADE YOUR FATHER TO ALLOW YOU TO VISIT AMERICA, MR. MANTA.
YEAH, AND I WAS SURPRISED WHEN ANNA ASKED ME TO BRING HER, TOO... EVEN IF IT WAS JUST TO SAVE ON AIRFARE.
BUT WHEN I HEARD MY FRIEND WAS IN BIG TROUBLE, I HAD TO DO SOMETHING.
Zzz
A SHAMAN FIGHT, EH?
YOU'VE EXPLAINED IT TO ME, BUT I STILL FIND IT HARD TO ENVISION.
haha
ha
I'M NOT SURPRISED.
IT MUST SEEM INCREDIBLE THAT THERE ARE STILL REAL SHAMANS AROUND TODAY.
BUT IT'S...
...PRECISELY BECAUSE WE LIVE IN TIMES LIKE THESE THAT SHAMANS ARE NEEDED, I THINK.
AND THAT'S WHY I HAVE TO SEE THIS FIGHT.
AMERICA...
mumble
BA-BUMP BA-BUMP
WHAT DO I DO IF I BUMP INTO TOM CRUISE?
TOMP
THAT'S NOT GONNA HAPPEN!!

Reincarnation 97: Enter the Ultra-Pompadour

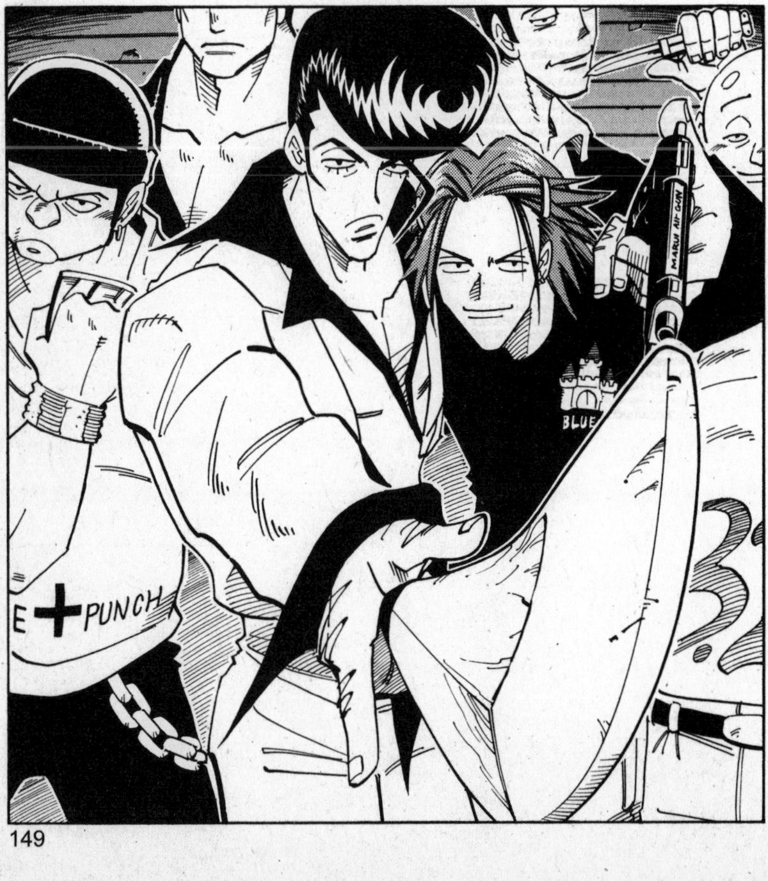
MARUI AIR-GUN
BLUE
E+PUNCH

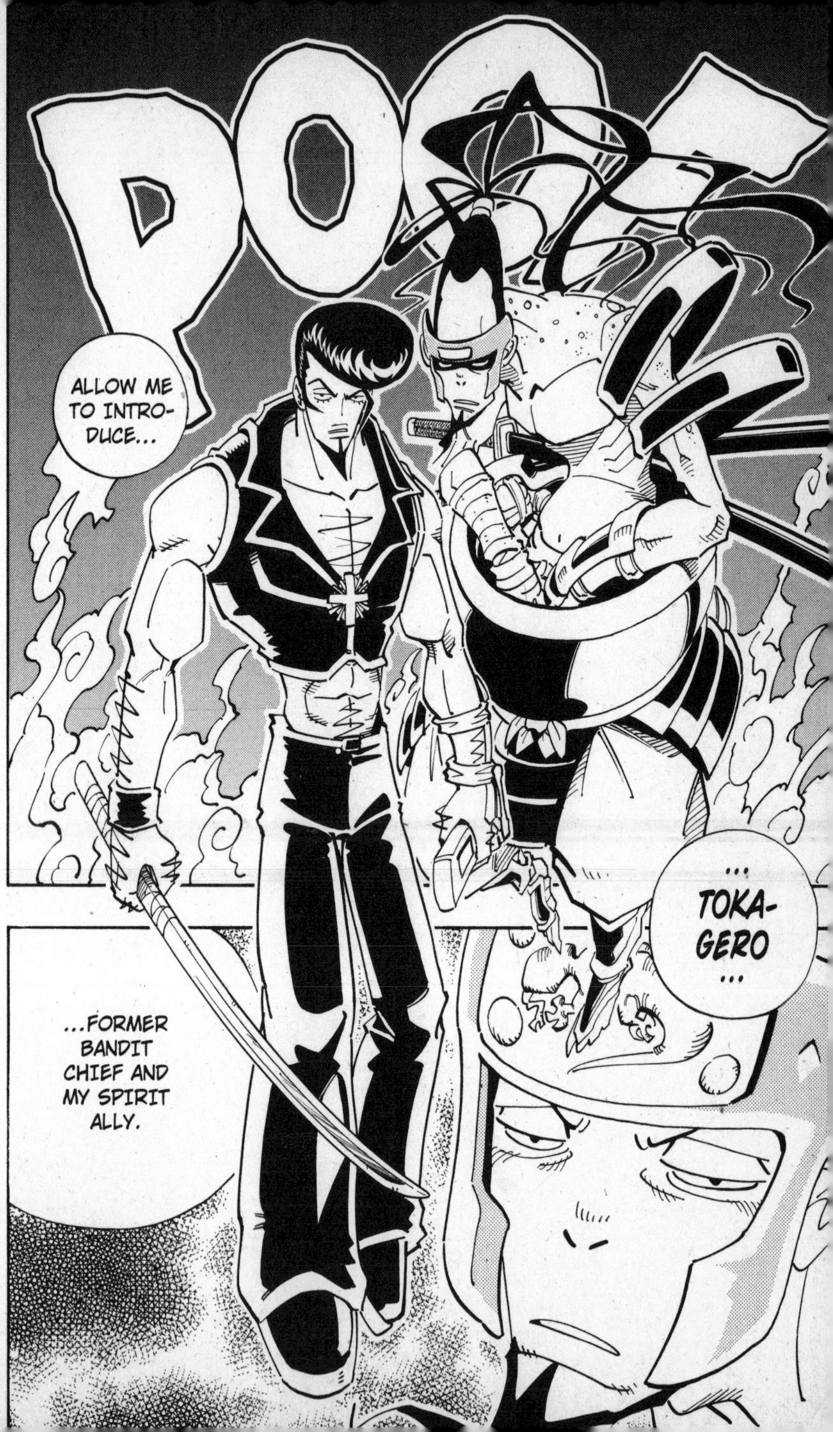
ALLOW ME TO INTRO-DUCE...
...TOKA-GERO...
...FORMER BANDIT CHIEF AND MY SPIRIT ALLY.

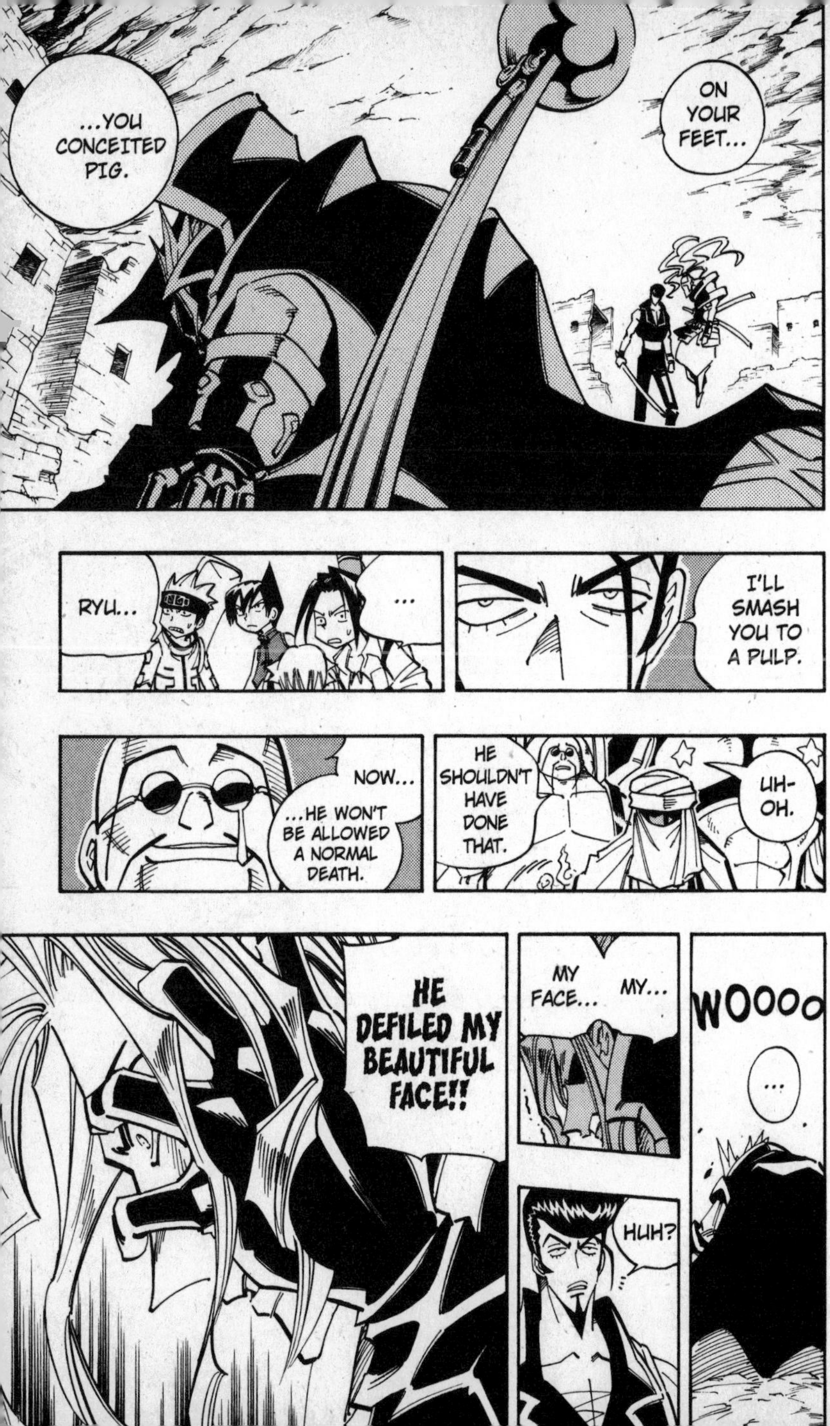
ON YOUR FEET...
...YOU CONCEITED PIG.
I'LL SMASH YOU TO A PULP.
...
RYU...
UH-OH.
HE SHOULDN'T HAVE DONE THAT.
NOW...
...HE WON'T BE ALLOWED A NORMAL DEATH.
WOOOO
...
MY...
MY FACE...
HUH?
HE DEFILED MY BEAUTIFUL FACE!!

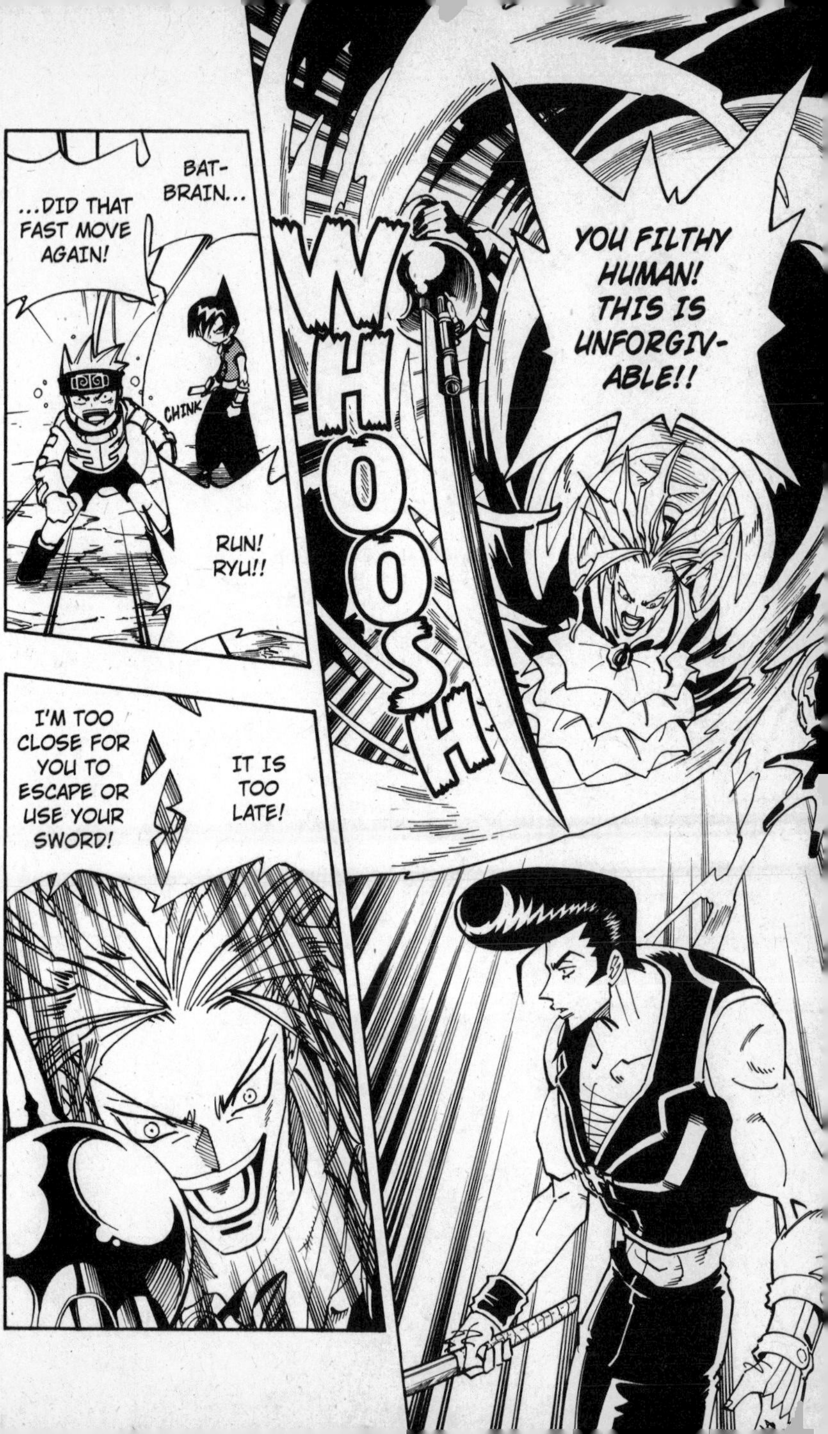
YOU FILTHY HUMAN! THIS IS UNFORGIV-ABLE!!
WHOOSH
BAT-BRAIN...
...DID THAT FAST MOVE AGAIN!
CHINK
RUN! RYU!!
IT IS TOO LATE!
I'M TOO CLOSE FOR YOU TO ESCAPE OR USE YOUR SWORD!

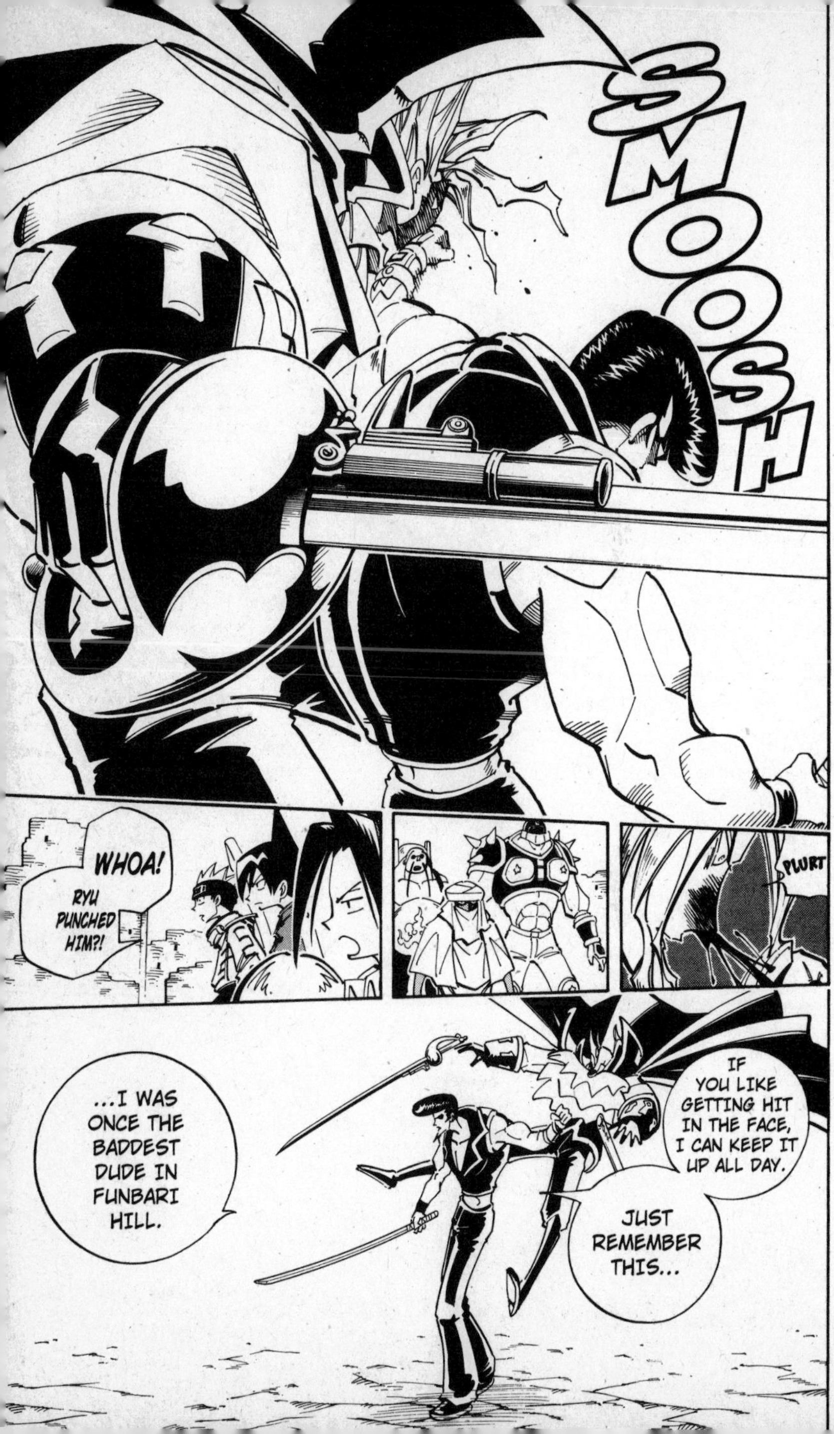
SMOOSH
PLURT
WHOA!
RYU PUNCHED HIM?!
IF YOU LIKE GETTING HIT IN THE FACE, I CAN KEEP IT UP ALL DAY.
JUST REMEMBER THIS...
...I WAS ONCE THE BADDEST DUDE IN FUNBARI HILL.

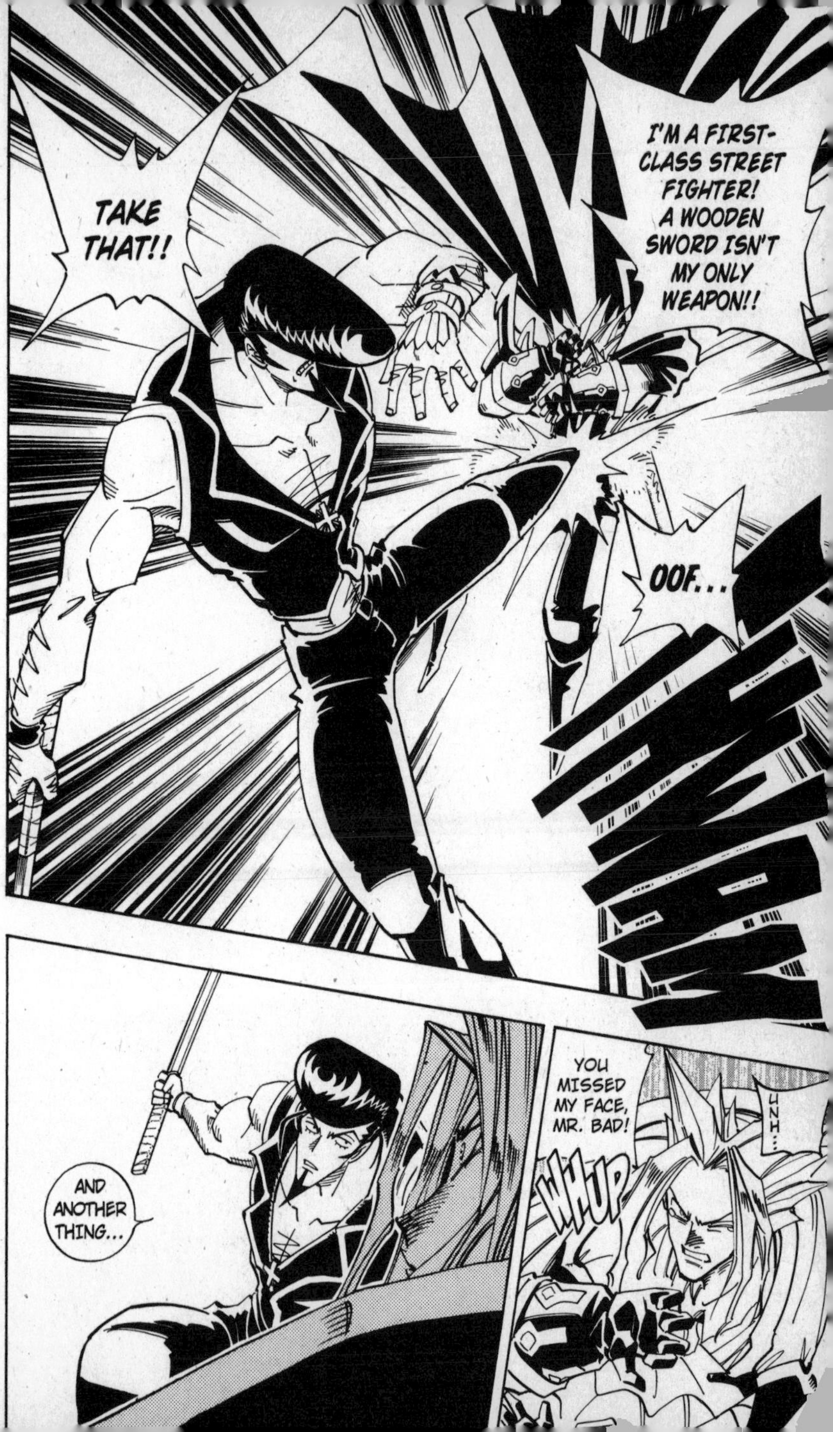
I'M A FIRST-CLASS STREET FIGHTER! A WOODEN SWORD ISN'T MY ONLY WEAPON!!
TAKE THAT!!
OOF...
UNH...
YOU MISSED MY FACE, MR. BAD!
WHUP
AND ANOTHER THING...

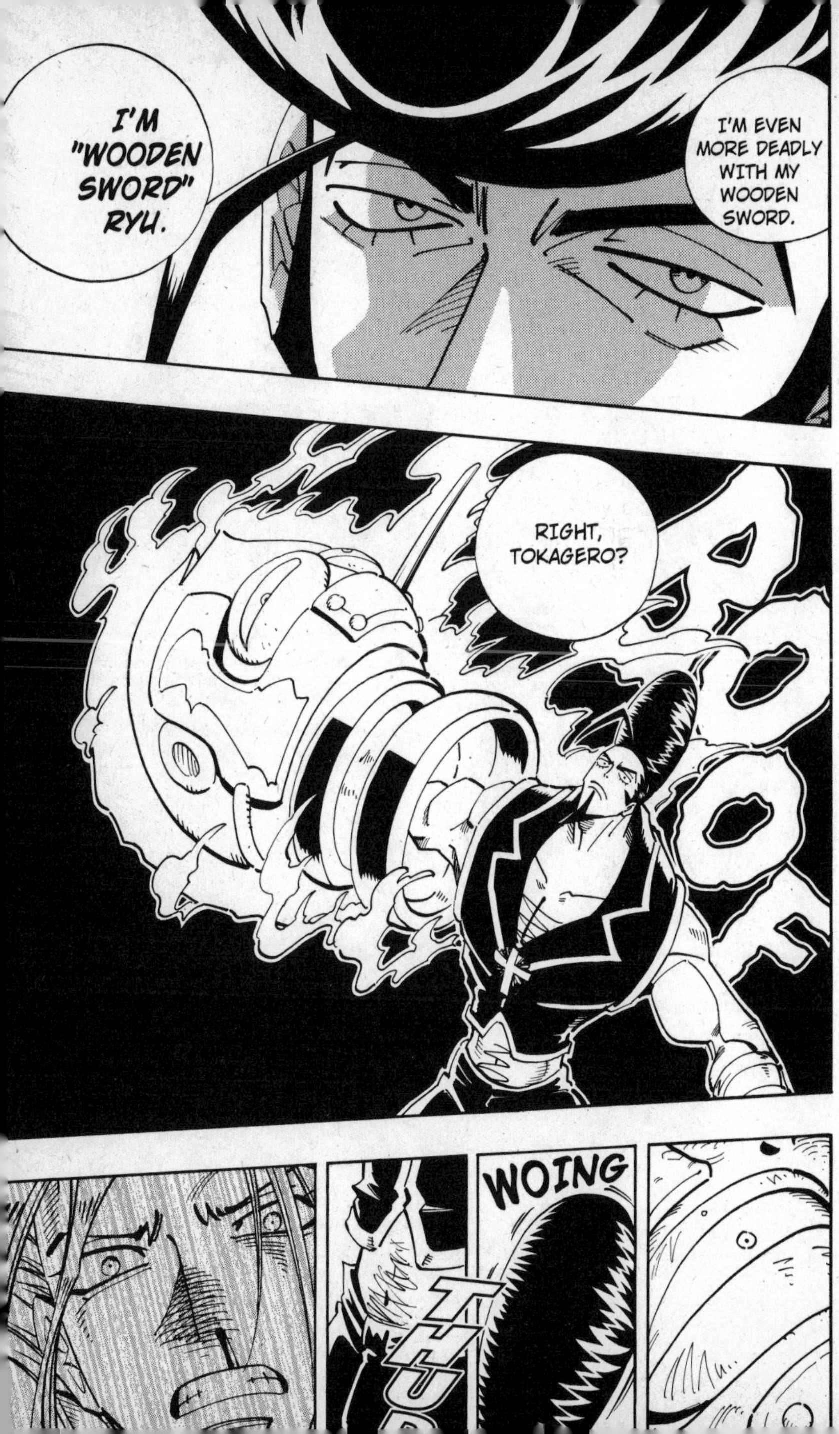
I'M EVEN MORE DEADLY WITH MY WOODEN SWORD.
I'M "WOODEN SWORD" RYU.
RIGHT, TOKAGERO?
WOING
THU

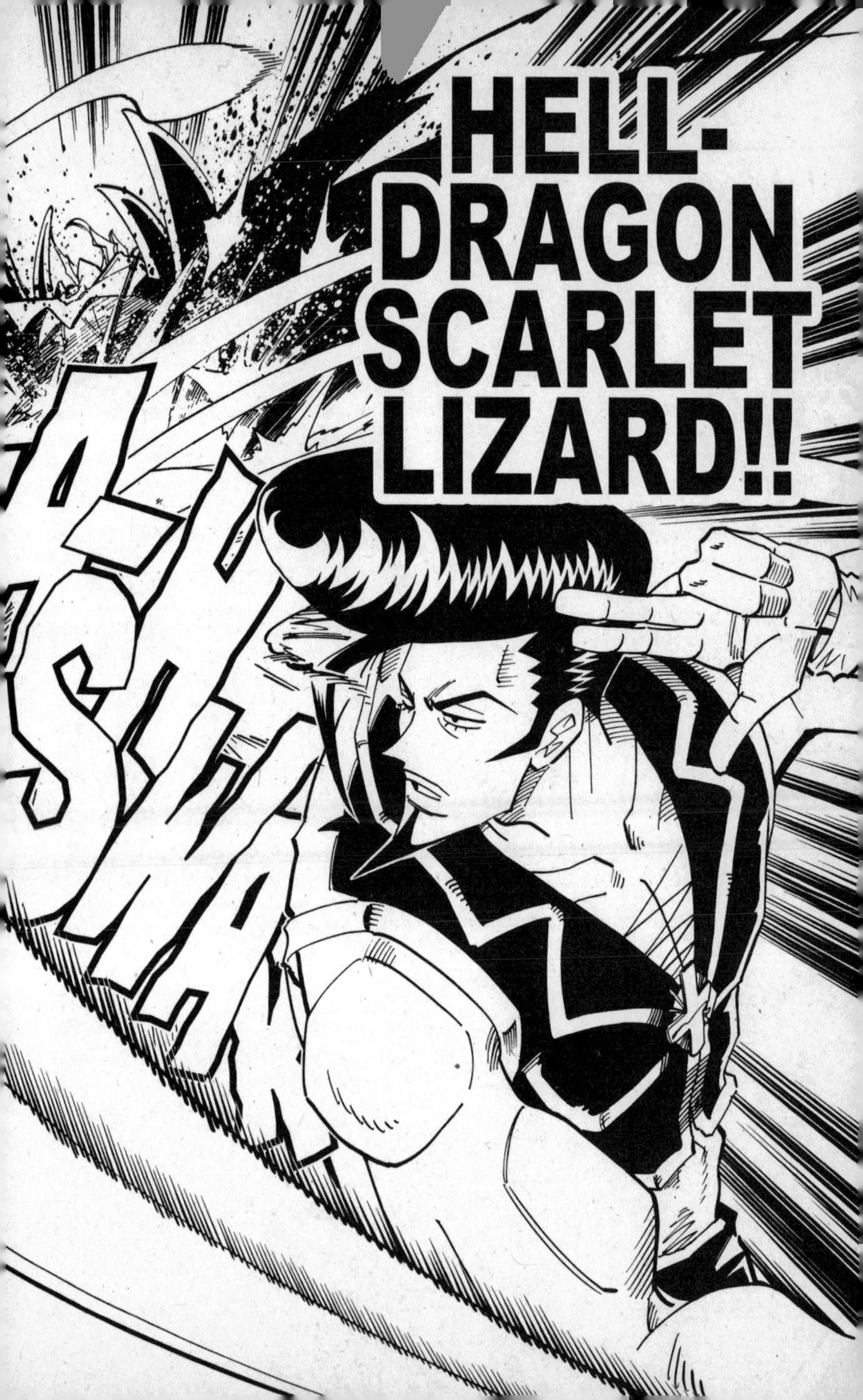
HELL. DRAGON SCARLET LIZARD!!

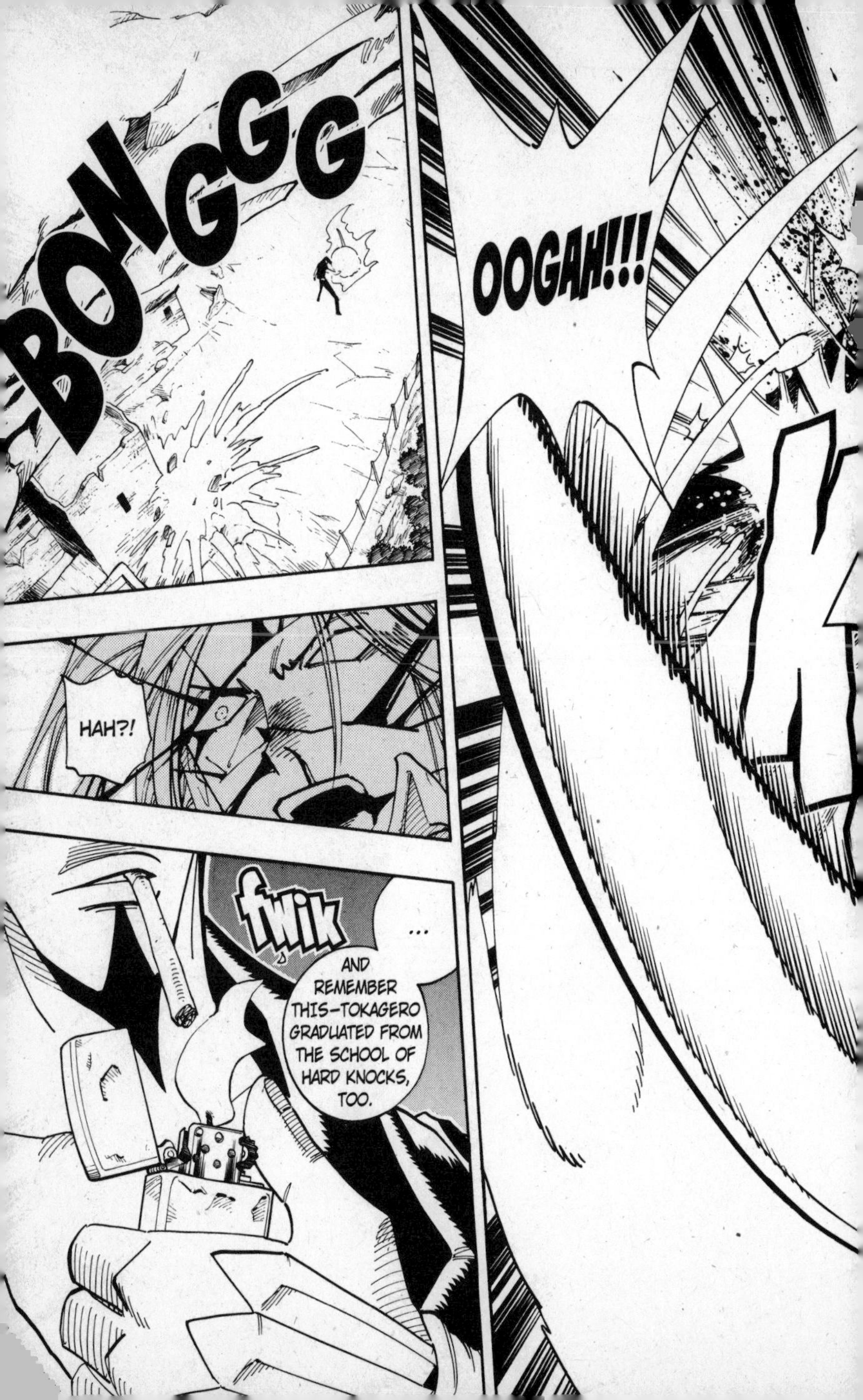
OOGAH!!!
BONGGG
HAH?!
fwik
...
AND REMEMBER THIS—TOKAGERO GRADUATED FROM THE SCHOOL OF HARD KNOCKS, TOO.

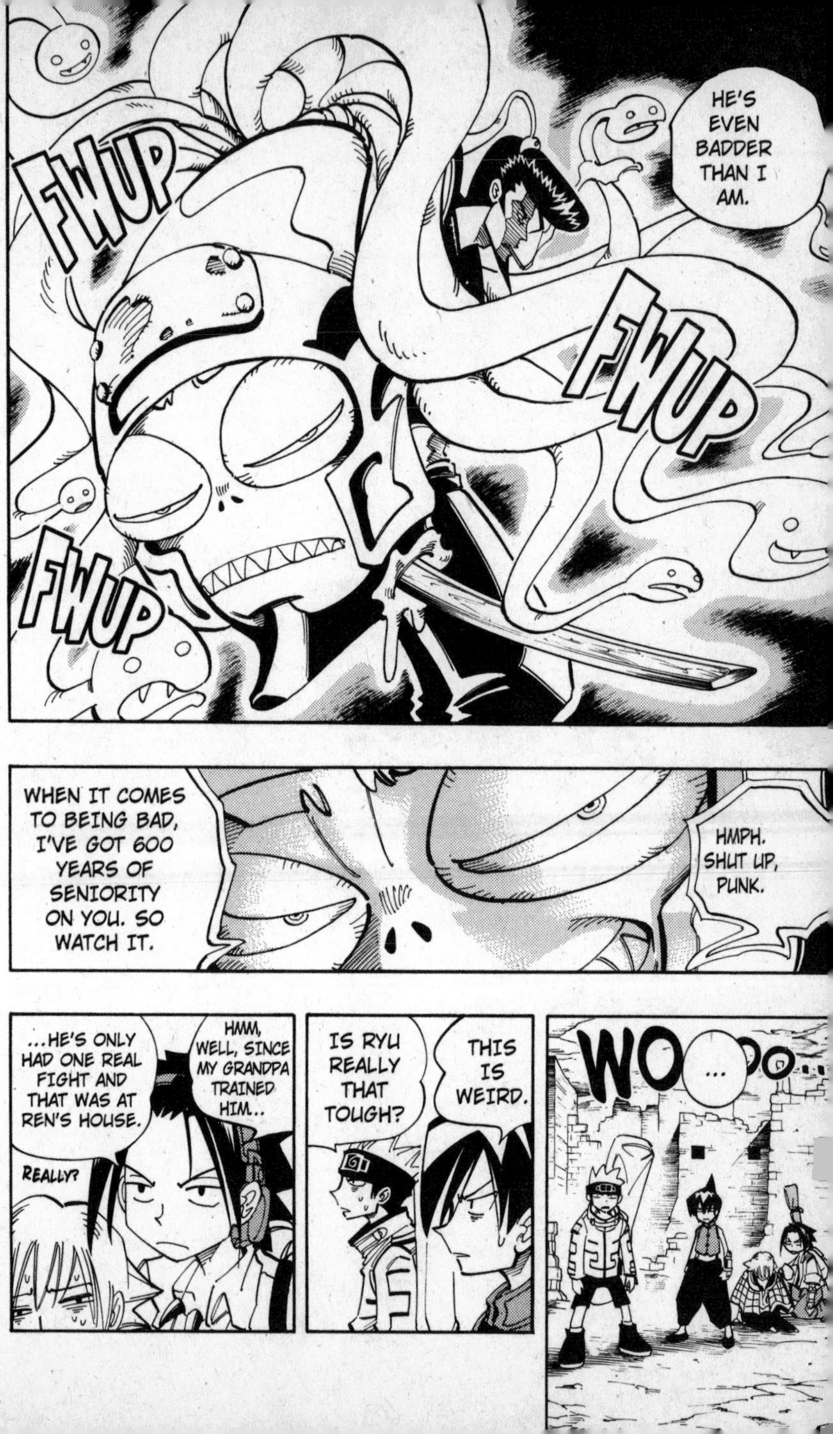
HE'S EVEN BADDER THAN I AM.
FWUP
FWUP
FWUP
HMPH. SHUT UP, PUNK.
WHEN IT COMES TO BEING BAD, I'VE GOT 600 YEARS OF SENIORITY ON YOU. SO WATCH IT.
WOOOO...
...
THIS IS WEIRD.
IS RYU REALLY THAT TOUGH?
HMM, WELL, SINCE MY GRANDPA TRAINED HIM...
...HE'S ONLY HAD ONE REAL FIGHT AND THAT WAS AT REN'S HOUSE.
REALLY?

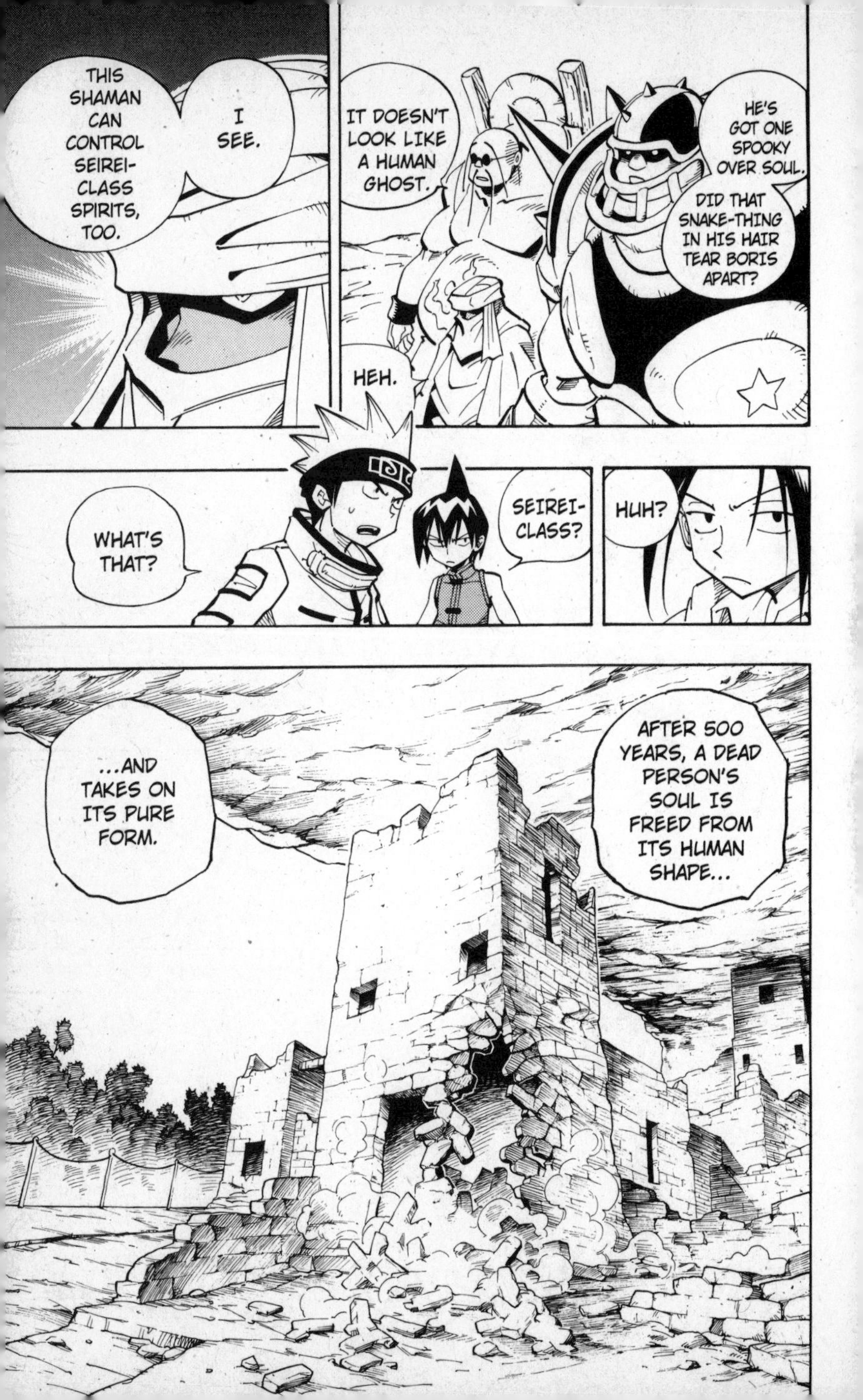
HE'S GOT ONE SPOOKY OVER SOUL.
DID THAT SNAKE-THING IN HIS HAIR TEAR BORIS APART?
IT DOESN'T LOOK LIKE A HUMAN GHOST.
HEH.
I SEE.
THIS SHAMAN CAN CONTROL SEIREI-CLASS SPIRITS, TOO.
HUH?
SEIREI-CLASS?
WHAT'S THAT?
AFTER 500 YEARS, A DEAD PERSON'S SOUL IS FREED FROM ITS HUMAN SHAPE...
...AND TAKES ON ITS PURE FORM.

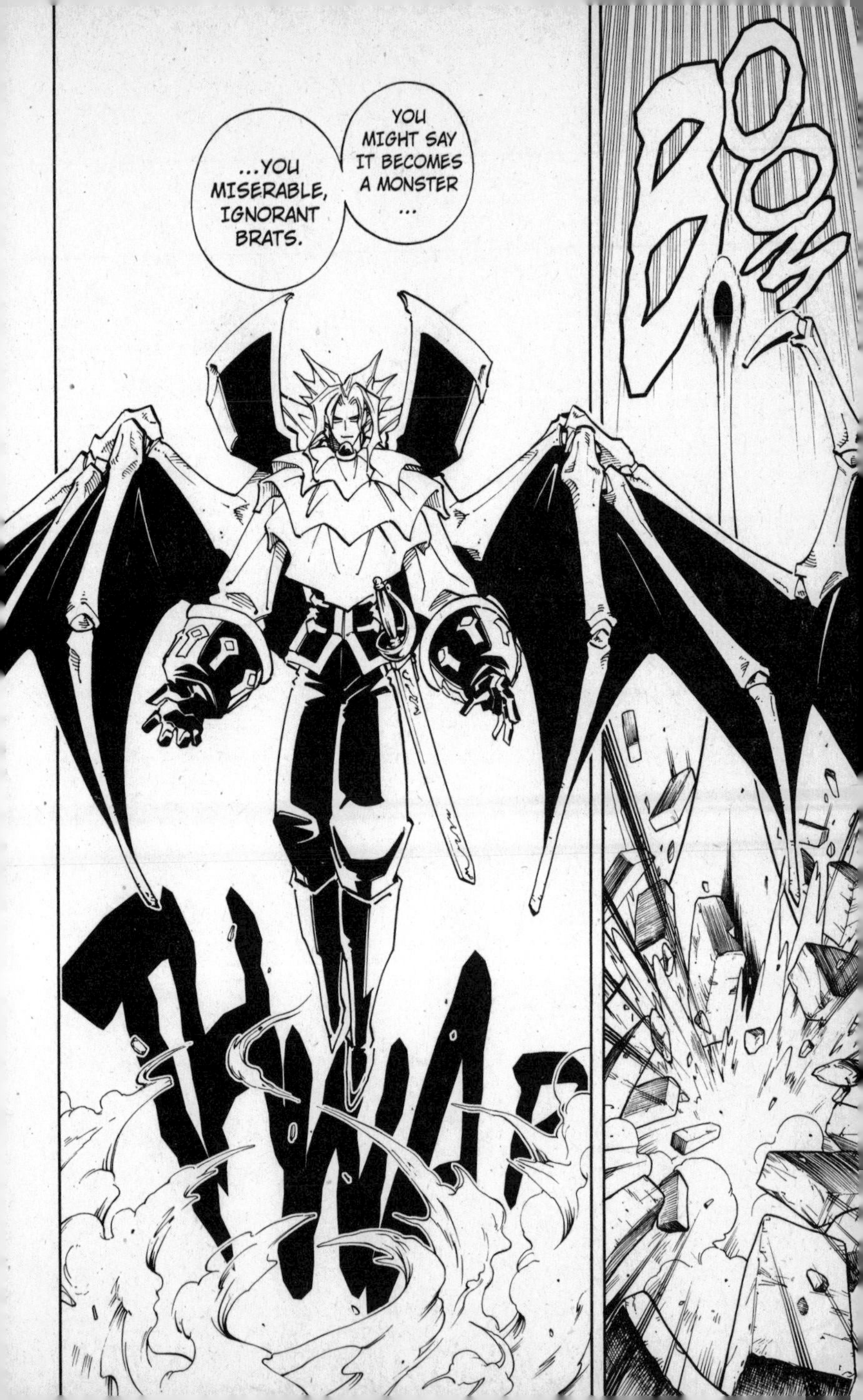
BOOOM
YOU MIGHT SAY IT BECOMES A MONSTER ...
...YOU MISERABLE, IGNORANT BRATS.

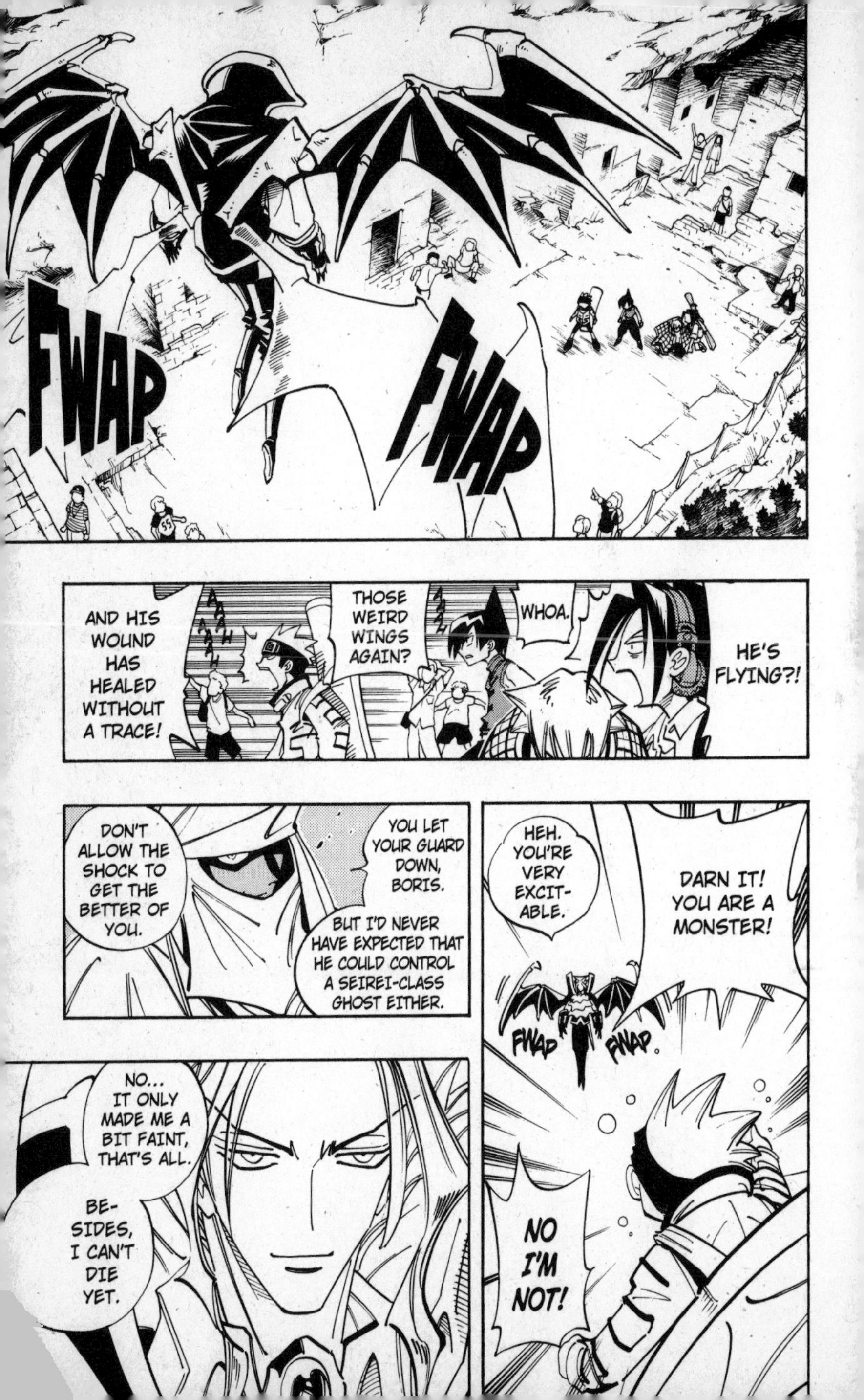
FWAP
FWAP
HE'S FLYING?!
WHOA.
THOSE WEIRD WINGS AGAIN?
AND HIS WOUND HAS HEALED WITHOUT A TRACE!
DARN IT! YOU ARE A MONSTER!
HEH. YOU'RE VERY EXCIT-ABLE.
FWAP
FWAP
NO I'M NOT!
YOU LET YOUR GUARD DOWN, BORIS.
DON'T ALLOW THE SHOCK TO GET THE BETTER OF YOU.
BUT I'D NEVER HAVE EXPECTED THAT HE COULD CONTROL A SEIREI-CLASS GHOST EITHER.
NO... IT ONLY MADE ME A BIT FAINT, THAT'S ALL.
BE-SIDES, I CAN'T DIE YET.

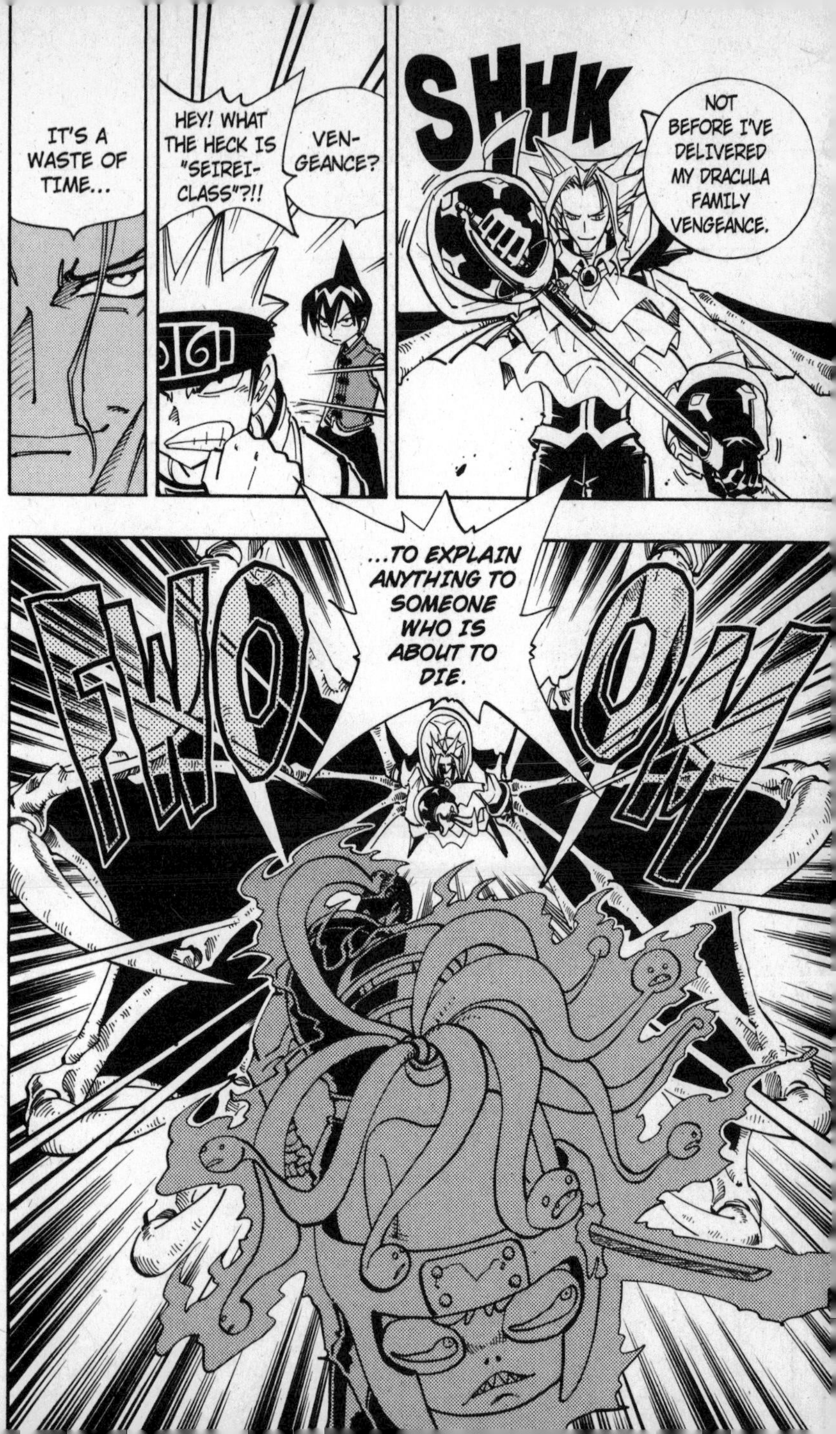
SHHK
NOT BEFORE I'VE DELIVERED MY DRACULA FAMILY VENGEANCE.
VEN-GEANCE?
HEY! WHAT THE HECK IS "SEIREI-CLASS"?!!
IT'S A WASTE OF TIME...
...TO EXPLAIN ANYTHING TO SOMEONE WHO IS ABOUT TO DIE.
FWOOM

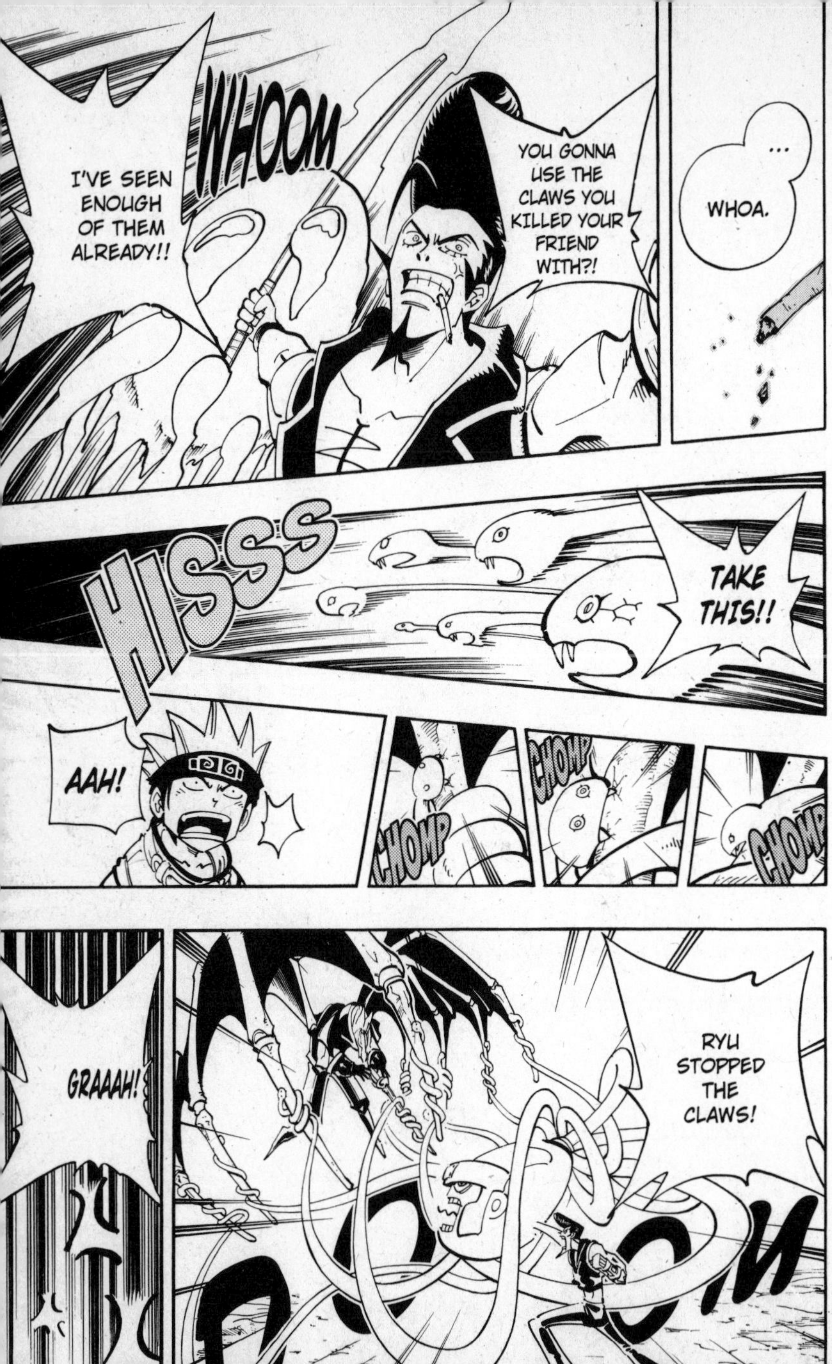
...
WHOA.
YOU GONNA USE THE CLAWS YOU KILLED YOUR FRIEND WITH?!
WHOOM
I'VE SEEN ENOUGH OF THEM ALREADY!!
TAKE THIS!!
HISSS
CHOMP
CHOMP
CHOMP
AAH!
RYU STOPPED THE CLAWS!
GRAAAH!

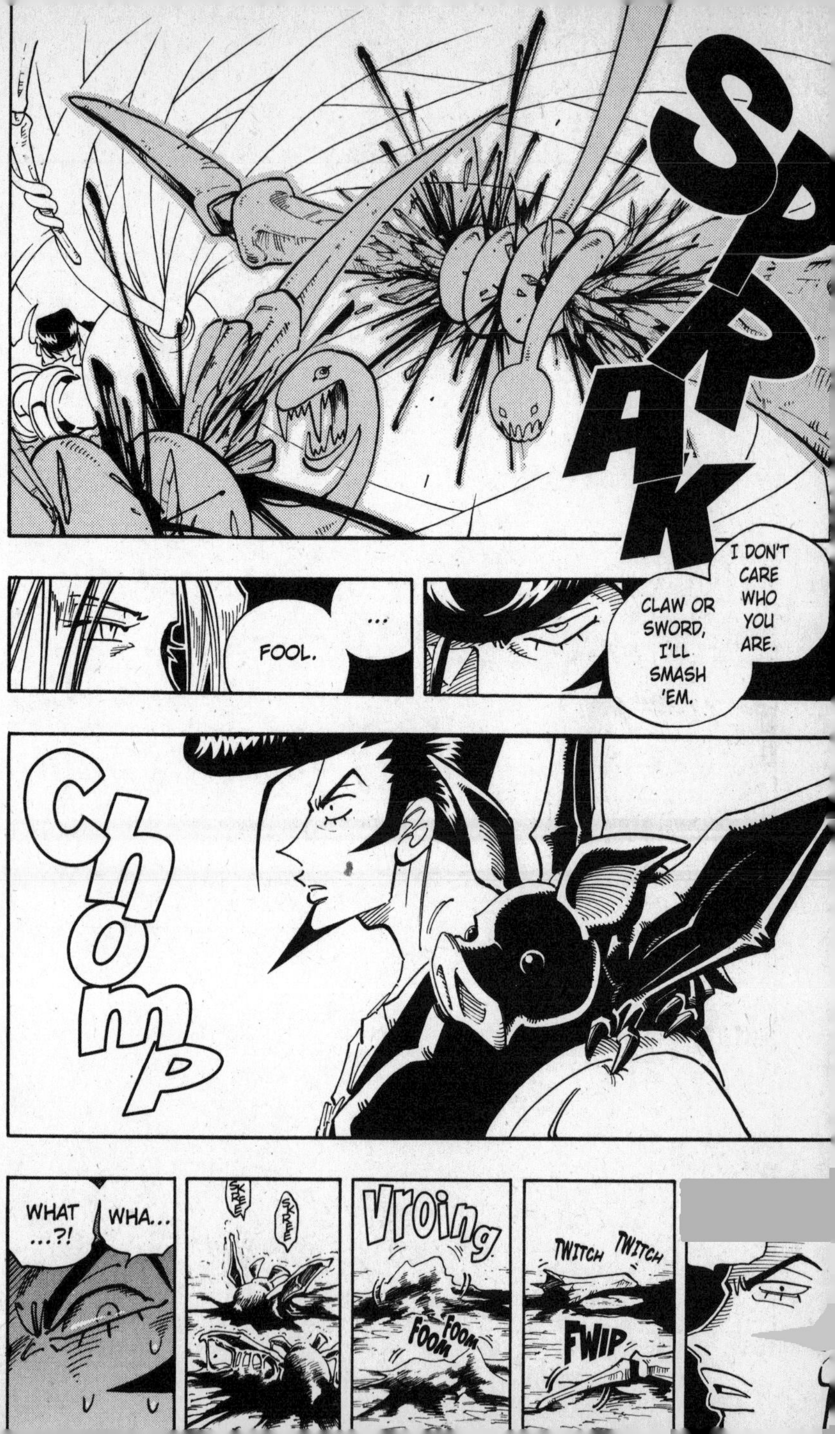
SPRAK
I DON'T CARE WHO YOU ARE.
CLAW OR SWORD, I'LL SMASH 'EM.
...
FOOL.
Chomp
TWITCH TWITCH
FWIP
Vroing
FOOM FOOM
SKREE
SKREE
WHA...
WHAT ...?!

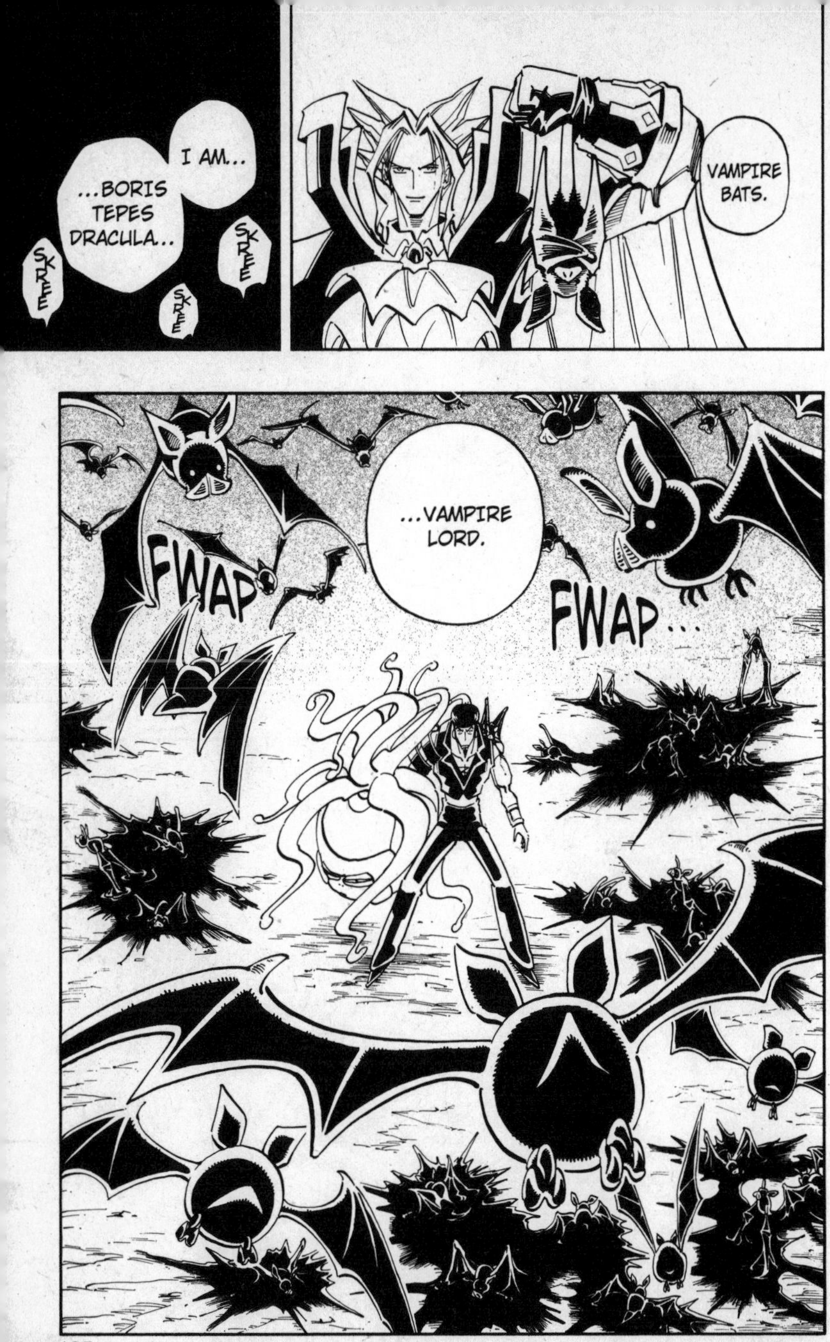
VAMPIRE BATS.
I AM...
...BORIS TEPES DRACULA...
SKREE
SKREE
SKREE
...VAMPIRE LORD.
FWAP...
FWAP

SHAMAN
KING
11

GUM

Reincarnation 98: The Smell of Sadness

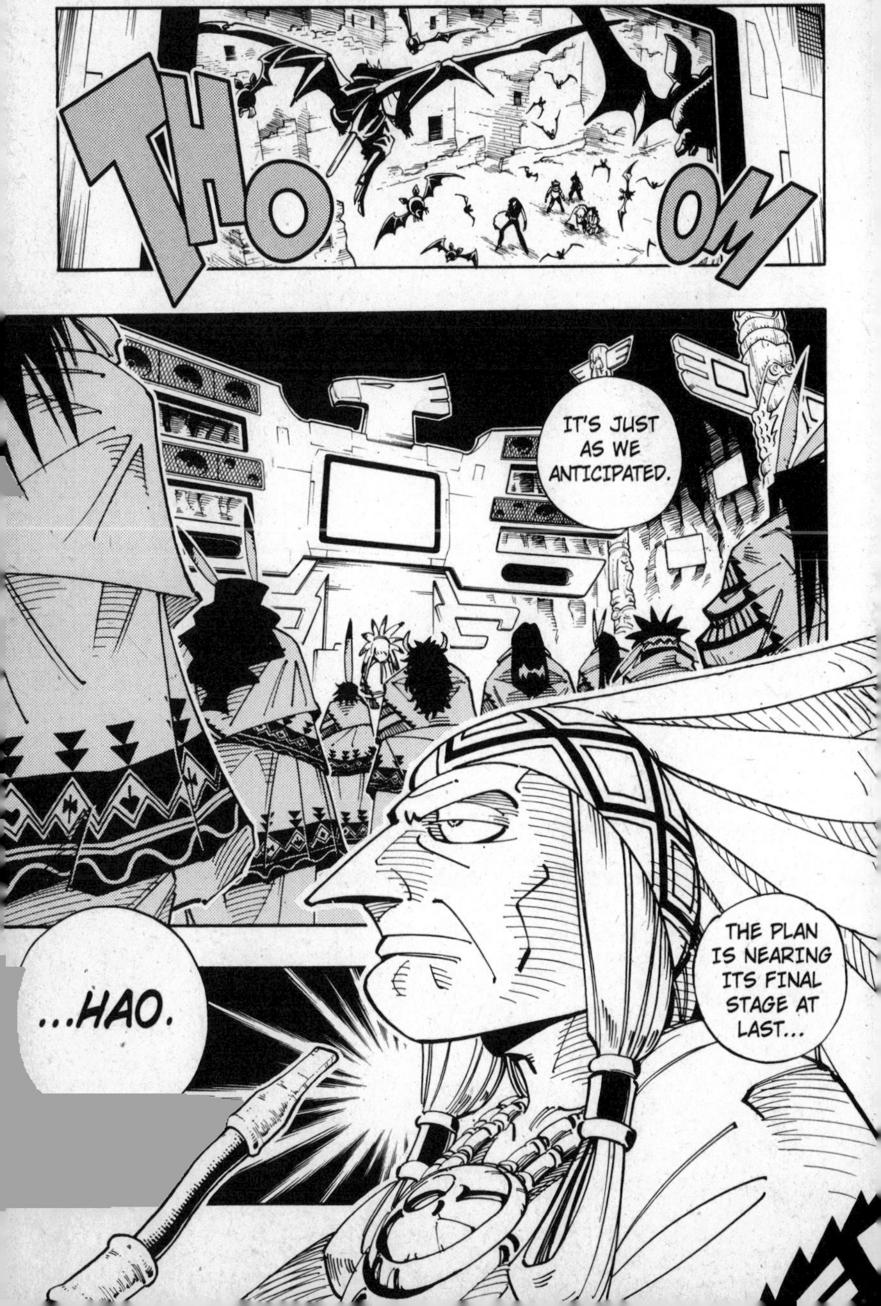
THOOM
IT'S JUST AS WE ANTICIPATED.
THE PLAN IS NEARING ITS FINAL STAGE AT LAST...
...HAO.

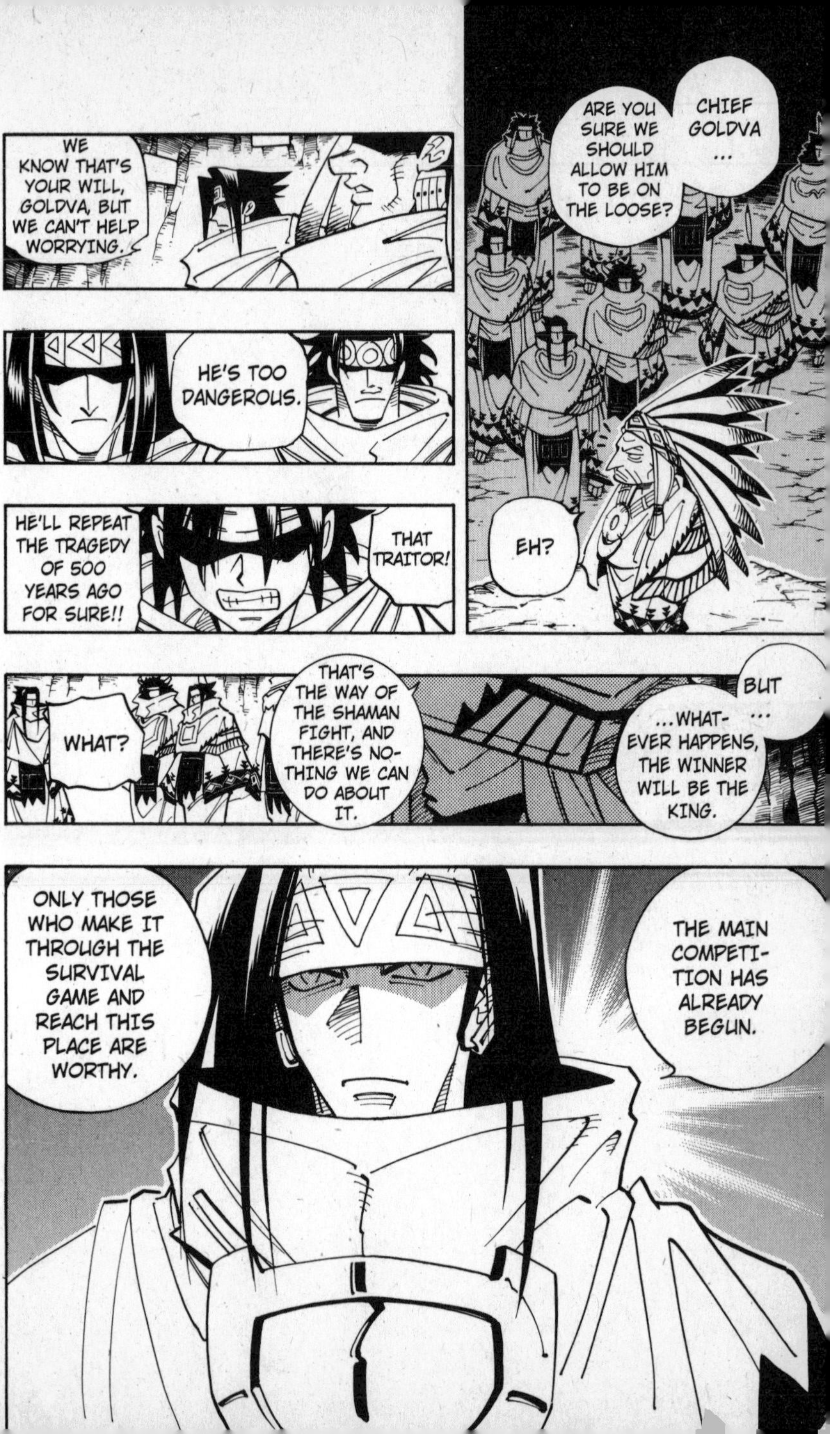
CHIEF GOLDVA ...
ARE YOU SURE WE SHOULD ALLOW HIM TO BE ON THE LOOSE?
EH?
WE KNOW THAT'S YOUR WILL, GOLDVA, BUT WE CAN'T HELP WORRYING.
HE'S TOO DANGEROUS.
THAT TRAITOR!
HE'LL REPEAT THE TRAGEDY OF 500 YEARS AGO FOR SURE!!
BUT ...
...WHATEVER HAPPENS, THE WINNER WILL BE THE KING.
THAT'S THE WAY OF THE SHAMAN FIGHT, AND THERE'S NOTHING WE CAN DO ABOUT IT.
WHAT?
THE MAIN COMPETITION HAS ALREADY BEGUN.
ONLY THOSE WHO MAKE IT THROUGH THE SURVIVAL GAME AND REACH THIS PLACE ARE WORTHY.

Reincarnation 98: The Smell of Sadness

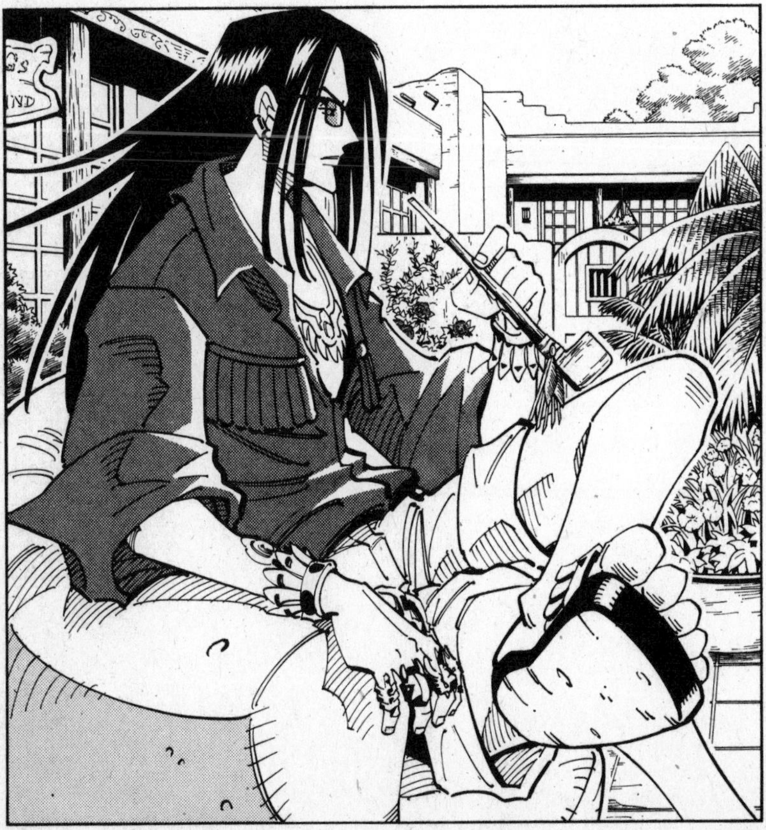

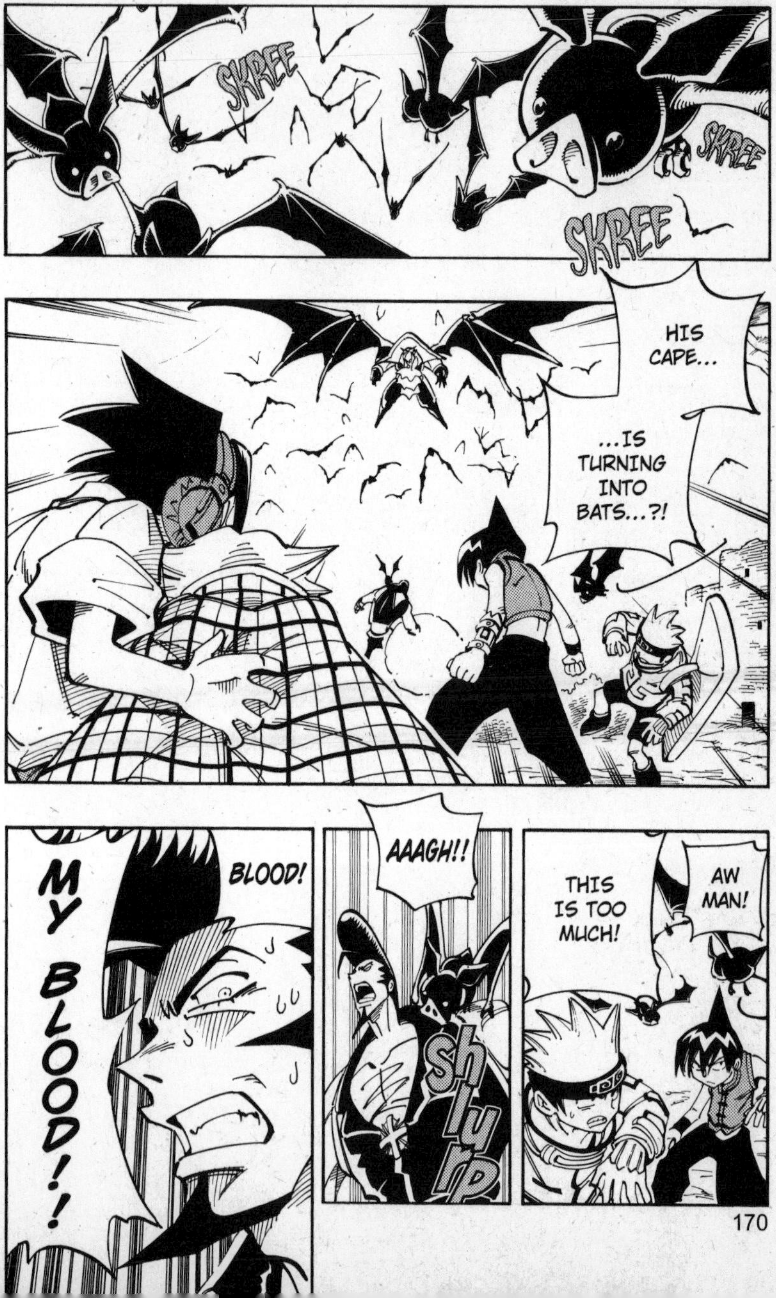
SKREE
SKREE
SKREE
HIS CAPE...
...IS TURNING INTO BATS...?!
AW MAN!
THIS IS TOO MUCH!
AAAGH!!
shlurp
BLOOD!
MY BLOOD!!

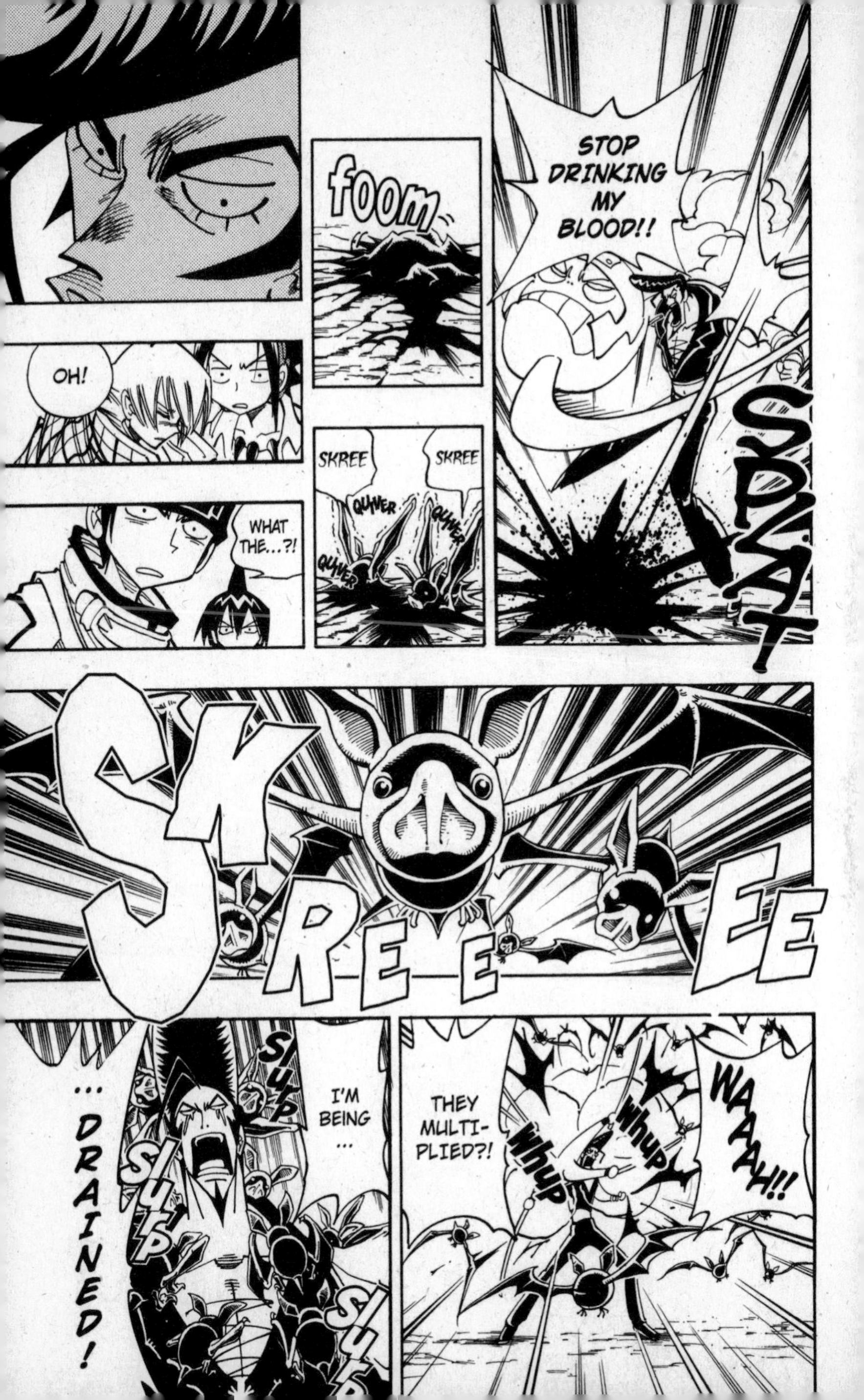
STOP DRINKING MY BLOOD!!
SPLAT
foom
SKREE
SKREE
QUIVER
QUIVER
QUIVER
OH!
WHAT THE...?!
SKREEEE
WAAAAH!!
whup
whup
THEY MULTI-PLIED?!
I'M BEING ...
... DRAINED!
SLURP
SLURP
SLURP
SLURP

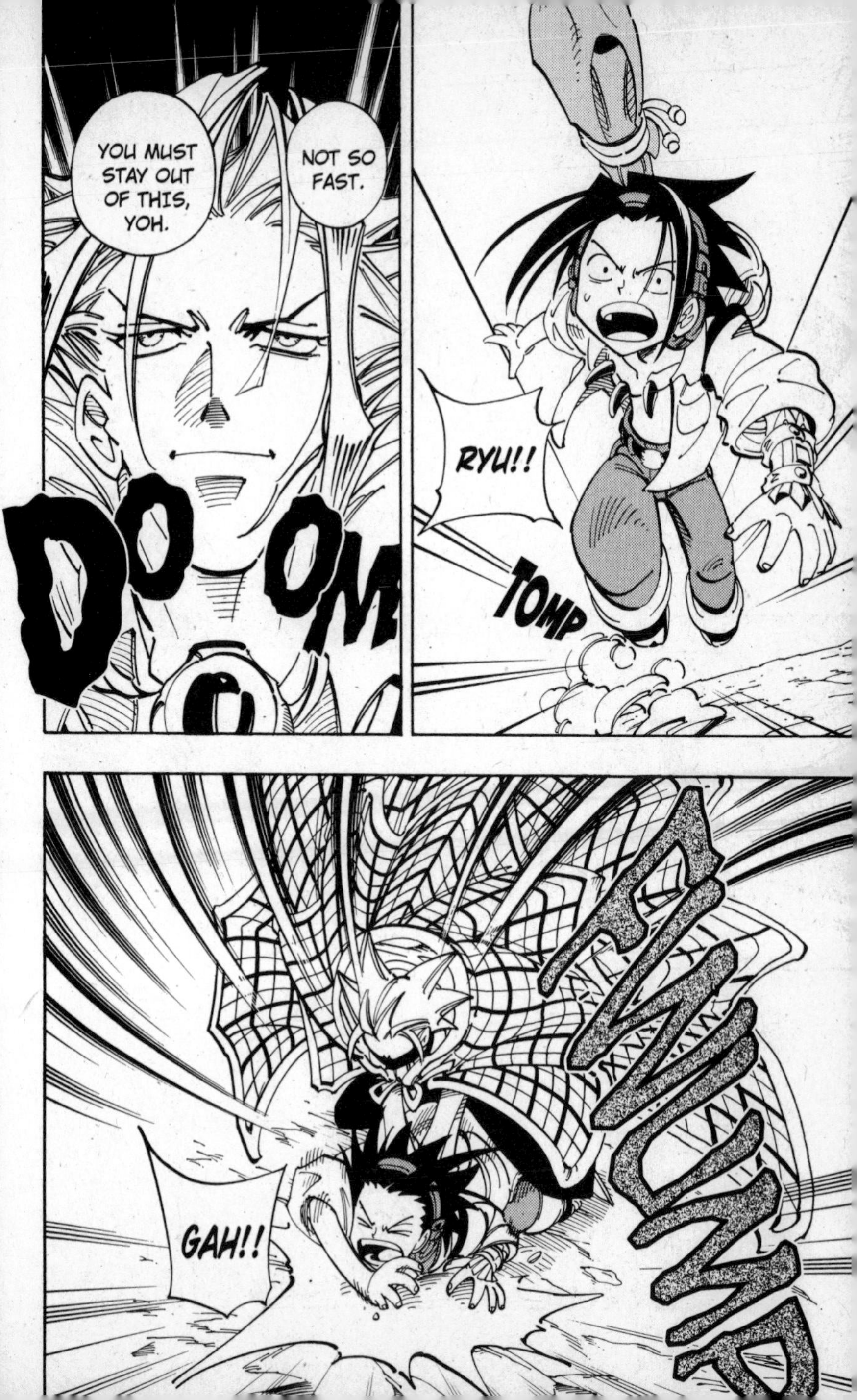
RYU!!
TOMP
NOT SO FAST.
YOU MUST STAY OUT OF THIS, YOH.
DOOM
GAH!!

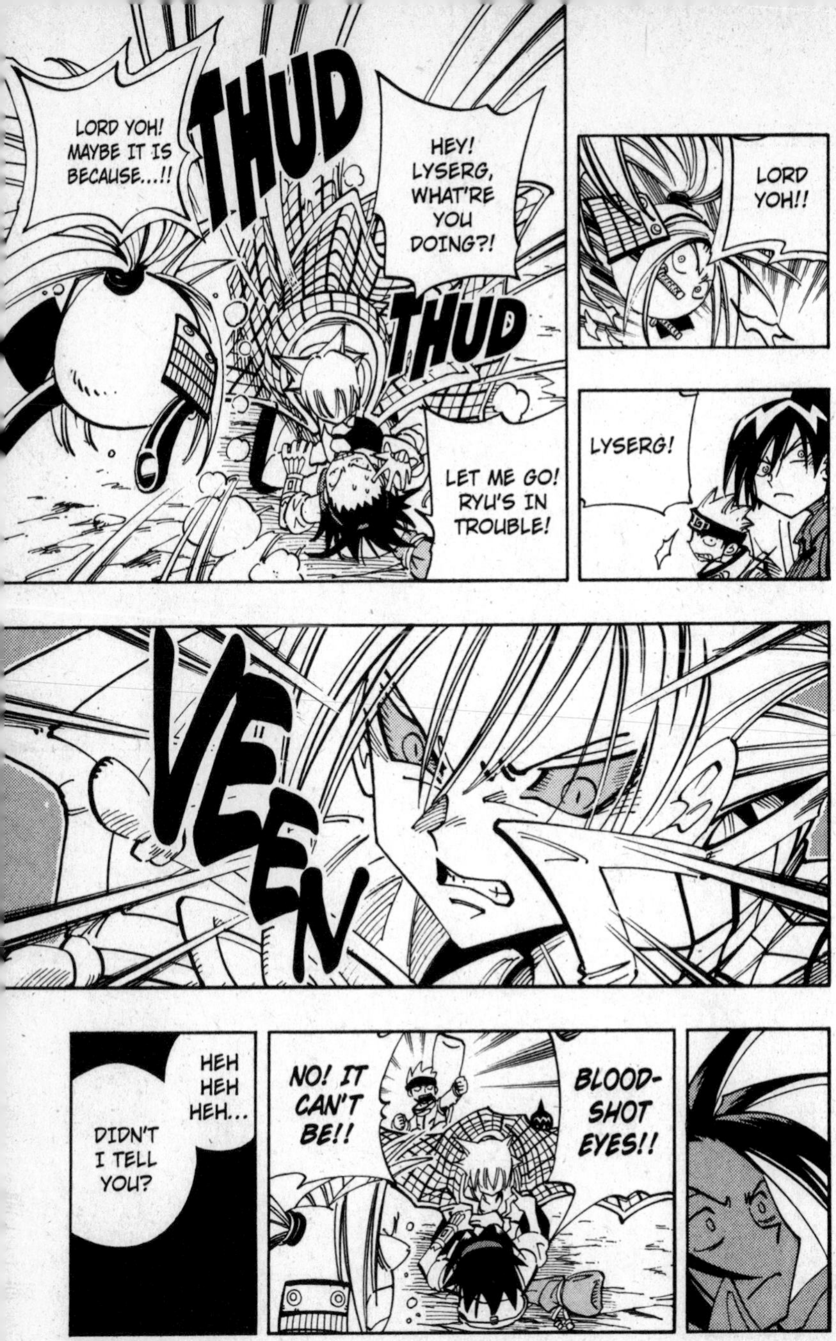
LORD YOH!!
LYSERG!
HEY! LYSERG, WHAT'RE YOU DOING?!
THUD
LORD YOH! MAYBE IT IS BECAUSE...!!
THUD
LET ME GO! RYU'S IN TROUBLE!
VEEN
BLOOD-SHOT EYES!!
NO! IT CAN'T BE!!
HEH HEH HEH...
DIDN'T I TELL YOU?

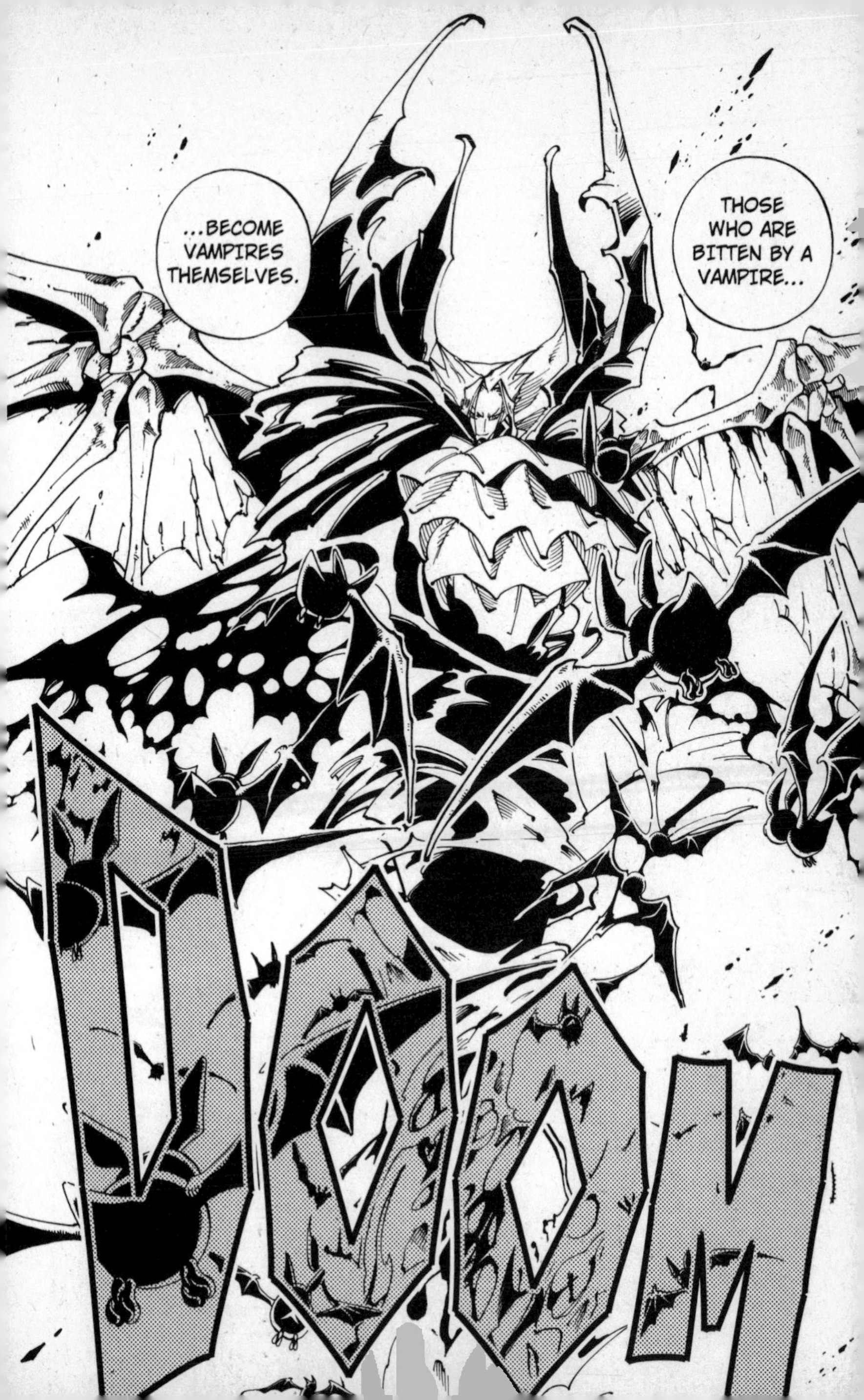
THOSE WHO ARE BITTEN BY A VAMPIRE...
...BECOME VAMPIRES THEMSELVES.
DOOM

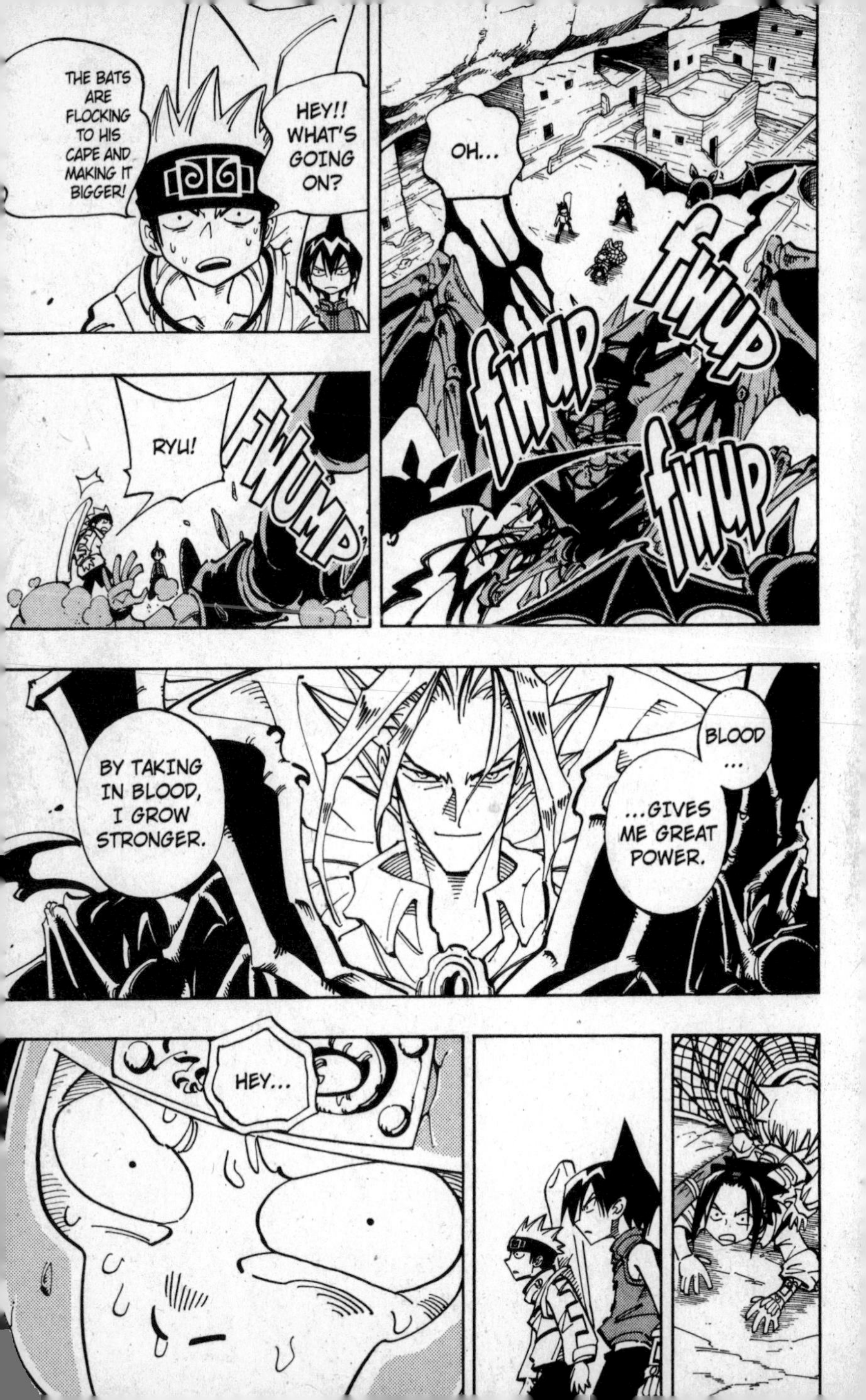
OH...
fwup
fwup
fwup
HEY!! WHAT'S GOING ON?
THE BATS ARE FLOCKING TO HIS CAPE AND MAKING IT BIGGER!
RYU!
FWUMP
BLOOD...
...GIVES ME GREAT POWER.
BY TAKING IN BLOOD, I GROW STRONGER.
HEY...

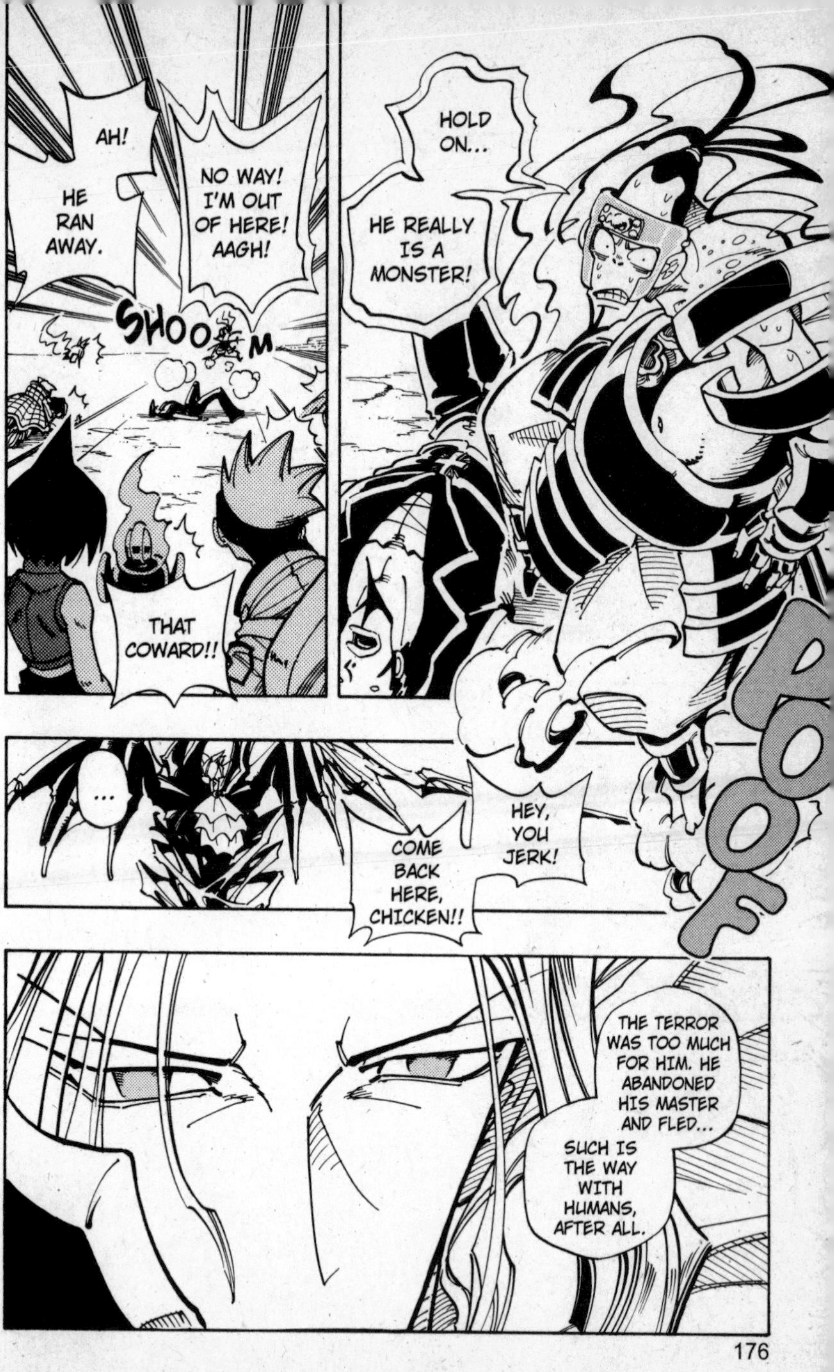
HOLD ON...
HE REALLY IS A MONSTER!
NO WAY! I'M OUT OF HERE! AAGH!
AH!
HE RAN AWAY.
SHOOOM
THAT COWARD!!
POOF
HEY, YOU JERK!
COME BACK HERE, CHICKEN!!
...
THE TERROR WAS TOO MUCH FOR HIM. HE ABANDONED HIS MASTER AND FLED...
SUCH IS THE WAY WITH HUMANS, AFTER ALL.

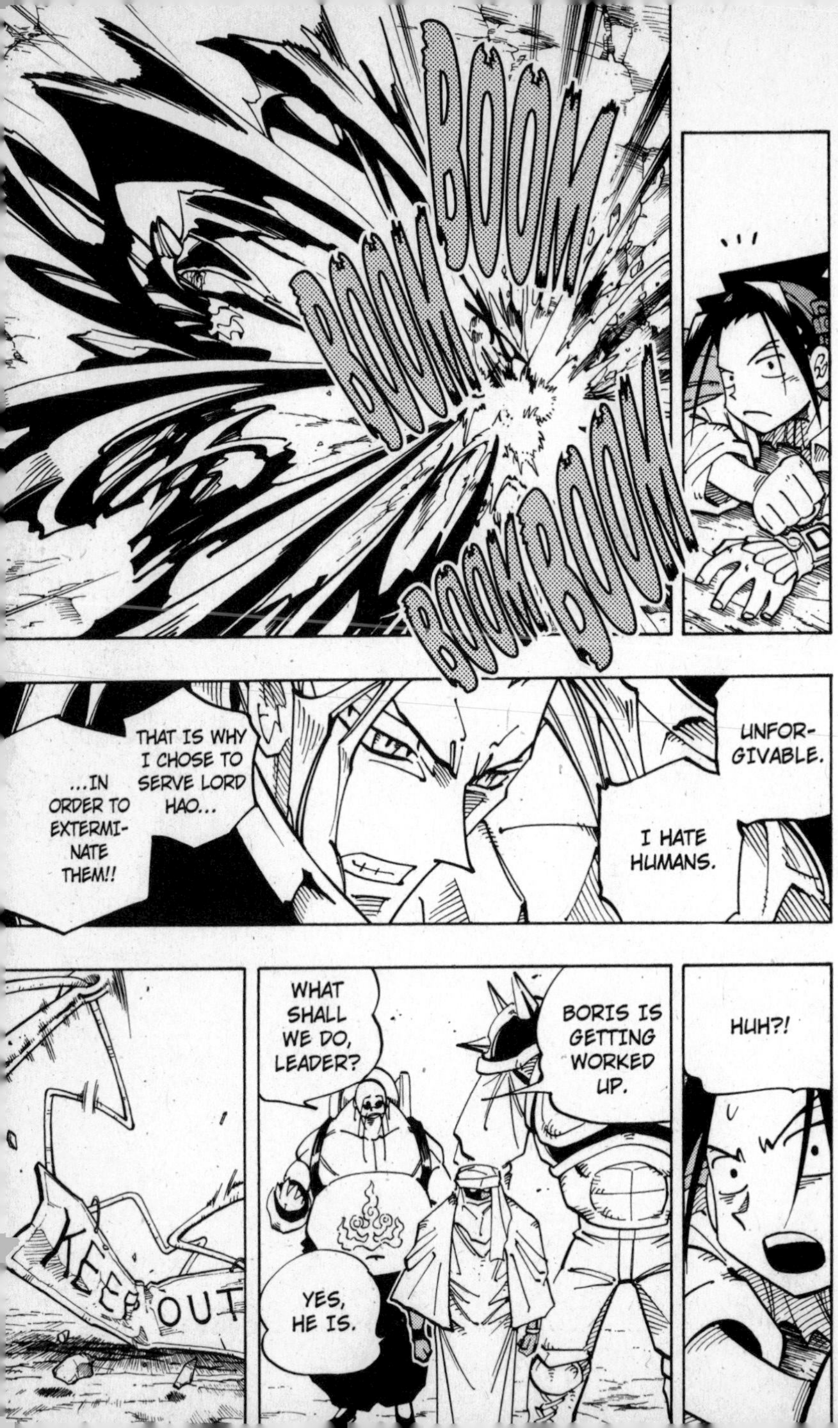
BOOM BOOM
BOOM
BOOM BOOM
UNFOR-
GIVABLE.
I HATE
HUMANS.
THAT IS WHY
I CHOSE TO
SERVE LORD
HAO...
...IN
ORDER TO
EXTERMI-
NATE
THEM!!
HUH?!
BORIS IS
GETTING
WORKED
UP.
WHAT
SHALL
WE DO,
LEADER?
YES,
HE IS.
KEEP OUT

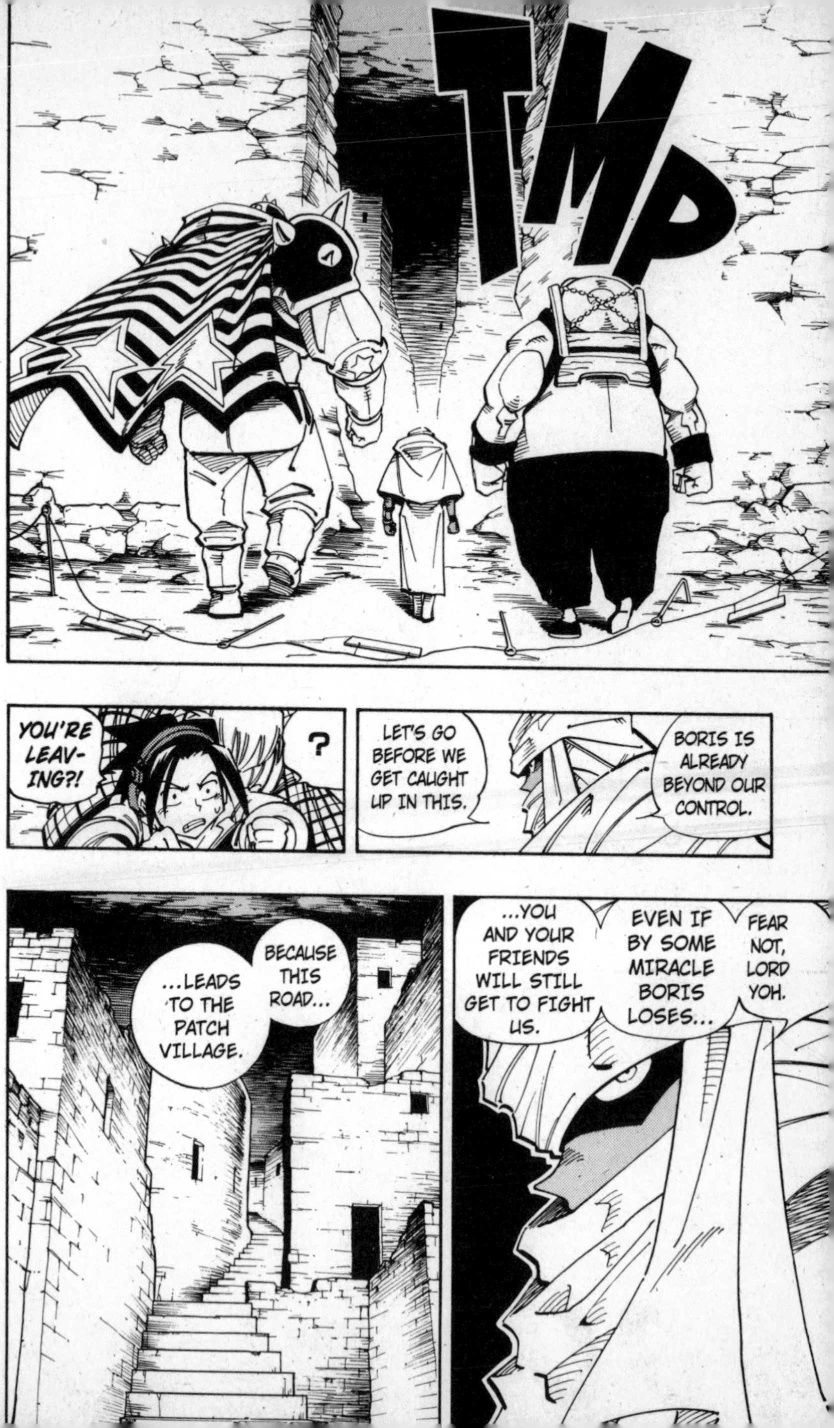
TMP
BORIS IS ALREADY BEYOND OUR CONTROL.
LET'S GO BEFORE WE GET CAUGHT UP IN THIS.
?
YOU'RE LEAV-ING?!
FEAR NOT, LORD YOH.
EVEN IF BY SOME MIRACLE BORIS LOSES...
...YOU AND YOUR FRIENDS WILL STILL GET TO FIGHT US.
BECAUSE THIS ROAD...
...LEADS TO THE PATCH VILLAGE.

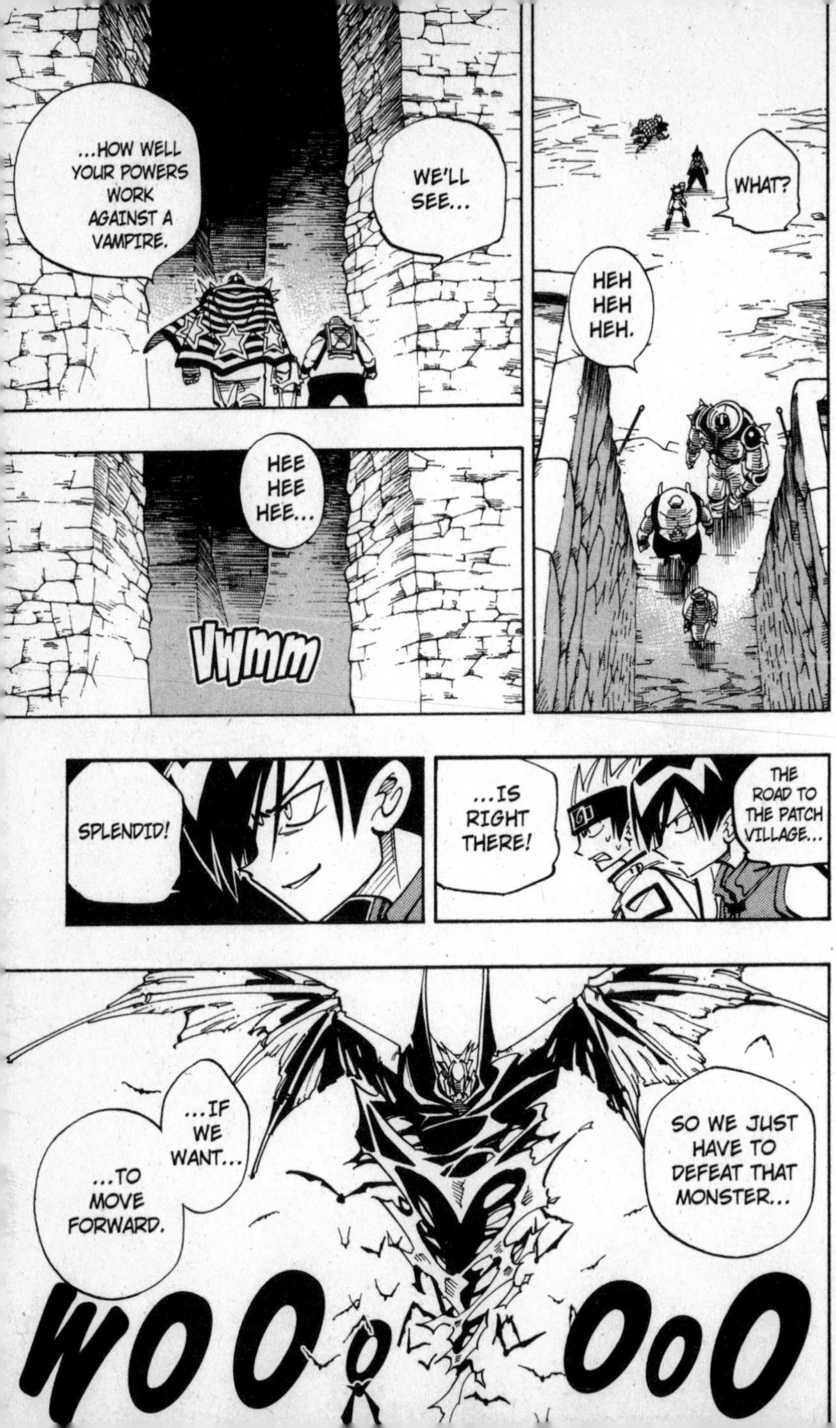
WHAT?
HEH HEH HEH.
WE'LL SEE...
...HOW WELL YOUR POWERS WORK AGAINST A VAMPIRE.
HEE HEE HEE...
VWMM
THE ROAD TO THE PATCH VILLAGE...
...IS RIGHT THERE!
SPLENDID!
SO WE JUST HAVE TO DEFEAT THAT MONSTER...
...IF WE WANT...
...TO MOVE FORWARD.
WOOoOOO

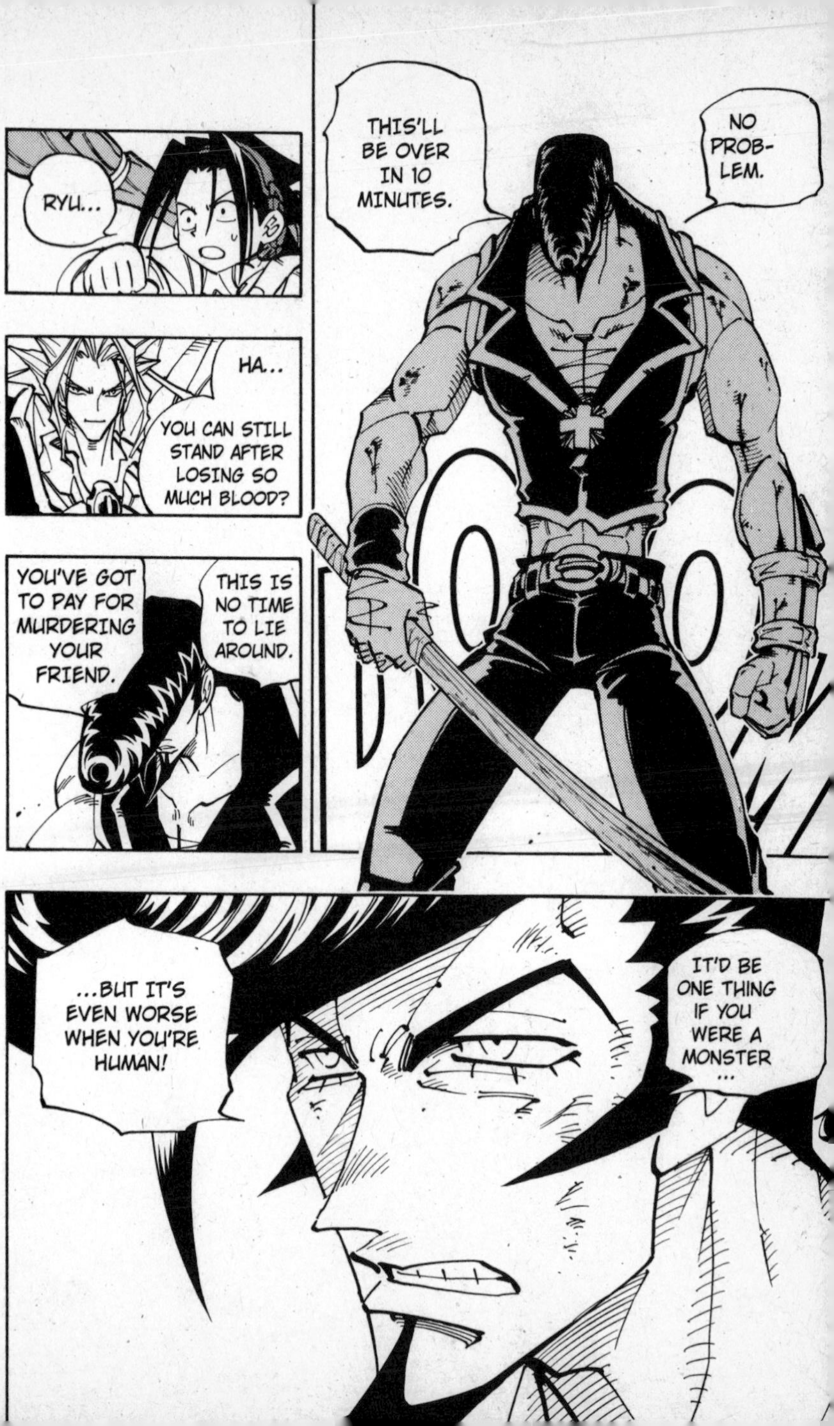
NO PROB-LEM.
THIS'LL BE OVER IN 10 MINUTES.
RYU...
HA...
YOU CAN STILL STAND AFTER LOSING SO MUCH BLOOD?
THIS IS NO TIME TO LIE AROUND.
YOU'VE GOT TO PAY FOR MURDERING YOUR FRIEND.
IT'D BE ONE THING IF YOU WERE A MONSTER...
...BUT IT'S EVEN WORSE WHEN YOU'RE HUMAN!

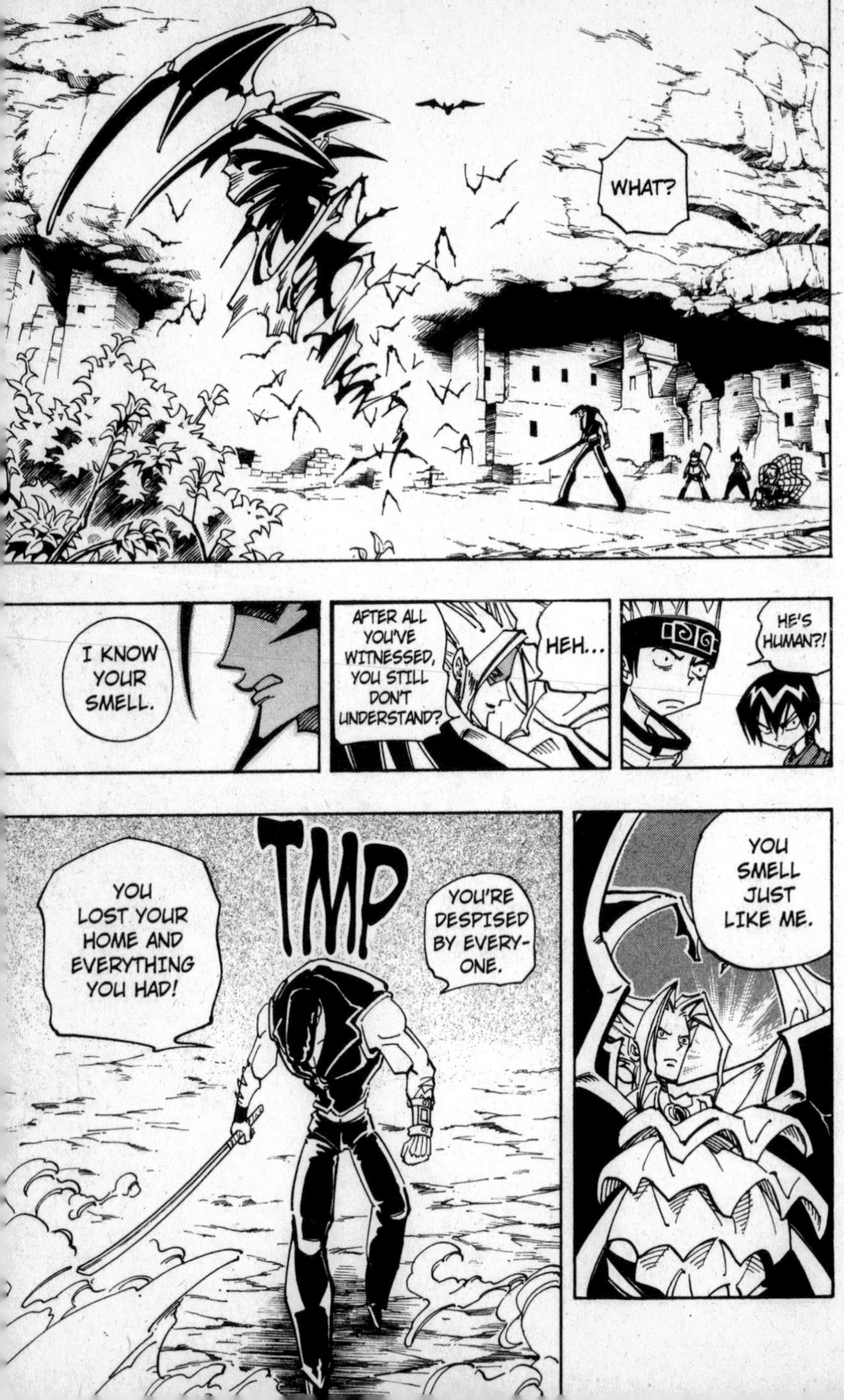
WHAT?
HE'S HUMAN?!
HEH...
AFTER ALL YOU'VE WITNESSED, YOU STILL DON'T UNDERSTAND?
I KNOW YOUR SMELL.
YOU SMELL JUST LIKE ME.
TMP
YOU'RE DESPISED BY EVERY-ONE.
YOU LOST YOUR HOME AND EVERYTHING YOU HAD!

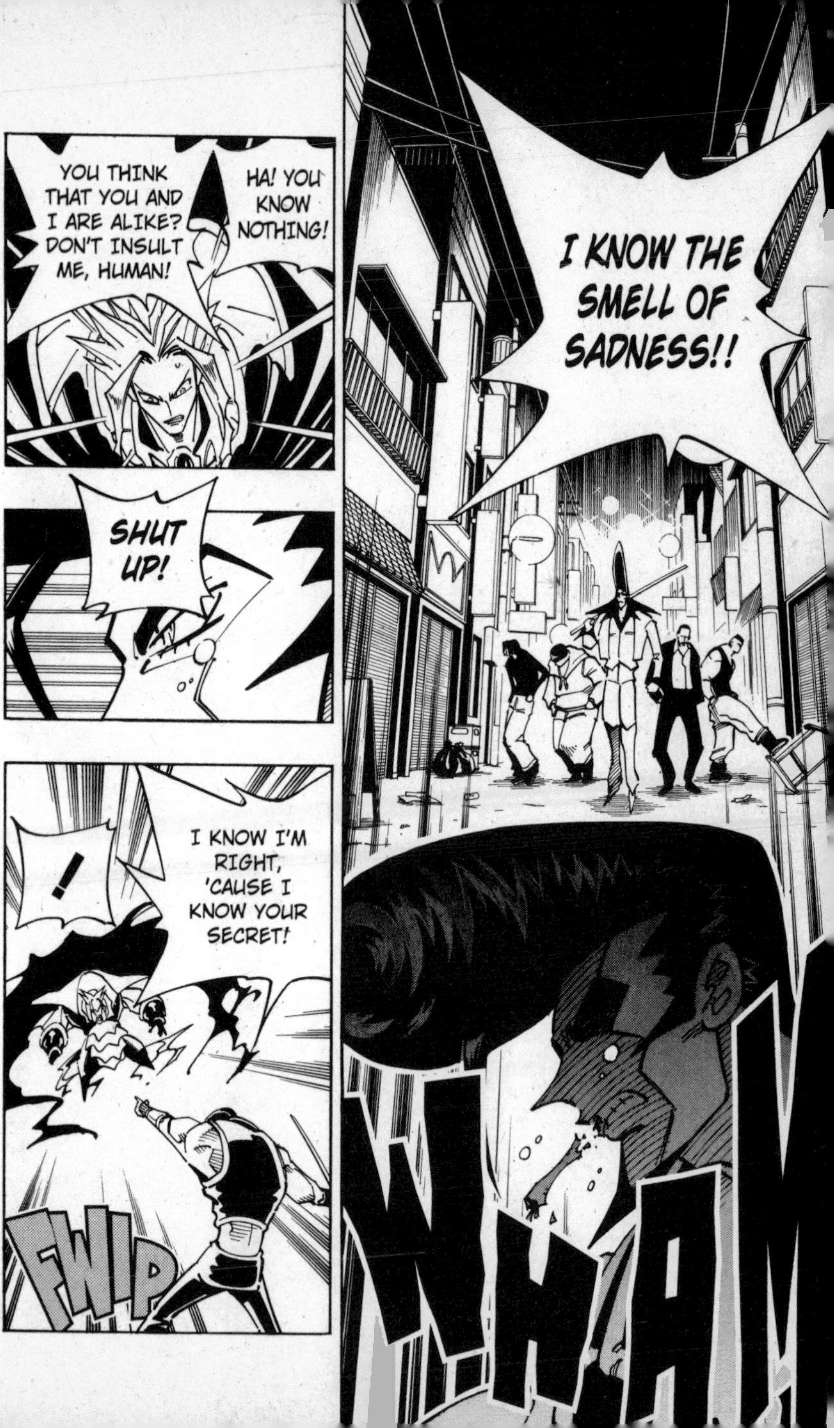
I KNOW THE SMELL OF SADNESS!!
WHAM
HA! YOU KNOW NOTHING!
YOU THINK THAT YOU AND I ARE ALIKE? DON'T INSULT ME, HUMAN!
SHUT UP!
I KNOW I'M RIGHT, 'CAUSE I KNOW YOUR SECRET!
!
FWIP

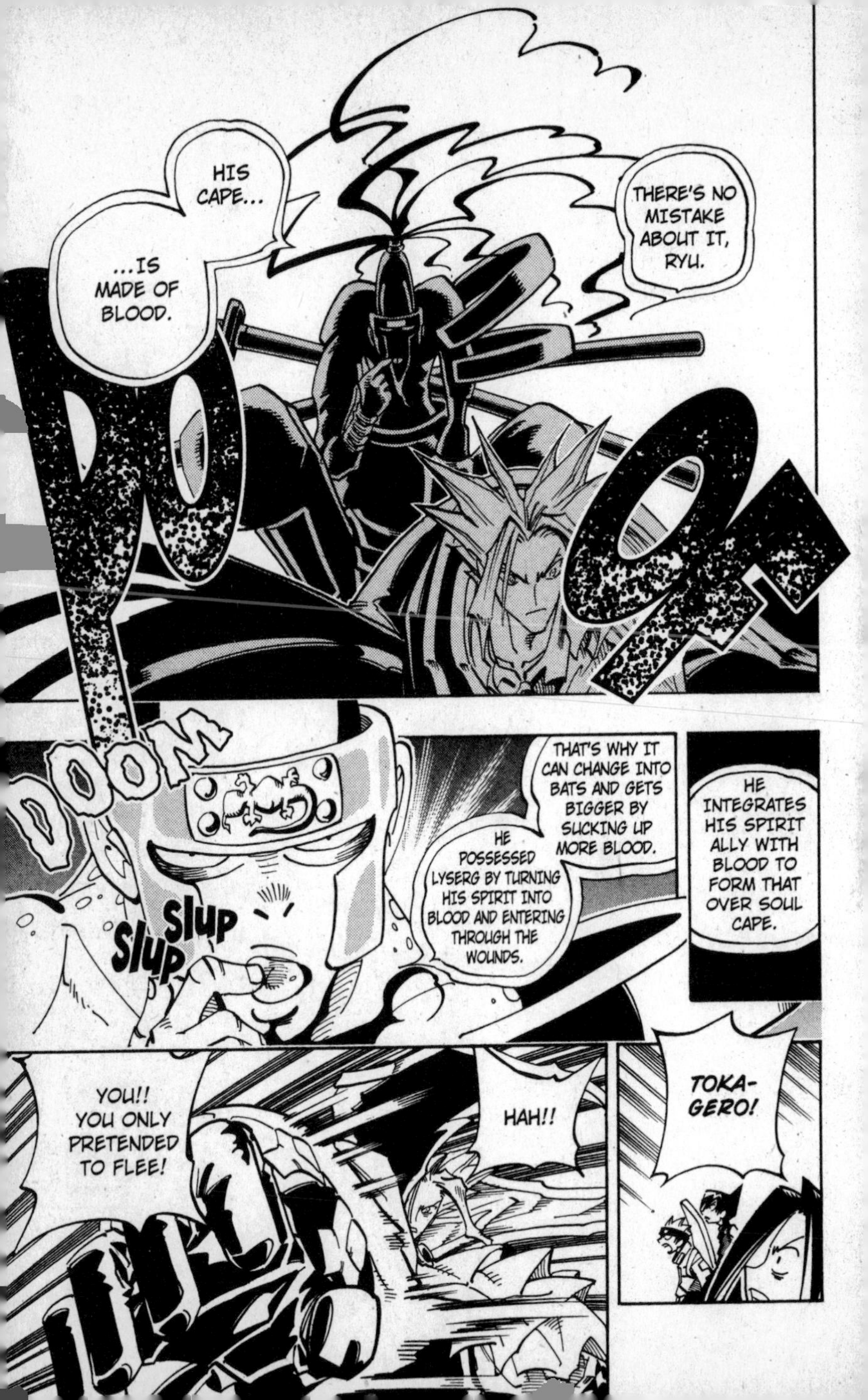
THERE'S NO MISTAKE ABOUT IT, RYU.
HIS CAPE...
...IS MADE OF BLOOD.
HE INTEGRATES HIS SPIRIT ALLY WITH BLOOD TO FORM THAT OVER SOUL CAPE.
THAT'S WHY IT CAN CHANGE INTO BATS AND GETS BIGGER BY SUCKING UP MORE BLOOD.
HE POSSESSED LYSERG BY TURNING HIS SPIRIT INTO BLOOD AND ENTERING THROUGH THE WOUNDS.
DOOOM
SLUP SLUP
TOKA-GERO!
HAH!!
YOU!! YOU ONLY PRETENDED TO FLEE!

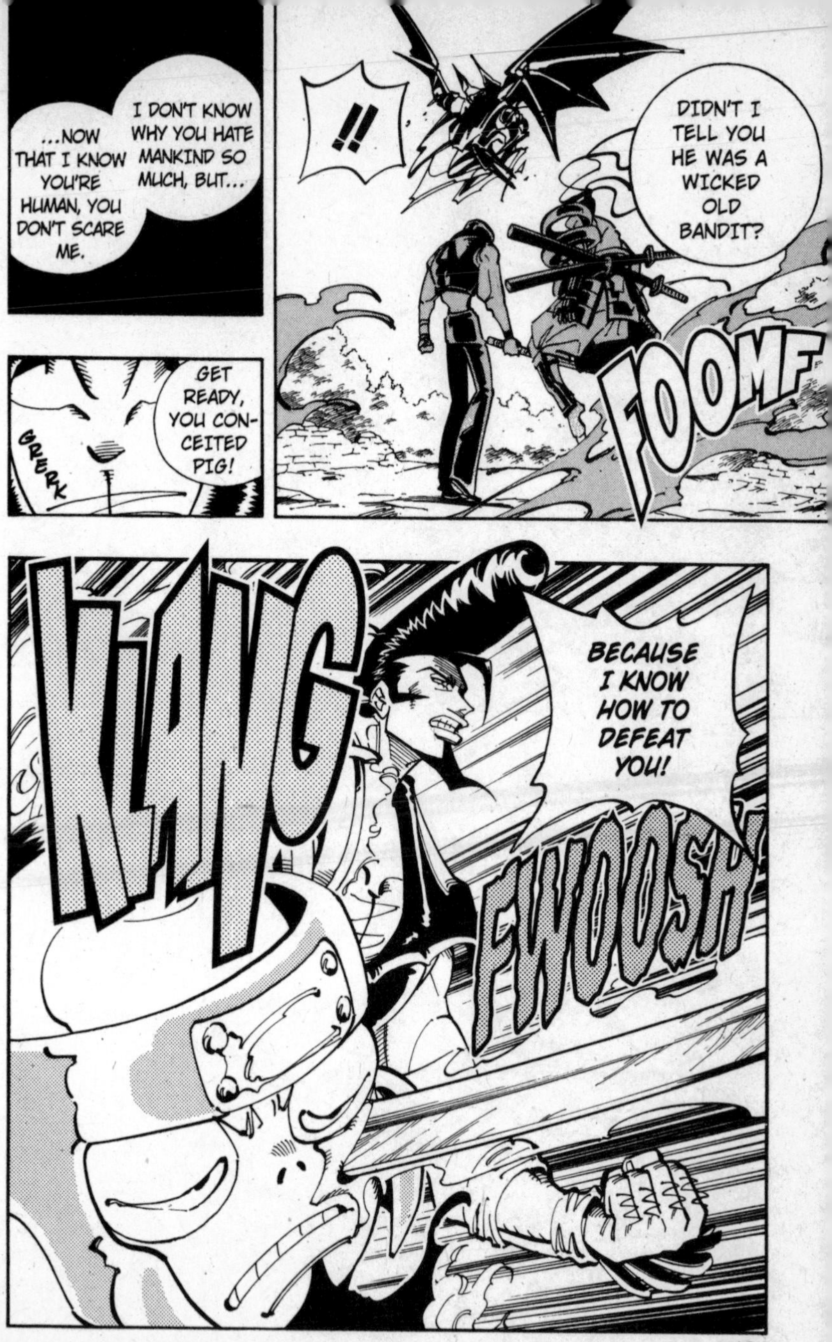
DIDN'T I TELL YOU HE WAS A WICKED OLD BANDIT?
!!
FOOMF
I DON'T KNOW WHY YOU HATE MANKIND SO MUCH, BUT...
...NOW THAT I KNOW YOU'RE HUMAN, YOU DON'T SCARE ME.
GET READY, YOU CONCEITED PIG!
GRERK
BECAUSE I KNOW HOW TO DEFEAT YOU!
KLANG
FWOOSH

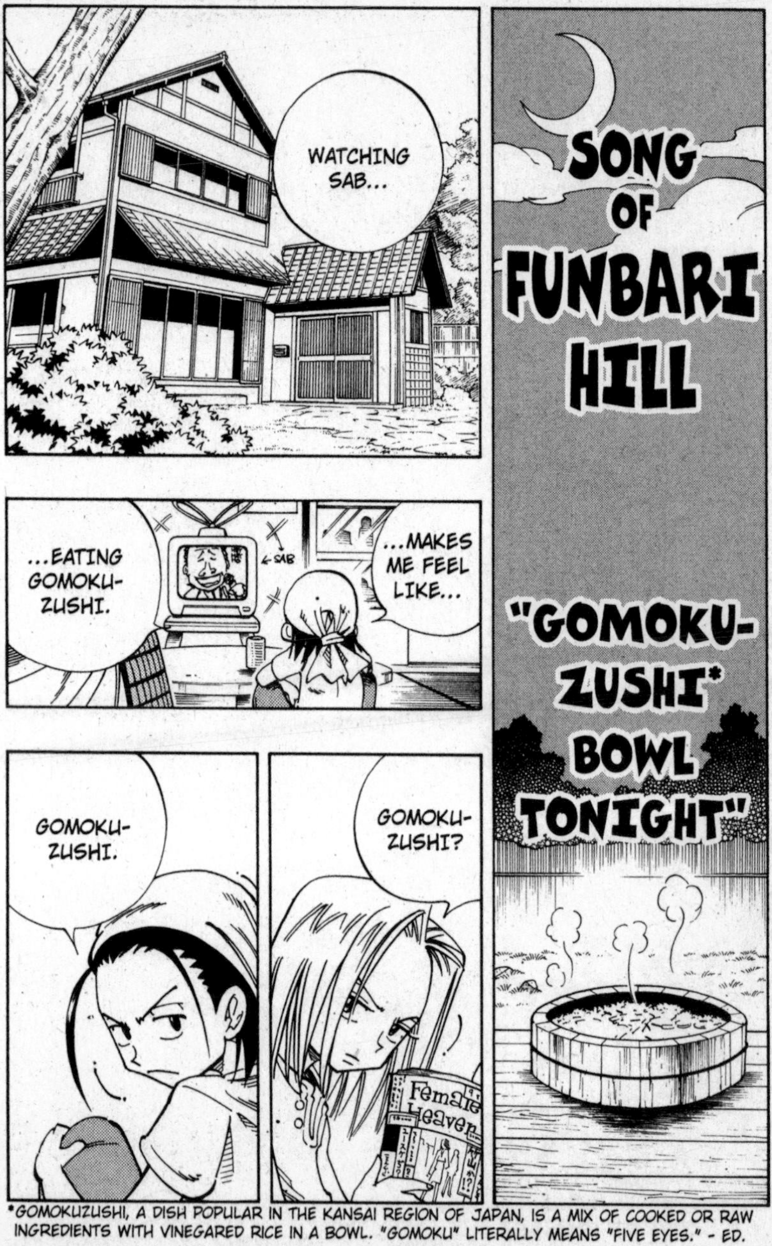
SONG OF FUNBARI HILL
"GOMOKU-ZUSHI* BOWL TONIGHT"
WATCHING SAB...
...MAKES ME FEEL LIKE...
SAB
...EATING GOMOKU-ZUSHI.
GOMOKU-ZUSHI?
Female Heaven
GOMOKU-ZUSHI.

*GOMOKUZUSHI, A DISH POPULAR IN THE KANSAI REGION OF JAPAN, IS A MIX OF COOKED OR RAW INGREDIENTS WITH VINEGARED RICE IN A BOWL. "GOMOKU" LITERALLY MEANS "FIVE EYES." - ED.

READ THIS WAY

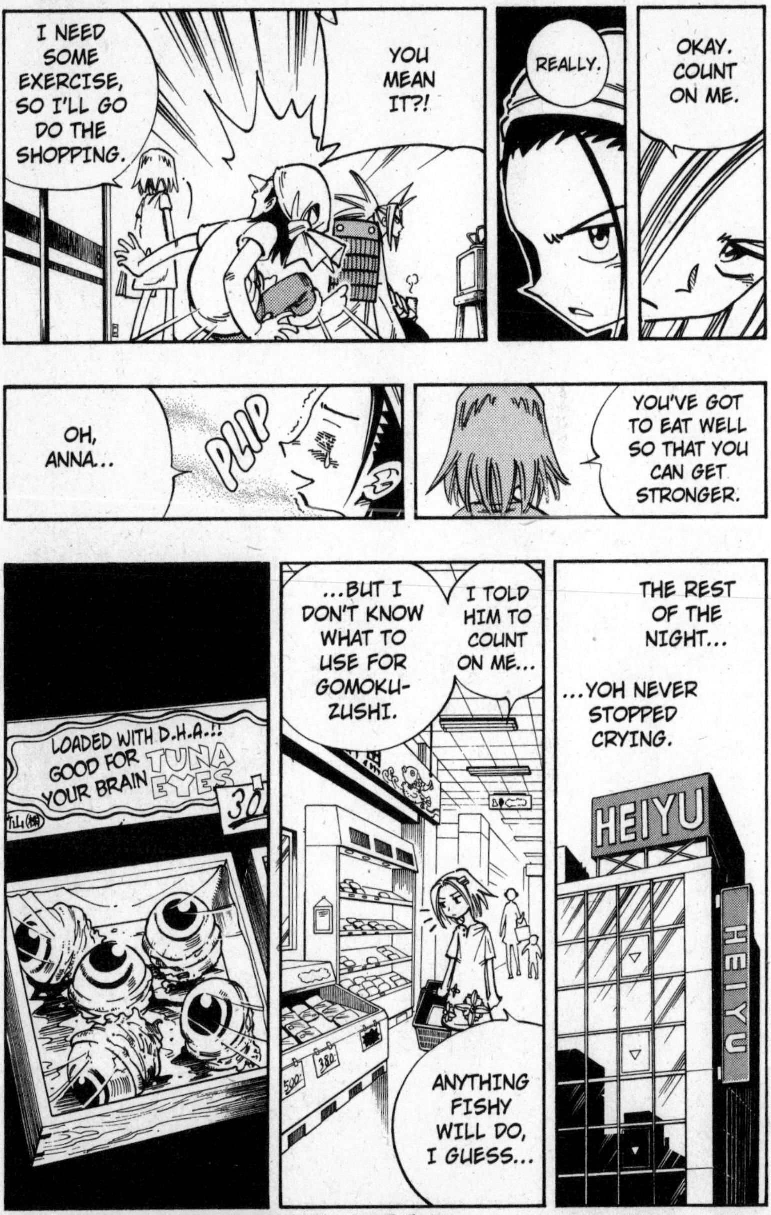
OKAY. COUNT ON ME.
REALLY.
YOU MEAN IT?!
I NEED SOME EXERCISE, SO I'LL GO DO THE SHOPPING.
YOU'VE GOT TO EAT WELL SO THAT YOU CAN GET STRONGER.
PLIP
OH, ANNA...
THE REST OF THE NIGHT...
...YOH NEVER STOPPED CRYING.
HEIYU
HEIYU
I TOLD HIM TO COUNT ON ME...
...BUT I DON'T KNOW WHAT TO USE FOR GOMOKU-ZUSHI.
ANYTHING FISHY WILL DO, I GUESS...
380
500
LOADED WITH D.H.A.!! GOOD FOR YOUR BRAIN
TUNA EYES

 SONG OF FUNBARI HILL (THE END)

SHAMAN KING CHARACTER FILE No.51

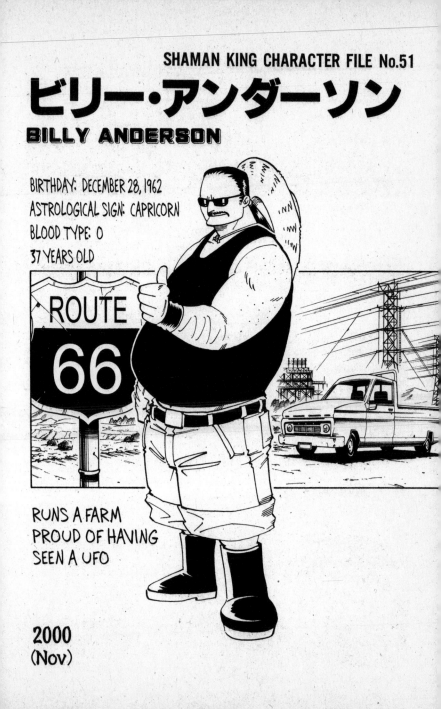

ビリー・アンダーソン

BILLY ANDERSON

BIRTHDAY: DECEMBER 28, 1962
ASTROLOGICAL SIGN: CAPRICORN
BLOOD TYPE: O
37 YEARS OLD

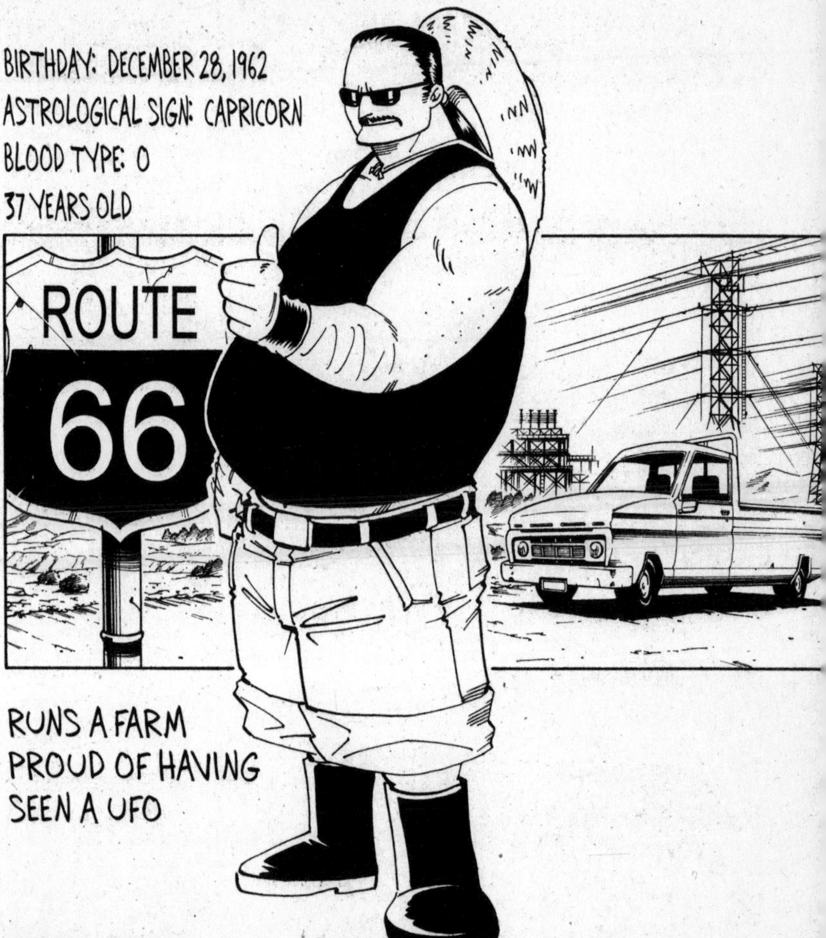
ROUTE
66

RUNS A FARM
PROUD OF HAVING
SEEN A UFO

2000
(Nov)

Shaman King™

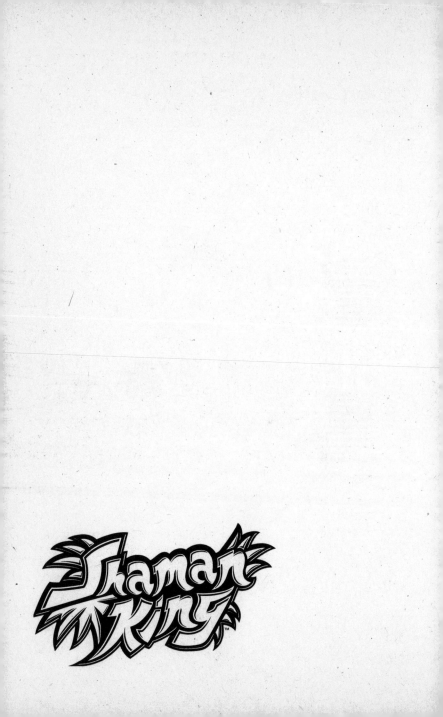

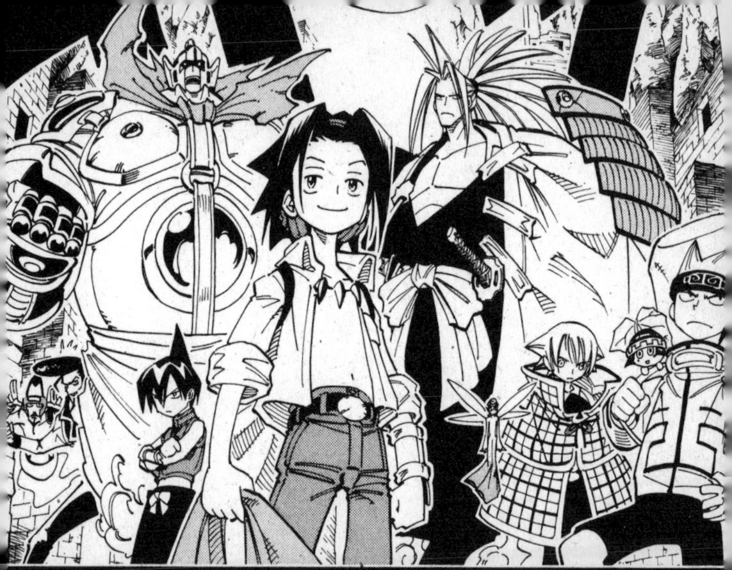

IN THE NEXT VOLUME...

Can a poor slacker ever catch a break?! Yoh and his merry band of Shaman King title contenders have made it to Mesa Verdede, where they think they'll find the hidden Patch village. But instead they find themselves face-to-face with one of Hao's most dangerous allies—Boris Dracula! Plus, a new team of shamans shows up. And they've got archangel Over Souls!

AVAILABLE MAY 2007!

Read it first in SHONEN JUMP magazine!

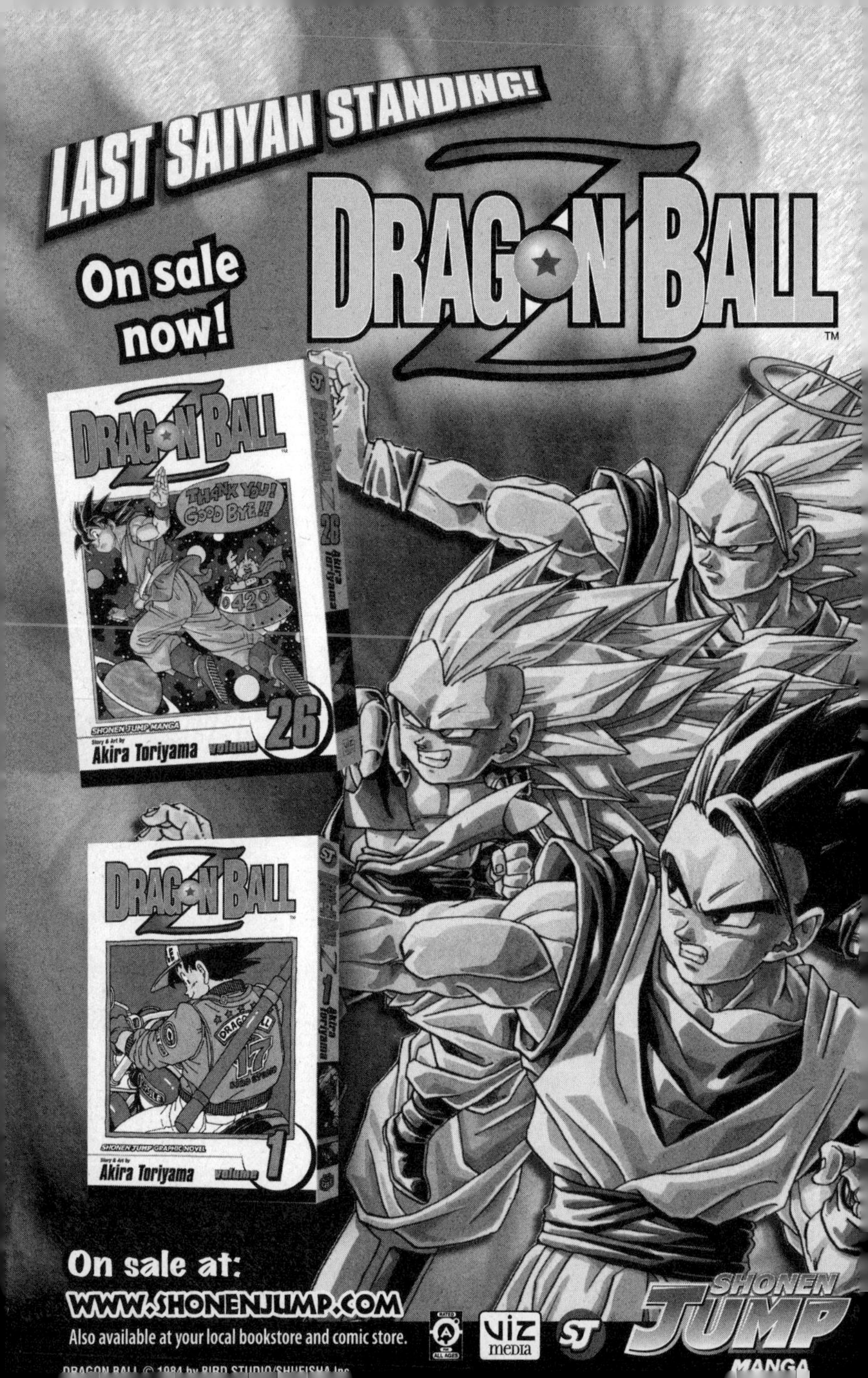

LAST SAIYAN STANDING!
DRAGON BALL Z™
On sale now!
DRAGON BALL Z
THANK YOU! GOOD BYE!!
SHONEN JUMP MANGA
Story & Art by
Akira Toriyama
volume 26
DRAGON BALL Z
SHONEN JUMP GRAPHIC NOVEL
Story & Art by
Akira Toriyama
volume 1
On sale at:
WWW.SHONENJUMP.COM
Also available at your local bookstore and comic store.
RATED A FOR ALL AGES
viz media
SJ
SHONEN JUMP MANGA
DRAGON BALL © 1984 by BIRD STUDIO/SHUEISHA Inc.

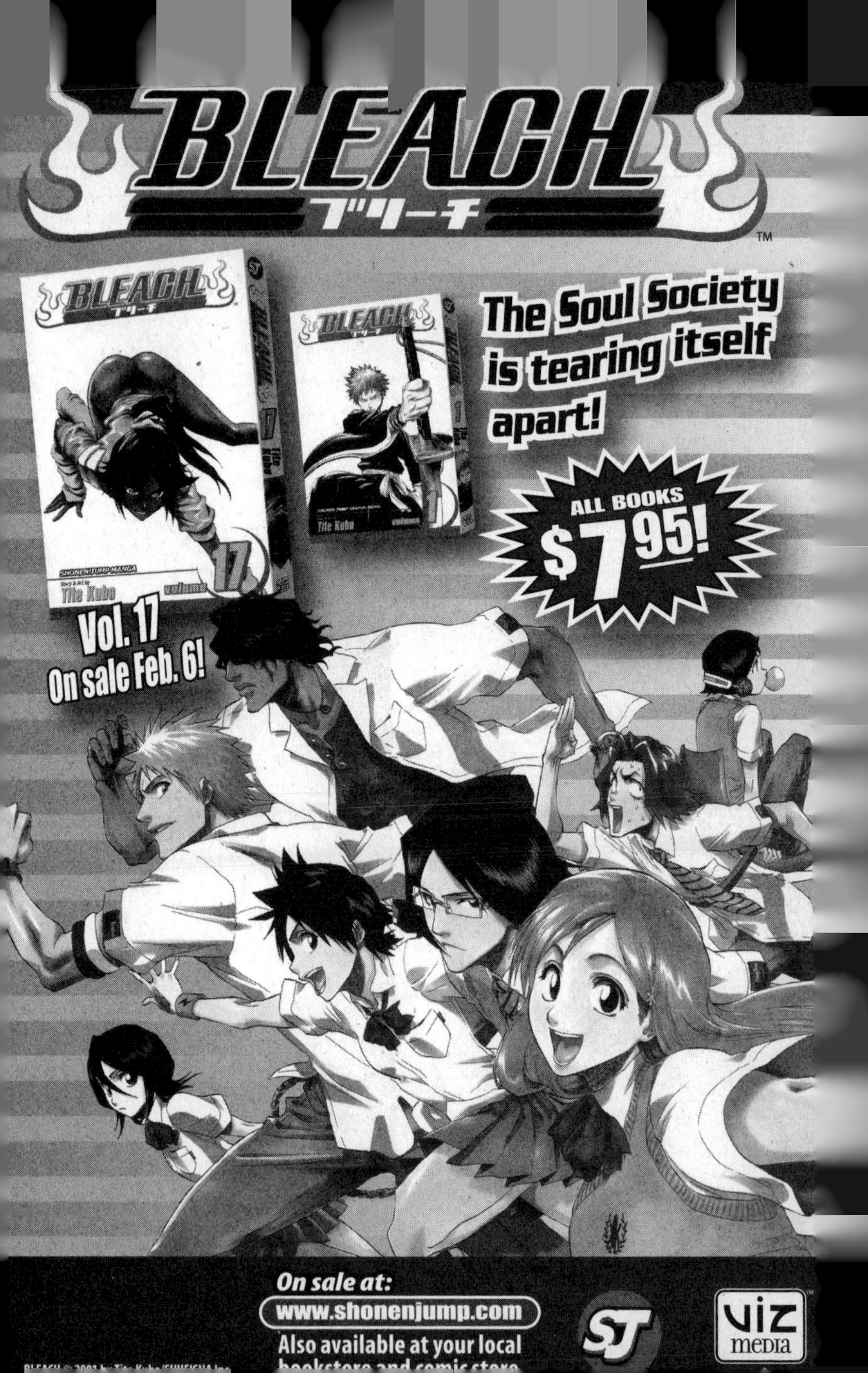
BLEACH
ブリーチ
™
The Soul Society is tearing itself apart!
ALL BOOKS
$7.95!
Vol. 17
On sale Feb. 6!
On sale at:
www.shonenjump.com
Also available at your local
SJ
viz media

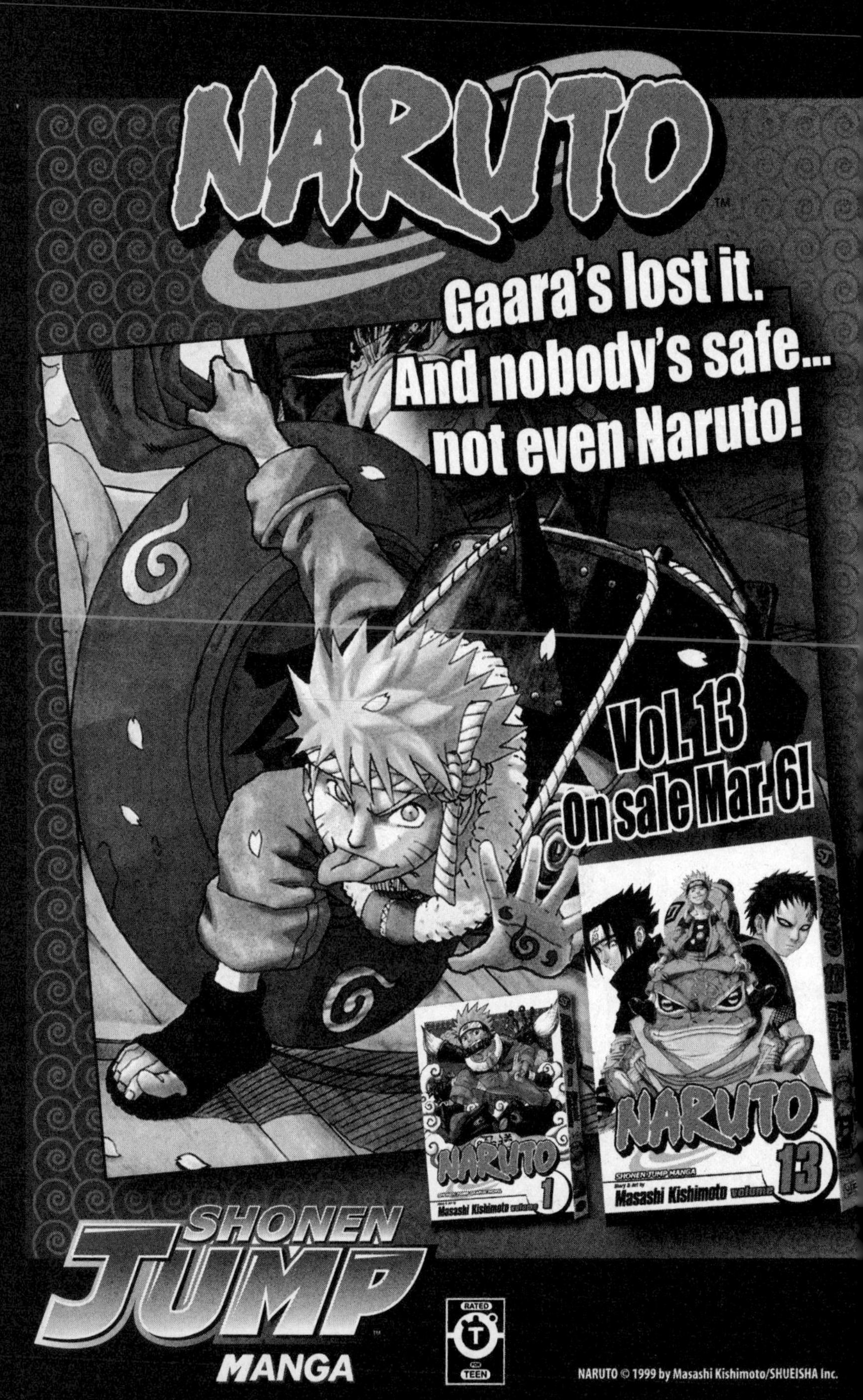
NARUTO
Gaara's lost it.
And nobody's safe...
not even Naruto!
Vol. 13
On sale Mar. 6!
NARUTO 1
Masashi Kishimoto
SHONEN JUMP MANGA
NARUTO 13
Masashi Kishimoto
SHONEN JUMP MANGA
RATED T FOR TEEN
NARUTO © 1999 by Masashi Kishimoto/SHUEISHA Inc.

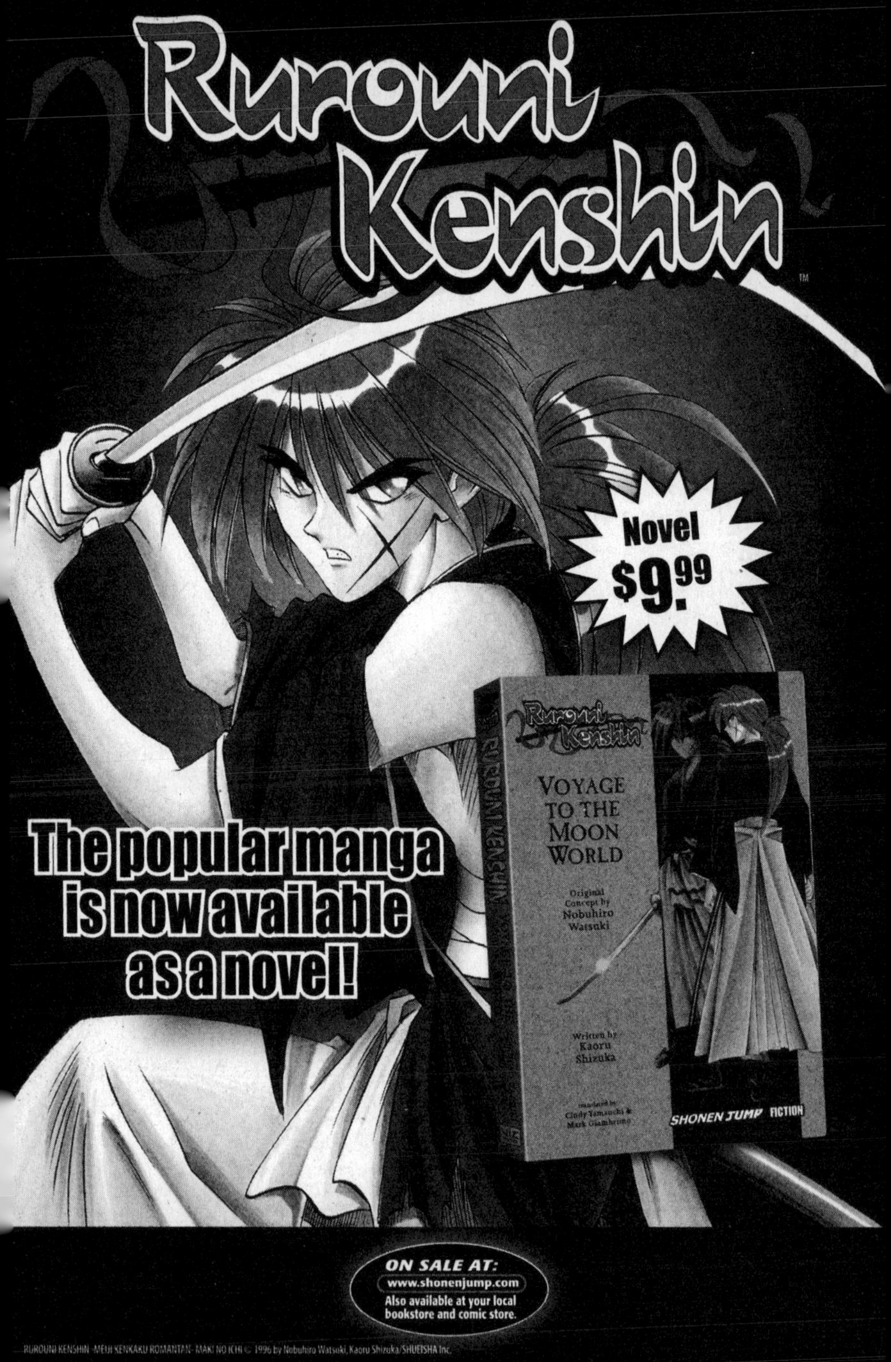
Rurouni Kenshin™
Novel $9.99
The popular manga is now available as a novel!
Rurouni Kenshin
VOYAGE TO THE MOON WORLD
Original Concept by Nobuhiro Watsuki
Written by Kaoru Shizuka
SHONEN JUMP FICTION
ON SALE AT:
www.shonenjump.com
Also available at your local bookstore and comic store.

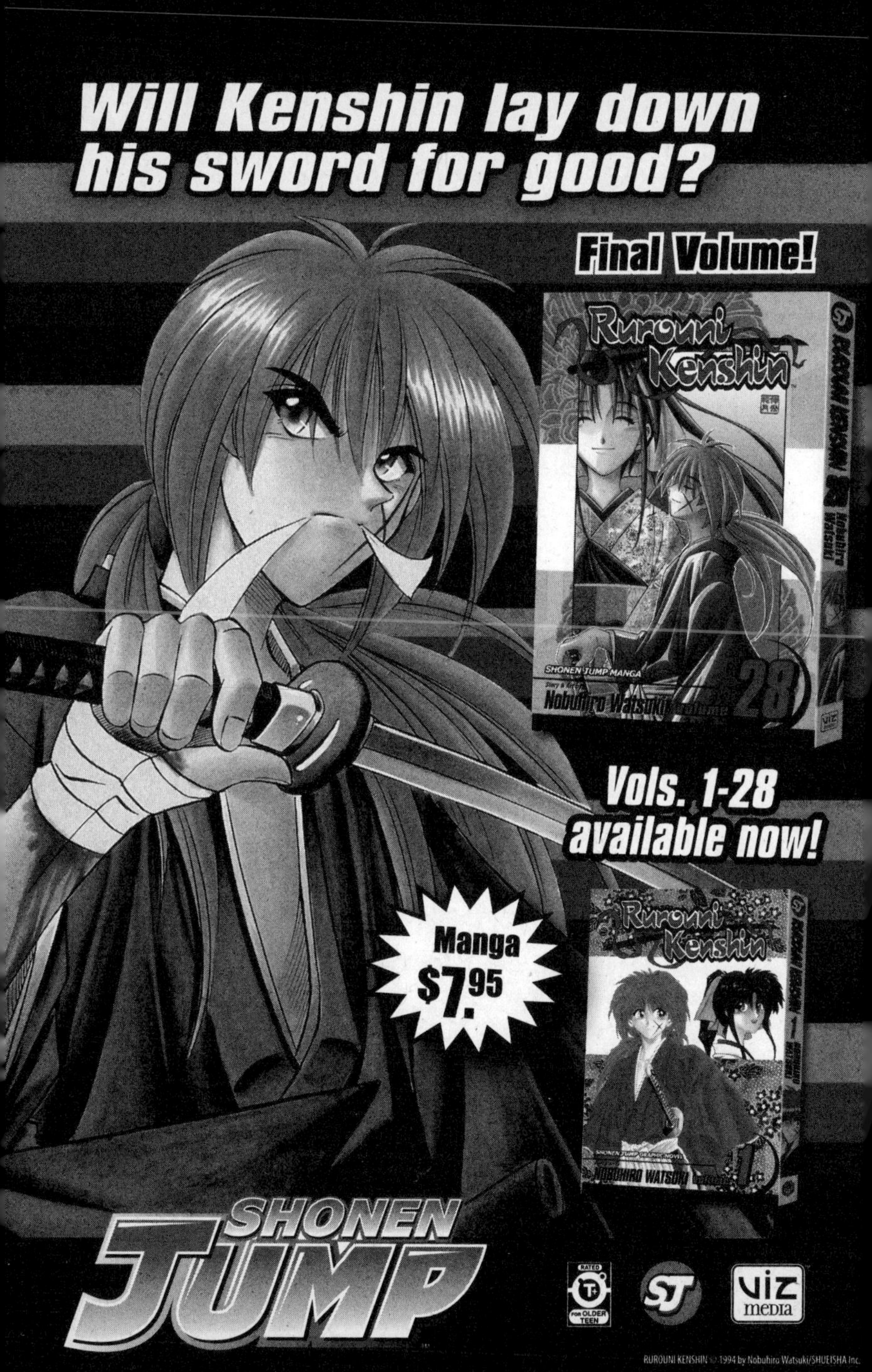

Will Kenshin lay down his sword for good?
Final Volume!
Rurouni Kenshin
SHONEN JUMP MANGA
Nobuhiro Watsuki
28
Vols. 1-28 available now!
Manga $7.95
Rurouni Kenshin
NOBUHIRO WATSUKI
1
SHONEN JUMP
RATED T+ FOR OLDER TEEN
SJ
VIZ media

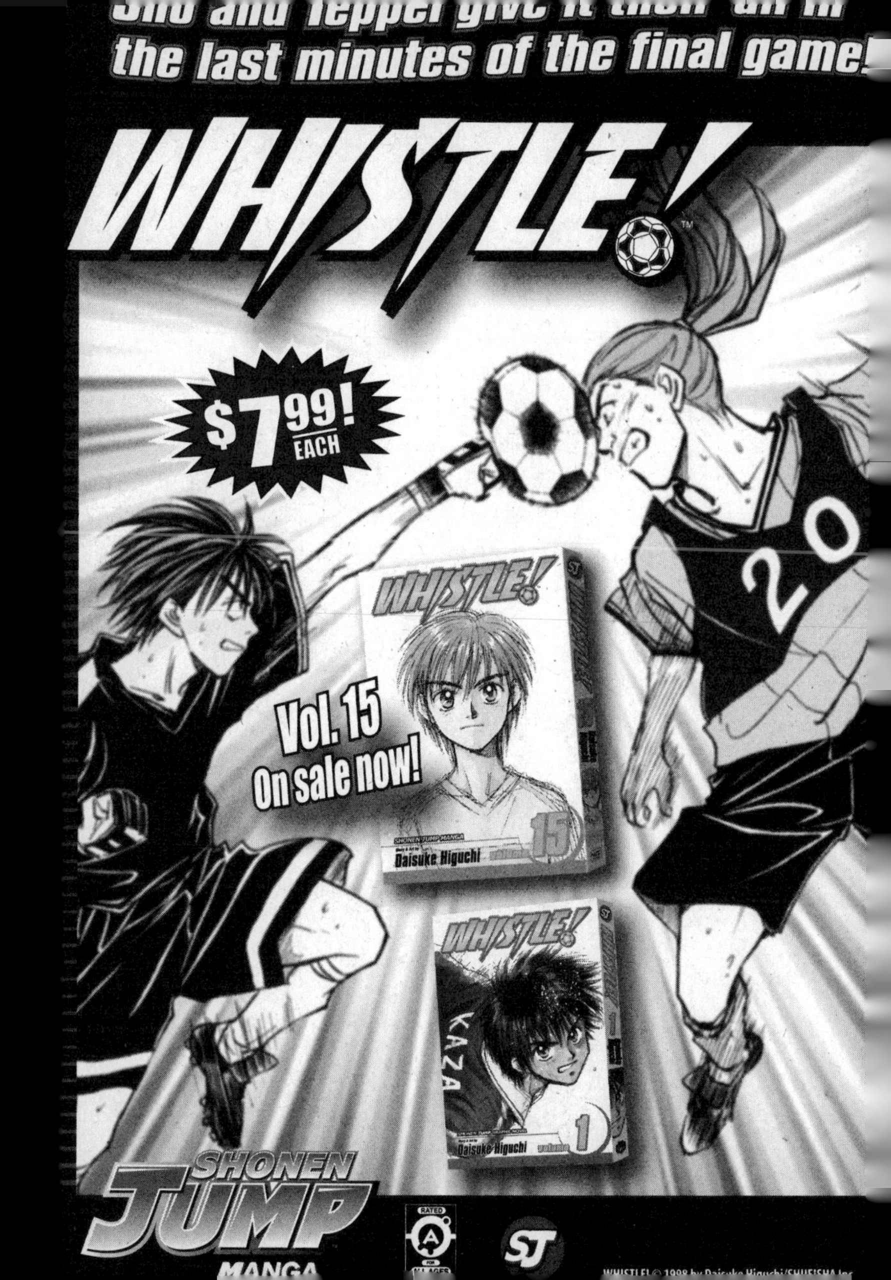

Sho and Tepper give it their all in
the last minutes of the final game!
WHISTLE!
$7.99! EACH
Vol. 15
On sale now!
SHONEN JUMP MANGA
Daisuke Higuchi
SHONEN JUMP MANGA
RATED A FOR ALL AGES
SJ
WHISTLE! © 1998 by Daisuke Higuchi/SHUEISHA Inc.